What Do You Do When You're Lonesome

What Do You Do When You're Lonesome

The Authorized Biography of Justin Townes Earle

Jonathan Bernstein

New York Boston

Da Capo
Hachette Book Group
1290 Avenue of the Americas
New York, NY 10104
grandcentralpublishing.com
@grandcentralpub

First Edition: January 2026

Da Capo is an imprint of Grand Central Publishing. The Da Capo name and logo are registered trademarks of Hachette Book Group, Inc.

The publisher is not responsible for websites (or their content) that are not owned by the publisher.

Da Capo books may be purchased in bulk for business, educational, or promotional use. For information, please contact your local bookseller or the Hachette Book Group Special Markets Department at special.markets@hbgusa.com.

Print book interior design by Amy Quinn.

Library of Congress Control Number: 2025944862

ISBNs: 9780306833274 (hardcover), 9780306833298 (ebook)

Printed in Canada

MRQ-T

10 9 8 7 6 5 4 3 2 1

For Dad

CONTENTS

Part III: Looking for a Place to Land

Forgive me for committing to suffering. I thought it might be the answer. That if I suffered loudly enough, for long enough, I would be owed something from somewhere holy.

—Hanif Abdurraqib

Ever wake up with the so different blues, anytime?
Ever wake up with the so different blues?
And you couldn't get on your Monday morning shoes

—Mance Lipscomb

INTRODUCTION

Nobody called him Justin Townes Earle. As a kid, his dad called him Cowboy. His mom and most of his family knew him as J.T. When he was a preteen, old enough to fabricate tall tales and spout nonsense, his friends coined the nickname Squirrelly Earle. When he began courting trouble as a gangly teenager touring with his father's band, a fellow crewmate referred to him, behind his back, as the Prince of Darkness. As an aspiring twentysomething singer-songwriter gigging around Nashville in the early '00s, everyone knew him, simply, as Justin Earle.

One day in December 2006, Joshua Black Wilkins, an aspiring photographer, showed Justin, then twenty-four, some album cover mockups for *Yuma*, Justin's first recording under his own name.

And there it was:

JUSTIN TOWNES EARLE

Justin's middle name came from Townes Van Zandt, the cult Texas songwriter known for his haunting country-folk poetry. Van Zandt had been a mentor, philosophical idol, and overall bad influence on Justin's father, country-rock star Steve Earle, who idolized Van Zandt so much he decided his firstborn son should bear his name.

Justin carried the name with pride and resentment. Van Zandt would eventually be revered as a musical genius. But Justin hadn't always cared for his father's destitute friend.

"He was just *boozy*," Justin once said, summarizing his childhood impression of Van Zandt.[1]

He noticed the way his dad constantly sought Van Zandt's approval. "As in a lot of these types of relationships," Justin once said, "the hero is the tormentor."[2]

After decades of alcoholism, Townes Van Zandt died of a heart attack at fifty-two in 1997, days before Justin's fifteenth birthday. After Van Zandt's death, Steve became the unofficial leader of the cult of Texas songwriters who idolized Van Zandt and worked to transform his life and music into something like a legend.

"In many ways I've wanted to be like Townes," Justin once said. "And in many ways I've *not* wanted to be like Townes."[3]

Glancing at mockups for *Yuma*, his debut EP, Justin considered it again: *Justin Townes Earle*. There was something eerie, something cursed with confidence, something almost comically predestined about a southern singer-songwriter embracing a name like that. The name was saturated with a legend so intertwined with his upbringing that it took years for Justin to label it.

But after getting sober in 2004 at twenty-two, Justin coined a term for it: *the myth*.[4]

The myth was a conception of art and music as a higher calling that requires suffering. It made young songwriters flee their families for the road, for the vans, bars, clubs, and motel room, any place that might draw them into depths of despair in the quest for mystical self-discovery.

According to the laws of *the myth*, self-sacrifice yields material, and pain is a currency cashed out in the form of two verses, a chorus, and a bridge. *The myth* prioritized song over selfhood, promoting the idea that the more one damages the latter, the more beautiful the former.

"Maybe she just has to sing for the sake of the song," Townes Van Zandt sang in 1968. "Who do I think that I am to decide that she's wrong?"

The name Justin Townes Earle conjured not one but two self-destructive songwriters—Steve Earle and Townes Van Zandt—both of whom embodied *the myth*. By 2006, Justin had long grappled with this archetype he felt he'd inherited. In his adolescence and young adulthood, he was seduced by the romanticized mythology of the tortured troubadour, pulling from it in his songwriting, adapting it for his own image, and exemplifying it in his lifestyle. But as he grew older, he became increasingly aware of its pitfalls and bore intimate witness to its curse.

"I believed *the myth* for a long time," Justin later said, "and I believed that I had to destroy myself to make great art."[5]

As a child of the early nineties, Justin saw *the myth* everywhere he looked. His hero, Kurt Cobain, went from generational voice to immortal icon after dying by suicide at twenty-seven in 1994. At that time, Justin was living as a preteen with his father—who was newly sober following years of rampant substance use—after a long separation; he saw the way Steve was celebrated for having courted death and survived with a song to sing. The books he read, on his father's advice, featured the self-destructive romance of beat authors like Jack Kerouac and William S. Burroughs. Many of Justin's favorite artists (the Replacements, Billie Holiday, Gram Parsons) were revered for their chemical-induced antics, for how their own tragic legends became intricately entwined with their art.

It was impossible to avoid the intoxicating fumes of *the myth* as the firstborn son of Steve Earle. Steve was, among other things, an evangelist and spokesperson for the generation of song-chasing Texas-associated geniuses a decade or so his elder: Van Zandt, Guy and Susanna Clark, Terry Allen, Jerry Jeff Walker. Steve often explained to anyone within earshot that these troubled artists left a permanent mark on popular music.

"Townes Van Zandt is the best songwriter in the whole world," Steve once remarked, "and I'll stand on Bob Dylan's coffee table in my cowboy boots and say that."[6]

The myth was old and persistent, something Steve Earle surely didn't invent, even if he stood on coffee tables and shouted it like the gospel.

As Steve's biographer, Lauren St. John, later put it: "He liked the idea of 'art at all costs.'"[7]

Later, especially once he embraced sobriety, Steve tried to deflate *the myth* even as he perpetuated it.

"I don't really see a correlation between creativity and killing yourself," Steve said in 2001. "I'm not sure that there are more self-destructive artists, proportionally, than there are self-destructive carpenters."[8]

The myth was not unique to Nashville, Tennessee, Justin's hometown, but it had long shrouded the country music city in a thick fog. Since the mid-twentieth century, the city had served as the American center for turning simple three-chord songwriting into industry. In the sixties, when songwriters like Bob Dylan and Joni Mitchell made it seem like pop songs were high art, a corresponding group of songwriters—Kris Kristofferson, Loretta Lynn, Dolly Parton, and Tom T. Hall among them—brought that spirit to Nashville. The perfect country song, the town insisted, was a noble pursuit worth celebrating, no matter its cost.

Justin lived his life reckoning with its cost. As a young boy he yearned for his famous father, who'd waved goodbye, hopped into a van, and didn't return. That's how Justin recounted growing up with his mother, Carol Ann: abandoned by his dad, struggling in his absence.

Justin wandered the hallways of his Nashville schools, where fellow children of country singers and musicians suffered the same absence. "In Nashville there's this whole group of girls my age that won't date a musician," Justin once proclaimed, "because they hate their fathers."[9]

The children's mothers—always the mothers, because even if they were also musicians, the women were the ones forced to sacrifice songwriting dreams to maintain the family—commiserated about their wayward husbands. In his thirties, Justin wrote a song about all this. It went, "Single mother / Absent father / Broken home."

As a teen, Justin rebelled in all the ways he thought he was supposed to. He roamed the streets of Nashville, popped prescription pain pills, and wrote songs. He started acting like a "mean little dope-dealing, pistol-packing shit," as he put it.[10] By late adolescence, he'd become yet another aspiring singer-songwriter pledging allegiance to *the myth*.

"I thought I had to live up to all these people," Justin said. "It was a really miserable existence."[11]

What began as preteen experimentation quickly descended into full-blown chemical dependency. "I believed I had to destroy myself in order to make great art," Justin said. "I used my music as an excuse to get high."[12]

Eventually, his young body failed him.

In July 2004, Justin, twenty-two, was admitted to the Vanderbilt ICU after having almost died from drug use.

Prior rehab stints had failed, but after his time in the ICU, sobriety stuck. Justin spent the next several years confronting his substance-use disorder. The twelve-step program, another subject of his father's evangelizing, played a transformative role in helping Justin see *the myth* for what it was.

"My life had become unmanigable," Justin wrote in a journal, "but it took me years to admit it to anyone most of all myself."

When Amy Winehouse died in 2011, Justin was devastated by the news. "I really take it personally when addiction takes one of us," he said. "It's a really hard thing . . . especially when you come from where I come from and know there's a fucking way out of it."

"*The myth*," he continued, "is going to continue to kill us."[13]

Yet, at the dawn of his career, how could Justin not have been seduced by the siren call of his full name?

Justin Townes Earle.

The name, it was quickly decided that day in December 2006, would be printed on the cover of *Yuma*, below a photo of him staring into the camera with his deep eyes. Soon after, Justin walked into a tattoo parlor and had six cursive letters, *TOWNES*, inked into his chest, just below his neck.

From there on out, Justin started building his own legend. He toured the country in a pickup truck. He shook hands and signed autographs and slicked back his hair and smiled wide. He started working and did not stop, releasing four records in four years, culminating in *Harlem River Blues*, which came out in 2010.

That album arrived at the precipice of the most successful period of his career. And although it also came amid a devastating personal crossroads, Justin's voice found its moment.

Harlem River Blues was a mix of rambling folk tunes about New York (subway conductors, cramped Brooklyn apartments, the FDR Drive) set to southern gospel. It was released in the shaky period following the Great Recession. In those years, old-time-conjuring music with banjos and fiddles enjoyed an unlikely resurgent mainstream popularity as groups like the Avett Brothers and Mumford & Sons presented bluegrass-infused music to pop audiences.

Justin Earle had spent his youth wandering through Nashville practically method acting the role of the wandering folksinger. After roots music boomed when the economy collapsed in the late 2000s, songs from a faraway American past, real or imagined, became popular as Americans, especially young adults, felt, themselves, rootless and burdened with economic anxiety.

Anchored by an upbeat sing-along title track about suicide, *Harlem River Blues* established Justin Townes Earle as the real-deal manifestation of this postrecession folk boom, a millennial Woody Guthrie type who sang his aimlessness back to a generation searching for somewhere to stand.

With his sharp sense of fashion, commanding charisma, bad-boy backstory, and knack for self-promotion, Justin Townes Earle seemed destined for the type of crossover stardom that would've plastered his six-foot-four frame on college dorm-room posters. He appeared on *Letterman*, won awards, packed large rock clubs, earned rave reviews, and was named one of the twenty-five "Most Stylish Men in the World" by *GQ*.

All the while, Justin shared stories and cigarettes with his fans, befriended bouncers and bartenders, won over grandparents with his southern manners, and seduced journalists eager to print his legend. Something about his mischievous grin and his disquieting openness about past demons made people fall in love with him.

"If he'd wanted to," said his longtime agent, Andrew Colvin, "Justin could have become governor."

To anyone who saw him perform in the late 2000s, stardom didn't seem far-fetched. Justin Townes Earle was a lightning bolt of magnetism: part vaudeville showman, part aw-shucks country rube, part Grand Ole Opry showbiz act, part Depression-era carnival barker, part revival-tent prophet.

He poured his heart out one song, wisecracked the next. His percussive, drop-thumb blues guitar picking produced a sound so full it left crowds wondering if he secretly played to a backing track. He talked ten miles a minute, stomped his boot on the down beat, danced around the microphone, and fixed his big eyes out into the middle distance of the crowd, as if he were focusing so intently on his songs about freight trains and cross-country rambling that he'd become entranced.

"I haven't strayed from Bruce Springsteen's formula of girls, cars, and sex," he told one enraptured crowd, before adding a qualifier: "Oh, and mama."[14]

Mama, always mama. The least rock and roll of song subjects, the one Justin couldn't stop writing about. Lurking behind his retro cadences and old-timey quips lay the twin subjects of so many of Justin's songs: *mom and dad*.

"Jason Isbell and I have a kind of friendly wager on who's gonna make a record first," Justin explained in 2013. "He's gonna make a record that doesn't have any daddy-issue songs, and I'll make a record that doesn't have any mommy-issue songs."[15]

By that point, Justin's career had already started to recede. Back in 2008, he'd shifted his hard-line definition of sobriety. He started smoking weed. Alcohol soon followed. Right as he was poised to seize his stardom, Justin succumbed, again, to the illness he'd been fighting since he was a child. He entered rehab in 2010, ten days after releasing *Harlem River Blues*.

The rest of Justin's life was a fight against and with his addiction. With the support of loved ones, Justin often made stunning strides and comebacks from places his addiction had brought him, even when many feared he'd never recover. He liked to claim, as a point of filial pride and connection with his father he so adored, that because Steve Earle had also survived many near-death scares, so too he, Justin Townes Earle, was invincible.

Like dad, Justin believed deeply in the power of sobriety, dishing advice and wisdom and serving as a model and inspiration for countless fans, fellow artists, and friends. But that didn't diminish his struggle.

In his last couple of years, the parts of himself he'd long fought to keep hidden started screaming to the surface. He began performing encores shirtless, his torso on full display, visibly incapacitated. The crowd stared at his middle name—*Townes*—etched into his body.

On August 20, 2020, Justin Townes Earle died at the age of thirty-eight after purchasing cocaine that he didn't know was laced with fentanyl. He'd grown estranged and detached from many of his friends and family, including his wife and young daughter, and was living alone in Nashville when he died in a sparsely furnished temporary apartment. His body was discovered three days later.

Long before *the myth* ended, yet again, in utter tragedy, Justin Townes Earle had begun the work of transforming his life into legend. The teller of that legend seemed unusually forthcoming, but those who knew Justin most intimately understood that the heartsick, smiley, bullshitting Nashvillian contained even more within him than what Justin Townes Earle disclosed in public. He was hilarious, hard-edged, stubborn, silly, solemn, generous, exasperating (gentle one moment, violent the next), kind, commandeering, compulsively chatty, and chest thumping. But beneath his bluster was a fragile yearning and a desperate desire to make his hurt heard.

Beneath the pistols, pickup trucks, whiskey, fistfights, and emotional barriers he put up was "a big kid trying to navigate the world," as one friend, Amanda Shires, put it.

Beneath the drinks and drugs that robbed him of reality in the last years of his life was a man, just shy of forty, who admitted he needed to finally face his demons but didn't believe he was up to such a daunting task.

The masks, tall tales, half-truths, and half-lies that Justin wielded and waved became a central part of his swaggering legend, a shield he formed around the profound beauty and deep truths of his best work.

"As much as Justin was trying to write great songs," said one old friend, Sean Locke, "he was trying to write the Justin Townes Earle story, too."

Justin was still revising that story on May 22, 2019. It was just after noon, and Justin was drunk, grinning, and staring into a camera in a Manhattan office as *Rolling Stone* asked him questions to promote what would end up being his final record.

Slurring his words, Justin jumped into the tale he wanted to tell: how he started using his middle name.

Telling the story made Justin smile.

As he explained, his friend Joshua Black Wilkins had lovingly encouraged him to do it when prepping *Yuma*: "He was like, 'So you wanna be Justin Townes Earle, right?'"

"I was just like, 'No, I'm Justin Earle.'"

"He goes, 'No you're not. You're Justin *Townes* Earle.'"

"And I go, 'You think I should do it *all*?'"

"And he goes like, 'I don't care what you want. That's what I'm printing on the formatting.'"[16]

The way he told it, Justin Townes Earle had no control over his destiny, no chance to tell the world who he was before the world told *him*, no way to articulate the difference between tempting and choosing his fate. And as was usually the case, even when Justin Townes Earle was bullshitting, he was more than a little right.

PART I

It's Cold in This House

CHAPTER 1

THE BABY BOY HAD BARELY LEFT THE HOSPITAL BEFORE HIS FATHER insisted on an important ritual. Steve Earle was going to make sure the first dirt his son's feet ever touched was bona fide Texas soil.

It was a common custom among members of the Lone Star State diaspora: Steve's father, Jack Dublin Earle, had performed the same ritual with Steve when he was born in southern Virginia 27 years prior.[1]

This wasn't ordinary Texas dirt. It had been gathered, so Steve claimed, from the San Jacinto battlefield outside Houston, where, 146 years prior, roughneck colonists defeated Santa Anna's army to win Texas's independence.[2] Steve lowered his newborn—eyes closed, face scrunched—into a yellow serving bowl filled with the soil.[3]

And there it was declared: This baby was an Earle, a Texan, spiritually if not literally, just like his father, grandfather, great-grandfather, great-great-grandfather, and great-great-great-grandfather Elijah Earle before him. The family had settled in East Texas in the 1840s and founded what still stands, nearly two hundred years later, as the unincorporated farming community of Earle's Chapel, Texas.[4]

Justin was born on January 4, 1982. His parents were overwhelmed with emotion when they brought their newborn back to their home in Nashville, on Seventeenth Avenue and Wedgewood, in the triangle between two universities (Vanderbilt and Belmont) and Music Row, where much of the business of country music was conducted.

Giving birth had been Carol Ann Earle's proudest moment.[5] She'd taken her pregnancy very seriously after having had an earlier miscarriage, refusing so much as a sip of coffee for nine months. Before then, the freewheeling twenty-five-year-old West Nashville pool shark spent her Friday nights beating men at billiards, working at bars after graduating high school early, and briefly attending Middle Tennessee State University.

Fatherhood also busted open Steve Earle's heart. "The entire world changed," he later said onstage, "when they handed me that little boy."[6] After Justin's birth, Steve, as the story goes, picked up a hospital pay phone and called his father. When Jack Dublin Earle picked up, Steve burst into tears, apologizing for "every fucking awful thing I'd ever done."[7]

Down the street from Baptist Hospital, a man everyone called Duffy was setting up microphones onstage at Springwater, the dirty dive where he tended bar. It was late afternoon on January 4 when an ebullient Steve Earle stormed in to issue a proclamation of biblical importance:

"Justin Townes Earle," Steve shouted to no one in particular, "is born into this world."

Barely anyone was at Springwater that afternoon. But that wasn't a problem for Steve. These were the days when a solitary bartender was a typical audience for the struggling songwriter. It was 1982, four years before Steve Earle had a number-one country album, the hard-edged *Guitar Town*; four years before the press proclaimed him country music's Bruce Springsteen; four years before he was credited, alongside stars like George Strait, Rosanne Cash, and Dwight Yoakam, for reviving the entire genre.

Eventually, Steve became a legitimate rock star, hanging around Hollywood with Guns N' Roses and brandishing his legend with outlandish statements and one-liners that made him seem like a supervillain out of outlaw-country central casting. "This is Steve," his answering-machine message warned at some point in the eighties. "I'm probably out shooting heroin, chasing thirteen-year-old girls, and beatin' up cops. But I'm old and I tire easily, so leave a message and I'll get back to you."[8]

Steve's fatherhood would become deeply complicated by fame, notoriety, addiction—first prescription narcotics, then heroin—and a series of altercations, alleged assaults, and arrests that eventually sent him to jail. But back in 1982, Steve was enraptured by his firstborn son, this screaming infant anointed in Texas dirt, who would one day inherit his father's talents and succumb to many of his father's struggles.

Although Carol Ann, Justin's mom, had first laid eyes on Steve Earle at Springwater, the first time the couple met was when she worked at a different bar called Villager, a Vanderbilt watering hole where students and aspiring songwriters chucked darts and danced to blues bands.

"He's a Capricorn, so he's winning, he's charming, he's intelligent," she said in Lauren St. John's Steve Earle biography, *Hardcore Troubadour*. "But I was afraid of guys like him. They would come running into your life, take over, and just dump you."[9]

Steve was married to someone else when he met Carol. But one glimpse of the tall, dark-haired woman slinging cheap beer, and soon he was returning to the Villager just to see her.

The year 1979 was a busy time in Nashville: The Radisson Plaza Hotel opened downtown, a rare sign of life for a neighborhood that had suffered since the Grand Ole Opry, the long-standing radio show and country-music institution, moved its operations to a patch of farmland on the city's outskirts five years before. A new boom in conservative evangelism was underway in America, and televangelists Billy Graham and Jerry Falwell held separate stadium-size rallies in the city, where the latter compared abortion to the Holocaust. That summer, thousands of fans flocked to Greer Stadium, the recently constructed home of the Nashville Sounds, the city's brand new minor-league baseball team. The team led the nation in minor-league attendance and won the championship that September. It was also the year of several important milestones: Descendants of the city's founding families marched to commemorate the two hundredth anniversary of Nashville's colonial beginnings. And there was a centennial celebration of Ella Sheppard Moore, a Black woman born into slavery who became a member of the traveling a cappella ensemble the Fisk Jubilee Singers, which had, according to an apocryphal legend, earned Nashville the nickname "Music City."[10]

Carol and Steve moved in together after Steve divorced his second wife. Carol, who worked part-time at a print shop,[11] was twenty-three. Steve was twenty-five. Their lives revolved around Springwater, a local institution, where they drank beers, sang songs, and spun yarns.

In 1979, a year after opening under its new name, Springwater was establishing a reputation as a go-to songwriter spot. Townes Van Zandt and Guy Clark performed on the bar's barely raised, red streamer–adorned stage. Steve played shows with his band the Gringos. On a weekly basis you could listen to John Prine's future guitarist or the guy who'd written Kenny Rogers's "The Gambler."[12]

When he wasn't writing songs or performing, Steve worked odd jobs building tennis courts and washing dishes at a short-lived restaurant with live boxing.[13] The couple was dissimilar in many ways—far too similar in others—but above all else, "they both wanted to have a baby," said Jack "Bullet" Harris, Steve's former drummer and friend at the time.

They married on March 22, 1981, at the Belmont Assembly of God Church on Music Row. The reception was—where else?—at Springwater. Carol soon became pregnant with Justin. Steve was elated, but, as Carol told Steve's biographer, pending fatherhood made him anxious. "He wanted children, but he was scared," she said. "He misbehaved the whole time I was pregnant."[14]

Steve wanted their firstborn's name to be an over-the-top tribute to two Texas songwriters—Guy Clark and Townes Van Zandt—who'd adopted him as their mentee when he'd first moved to Nashville as an overeager aspiring songwriter.

Guy Townes Earle would be his name.

Carol intervened. Really, she had another musical hero to honor.

Ever since her high school prom's theme had been based on the 1967 Moody Blues song "Nights in White Satin," Carol had wanted to name her future son after the band's strapping singer Justin Hayward.

The compromise: Justin Townes Earle, or J.T., as everyone soon called him. It still had layers of tribute. J.T. was not only the name of Townes Van Zandt's own son, born twelve years earlier, but actually Van Zandt's name, too: John Townes Van Zandt.

The couple announced their child's birth in the *Tennessean*, Nashville's morning paper, and embarked on the balancing act of being a Nashville showbiz couple with a baby. Carol accompanied Steve to the hand-shaking events one must attend when seeking stardom. "Carol Earle, wife of rockabilly newcomer Steve Earle, was stately in a black satin floor-length dress," noted a reporter at a glitzy music-industry ballroom banquet in 1983.[15]

Those who spent time with Steve and Carol during Justin's infancy were struck by Steve's dedication to the daily realities of parenthood. "Steve was a good father," said Carol's sister, Judy Hilton, one of many who observed his attentiveness and day-to-day devotion to his son. Carol eventually went back to work, and when she got home, she cared for Justin and made home-cooked meals for any friends who happened to stop by.

Steve, still struggling with his music career, stressed over finances. When he wasn't rocking his newborn to sleep, he was writing songs for publishing income. The family otherwise relied on food stamps. During these first few years, Justin formed what he later claimed were his earliest memories: his father holding him up in the air on a big yellow pillow; playing with his Alvin and the Chipmunks doll.[16]

"There was so much love in that house," said Bullet, Steve's friend who spent time at their home.

Eventually, Steve began getting bigger gigs. A few of his songs were cut by better-known singers and became minor hits. Career momentum started building. He began spending more time away from home. He started drinking more.

"Steve was obsessed with becoming a star and being a writer," said Robert Jetton, Steve's friend. "And he didn't leave much time for [Carol]."

Carol and Steve began to yell and fight. "They just didn't mesh," recalled Carol's sister. "They both needed a lot of attention." Neither was getting enough from the other.

It was a freewheeling time in their neighborhood, just south of Music Row, nestled between Belmont University and the neighborhood of Hillsboro Village. Twentysomething musicians and bohemians had settled in the affordable, middle-class extended area. If Steve and Carol's friends and neighbors weren't in bands themselves, they went out to hear music at night, spending their extra cash at the end of the week at the cluster of bars on Elliston Place, known as the "Rock Block," where they'd hear loud guitars at Exit/In and stay up late drinking margaritas and eating bean rolls at the Gold Rush.

Justin's mom was overwhelmed by her new life. She often found herself alone with a toddler. She was barely twenty-six and married to an increasingly absent aspiring rock star.

Carol Ann Earle had always wanted to escape West Nashville. The two-bedroom house, in the neighborhood of Charlotte Park, where she'd grown up with her parents and younger sister, was a volatile place. Her father, Horace Hunter, worked at a cement-manufacturing company and spent many evenings at a nighttime competitive bowling league. He suffered from alcoholism and bouts of violence, which were directed at his wife and two girls. "He was a problem," Judy Hilton, Carol's younger sister, said of their father. "He was not good to the family."

"I was an abused child," Carol later told Steve's biographer.[17]

Carol's mom, Norma, was a loving, churchgoing woman who was a nurse before she got a job at the United States Postal Service during the Vietnam War. Norma worried constantly about her eldest daughter: As a young girl, Carol came down with a bad case of spinal meningitis that left her hospitalized for an extended period. "With my mother, it was always, '*Carol, Carol, Carol*,'" said Judy Hilton. "She was always concerned about her."

After a federal judge ordered that Nashville increase its use of busing to desegregate its school system in 1971, Carol switched from the segregated Hillwood High School to Cohn High School.[18] She was taller than her classmates and felt alienated by high school, where, she said, teachers picked on her. "Carol always felt she was different from everybody else," her longtime companion, Michael O'Brien, said.

As teenagers, Carol and her sister spent their allowance on Elton John and Jethro Tull concerts downtown. Her parents eventually divorced. Carol took enough summer-school classes to graduate high school at age sixteen, after her sophomore year. In her sophomore class photo, from 1972, Carol has long brown hair that goes past her shoulders. Of the thirty-seven students on her page of the yearbook, Carol is basically the only one not smiling. Her long face and deep eyes gaze into the camera with a look of resigned intensity she'd one day pass on to her son.[19]

Carol had, like Steve, already been married. In 1973, at age seventeen, she wed an electrician's apprentice from Texas. They divorced before she married Steve.[20]

Having already weathered the disintegration of one marriage, Carol managed as best she could as Steve's career gathered steam, calling landlines around Nashville trying to track down her husband. At some point, she realized that Steve was cheating on her.[21]

Forty years later, Carol needed only a few words to sum up the father of her only child: "Steve was a good guy," she said, "and a wild man."

Their fights were terrible. One night, in the middle of a dispute on a drive home, Carol leaned over to Steve, who was driving, and punched him in the face. Steve, and subsequently Justin, who inherited his father's penchant for exaggeration—both of them abiding by the adage to "never let the truth get in the way of a good story"—later relished telling this story. (In the *Earle-ification* of the tale, Carol's blow detached Steve's retina.)

As an adult, Justin shared that story as an example of his mom's no-bullshit toughness. The reality is that, at that time, Carol was barely hanging on.

"I was so out of it and so afraid and so scared," she told Steve's biographer Lauren St. John. "I was *not* strong. . . . I cried all the time. I was a nutcase. . . . I did not know how to raise a little boy by myself."[22]

There's a photo from around this time of Justin, age two or so, towheaded with giant blue eyes, dressed in a onesie and a red-and-blue-striped shirt, nestled safely in the arms of his dad. Steve, wearing flannel, a jean jacket, a bushy mustache, and long brown hair that fell over his eyes, stares down at his son with a look of adoration and amazement.

Twenty or so years after it was taken, Justin showed this photo to a girlfriend. It was the time he was truly happy, the *only* time, he explained, and it's how he wanted her to remember him.

"Look at this," he said of the photo. "This is before it all went to shit."

In Justin's memory, in the stories he later recounted, recited, molded, and mythologized, what happened next was a painful parting, the beginning of a life of sorrow. He recalled staring through the front door's paneled glass as his father left the house, waved at him, and hopped into his touring van.

"I remember the day he left very vividly," he told a journalist in 2010.[23] Once he became a public figure with his own platform, Justin never passed an opportunity to correct anyone who suggested his famous father raised him:

"I am not a product," he loved saying, "of an asexual science experiment involving songwriter Steve Earle."[24]

In Justin's telling, his dad departed and wasn't heard from again for years. The reality of Steve and Carol's split wasn't nearly so black-and-white. Around the time Steve moved out, his friend Robert Jetton received a phone call: Steve and Carol were going through it, and Steve needed a place to crash.

"Steve moved in with me," said Jetton. "I didn't realize, at the time, that J.T. was also moving in."

Jetton's two-bedroom apartment was around the corner from Brown's Diner, which was where most disheveled songwriters loved to scarf down a burger. When John Prine or Townes Van Zandt went to Brown's, the musicians stopped by Jetton and Steve's spot afterward, singing songs while Justin slept in the bedroom he shared with his dad. (Steve shared parental duties with Carol, bringing Justin, age three or so, back and forth between the two homes.) By all accounts, it was Justin's mother, not

Steve, who struggled most with the responsibilities of being a new parent in Justin's first years.

"At that point, Steve was pretty responsible with J.T.," Jetton recalled, decades later. "And then the record deal, and money, kicked in, and all of a sudden Steve went off the rails."

The arrival of Steve Earle's debut album, *Guitar Town*, in 1986 changed his life, catapulting him into the stardom he'd long craved. The title track, which became a top-ten country hit, tells the story of a rambling musician tearing through Texas with his band, enthralled by the touring life. The song is written as a vague promise to a woman at home: One of these days, the narrator assures her, he will settle down and return to her. But not while the road was still calling.

Steve also folded his fatherly absence into the album. The ballad "Little Rock 'N' Roller" tells the story of a boy who eagerly picks up a ringing telephone. On the other line, his distant dad, calling from an Arkansas truck stop, takes a few minutes to check in on his son, to tell him something that might make him feel better: One day, when you're a little bit older, he promises, you can join Daddy on his tour bus.

"Little Rock 'N' Roller" marked the beginning of Steve Earle's penchant for mythologizing his complicated relationship with Justin, a showcase of sympathetic self-awareness (the tale of a guilt-ridden, homesick dad), honesty about his shortcomings, and a convenient papering over of the dark realities his absence wrought.

Around this time, a fellow dad was watching his kid play T-ball in Nashville. It was a typical suburban scene, parents in bleachers cheering on their four-year-olds. Only one element was out of place: a solitary figure sitting out in the parking lot, far from the other parents.

"I look way out, beyond the outfield, and there's Steve Earle on a Harley-Davidson with his legs stretched over the handlebars," said the dad, a man named Jody Williams. It took him a moment to realize why this nascent country star was staring at a suburban Nashville ball field: to watch his little rock 'n' roller play.

By this point, Steve was involved with the woman who'd become his fourth wife: Lou-Anne Gill. She worked in the music business and had a daughter Justin's age. Steve eventually moved in with Gill, insisting Justin stay with them on weekends. Separated but not yet divorced, Steve and Carol began disagreeing about how to raise their preschool-age child: under Carol's supervision, Justin was diagnosed as having ADD. "It was a focus problem," said Carol. "He had so much on his mind." Suspicious of the rise of ADD diagnoses, and fearful of his own troubled relationship with substances, Steve didn't want to medicate Justin.

The very young child Gill was introduced to at that time was already, she sensed, fractured and vulnerable. "The trauma he had when he was little was because the adults in his life were paying attention to what was going on in *their* lives and *their* trauma and not paying attention to how it was affecting kids," she said years later.

As a young child, Justin courted danger and tested every boundary: When his stepsister, Amy, concocted a potion with nail polish and household products, Justin drank it willingly. By age five, "he was like, 'I can do anything; I'm invincible,'" said Gill.

Justin was often surrounded by aunts, uncles, grandparents, and cousins, in addition to his step-sibling and his half brother, Ian Earle, who was born to Gill and Steve in 1987. The commotion and warmth of Justin's new family did nothing to curb Justin's knack for kicking up chaos: During dinnertime, Justin's stepmom would spend an hour coaxing Justin to eat while he ran around the house. When Steve enrolled Justin at a Montessori preschool, Justin was kicked out; he couldn't sit down or stay quiet.

As a young boy, said Gill, Justin was "very much like his dad: If everything was going along smoothly, he had to blow something up."

But Justin also exuded an innocent sweetness. When he showed up to Easter at his relatives' home in a crisp white suit Carol dressed him in, he wandered around the front lawn, lost, while his older cousins raced around finding eggs. When Justin was about six, he brought home a wounded kitten. "He was determined to save the cat," said Gill. "When the cat died, he cried and *cried*."

When Justin was with his stepmom (he never called her mom, always "Lou") and siblings on the weekends, his father was often on tour. When Steve came home, he gave his kids presents and riled them up by blaring Guadalcanal Diary's song "Watusi Rodeo" or playing Elvis on his guitar as the kids danced around the living room.

Justin adored and began to mimic his father. He boasted about his dad, telling classmates his father was a rock star, starting fights if they didn't believe him. "I'd brag my ass off about it," Justin remembered. "I thought it was big shit."[25]

Gill saw the way her and Steve's behavior rubbed off on their kids, none more than Justin. Steve was constantly fighting—with his wife, his record label, his bandmates, his manager. "It was always someone that he had to be mad at," she said. "The kids saw that."

Steve and Carol legally divorced in 1987, and Carol got a job as an administrative assistant at a music publishing company. She switched jobs often, but she was beloved by her colleagues at one of her most long-standing gigs: working as a stagehand and lighting technician for concerts at big venues like the Starwood Amphitheatre.

She remained overwhelmed by single motherhood, by the way her independence had been stripped from her. She did her best to hold on to her life, letting her son spend weekends with relatives so she could go out.

But it remained hard. From a young age, Justin sensed the way his presence could disturb, disrupt, or fluster his mother. When he grew old enough to face difficulties in school, old enough to need lunch money, old enough to be scared in his bed at night, he kept those needs, fears, and problems to himself. He never wanted to upset or burden her.

"There's a lot of things that I didn't tell my mom," he explained, "because, even as a kid, my mom did not need the stress."[26]

Carol tried to keep Justin engaged, enrolling him in karate, where he dressed up in a white gi and kicked around the studio, and taking him to Pop Warner football tryouts. Justin took to sports—basketball, soccer—particularly excelling at the latter, but he "didn't stay with anything," said Carol.

In class Justin was rambunctious and hyper. He attended Eakin Elementary School, the neighborhood public school, where many of his classmates' parents either were connected to Vanderbilt University or had ties to the music industry. Eakin was an arts-focused, nationally recognized public school; the music teacher once played in the Charlie Daniels Band.

Across the street from Eakin, he ran around Fannie Mae Dees Park, called "Dragon Park" for its serpent-like sculptures. From young childhood to adolescence, Dragon Park became the center of Justin's social life, the location for a series of progressively less wholesome pastimes as Justin and his friends grew from boys to punk teens: from running around the park's field to skateboarding to bottle-rocket wars and drinking forties. (The park served as the backdrop for the cover of Justin's 2014 album, *Single Mothers*.)

From a young age, Justin made up stories and spun tales to adults and classmates. He became so talented at weaving together these imaginative stories that his aunt Judy Hilton thought, "He's going to be a songwriter, like his dad." (As an adult, Justin explained how songwriting suited his penchant for truth bending: "I got into a business where I could apply my bullshit everyday.")[27]

Steve Earle released his third album, *Copperhead Road*, in 1988, establishing himself as a bona fide rock star. He used his heightened celebrity to work out his feelings about fatherhood in public. Steve cofounded a nonprofit for homeless children, lamented missing his younger son Ian's early milestones, and vowed to stop touring altogether once Justin turned thirteen.

"The only people I think who are really worthless in this world," Steve told a reporter in 1988, "are the people who won't take care of their children."[28]

Steve was also developing a raging addiction to all sorts of drugs. As a result, seeing his dad around this time could be a disturbing and destabilizing experience for Justin. Shortly after *Copperhead Road*'s release, Justin witnessed an altercation between his dad and Gill, who'd separated after Steve had, once again, cheated on his wife. The couple got into a fight in their bedroom, their children "screaming outside the door," as Gill told Steve's biographer.[29] Afterward, Gill filed assault charges against her soon-to-be ex-husband. She later dropped them.

"It was a volatile time," she said years later. "Steve didn't abuse me physically; he abused me with his behavior, just like he abused Justin with his behavior."

The chaos in Justin's home life started manifesting at school. One classmate recalled that Justin "would sneak up behind me, slap the back of my head, then go running down the hall." Justin was hyperactive and struggled to focus. He had difficulty learning. Years later, he explained that he was dyslexic.[30]

To his classmates, Justin was the boy whose father once showed up to a bring-your-parent-to-school day, dressed in a leather vest and sunglasses and told the class, "I play in a band called Steve Earle and the Dukes."

One day in third grade, Justin's class clowning ascended to new heights. He decided to stick a metal object into an electrical socket.[31] "We saw that dude jerk," said his classmate Tommy Anderson. "And then the lights went out." Justin's teacher grabbed him by the cheeks to discipline the unruly boy. Justin soon left Eakin Elementary.

Justin and his mom regularly switched homes. They didn't move as often as he later claimed, and their economic situation wasn't quite as desperate as he later made it out to be. But Justin's childhood was defined by a general sense of precarity.

In the telling of his own story, Justin emphasized his mother's working-class struggles and minimized, or outright erased, his father's financial role in his upbringing. Growing up with no money was a story Justin told that was simpler, perhaps, than articulating what he *did* lack: consistent care, supervision, structure, stability, and attention. "Steve gave us money," Carol explained in *Hardcore Troubadour*, "but the money made no difference when it came to the emotional well-being of a child."[32]

One memory Justin couldn't shake: the day he asked his mom for two dollars and was told no, because Carol needed to buy milk.[33]

Justin summarized his scarred childhood memories in a never-released song he wrote before his career took off called "Uncertain Tears." It offered his response, of sorts, to the tender imagery of his father's "Little Rock 'N' Roller," and obliquely referenced his mother's frenzied absence: "Waiting late nights by the phone / Ah, but daddy never called," he sang. "And mama's busy climbing up the walls / So I just got used to being on my own."

"When I was a kid, just everything hurt so bad," Justin said during a series of extensive interviews with an Associated Press reporter named Chris Talbott in 2011. "I was abandoned by my father and left with my mother, who, because we'd been abandoned, had to work all the time. And, so, against my mother's will, she had to abandon me. . . . I was a real hyperactive kid who said things that were really weird. . . . I got made fun of a lot in elementary school and beat up. And the whole time, I was alone. I'd always go home and I'd be alone."[34]

Then again, sometimes being alone was a best-case scenario.

"My mom, something she feels terrible about, had this string of drunk boyfriends," he told the journalist. "One of them used to beat me up. So I never even felt safe when I went home."[35]

Justin remembered walking himself to the bus stop in the morning, wandering home after school, scrounging for lunch money, fixing his own food. He clung to his mother when he could, hoping she'd stay with him when she had other places she needed to be. He found solace in rare moments of undivided care he received from his maternal grandmother, Norma, who sat quietly beside him at Greer Stadium, teaching him how to keep a box score at Nashville Sounds baseball games.

But for much of his childhood, Justin was, in fact and feeling, alone. It was an aloneness that settled in so quickly and deeply it wasn't ameliorated when Justin, age five, got a younger brother and a stepsister when his dad married Lou-Anne Gill. It was an aloneness that Justin resented and revisited for the rest of his life, an aloneness he alluded to in his songs about cold houses and faraway fathers and mamas who tended to look the other way.

"I learned to be brave," Justin said in his early thirties, promoting his album *Single Mothers*. "But I was lonely. I was lonely for a long time."[36]

In his midthirties, Justin Townes Earle disappeared to a remote seaside village thousands of miles from Nashville and filled a notebook with verses about his hometown. In one song, called "Kids in the Street," Justin revisited the faces, sights, and smells he encountered wandering Twenty-First Avenue as a preteen. In one unpublished couplet, he wrote:

Once I thought the world revolved
Around these sixteen city blocks

Those sixteen city blocks—the quadrants of Justin's preteen latchkey universe—encompassed the apartment complex where Justin and his mom lived on the corner of Portland and Twenty-First Avenue and Brown's Diner, the famous Nashville greasy spoon John Prine used to frequent.

There was a Jim Dandy convenience store, where Justin and his friends bought twenty-cent ice-cream sandwiches and from which they were eventually banned after stealing *Playboy* magazines. Across the street was the grocery store, Compton's Foodland, where they purchased ramen noodles they ate raw and Kool-Aid mix they poured down their throats. Friedman's, the army-navy surplus store where Justin and his friends admired the guns for sale in glass cases, was down the street. At night, in the open field next to Justin's apartment, the neighborhood kids played German Spotlight, hiding in the bushes in the dark and shining flashlights at each other.

Many of Justin's friends lived nearby. Left with no babysitter (his mom couldn't afford one, he said),[37] Justin hosted friends at his unsupervised home. In his bedroom, beneath his Guns N' Roses poster, they huddled around his computer—Justin was the rare kid who owned one—and giggled as they played *Leisure Suit Larry*, an adult-themed video game featuring a middle-aged man trying to pick up women that, to eleven-year-old boys, functionally served as pornography.

"I had the shaved head and the rat tail and wore the Jams and Air Jordans and got ringworm just like every other kid that rolled around in the grass at Sevier Park," Justin recalled, referring to the then rough neighborhood park.[38]

On Saturdays, Carol often took Justin to Baskin Robbins after lunch (his favorite flavor: "Daiquiri Ice"). But on weekdays, the feral kid who missed Mom would wander.

"Justin would come home to sleep and eat, basically," said his close childhood friend Adam Williams. "Other than that, he wanted to get out and raise hell."

Justin's unchaperoned childhood was not unusual. Neither was his family's connection to the music business. Many of Justin's classmates had fathers in the music industry: One kid's stepfather was "Small Town Saturday Night" country hitmaker Hal Ketchum; another kid's dad ran Capitol Records.

On the contrary, Justin's lonesome upbringing was an unspoken connection he shared with his friends, many of whom came from similarly unstable families.

"We just kind of did what we wanted," said one neighborhood acquaintance. "You grow up in an atmosphere, in Nashville, at least in that area, in that time, where *everybody* does drugs. . . . Among the people Justin knew, everybody had a nontraditional-upbringing lifestyle."

The sixteen city blocks that formed Justin's childhood stomping grounds spanned several overlapping neighborhoods: Hillsboro Village, Belmont, and, farther south, Hillsboro and Green Hills. The adjacent neighborhoods were known for their affordable real estate, proximity to downtown, and businesses that catered to college students. Even as Nashville families left for the suburbs in the early nineties, the area's population grew by more than 50 percent.[39]

North Nashville, just some half-dozen miles away, was predominantly Black and eventually had the country's highest rate of incarceration.[40] There, just driving home from work could result in a police stop.[41] But Justin's whiter middle-class neighborhood was much less policed, a part of town where parents had no fear about letting their kids run wild between school and dinnertime.

It was the early to midnineties, the age of *Beavis and Butt-Head*, Nirvana, and Snoop Dogg's *Doggystyle*. Justin dyed his hair green, skateboarded around town, stole cigarettes, and got into graffiti (his tag: *KUJI*, short for "Cool G"). He and his friends tried to make napalm, hoarded nondairy creamer because they heard it was flammable, turned lighters into makeshift flamethrowers, and set a garage roof on fire. When they were old enough, they biked to Lucy's Record Shop, the all-ages venue where Nashville punks hung out and where teenagers sniffed glue and drank Mad Dog 20/20 in the back alley.

As a preteen, Justin loved Pearl Jam, Nirvana, Dr. Dre, Beastie Boys, Eazy-E, and the frenetic Chicago rapper Twista. Some of his childhood pop-music education came via his dad, who'd relocated to Los Angeles with his fifth wife—a record executive named Teresa Ensenat—and occasionally sent records home: AC/DC, Nirvana's *Bleach*, Ice Cube's *Lethal Injection*.

Before he expressed interest in guitar, preteen Justin talked about wanting to be a rapper. One of his neighborhood friends can still remember the day Justin began to freestyle. He didn't get through his rap before his friends started making fun of him: Most every line he rapped was taken from a popular hip-hop song of the day.

But he absorbed all types of music. He discovered heavy metal. Classic British punk was next. The first band he ever saw live, he claimed, was Kiss. He started a band with a cousin called Sheep Hill, where he thrashed around on guitar.

"I was playing in bad punk bands from the age of 11 or 12," Justin said, "and doing what guys in bands do: smoking dope and drinking liquor."

Throughout his adulthood, Justin told outlandish stories about how frightening his childhood had been. There was his story of seeing crack cocaine for the first time in a parking lot at age nine, his story of his father leaving him at a crack house, his story of smelling crack for the first time on a trip to Disneyland at age six or seven.[42]

Late in his life, he started claiming he first shot up heroin as a twelve-year-old. "When that plunger went down," he said in one version of the story, "it was like a warm blanket wrapped over me."[43] Those he grew up with—including friends with whom he *did* soon start to experiment with drugs—believed that was a wild exaggeration.

But he also told a more plausible origin story of his introduction to narcotics. This was the story of a twelve-year-old with impulse-control issues stumbling upon a dangerous object for his appetite: his grandmother's pill case. More specifically, he claimed he discovered Dilaudid, or hydromorphone, a highly addictive opioid prescribed as a painkiller.[44]

"Opioids were always my first and foremost drug," he later said.[45]

"I just remember getting hit with it and it just felt like everything was just going to be OK," Justin said many years later, reflecting on his history with addiction in an interview he gave shortly after relapsing. "I wanted to go back and capture that feeling again."[46]

CHAPTER 2

THE FIRST TIME JUSTIN LEFT NASHVILLE, HE DIDN'T MAKE IT PAST the suburbs. Steve had purchased a country home in Fairview, a small town thirty minutes outside the city, while dividing his time between Tennessee and Los Angeles. In 1992, he divorced Ensenat, his fifth wife, and the next year *remarried* Lou-Anne Gill. Gill and Steve settled in Fairview full-time with their son, Ian, and Gill's daughter, Amy.

Fairview was a much more conservative place than Nashville. High school football and church ruled supreme; Gill recalled that when she moved there, it felt so provincial, she felt like she'd arrived at the edge of the universe.

When Steve was previously married to Ensenat, Justin had spent time in Fairview on and off, and Steve's younger sister Stacey Earle had moved in to keep the household afloat. Speaking with author David McGee for his Steve Earle book *Fearless Heart, Outlaw Poet*, Stacey set a stark scene: "There's needles laying everywhere, blood I'm washing off the mirrors," she said. "I'm feeding the kids with cereal spoons he'd been using to cook crack."[1]

When Steve remarried Gill in 1993, Justin moved out to live with his dad full-time. The idea was to reconvene the family unit that'd briefly lived together—and had been relatively stable—during Steve and Gill's first marriage. The reality was much different.

"It was like controlling a circus of meth addicts," Gill said.

The decision for Justin to move to Fairview was one both father and son later mythologized to their own ends, each one claiming *they* made the decision to save the *other*. Justin said he moved in because he was worried his heroin-addicted father might die. Steve said he brought his preteen son to Fairview because he was worried Justin was spiraling into delinquency.[2]

"He was stealing shit, he was not going to school, and he was taking drugs," Steve recalled.[3]

Carol believed Justin needed discipline only his father could provide. "He had started being defiant," she said.

But the household Justin joined was "absolute fucking mayhem," as Justin later put it.[4] His father was in the depths of his addiction. Dad had declared his bathroom forbidden to everyone else. Dad subsisted on frozen White Castle burgers and Dr. Pepper. Dad disappeared for days. Dad crashed into a pickup truck on I-40.[5] Dad screamed at his wife.

"Chaos controlled everything in our house and in our lives. It was chaos and trauma," said Gill, who tried maintaining order even as she herself struggled with her own substance use.

Justin later told a similar story. "You never knew what the fuck was going to happen in that house," he said. "I was living out in the country with a wild-ass dad and a fucking slumped over step-mother, doing what I thought was taking care of my kid brother and sister, which I wasn't, I was just being an idiot."[6]

As Steve tried to kick heroin, Gill drove him every morning two hours to a Chattanooga methadone clinic. But one day, as both Gill and Justin's friend Adam Williams, recalled, Steve drove himself. On this particular day, Williams had slept over in Fairview; Steve woke him and Justin and ordered them into his car. Williams remembered driving two hours, then waiting in the car as Steve went into the clinic.

He also remembered falling asleep, then being awoken on the ride back to Fairview.

"Next thing I know, I pop up, and the car is jumping around," said Williams. "Steve had nodded off at the wheel and we were driving off the road, and I swear he stopped and probably thirty feet ahead of us was this big embankment."

Justin cycled through preadolescent phases: white rapper, basketball jock, graffiti punk. But when he moved out to Fairview full-time, Gill remembered him as a "clean cut soccer player." In the 1995 Fairview Middle School yearbook, Justin, thirteen, smiled for the camera with a blond bowl cut.

Through his stepsister, Justin found a group of Fairview outcasts who gravitated toward flannel, hair dye, and loud guitars. "We were all going through that same grunge phase," said Sara Connell, Justin's middle school girlfriend.

With his tall-tale stories, easy smile, and rowdy sense of humor, Justin established himself immediately in the friend group. When Connell remembered Justin, she remembered a "six-foot, tall, goofy guy with the hot pink bowl cut" always making his friends laugh.

One of their foremost obsessions was Beck, a Los Angeles street musician who blended blues, folk, and hip-hop and was the son of a noted musician and string arranger. In 1994, Beck was experimenting with field recordings and his own version of contemporary acoustic blues on his albums *Stereopathetic Soulmanure* and *One Foot in the Grave*.

From his basement bedroom in Fairview, Justin felt his way through Beck's acoustic songs, like "Puttin' It Down," pondering, perhaps, how this twentysomething white California kid used harmonica wheezing and toe-tapping and an affected southern accent to make himself sound like a sage bluesman.[7]

Sitting next to Justin in his bedroom, often, was Chaz Moore, a fellow Fairview troublemaker. The two boys became fast friends, responding to pubescent woes the same way many pissed-off eighties and nineties teens responded to those feelings: they started a punk band.

Theirs was short-lived, existing entirely within their bedrooms and primarily in their own minds. They called themselves Fucked Up Smiley Faces, and Moore claimed the band got as far as recording a scratchy home demo. The boys got the cassette tape in the hands of a family friend who worked at a radio station, Moore remembered, and that family friend promptly told them, "I can't play something from a band called Fucked Up Smiley Faces."

This was a blessing. "It was probably some of the worst music anybody ever heard," said Moore.

As Justin worked through his feelings making music in the basement, upstairs Steve remained tormented by his illness. His addiction had left him barely functioning. In September 1994, he was sentenced to a year in jail for heroin possession after a series of drug arrests and failures to appear in court. After eight days in a Nashville jail, he was transferred to Buffalo Valley, a drug-treatment center outside Nashville. He spent a month there before being transferred back to jail and was released on the condition he attend outpatient treatment.[8]

The experience saved Steve Earle's life and changed it permanently. He kicked heroin and made a lifelong commitment to twelve-step recovery, a practice to which he remains devoted.

"I guess the fog cleared," Steve said on NPR's *Fresh Air* in 1996. "I actually had been physically restrained from taking drugs for several weeks, and that hadn't happened to me in years. I just probably wouldn't have gotten clean if I hadn't gotten locked up. . . . I would have just died."[9]

The story of Steve's brief stint in treatment and jail soon became a tidy tale of roughneck redemption: outlaw lands behind bars, then turns his life around. He detailed his experience of withdrawing in jail and talked up the power of recovery in interviews. "What I do," Steve said in 1996, "is get up and get my ass to meetings, pretty much every day. I don't know how other people deal with their addiction, but this works for me."[10]

Publicly, Steve credited his new sobriety as a turning point for him as a father. "I've been there every fucking day since I got sober," Steve said in 2009. "I've saved it up and showed up as a parent."[11]

For his family, the reality was more complicated. Steve's reappearance after quitting heroin provided its own world of hurt. "When Steve came out of treatment, we all expected this nice, clean, shiny start," said his then-wife, Gill.

Instead, Steve was irritable, impulsive, and he fought bitterly with his family. When he disagreed with a decision his record label made about sequencing his first postjail record, *Train a Comin'*, he shot a copy of the album with a rifle, riddling it with bullets.[12]

This behavior was, in ways, even more devastating to family members than his using. "Well, he's clean now," Justin remembered thinking to himself. "Where the fuck is he?"[13]

Justin's middle school girlfriend, Sara Connell, remembered the sole occasion Steve engaged with his children while she was over at the house: Steve summoned his kids and their friends, squeezing them into the backseat of his Cadillac, and drove them to a gas station to buy candy, blasting "Sabotage" by the Beastie Boys.

Justin experienced his father's postsobriety instability as yet another type of abandonment. He bristled and rebelled. He ran away from the cops. He ran away from home. He was brought to a therapist and, according to Gill, at one point, a psychiatric hospital. He lashed out at authority figures in school, calling one teacher a Nazi and later, according to both a classmate and his stepmom, jumping up and spitting on that same teacher's desk. This, Gill remembered, got him kicked out of Fairview Middle School.

Justin landed at the Dede Wallace campus at Centerstone, a social service agency that housed an alternative education program in North Nashville for children with emotional and behavioral issues. "It was a jail, basically," Justin said. "There were these big guys that roamed the halls who were just bouncers. They had a cell in each room [that] had slide locks on it. They'd throw your ass in there and lock you up if you were causing trouble."[14]

Justin, now thirteen or so, eventually moved back to Nashville. Lou-Anne Gill divorced Steve for a second time (she'd again suspected, correctly, that he'd been cheating), and Justin joined Gill, his half-brother, and his stepsister at Gill's new home in the city. It was, briefly, a more stable environment, with Justin's friends coming over for sleepovers and movie nights.

But it did not last. Eventually, Gill noticed what seemed to be several stolen car radios in the back of Justin's closet. And she remembered Justin, after hearing their neighbor was being physically abused by her husband, going out to smash the window of a car he thought belonged to the abuser (he wrecked the wrong car). She didn't know how to handle him.

Justin was sent, once again, back to Fairview. Back with his dad, Justin sought new levels of mischief with friends. They smoked weed underneath their parents' decks, threw ragers at Steve's largely unsupervised house, drove go-karts around Steve's front lawn, goofed around with Steve's expensive guitars, drank Wild Turkey, committed petty theft, blasted Marilyn Manson and Nine Inch Nails, and lit fields on fire.

Justin was angry that his dad had, once again, broken up a family unit, angry that his dad quitting heroin hadn't made things better, angry that in some ways, his dad seemed even less available than when he was using.

Justin sought out new ways to piss off Steve. He developed a passing interest in golf, knowing Steve despised the sport. (When father and son agreed, years later, to a joint interview with NPR, Steve recalled coming home to Justin wearing jeans and a too-short Nirvana T-shirt, launching golf balls into a cow pasture from their front yard.)[15]

Justin also knew his dad kept a nine-millimeter pistol underneath his mattress, a holdover from Steve's days of heading into rough parts of Nashville to score drugs. So Justin stole it.

It was a story Steve told for years, one that became his sound bite for why he changed his mind in favor of gun control.[16] Justin hid the loaded gun behind the basement shower. When Steve realized Justin had stolen it, he panicked, scouring the house, demanding Justin tell him where it was.

Finally, Justin had his father's full attention.

Steve couldn't find the gun. Justin wouldn't say where it was. Eventually, Steve decided Justin should be sent away to the same place Justin's cousin had been sent years prior after getting into serious trouble. Steve called his brother, Patrick, and the two men forcibly placed Justin in a car—"like trying to wrestle a live deer into your truck,"[17] Steve said years later—and drove him forty miles to the Three Springs–Duck River wilderness camp in Centerville, Tennessee.

DOES YOUR SON NEED HELP GETTING BACK ON TRACK?

Thus read a 1995 advertisement[18] for Three Springs–Duck River, the central Tennessee location of a fast-growing corporation that, by the midnineties, sold a seductive solution to parents in the Southeast: If they sent their unruly teenage boys to an educational camp where they had to do physical labor and engage in group therapy, they'd be reformed by the hard lessons and harsh realities of living in the woods.

These so-called wilderness camps were the latest trend in the "troubled-teen" industry, which was becoming big business. Founded in 1985, Three Springs opened eighteen locations in six states and commanded roughly $13 million in annual revenue by the midnineties, earning a spot on *Inc.* magazine's list of fastest-growing companies in the country.[19]

When Justin arrived, he was searched for contraband, assigned to a group (Wakpa Tate, crudely translated from Dakota as "river wind"), and given a handbook that outlined what he could expect from his time in the woods.

"Dear New Resident," the book began. "We realize you may be experiencing a lot of different emotions as you enter treatment. . . . It is our sincere hope that you will choose to use your time here in a constructive way and make some meaningful changes."

Three Springs was divided into a series of isolated campsites. During the week, groups of teens congregated at the mess hall for meals and classes. On weekends, each group worked on tasks around their campsite, like building a new latrine or constructing a rainproof cover for the firepit.

Justin arrived at Three Springs as a tall goth-looking outcast. He soon adjusted to the rigid schedule: waking up at 6:00 a.m., cleaning their quarters, breakfast at 7:15, classes all morning, vocational projects and phys ed in the afternoon, dinner at 5:00 p.m., showers at 5:30, group therapy and homework at 7:00 p.m., bedtime at 10:00. Twice a week, he met for one-on-one sessions with a psychologist.

It remains unclear exactly how long Justin attended Three Springs. In Steve's telling, Justin called his dad the day after being sent away and told him where his gun was. After that, Steve recalled Justin returned home soon after.[20] But multiple people at Three Springs, including one of Justin's clinical supervisors, remembered him spending somewhere between three and six months at the camp.

They remembered him as a well-behaved, quiet kid who followed the rules. He shivered through the cold country evenings. He did his chores, said the right things in group therapy, and helped out with the kids' shared tasks. And while he likely felt fearful and alone living with strangers in the woods as a fourteen-year-old far removed from friends and family, Justin was, by several accounts, largely spared the type of severe physical and emotional abuse that would be revealed in subsequent decades to be commonplace at other such adolescent wilderness camps.

When one fellow group member, Clayton Kidd, remembered Justin at Three Springs, he pictured him lugging around a bright-orange five-gallon Gatorade cooler filled with drinking water. But his main memory was of Justin repeatedly singing the opening lines to "Sound System," a song by West Coast punk band Operation Ivy: "Sound system gonna bring me back up / One thing that I can depend on."

Justin had definitely left the wilderness camp by early January 1997. On New Year's Day 1997, his namesake, Townes Van Zandt, died of a heart attack at fifty-two. One of the first things Justin did when he was back from Three Springs was accompany his father to Van Zandt's memorial service.

"I booked this gig thirty-something years ago," Van Zandt's dear friend and fellow musician Guy Clark said from the podium, as Justin looked on.[21]

The affair was held at Nashville's Belmont Church on January 5, the day after Justin's fifteenth birthday. A cadre of songwriters—including

Emmylou Harris, Lyle Lovett, Nanci Griffith, Rodney Crowell, and Susanna Clark—showed up. Van Zandt had suffered in his last few years, strung out from alcoholism, playing to tiny crowds, no longer able to write the kinds of songs on which his legend depended.

As a kid, Justin had always wondered why he'd been named after the drunk, disheveled friend of his dad's, a guy whose music his mother loved but whose persona his mother despised, a guy who had stumbled into Justin's life on a few occasions to tell him some scary story but whose music had seemed, frankly, boring. "I didn't give a fuck about Townes Van Zandt," Justin told a music blog years later.[22]

But at Van Zandt's memorial, it began to make sense. Van Zandt hadn't been a stand-up member of society, maybe, but, judging by the reactions to his death, his music must've touched and shaped a lot of people.

Justin listened to his father's eulogy. "He went into the dark, scary places we couldn't go," Steve told the packed church. "Sometimes I think he went there so we didn't have to."[23]

It'd take Justin another ten years to release his own music. But sitting in Belmont Church, the fifteen-year-old finally understood why his father gave him his middle name.

"That day," Justin said, "I got more of an idea of the greatness of him than ever before."[24]

One story father and son both loved telling: Sometime around 1995, before Justin was sent to Three Springs, he became one of several million American teenagers to fall in love with Nirvana's *MTV Unplugged in New York*.

Justin was particularly enamored with the album's closing song, "Where Did You Sleep Last Night" (also known as "In the Pines"). Kurt Cobain sings the haunting ballad with an ache that escalates into wails of loss and confusion. The song was cemented in Nirvana's canon, and Cobain's legend, in part because it was recorded just five months before Cobain's death at age twenty-seven.

Justin couldn't stop listening.

One day, overhearing Justin blaring the song, Steve Earle popped into Justin's bedroom to offer some fatherly folk knowledge:

"You know that's a Lead Belly song, right?" Steve asked Justin.

"No," Justin insisted. "Kurt Cobain wrote that."

Steve promptly took Justin upstairs and put on a Lead Belly record.[25]

Hearing Lead Belly was, by Justin's telling, his musical big bang, like Bruce Springsteen watching Elvis shake his hips on *Ed Sullivan*, or Mavis Staples hearing the voice of Mahalia Jackson, or Steve Earle first hearing Jerry Jeff Walker in high school.

Long recognized as an icon of the American blues and folk-music tradition, Huddie Ledbetter—or Lead Belly—was born on a plantation in Northwest Louisiana in 1888. A series of convictions had led him in and out of prison as a young man (as the legend goes, his music earned him a pardon from the Louisiana governor). His music was eventually introduced to white audiences by folklorists John Lomax and his son Alan, who also shaped the careers of mid-twentieth-century folksingers like Woody Guthrie and Pete Seeger. As with Guthrie and Seeger, Lead Belly sang and recorded many songs he did not write.[26]

One of those songs was "In the Pines." In 1944, a few years before dying at sixty-one, Lead Belly recorded his version of the song, turning the traditional Appalachian mountain tune into a gothic blues ballad.

Discovering Lead Belly, Justin said, was like "getting a bomb dropped on you."[27] Like Beck, Steve Earle, and countless other white musicians before them, Justin's life changed the moment he discovered southern Black music. The tone, honesty, and sparseness of this impossibly old-sounding voice singing through the static set Justin's teenage mind ablaze. Suddenly, he said, life felt different.

For years, as Justin remembered, an acoustic guitar his father gifted him at age nine had sat unused in his closet. "At that point," Justin said, "I thought music was the reason my family was broken up."[28]

Steve had missed birthdays, graduations, parent-teacher meetings, soccer games, karate demonstrations. What would've happened if he'd missed his son blaring Kurt Cobain? Is the fact that he *didn't* miss it, that he'd been present for that moment, one of the reasons both father and son so loved telling this story? Is that why Justin and Steve both crystallized this instance as the beginning of the Justin Townes Earle story?

Lead Belly led Justin to other Black midcentury folk-blues singers like Sonny Terry and Brownie McGhee, which led him to Guthrie. Next came the southern country-blues pickers who'd soon form the basis of Justin's guitar playing: Mississippi John Hurt, Lightnin' Hopkins, and Mance Lipscomb.

Suddenly, Beck and Metallica and West Coast rap didn't seem nearly as interesting. This southern music now spoke to him far more than grunge or goth. Justin wanted to learn what these old songs meant, *how* they sounded the way they did. If he was willing to be taught, his dad was right upstairs.

The musicians he tried to emulate most were Lipscomb and Hopkins, both of them introduced to him via documentarian Les Blank's films about the two bluesmen: *A Well Spent Life* and *The Blues Accordin' to Lightnin' Hopkins*. When Steve wasn't around, Justin remembered using a secret spare key to sneak copies of the films from his dad's locked closet full of old CDs and music VHS tapes. He watched footage of these old musicians, who enraptured him just as they'd enraptured Steve decades prior.

Justin was particularly fascinated by Lipscomb, who was born in 1895, the son of an enslaved man who became a professional fiddler.[29] His name, "Mance," was short for *emancipation*.

One song, in particular, caught Justin's attention: "So Different Blues," an obscure number with an impossibly complex, ragtime-influenced guitar riff interspersed with Lipscomb's signature dead-thumb fingerpicking. Lipscomb knew that replicating the guitar part he'd composed for "So Different Blues" was a physically demanding task: "Nobody can pick it up to save their lives," he once said of the song.[30]

When Justin heard "So Different Blues," he embraced the challenge.

"My dad showed it to me, and he was like, 'You're not going to be able to do that,'" he remembered.[31]

Justin was determined to prove his father wrong, sitting in his bedroom for a week trying to figure out how Mance Lipscomb moved his fingers.

When he emerged, having mastered the song, his father couldn't believe it.

"Next thing I knew," Steve wrote, remembering the moment years later, "he was playing stuff I'd been trying to sort out for years."[32]

Justin kept his new passion close to the chest. This was a secret he shared with his dad. When his peers caught him listening to this ancient-sounding folk music, Justin remembered their teasing: "Turn that honky shit off."[33]

"My friends thought I was weird," he explained. "But my heart would beat fast listening to Lead Belly. It made me feel different than any other kind of music. That's what made me realize I could actually write songs."[34]

CHAPTER 3

THE OLD MUSIC JUSTIN EARLE DISCOVERED IN FAIRVIEW EXISTED IN his own private universe until he encountered the Chicken Shack.

In the 1990s, a songwriter turned carpenter named Bill Schleicher built several small, one-room wooden cabins for musicians around Nashville. These little sheds, tucked away in backyards, were used for recording and songwriting.[1] One of them was located in the backyard of a redbrick home on Warfield Drive in Green Hills, a nice neighborhood near where Justin grew up. In 1998, a woman named Jennifer Patten, recently divorced from singer-songwriter Kevin Welch, moved into the home with her three kids. Her eldest, Dustin Welch, was a soft-spoken, bookish boy who blared music and banged around on guitar. It was mutually decided that the backyard shack would become Dustin's bedroom. Everyone called it the Chicken Shack.

Welch, seventeen at the time, would soon become fast friends with Justin Earle; the Chicken Shack eventually became a nearly mythical meeting space for them and for a generation of young Nashville roots musicians. But before that, Welch left high school and used his backyard bedroom as a creative classroom. It was where he did his homeschooling work, and where he painted, wrote songs, devoured the novels of Steinbeck and Bukowski, and taught himself how to play banjo.

Over time, he transformed the one-room shack into his own teenage clubhouse, bringing in paintings, instruments (guitars, banjo, drums, bass, tambourine, trombone, mandolin, washboard, lap steel guitar, even, somehow, an upright piano). He constructed papier-mâché objects out of chicken wire, hung up dream catchers, filled shelves with yellowing paperback books and vinyl LPs, tacked up crooked pieces of cheap art and old jug-band posters and a red Pegasus sculpture, and filled the room with as much audio equipment and recording gear as he could find. He hung an upside-down rubber chicken from the rafter.

He filled the fridge with PBR and Busch Light, burned sage, and spent hours reading. The Chicken Shack was "probably what the inside of Dustin's brain looked like," said Angela Schmidt, one of many friends and girlfriends who'd pass through on nights and weekends. She remembered sitting on a cramped couch reading *Calvin and Hobbes* while other kids played music.

Earlier in his adolescence, Welch was in a hippie rock band called the Groundlings, which included his childhood friend Cary Ann Hearst, who would later form the band Shovels & Rope. But in the Chicken Shack, Welch formed a musical group that would change the trajectory of many lives.

All the boys in the band had fathers who were, in one way or another, musicians—Willie Domann was the son of gospel songwriter Lee Domann; Andy Moore was the son of semiprofessional blues singer Rick Moore; Cory Younts was the son of drummer Bob Younts; Travis Nicholson was the son of songwriter Gary Nicholson; Skylar Wilson was the son of hit producer Wally Wilson. In one early iteration, they called themselves Lefty Loosy and the Screwdrivers. The group performed at a classmate's graduation party in the spring of 1998, their sole gig. "People hacky-sacking while we played the blues," as Travis Nicholson remembered.

Welch, Younts, and Nicholson had begun going to the Chicken Shack to sing more roots-based tunes as a trio while they were still in school. After much of that band graduated from Hillsboro High School in 1998, everyone started spending more time at the Chicken Shack. (Hillsboro High graduated many other fledgling Nashville artists in that decade, including filmmaker Harmony Korine, then a straight-edge punk, who was encouraged by his creative-writing teacher to apply for a grant to make a film and would go on to write the dark cult-classic 1995 New York City film *Kids*.)

The Chicken Shack quickly evolved from Dustin Welch's personal classroom-bedroom into a multipurpose space: clubhouse, crash pad, weed den, teenage hostel, party house, multimedia art center, movie theater, and recording studio.

There was an open-door policy; if Welch was finishing up his shift in the kitchen at the Bluebird Cafe, the legendary singer-songwriter venue down the street where he worked, his friends could arrive and start jamming without him.

For an art-minded Nashville teen who couldn't yet get into bars and had nowhere else to go, the Chicken Shack was a "little pocket universe in Green Hills," recalled Jenn Ramsey, one of many fellow Hillsboro alumni who drank and listened to music there.

"When you entered the doors of the Chicken Shack, it was like there was no other world, that's literally what it felt like," said Jared Tyler, a Dobro player who worked with Welch as a barback at the Bluebird. To Welch's younger sister Savannah, the shack behind her house felt like Neverland. "Me and my friends would sit on the trampoline in the backyard, get stoned, and wait for an invitation to the party," she said.

Once inside, Dustin's bandmates impressed Savannah's friends with their wistful country covers. When one of those friends, Melinda Baker, thought back on the Chicken Shack years later, she said, "I just remember it glowing."

The song swapping and guitar pulling had started informally, what you might expect from a group of white southern high schoolers raised by baby boomers. Travis Nicholson covered John Prine and Tom Petty; Dustin Welch dug Texas songwriters like Guy Clark and Townes Van Zandt; Cory Younts pushed the jams toward the high harmonies and rootsy arrangements of the bluegrass music he listened to. Everyone sat around singing Gram Parsons or old-timey humorous country tunes like Roger Miller's "My Uncle Used to Love Me but She Died." They soon started imitating anything from their living idol, songwriter Malcolm Holcombe.

For the Chicken Shack boys, playing this music was a form of bonding. They shared a love of the old and obscure, which they had ready access to via their fathers' record collections. Their high school English teacher, Jeffrey Marks, introduced many of them to *Viper Mad Blues: 25 Songs of Dope and Depravity*, an obscure 1991 compilation of drug-themed jazz and blues tunes from the twenties and thirties. The Chicken Shack teens fell hard for the album, for the scratchy sounds and salacious tales they heard on songs like "Cocaine Blues" and "Take a Whiff on Me." The compilation introduced them to folk-blues pioneers and Black jug bands: Cats and the Fiddle, the Memphis Jug Band, Gus Cannon. Songs about knife fights and reefer and moonshine, recorded long before their parents were born, sounded foreign and far more thrilling than the middle-class lives the boys lived. They started studying, then imitating groups of Black musicians from the minstrel and vaudeville circuits who formed bands in southern cities like Memphis and Louisville in the early twentieth century. Jug bands were focused on entertaining, injecting humor and showbiz into their sets. They played makeshift instruments, most famously, ceramic jugs, which would be blown as horns. *This*, the boys felt, was original. There were plenty of eighteen-year-olds skulking around Nashville cafés singing Guy Clark and John Prine. There were far fewer performing jug-band blues renditions of "Chittlin' Cookin' Time in Cheatham County," a song popularized in 1936 by Fiddlin' Arthur Smith. It quickly became their signature song.

This music felt like the boys' own private discovery. They decided to start playing public domain songs—"stealin' stealin'" them, in the parlance of one Memphis Jug Band song they adored—adopting old, forgotten tunes as their own. The boys settled on a band name that spoke to its love-and-theft premise.

They called themselves the Swindlers.

The Swindlers studied old records by putting their fingers on the vinyl to slow them down and better understand how they worked. On Monday nights, they headed to the Bluebird, where they listened, mesmerized, to guitarist Mike Henderson.[2] On one of those outings, as former Swindler Andy Moore remembered, Henderson brought his friend Mark Knopfler to the stage.

"Oh, it's the little blues boys," Knopfler said, noticing the group of eager teens in the back.

Not long after Justin was obsessing over Lead Belly thirty miles outside of town in Fairview, the Swindlers were learning Lead Belly–popularized standards like "Midnight Special." They learned Tin Pan Alley classics like "Shine on Harvest Moon" via the oddball vaudeville revivalist Leon Redbone. They picked their way through songs from jazz guitarist Django Reinhardt and blues pioneer W. C. Handy and Hank Williams. They took up folk traditionals like "Moonshiner" and "Shady Grove." They absorbed Dixieland jazz tunes like "Bill Bailey" and big-band blues like "Stormy Monday Blues" and western swing numbers like "Old Fashioned Love" and bluegrass classics like "I Truly Understand That You Love Another Man." They sat in the Chicken Shack, rewinding a VHS of *Three Amigos* in order to write down the lyrics to "Blue Shadows on the Trail," Randy Newman's cowboy pastiche of old Roy Rogers westerns.

Aspiring singers, songwriters, and musicians soon got word of the Chicken Shack and began making pilgrimages: Jason Isbell, Cary Ann Hearst, Willie Watson, Malcolm Holcombe, and instrumentalists like Chris Scruggs (banjo legend Earl Scruggs's grandson), Jared Tyler, Fats Kaplin, Derek Pell, and Josh Graham all visited the backyard cabin at some point.

But the constants were the Swindlers, a rotating cast of friends who stayed up playing music until 4:00 a.m. and then all slept over. Welch would board up the Shack's two windows, turn on the ceiling fans painted with glow-in-the-dark-stripes, throw on a Dvorak concerto to calm everyone down, and everyone would fall asleep.

Welch was the group's leader, the guy handing out band business cards at house parties and trying to convince strangers to take them seriously. He fastened a kick drum and tambourine to a pickle bucket and attached the pickle bucket to a wooden box that spelled out the band's slogan in red and white paint:

The Swindlers: Old Fashioned Ruckus Busking

When the boys would wake up, Welch might suggest they go out for a day's work. That meant packing their pickle bucket, banjos, washboards, and mandolins into a truck and driving downtown to Second Avenue, where they busked—first in overalls, later in musty suits—to tourists in search of cowboy boots and country music. Welch fixed a spittoon to the top of the pickle bucket as a tip jar.

Nashville's country-music industry had enjoyed a decade of mega expansion in the 1990s by emphasizing the suburbs-friendly sounds of artists like Garth Brooks, Kenny Chesney, and Faith Hill. With 1999's *Fly*, a trio from Texas who called themselves the Dixie Chicks toppled conventional wisdom by turning traditional bluegrass-inflected music into a blockbuster. But the industry was still printing money with pop-friendly crossovers: 1999's biggest-selling album was Shania Twain's two-year-old *Come on Over*; the top-selling song was "Amazed" by the boy-band-adjacent Lonestar.

All this money had only recently started to flow back to Nashville's downtown, which was finally attracting tourists for the first time in more than a decade. Since the Opry left the famed Ryman Auditorium in 1974, much of the city's country-music tourism had been redirected to what became known as "Music Valley": the series of motels, souvenir shops, restaurants, and parking lots sprouting up outside the city off the highway near the new Opry. But by the midnineties, the deserted streets of downtown Nashville—populated by sex shops and drug activity—began transforming: The Ryman reopened in 1994. Chains like Hard Rock Cafe and Planet Hollywood and NASCAR-branded restaurants soon followed.[3] It would still be several decades before the city's downtown streets became littered with bachelorette pedal pubs and celebrity-branded honky-tonks, but change was underway.

"Molding Music City to Become Tourist Mecca" read a 1993 headline announcing several major commercial developments, including a downtown arena and an Opryland amusement-park expansion. The key to turning the city into a major metropolis like Atlanta would be selling its music history: "That identity, if pushed in advertising, marketing, and by individuals," read the *Tennessean*, "will be as identifiable to Nashville as Mickey's ears are to Orlando."[4]

Around this time, a throwback country-rock band called BR549 began performing on Lower Broadway, the main thoroughfare, at a newly opened traditional honky-tonk called Robert's Western World, bringing throngs of locals downtown to hear live music for the first time in years.

Three blocks away, Second Avenue was lined with buskers performing "Ring of Fire," "Jolene," and "Friends in Low Places" to streams of tourists. The formula for success was simple: the more likely a passerby was to know a song being strummed by a street performer, the more likely they were to drop change into their guitar case.

The Swindlers, with their Depression-era tunes about chitlins and moonshine, cared not for this equation. Even if they busked there for beer money, Nashville wasn't downtown for these postgrunge nineties teens.

Their lives revolved, instead, around places like Bongo Java, the coffee shop on Belmont Boulevard, the first proper one in town, which had recently become internationally famous for selling "Nun Buns" after an employee noticed one of its pastries bore an uncanny resemblance to Mother Teresa.[5]

And nowhere was more important than the Circle K gas station two doors down from Bongo Java. That's where you'd run into someone buying cigarettes, or meet a friend before heading to Athens, the late-night Greek spot down the street, or gather before walking to Brown's Diner. "The center of the universe," is what Jenn Ramsey, Steve Earle's goddaughter and a sisterlike figure to Justin, said everyone called the gas station.

The Circle K had also been scouted by Harmony Korine for his film *Gummo*, circa 1996, when he was back in Nashville looking for rundown locations and feral teenagers to play key roles in the movie (Justin's childhood friend Jacob Sewell was cast as "Bunny Boy").[6] The film was shot in West Nashville, a working-class part of town far removed from the gradually developing downtown. So even though Korine changed the film's setting to Ohio, the story was a depiction of a side of his home city in the 1990s—one of small-town listlessness and proximity to rural poverty, the exact opposite of the image the city's boosters and developers were trying to project.

In 1997, Justin returned to Nashville, living full-time with his mom for the first time in years. At some point—it's not exactly clear when—he also briefly attended Hillsboro High. By his own recollection, Justin attended for a total of two weeks.[7] By early 1997 he'd enrolled at Benton Hall, a small private alternative school for students with learning disabilities that Justin also remembered having briefly attended in middle school. There, Justin "had a decent year trying to turn it around," according to a teacher, James Purcell. But he continued to struggle academically. By his second semester of his sophomore year, in 1998, he'd entirely dropped out.[8]

Steve blamed the education system for his son's classroom struggles. "They really dropped the ball on him in school," Steve later said. "They declared him learning disabled, and then they gave up on him."[9]

As Justin would later tell the story, he'd decided, with his parents' blessing, that he wanted to play music for a living. He'd grown up around his father's life in music and would accompany his mom to the venues where she worked as a stagehand. "He was intrigued; my work, his dad's guitars, everything," said Carol. Justin settled on his fate: He'd join the family business.[10]

Years later, a journalist asked if he graduated high school.

"I barely even started!" he said. "I skipped out after three months in the ninth grade."

Is that legal?

"I don't know," Justin said. "It was Tennessee."[11]

He'd spent the past couple of years scooting between houses, apartments, and juvenile institutions. Back in Nashville, Justin remained restless, constantly roaming the streets. He bounced his way around the neighborhood, listening to Three 6 Mafia and Hot Boys and dropping into his mother's two-bedroom apartment. His childhood had been defined by constant commotion and unpredictability. Now he sought it out. "Change and uncertainty," as he later put it in a song.

Each morning, he joined his buddies to smoke in the alley next to the Donut Den across the street from Hillsboro High. When everyone else went to school, Justin would vanish. No one ever knew where he went.

Carol was down-to-earth, sweet, and loving. "That woman had one of the biggest hearts of gold I've ever seen," said her former boss John Orchard. But as Justin grew more unruly, she struggled to be fully present for his fast-growing set of issues. After he dropped out, she had an even harder time keeping tabs on him.

By his own grand telling, Justin began writing his first real songs and performing around town after leaving high school. He maintained that he wrote three of his signature songs at age fifteen: "South Georgia Sugar Babe," "Halfway to Jackson," and "Ain't Glad I'm Leaving," the last song a straight-country number Justin claimed he wrote after overhearing a man in a Waffle House booth say to his girlfriend: "If you ain't glad I'm leaving, girl, you know you oughta be."[12]

Eventually, he scored an amateur gig playing blues covers at the Springwater Supper Club & Lounge, the dive his parents once frequented.

As Justin told it, he weaseled his way into all-day gigs every Sunday and Tuesday, playing Lightnin' Hopkins and Mississippi John Hurt songs he learned from his father's record collection.[13] (Later concert listings from 1999 show a seventeen-year-old Justin Earle—categorized as "blues"—indeed playing multiple Sunday-afternoon Springwater sets.)[14]

"I totally jived my way into it," he said. "I did not know that much material. . . . Every week I had to keep learning new songs . . . so I kind of bullshitted my way into a music education really fast."[15]

Justin's newfound hobby was a mixed blessing for Steve Earle, whose relief that his son had found a passion contrasted with a universe of emotions—fear and guilt likely among them—that came with knowing he'd passed down his own obsession. "When I saw Justin not preparing himself to do anything else," Steve told NPR years later, "I knew what that looked like."[16]

Justin baffled his friends. He was hard to pin down, a sensitive soul who acted out his aggression, a childlike bragger who acted older than any of them, and a "spoiled rich kid that didn't have the amenities of most rich kids," as one of his teenage pals, James Crenshaw, put it.

And if Justin was writing world-class honky-tonk music while his friends were in chemistry class, it wasn't something he shared with them. Friends at the time don't remember the sixteen-year-old Justin Earle as a focused future star whose dreams couldn't be contained by classrooms. To them, Justin was the bullshitting, tall tale–telling mess of a friend with a penchant for wreaking havoc. "He wouldn't lie to manipulate people or get one over on anyone, but he just made up stories about stuff he did all the time," said another of his friends who'd known Justin since they were preteens, Richard McBride.

In his adolescence, Justin's behavior and substance use started to alienate and scare his peers. He projected a veneer of tough-edged fearlessness. "I was one of those kids . . . scared of thunderstorms . . . I was scared of the dark," he once explained. "And then, one day, for some reason, when I was eight or nine, I just stopped being afraid of everything."[17]

Justin tested his friends' boundaries, showing up to their houses drunk or high, turning weed-and-beer high school hangs into something darker. He and several other boys had started experimenting with cocaine. Justin took it further than anyone. One time, a group of friends was hanging out at Adam Williams's dad's house when Justin showed up with a twelve-pack.

Williams didn't want Justin causing trouble. So the boys grabbed sleeping medication lying around the house, crushed up the pills, then slipped them into Justin's beer.

Justin noticed his drink had more foam than usual. Then he shrugged, chugged the beer, and soon after fell asleep. By Justin's own telling, he was also, at the time, regularly getting high on Dilaudid, nodding off on the drug during his marathon Springwater sets.[18]

This group of friends often hung out at Richard McBride's mother's house on Beechwood Avenue, near Sevier Park. As the legend goes, one night around 1997 or 1998, Justin showed up in a frenzied state. He told his friends a startling, scary tale, this one more outlandish than usual: According to two boys at McBride's house that night, as well as a half-dozen or so neighborhood friends to whom Justin eventually told this story, when Justin arrived at the Beechwood house, he claimed he and a fellow teenager had just robbed someone at an ATM in a Green Hills shopping center at gunpoint.[19]

Justin had started using so much cocaine, he told his friends, he'd needed money to buy more. He said he'd recently bought the handgun he'd used for the robbery from a friend and had been aware it was missing a firing pin, making it nonfunctioning.

Justin was never caught or arrested for the self-proclaimed crime that soon became neighborhood lore. When he told another friend, Ian McCall, about it, Justin expressed remorse about having robbed an innocent stranger. "The whole time I was doing it," McCall remembered Justin telling him, "I felt horrible."

To some of Justin's friends, his purported robbery was a comical farce, the story of a well-off kid masquerading as a criminal. To others, it was proof Justin's adolescent substance use was driving him to darker, more desperate places than anyone was comfortable with.

What was clear is that Justin's cocaine use started isolating him from his friends. He wandered the streets late at night, strung out, alone, and likely ashamed to show up at his mom's. He often fell asleep on whatever couch or closet he wound up in at the end of the night.

Shortly after leaving rehab and prison, Steve Earle founded a record label. He called it E-Squared and opened up an office in Nashville. One of his interns was a young musician named Joie Todd Kerns, who played in a local band called Les Honky More Tonkies. Now that Justin had dropped out of school, he began spending much of his spare time at the offices of his dad's label. Eventually, Steve tasked Kerns with serving as Justin's unofficial babysitter.

Kerns witnessed Justin's evolution from hip-hop teen to grunge kid to blues picker. For hours on end, Justin sat in Kerns's office noodling around on acoustic guitar. In the evenings, after a full day of hassling Kerns, Justin often followed him home to crash on his couch, wearing ripped-up jeans scuffed at the bottom from where he'd stepped on them.

When a college senior named Andrew Colvin first encountered Justin Earle during his own internship on the same floor as E-Squared, he was taken by the teenager. But he could sense he was trouble.

"Justin was, I mean, you could feel it: He was like a criminal," said Colvin.

Justin often needed someone to drive him around. In the summer of 1999, that someone was Colvin. Sometimes he'd drop off Justin at E-Squared, where Justin was supposedly "working," or pick him up at Steve's apartment off Music Row, another place Justin sometimes crashed. The apartment was barely furnished: guitars, a boom box, spill-over Steve Earle merchandise, a room with bunk beds, and, for some reason, a grocery-store shopping cart in the kitchen. The only decoration on the wall, one friend remembered, was a wooden snake.

Justin invited friends over for parties at the unsupervised apartment. One of them, Ian McCall, took pleasure in repeatedly taunting Justin: He would pick up an acoustic guitar, stare at Justin, and play the opening riff to Steve's biggest hit, "Copperhead Road."

Released in 1988 as the title track to an album with a skull-and-crossbones cover, "Copperhead Road" had taken Steve Earle's image from trailblazing country kid to bad-boy rock star. Based on an actual country road in East Tennessee, the song tells the story of a son who comes from three generations of backwoods outlaws. Like his moonshine-selling father and grandfather before him, the Vietnam-vet narrator flouts the law by, in the narrator's case, growing weed in the hollers of Johnson County. The song became a rock-radio staple and a line dancing standard. Its hard-edged sound also drew bikers and rock fans into Steve Earle's fan base, crystallizing the singer's image as a rule-breaking renegade.

Justin's own guitar playing was improving so much during this time that it now commanded the attention of strangers. One such stranger was an aspiring songwriter in his late twenties named Sean Locke, who lived across the parking lot from E-Squared. Locke could hear the sound of blues guitar across the street. At first, he didn't interact with the kid playing guitar, but he could tell "just from his mannerisms and his talking two hundred miles an hour" that the fingerpicking kid must be the son of Steve Earle.

One afternoon, Justin was in front of E-Squared fingerpicking Mance Lipscomb's "So Different Blues."

"I was like, 'My god, listen to the *thumb* on this kid,'" Locke remembered thinking.

He walked across the parking lot to introduce himself. Justin made an instant new friend. Better yet, he'd found another place to stay. Justin and Locke grew close, spending endless nights driving around Nashville, trading songs, sharing stories, snorting cocaine, drinking warm beer and then chucking the empties off the roof of Locke's apartment. It was a period Justin later remembered, with unusual warmth, as "a songwriting slumber party every night."[20]

Locke's apartment was just another one of the many places Justin crashed in his adolescence. He stayed on high school friends' couches for weeks at a time. When he befriended Old Crow Medicine Show singer-guitarist Willie Watson, he sometimes passed out in Watson's closet after a late night at Springwater. When no couch or closet availed itself, Justin slept in a green van in the Springwater parking lot, or across the street, in a hammock, in Centennial Park. After he was introduced to the Chicken Shack crew, he'd often stay there, too.

He also still crashed with his mom frequently. She'd moved in with her boyfriend, Michael O'Brien, around the corner from Springwater and was completing her college degree—a bachelor of science—from Middle Tennessee State University. With O'Brien frequently out of town, it was often, once again, just Justin and his mom. It was tough for Carol to see her son so aimless. Eventually, he'd leave and continue his wandering.

"I was just banging around town," as he later put it, "without any particular direction."[21]

The first time Dustin Welch saw Justin play was at an open mic night at a twenty-four-hour coffee shop called Cafe Coco, sometime around 1998. Welch was eighteen and Justin sixteen. The Chicken Shack ringleader was transfixed by the teenager performing Mance Lipscomb's "So Different Blues." Who was this kid singing about railroad tracks and empty money sacks?

"I was completely trashed and was wearing these blue cabana-boy slacks, a black short-sleeve button-down shirt, a straw hat, and god knows what kind of horrible Beatle boots," Justin recalled of their first encounter. "Dustin told me later that the first thing he thought was, 'Who the fuck does this guy think he is?'"[22]

Soon after, Welch introduced Justin to his band—and to the world of the Chicken Shack.

From the moment Justin Earle stepped foot inside the one-room cabin packed with guitars, hand-rolled cigarettes, and blues records, he was transformed.

His presence also transformed the Swindlers. In Justin, they'd instantaneously found a new lead singer and primary songwriter with a hardcore backstory to boot. Almost overnight, the band became Justin Earle & the Swindlers.

The Swindlers could hardly believe their luck. They'd been messing around with scrappy jug-band covers for the past year or two, trying to sound as authentic and raw as a group of middle-class white kids in suburban Nashville possibly could. To them, the arrival of Justin Earle, who brought them songs he wrote that sounded like they came from the same far-off early twentieth-century America they all romanticized, felt like divine intervention.

"It was like a messiah had come," said Skylar Wilson, who joined the Swindlers after returning home from college in Memphis. "We no longer had to do Big Bill Broonzy covers; all of a sudden, it was like, 'Oh, this guy just wrote this song yesterday.'"

Justin had been learning Lipscomb's fingerpicking and practicing Lead Belly, but the Swindlers had already amassed a depth of obscure musical knowledge he'd barely scratched the surface of.

"I didn't know about old-timey music when I joined the band, and I thought these guys had written all these songs," he once said of the Swindlers' musical repertoire. "And then they started playing me all these records, and I realized that all these songs were . . . recorded, you know, 160 years before these guys were even born."

Justin may have been exaggerating about just how old the records that inspired the Swindlers really were, but the American roots music that influenced him and his band pulled from much deeper traditions. The Swindlers studied the sounds and styles of music that had inspired the early jug bands they modeled themselves after. Those genres—the country blues, jazz, vaudeville, ragtime—were all shaped by if not directly sourced from Black music from the American South that had its roots in slavery. ("When it comes right down to it," Justin said much later, in 2017, "what I do is make music invented by Black people.")[23]

The Swindlers were hardly the first generation of white teenagers to have their lives changed upon discovering these sounds. Nor were they the first white artists to then fashion themselves after music pioneered and innovated by largely forgotten Black forbears.

Their *fathers'* generation—Eric Clapton, Bob Dylan, Steve Earle—had been drawn to southern acoustic bluesmen of the twenties and thirties. But, consciously or not, the jug bands the Swindlers obsessed over pointed them toward an even earlier time, to a more vaudevillian tradition, music that was popular before the modern recording industry became segregated and marketed along racial lines. Just as the Swindlers conceived of themselves as a modern-day jug band, Justin, as he grew older, would fashion himself after artists who saw through arbitrary genre boundaries, whose music drew on the heavily Black-influenced, culturally diverse sounds of a much earlier time: Lead Belly, Hank Williams, the Staple Singers, Townes Van Zandt. "I make Black American music," Justin continued in the same 2017 interview, "as it was created in the early twentieth and late nineteenth century."

Back at the Chicken Shack, Justin developed a deep bond with this group of teenage jug-band music weirdos. Their relationships were held together by some shared trauma, though that's the last thing any of them would've called it. All the "Music Row brats" in the Swindlers shared a passion for music with their fathers, whom they idolized yet rebelled against.

Many of them grew up with a father who'd spent more time on a tour bus or recording studio than at home. But the records they unearthed and played over and over in the Chicken Shack were their fathers'. The recording gear Welch used to produce makeshift Chicken Shack recordings was from his dad. The music they loved—old folk and blues and Texas singer-songwriters—was introduced to them, and similarly worshipped, by their dads.

"All of them were trying to impress their parents," said Willie Domann, the Swindlers' bassist, whose father, Lee Domann, was a songwriter. For Domann, who'd known Justin since elementary school and came from a similarly unstable home, the Chicken Shack was a safe haven. "I'd never experienced the amount of emotional support and family that was available through hanging out with them," he said.

For Justin, it was a revelation. In a room full of kids whose dads were all successful musicians, having Steve Earle as your father was barely worth mentioning. Not sticking out because of his dad—this was a new feeling.

Justin and Welch soon became inseparable.

"It was an intense bond, and a necessary one," Dustin's sister, Savannah

Welch, recalled of her brother's connection to Justin. Both Steve Earle and Dustin's father, Kevin Welch, included on their debut albums tender ballads to the sons they'd left behind. Dustin and Justin shared the pains of abandonment, the joys of music making and self-expression, and a penchant for laughing through it.

"There's a quality to having a father who's a songwriter and performing, but also pursuing that in your own way, too, that's really hard to explain or put into words," said Savannah. "When somebody else gets it, you don't even have to talk about it. You just keep those people close."

Justin had amassed a repertoire of blues and folk standards, but singing other people's songs was never his goal. He wanted, like his dad, to write his own. He was now doing that at a feverish pace, bringing new songs to the Chicken Shack practically every week—studied exercises in forties and fifties country, folk, and blues.

The earliest tunes were tales of train hoppers and troublesome women and rough-and-tumble troubadours. They were clean and concise, never more than three verses or minutes. They closely followed the conventions of whatever genre Justin was emulating in a given song, though he found ways to play with the tropes he was mimicking.

"Roses are red, and violets are little, babe," he sang in one Swindlers staple, "Hard Livin'." "Why do you always gotta speak in riddles?"

These early songs taught Justin an invaluable lesson: If he dressed up his innermost feelings—his fears, uncertainties, and resentments—in the veneer of old-sounding, tough-edged genres, audiences were less likely to assume he was singing about himself. Classic country caricature, blues bravado, and folkie romanticism provided cover and plausible deniability that allowed Justin to sidestep his own vulnerability and expose the rawness of his interior life without anyone—himself included—thinking twice.

When busking downtown, the Swindlers now had original material, slipping in songs Justin had written to see if anyone noticed the difference between the early twentieth century tunes they typically performed and the ones written by a teenager the previous week. No one did. One of their earliest shows at a proper venue with Justin as lead singer took place at Springwater. The hand-scribbled set list had nineteen songs, a mix of standards like "St. Louis Blues," singer-songwriter favorites like John Prine's "Please Don't Bury Me," country classics like Hank Williams's "Lovesick Blues," and a handful of Justin Earle originals.

The beer-only dive soon became the Swindlers' main haunt. (Justin insisted on calling the bar by its full name: the Springwater Supper Club & Lounge.)[24] Too young to legally drink, the boys hid a bottle of whiskey in the rafters to pull from during their set. Their shows were often sloppy: The band constantly rotated between lineups and members, and at Springwater, where they were frequently wasted, they often sounded unrehearsed and out of key.

But once the Swindlers began performing at Springwater, their dads—Wally Wilson, Steve Earle, Kevin Welch, Gary Nicholson—started showing up at gigs in leather jackets. They watched with their arms crossed, from the back of the bar. It was, Dustin Welch recalled, "like they were coming to our Little League games."

CHAPTER 4

Even as Justin found a new home at the Chicken Shack, among the Swindlers he remained an enigma, keeping himself at a distance from the close-knit group. If he wasn't physically present at the Shack, the Swindlers typically had no idea where he was.

He was prone to wandering farther and farther outside of Nashville for weeks or months at a time. Around when Justin discovered the Chicken Shack, he also started traveling to Johnson City, a small city four hours east of Nashville and about an hour or so west of the real Copperhead Road.

The Appalachian town became an integral part of the story Justin later told about his own legend: It was, he claimed, where he learned bona fide mountain music, where he studied with anthropological curiosity the musical traditions of the hill people in the region, where he partied with women who went to Eastern Tennessee State, and where he deepened his drug dependency.[1]

"Pain pill heaven," he later called the area.[2]

Justin's connection to Johnson City was a songwriter seven years his senior named Scotty Melton. In 1998, when Justin was sixteen, Melton was a promising up-and-coming folksinger-songwriter with a debut album called *Unknown in San Antone*. He played frequently at the Down Home, a cozy venue with low ceilings, wood chairs, wood tables, and wood floors that served as the area's go-to folk club.

The Down Home is where, on June 26, 1998, Melton first remembered encountering Justin. Justin was in town to see his aunt Stacey Earle play a gig after the release of her debut album, *Simple Gearle*. In the bathroom, Melton found the teenage boy trying to make sense of some graffiti: *Steve Earle is the messiah; Steve Earle is a prolific fathead.*

Justin remembered their first meeting differently. The way he told it, Melton appeared out of nowhere in Nashville as his savior, an older, more serious songwriter who took the troubled teenager under his wing.

As Justin recounted, Melton was staying at the house of Justin's E-Squared babysitter, Joie Todd Kerns, and the two of them immediately hit it off, getting wasted and singing songs together.

"[Scotty] was like, 'Hey, you should open for me tomorrow,'" Justin recalled. "I was like, 'Hell yeah.' It was my first real show."[3]

Justin played his first documented solo set—sharing a bill with Melton, Les Honky More Tonkies, and Emmylou Harris's daughter Meghann Ahern—at a club in Nashville called the Sutler on March 14, 1999.[4] He had just turned seventeen. He celebrated by "getting really fucked up" afterward.

The next morning, when he woke up on the floor of the living room, he recalled Melton nudging him with his foot and asking:

"What are you doing?"

"I'm not doing anything," said Justin, barely awake.

"Well," said Scotty. "Then you should come with us."[5]

Justin got into the car. This started a pattern where the two would spend weeks together bouncing between Nashville and Melton's family home in the Johnson City area, writing songs, drinking beer, and talking about their shared songwriting heroes.

Justin's memories of Johnson City were vivid and precious to him.

"I was waking up every morning at 7:00, hungover, making a cup of coffee, and sitting down with my guitar," he said. "Writing for six hours, then taking a little nap, getting up, and writing some more. Then at night, we'd all get together and play. I wrote constantly, constantly, constantly."[6]

Much of it took place in the spacious parlor living room of the Meltons', with Scotty's dad—"an old biker kind of cat," Justin called him[7]—presiding over the proceedings.

Justin never actually resided in Johnson City, despite a multitude of interviews in which he claimed he lived there for two years. But he did go there frequently for several years as a teenager and young adult, sometimes staying for long stretches.

In Melton, Justin found his first true mentor. He may have been dishing the same advice Justin's dad had tried to give his son for years—work hard at your craft, don't let partying get in the way—but Justin felt unjudged by Melton, who treated him like a peer.

In Justin, Melton found an uncommonly talented songwriter, even if not everyone else saw it. "When I first met Justin, I thought, 'This kid is a hell of a bullshitter,'" said Melton. "He mythologizes a little bit, but that's what his job was. . . . In good bullshit, and in mythology, there's a deeper, more profound truth."

At the Down Home, in Johnson City, Justin met one of his heroes, Malcolm Holcombe, an eccentric, economical songwriter whose voice reminded journalist Peter Cooper of "an Appalachian Keith Richards with strep throat."[8]

Holcombe was a mystical figure to Justin and everyone else at the Chicken Shack—an enigmatic genius who'd eluded fame and success but whose gravelly singing and distinctive guitar playing was legendary among those in the know. As with so many of his musical interests, it was no mystery how Justin discovered him: Steve was a prominent Holcombe advocate, having once dubbed him "the best songwriter alive today."[9]

Born in 1955 and raised in western North Carolina, Holcombe eventually moved to Nashville and performed around town when he wasn't flipping burgers in the kitchen of a café called Douglas Corner. According to lore, Holcombe sometimes took off his apron, stormed out of the kitchen, walked onstage to stun the crowd with a few songs, and then put his apron back on and resumed his oversight of the grill.[10]

In 1999, Holcombe released his major-label debut, *A Hundred Lies*, which earned a four-star rave from *Rolling Stone*'s David Fricke.[11]

By Justin's account, he was introduced to Holcombe, by Melton, as "Steve Earle's son."

"Well, who gives a fuck," Justin remembered Holcombe saying.[12]

Justin was honing a distinct guitar-picking style by picking up techniques from a variety of inspirations. "I'm kind of a collector of picking styles," as he put it in 2011. In addition to perfecting Mance Lipscomb's one-finger "dead-thumb" picking, Justin practiced various two-finger folk-blues picking styles pioneered by singers like Mississippi John Hurt and Reverend Gary Davis that he and others often lumped together as "Travis picking," after the forties country singer Merle Travis, as well as clawhammer banjo–picking style, and a rhythmic style preferred by his aunt Stacey. Justin had developed such an aggressive rhythmic bass-note picking with his thumb that his father's friend, the legendary songwriter Guy Clark, compared Justin's thumb to a sledgehammer.[13] Dustin Welch's dad called Justin's right hand his "Hammer of God."

But it was witnessing Malcolm Holcombe's guitar playing in person that Justin credited with revolutionizing his guitar style.

"I watched Malcolm play, and I was just floored," he recalled. "He had this thing where he kept the rhythm with his thumb on the low strings and picked a part with his index finger on the high strings, while holding the rest of his fingers like a claw, like you would to play a clawhammer [banjo]. And then he'd strike the strings with that claw, really making a lot of noise. So I went home that day and tried to play like that."[14]

Other regional influences included two little-known blues guitarists of his father's generation, Frank Schaap and Joey Broughman. Occasionally, Justin would drive out to Lexington, Kentucky, where they lived.

In December 1999, Justin earned one of his first reviews opening for Schaap at a Lexington blues club called Lynagh's.

"Seventeen-year-old Nashville bluesman Justin Earle showed off an impressive and mature understanding of blues basics by giving fresh solo guitar interpretations of classics by Mance Lipscomb and a breezy, earthy tone popularized by the Rev. Gary Davis," wrote the *Lexington Herald-Leader*'s Walter Tunis. "There was also considerable buzz at the club over one especially appreciative patron—the singer's dad, songwriter

Steve Earle—who sat without ceremony in the crowd, chatting with fans between sets."[15]

With Scotty Melton's help, Justin started writing songs that were more vulnerable and introspective than his earlier, rough-edged retro tunes, including a ballad called "Turn Out My Lights." It sounded like it could've been about a girl but was, in fact, one of several songs Melton and Justin would write about the opiates they were using. To drive home the druggy subtext, Justin insisted on making the refrain "turn out *my* lights" rather than "turn out *the* lights," Melton recalled.

The song taught Justin another lesson: If a tune was written cleverly enough, there wasn't much difference between a torch song about a woman and an ode to pain pills. Justin could write about both if he concealed more than he revealed. "Nobody wants to hear poetic war stories about bad needles," he later said. "I rarely ever try to talk about the actual function of being a drug addict as I do the emotions of it."[16]

Another heartbreak-and-heroin song they wrote, "Far Away in Another Town," was inspired by a shared crush on a woman named Darcy Cooke, but the first line was an allegorical depiction of the rush of injecting heroin: "Well I'm leaving, tonight, babe, on a midnight train."

Justin sets up the song's refrain by singing about a woman "who can't do nothing but bring me down." By the time he sings the chorus, he's established a double meaning: perhaps the song's narrator simply hopped on a train to flee a love interest, or perhaps opiates have cut them off from the world.

When the duo finished writing the soul ballad, they were so ecstatic they started daydreaming about Ray Charles recording the song.

Still, Melton remembered trying to steer Justin away from what was becoming his favorite songwriting topic. "I was always like, 'Justin, we can't always write about drugs,'" he said.

In later years, Justin alternated between rose-colored nostalgia and harsh honesty about his and Melton's deepening substance use when reflecting on Johnson City. Sometimes, the period represented the apex of the bohemian life that enabled him to discover his voice.

Other times, he hinted at the cost of what such a life had entailed.

"We were both going through the same things about the same time," Justin said, elliptically, in 2008, promoting his first full album, which contained three Melton cowrites. "It represented the beginning of us slipping in our life."[17]

The next stop in Justin's journey was Chicago. In the early winter months of 2000, Justin showed up in the city with his father, who'd arrived for a new gig teaching a class on folk music. The opportunity, as Steve explained when he showed up in town, was merely an excuse for some father-and-son bonding: "It was a chance for Justin and I to spend some time together."[18]

Justin, eighteen, lived in Chicago for roughly six months in the first half of 2000.

His time there, at least as it's remembered by many friends, fellow musicians, bandmates, and brief mentors who knew him during this period, offers a stark contrast to the desolate image Justin would later convey of his stint in town. The picture these acquaintances paint was a period of near-constant companionship and camaraderie, one where Justin was exposed to like-minded music geeks by way of one of the city's most renowned musical institutions: the Old Town School of Folk Music. Songwriters like John Prine and Steve Goodman made the school famous back in the seventies, and it'd retained its reputation as a ramshackle community for teachers and students alike ever since, offering classes and hosting concerts for amateur musicians.

Justin was, perhaps unsurprisingly, uninterested in the *school* element of the Old Town School of Folk Music. "I was a total slacker," he recalled. "I think I went to a class maybe two or three times, and then I started chasing after the girl who worked at the snack bar."[19]

Steve Earle taught a class called "The Relationship Between Traditional Material and Contemporary Songs; or, The Cool Shit to Steal, Tracing the Roots of American Music."[20] The class traced a curated folk canon from Woody Guthrie, Hank Williams, and Harry Smith's

Anthology of American Folk Music up through Bruce Springsteen and Bob Dylan. Eleven hundred applicants reportedly applied to take the ninety-person lecture.[21]

Steve wanted to expose Justin to the Old Town School. During Steve's several-month-long class, he talked up his son at every opportunity, parading him around to promotional appearances.

"He's becoming really interested in a lot of music that he can learn a lot about at this school," Steve explained in Chicago. "He fingerpicks better than I do now."[22]

Steve and Justin duetted on "So Different Blues" by Mance Lipscomb, father and son singing and playing in unison, in front of a camera crew at a Chicago guitar shop. Justin sat quietly smoking Marlboros in a Chicago diner as his father boasted about him to an *Esquire* journalist: "He wrote a song last week that I would put on one of my records."[23]

Justin surrounded himself with fellow musicians, soaking in the energy from an entirely new world of aspiring artists in their twenties and thirties.

Most who encountered the eighteen-year-old Justin in Chicago remember a deeply motivated, cocksure young kid, one who masked his ambition with an aw-shucks affect but was nevertheless eager to collaborate. He worked, briefly, as an assistant for Steve's friend, the visual artist Tony Fitzpatrick. He recorded demos at the Old Town School library, hung around more established bands, and held court on the wooden bench in the school's main lobby, sitting for hours telling tales of Nashville, covering Gram Parsons, preaching about Townes Van Zandt, or just singing Van Zandt's songs: "Mr. Mudd and Mr. Gold," "Quicksilver Daydreams of Maria," "Fare Thee Well Miss Carousel."

Justin seemed eager to impress his new audience, determined to make the most of what was, essentially, his street-musician version of a semester abroad: He charmed, flirted, and fell for older women; told stories that betrayed his age; and talked up new friends whose songwriting he admired to promoters around town in an effort to get them booked. He outlandishly claimed he'd written two hundred songs by age eighteen.

"What I remember most," said Susan Moffett, an Old Town School employee who got to know Justin well enough to see past his bravado and big stories, "was that Justin was really hungry for love."

Moffett was working the front desk that winter, signing students up for classes and selling concert tickets. One day she showed up to work, and there stood the shaggy-haired son of Steve Earle. Justin was "like a mythical creature," she remembered, a hillbilly Huck Finn type: wafer thin, worldly seeming, with deep eyes that made him look as old as his hard-nosed stories about his rough-and-tumble past made him seem.

Justin started gigging around town: the Hideout, Winner's Bar & Grill, Uncommon Grounds, "all the little shows I could get my hands on," as he later put it.[24] At the Hideout, where he played repeatedly, Justin waited in the greenroom until taking the stage because it was illegal for him to be in the bar as an underage patron. He asked older musicians to tune his guitars and told them his dad called him "thunder thumbs" for the way he played, explaining that the nickname was not necessarily a compliment.

Justin also hung around a group of men who played in a country-rock band called Old Number 8. He watched them rehearse, volunteered to carry their gear to and from gigs, and, after his father left town, moved into their bandmate Charlie King's spare bedroom in his Rogers Park apartment.

The gentrifying Northside neighborhood was quiet, diverse, and far from downtown, with huge prewar apartments and cheap rent. Justin brought his guitar, suitcase, and not much else to King's spot on Touhy and Greenview, where he crashed for a few months. He spent time in his room alone, setting the scene for a song he'd soon write about his time in Chicago.

"Rogers Park," written with Melton in 2002, was his launching pad for that story. The song chronicled a hopelessly alone narrator who comes to Chicago full of hopes and dreams, only to spend his time staring out their window at the Lake Michigan chill of a cold, uncaring city. It was a beautifully broken ballad of misery and alienation that represented a giant leap forward for Justin as a songwriter.

Remaining in Chicago after his father left, Justin must've felt overwhelmed by the scale of his new surroundings. The self-mythologizing folksinger living out his rambling journey was, also, an eighteen-year-old boy far from home for the first real time. He might've been scared by his growing capacity for self-obliteration, terrified by how quickly his life was hurling forward. He might've felt, as he put it in "Rogers Park," in a line that referenced a song by Townes Van Zandt, like he had no place he could fall.

He could keep up with, and in many cases outpace, the musicians he hung around, drinking whiskey, smoking weed, and snorting coke. When he told these adults a story about how he'd already developed a hole in his septum from all the cocaine he'd done, some grew concerned, though not enough to stop partying with him.

Justin eventually narrativized his stint in Chicago as a desperately lonely time of drug addiction, a hazy period blanketed by crack and heroin. Chicago, as Justin told the tale, was the big city where the young man arrived, fell prey to its temptations, realized how plentiful and cheap its strong drugs were, then fled town in a panic.

Yet none of the many friends and musicians with whom Justin spent time remember witnessing, hearing about, or getting any sense that Justin was smoking crack, or using any type of heroin while in Chicago, as he would darkly proclaim for years to come. King, his roommate, never once encountered any needles, spoons, or pipes in their apartment.

What King does remember is that, after Justin fell behind on his meager rent, he offered up his father's mandolin as payment. (King accepted.)

While in Chicago, Justin informally joined a band called Lubbock. The group was the brainchild of Russel Brown O'Brien, a gregarious, tall, thirty-eight-year-old, red-haired Irish whiskey–drinking singer and performance artist who'd spent time in Nashville and immediately took to Justin. When Justin played with them, he sang Gram Parsons's "Hickory Wind" and his own song, "Lonesome and You," a classic country tune written in the style of fifties honky-tonk singer Ray Price.

The band was relatively unfocused, covering everything from Doc

Watson to Pat Benatar. "I think we collectively wrote one song," said October Crifasi, an Old Town School teacher and musician who played guitar and sang in Lubbock. "It was kind of a metal thing. It wasn't all that fabulous."

That spring, O'Brien finagled a headlining out-of-town show at 12th & Porter, a several-hundred-person club in Nashville, Lubbock's biggest gig yet. This, he told the band, was going to be their big break. The date was set: April 22; six-dollar cover. Posters were printed. The word was spread. Promises about who might show up—Emmylou Harris, Steve Earle—were made.

"He is risen!" read the concert poster. "Russel Brown O'Brien, bored to and by his own death, returns to Nashville with his band." One of four bandmates listed was "Justin Earle (guitar, dobro & voice)."

For Justin, the prospect of a Nashville return wasn't nearly so exciting. In the weeks leading up to the show, he warned Crifasi that "Nashville's gonna get ugly," that if his friends showed up there would be too many temptations. Given those circumstances, he was nervous about playing in front of his grandfather Jack Dublin Earle, who he said might attend.

Crifasi was worried about Justin's drug use: Their friends and family were traveling a long distance for the show.

Please, she begged him. *Can you wait to party until after we perform?*

Justin found his own way to Nashville, so Crifasi didn't see him until right before the show, when he pulled up to the venue in a dark car with tinted windows.

"The door opens, all this smoke pours out, and then this long, jeaned leg sticks itself out, and, slowly, Justin Earle pours himself out of the car," she remembered. "In that moment, I knew. . . . He was so fucked up, *so* fucked up."

Crifasi was crestfallen watching Justin fumble through the show, forgetting words to his own song. "I knew how good he could be," she said. He barely got through the gig, strumming along as the band covered everything from Steve Miller's "The Joker" to the standard "Mack the Knife."

Afterward, Justin invited Crifasi to go play tunes and drink at a friend's place.

Despite the mess that'd just transpired, Crifasi agreed. She soon noticed a much different Justin than the one she'd seen forgetting lyrics a few hours prior. Perhaps he'd come down from the peak of his high. Perhaps he was relieved that a stressful gig was over. Whatever it was, she noticed how comfortable, how *himself*, Justin seemed sitting in a small room with a few people sipping beers and trading songs back and forth on guitar.

The 12th & Porter show had been a bust. Jack Dublin Earle, Justin's grandpa, attended, but none of the other music biz VIPs O'Brien promised had. Lubbock didn't get their big break, lasting only a few more months as a band.

Justin returned to Chicago, but he didn't stay much longer after that. No one remembered exactly why, or even when, but Justin disappeared from Chicago without fanfare or notice, leaving a suitcase in his rented Rogers Park bedroom that he never came back to claim.[25]

He was journeying once again back to Nashville, the city that, for better or worse, he'd always call home.

CHAPTER 5

IN THE MID- TO LATE NINETIES, JUSTIN EARLE FOUND A NEW WAY TO skip town: He packed his scattered belongings; said goodbye to friends, girlfriends, and bandmates; and set out, for weeks or months at a time, on Steve Earle's tour bus. Since Justin had dropped out of school, Steve started bringing his son on the road, figuring it was the best, or only, way to supervise him.

Sometime around 2001, Justin slipped a note through the window of his friends' house on Douglas Avenue before one of Steve's tours.

> Hey Guyz,
>
> I'm takein' off
> on the road Friday
> For a long while
> So any one who
> aint a pussy come
> To Springwater this
> Thursday for the last
> Waltz
>
> Forever lost
> Justin

Carol was not thrilled with the arrangement. "She would go out of her way to make sure Justin didn't end up anywhere near Steve," remembered John Orchard, Carol's longtime boss at the stagehand production company she worked at. The idea of Justin joining his dad's rowdy rock tours several times a year filled Justin's mom with dread.

On tour, Justin was employed as a roadie and, later, a guitar technician. He slept on a bus with a small crew that ensured Steve's show functioned without hiccups.

This was just one way Steve had begun introducing his teenage son to the music industry and pulling him into his own artistic orbit. Justin's first appearance on a record came when he was eight, singing backup on Steve's 1990 "Regular Guy" alongside other family members. In 1997, Steve enlisted Justin, fifteen, to play electric guitar on the proto–Green Day rocker "Here I Am." That same year, Justin, already taller than his dad, appeared in the music video for "Telephone Road," riding shotgun alongside both his father and a monkey in a convertible.

Even when he was still technically in school, Justin had stood onstage in suburban Chicago in front of thirty thousand fans at Farm Aid shredding guitar alongside his father. "Nobody else makes noise like that," Steve told the crowd, "so he had to come out and play with me."[1]

In 2002, the *Nashville Scene*, the city's alt-weekly and local arts bible, became the first prominent publication to interview Justin. The subject of the story was Steve, whom Justin flooded with praise. "I couldn't be more proud of my father for what he's done," Justin said. "He's come out of the darkness and is doing the best to make up for it." They'd put the past behind them, Justin explained, crediting his dad for teaching him much of what he knew about being a musician. "I have a relationship with my father that most kids wish they could have," Justin said. "We sit around and we just act like friends."[2]

On tour, father and son were not friends but, rather, employer and employee, and, sometimes, adversaries. "Justin was trying to make up for a lifetime of [his dad] not being there," said Brian Willis, a guitar tech who roomed with Justin on Steve's 2003 tour. "This was his opportunity to get back at him."

Rebelling and slacking off on tour in his dad's presence served a number of potential emotional purposes for Justin: It might've made his dad angry, it might've been a form of mimicry of a father he deeply admired, or, in reenacting his dad's youthful misdeeds, it might've made Justin feel close to someone whose presence and approval he constantly craved.

"It was like, 'You think I could cause trouble at home?'" said Matt Svobodny, a longtime Steve roadie. "'Watch *this*.'"

Steve's idea had been to keep Justin close and, in theory, employed. The reality is that "working" for his father exposed Justin to an entirely new arsenal of vices and troublemaking that came with an international rock tour. Suddenly, Justin had new staging grounds—tour buses, hotel rooms, greenrooms—for his misbehavior.

The crew was exasperated with the boss's son. At first, Justin was reluctant to do any work at all. He showed up late, slept through load-ins, staggered into sound checks, disappeared without warning, and never knew when showtime was. "I'm usually the guy that's running around asking," he once said on tour with his dad, "and everybody's telling me to get a fucking watch."[3]

Son was exactly like father: You could not, under any circumstances, tell him what to do. Svobodny, Justin's supervisor, devised a new managerial strategy: showing him respect. He explained that he was part of the team, treating Justin like an autonomous crew member.

"You couldn't just drill-sergeant Justin," Svobodny explained. "If it was some new kid on their first tour, I'd be a hard-ass with them until they got it, and then they'd get the respect later. With Justin, it was the other way around."

Slowly, it began to work. With each tour, Justin evolved more and more into a semiresponsible crew member. When the respected roots-rock guitarist Eric "Roscoe" Ambel joined Steve's band as lead guitarist in 2000, he was assigned Justin as his guitar tech. The Justin that Ambel encountered was earnest and eager to learn the job, if also a bit careless about the thousands of dollars of equipment he was in charge of transporting.

Ambel became a mentor to Justin, recommending him books about Ernest Hemingway and the Beatles and showing him albums like *West Side Soul* by Chicago blues singer-guitarist Magic Sam. He loaned Justin a guitar so the teenager could rehearse his own songs during downtime.

In certain regards, Justin remained an ineffectual roadie, breaking Ambel's pedal board and permanently scratching several of his guitars. In other ways, he showed new levels of care and dedication: He taught Ambel an ingenious workaround method he'd devised to restring the vibrato tailpiece on his guitar. And he implemented a nightly ritual with the guitarist: When the musician switched guitars before "Copperhead Road," Justin had a packed bowl of weed, ready for Ambel to take a quick hit from the side of the stage.

Eventually, Justin graduated from roadie to a part-time member of Steve's band, the Dukes, playing guitar or keys during shows.

Buffalo journalist Jeff Miers wrote about watching Justin onstage in 2003. "When Steve Earle rolled into [town] . . . he had in tow an auxiliary musician who haunted the rear and fringes of the stage throughout the set, handing the musicians their guitars and occasionally stepping forward to add a keyboard part or an extra rhythm guitar. . . . The kid looked a bit dazed, it must be said, as if he was unsure of his role in the whole affair."[4]

It was clear to the roadies how much Justin idolized Steve. During an unexpected night off, the band and crew took over an empty music venue and spent the night performing songs for each other. When it was Justin's turn, he performed a note-perfect imitation of his father's cover of the Rolling Stones' "Dead Flowers," including the ad-libbed "*think* about it" line with which Steve sometimes used to end the song.

Justin also carved out as much space for his own self-expression as he could on his dad's tours, often to the chagrin of his colleagues. During sound checks, he pretended the spotlight was on him and not his dad, turning empty clubs into his own private rock show as he used Ambel's guitars to test out blues licks and his drop-thumb percussive guitar style.

Steve continued to fold his son into his own professional life, to encourage and support Justin's own aspirations by offering his son every platform he could.

In 1999, during a joint set with Guy Clark at Merlefest, Steve brought up his seventeen-year-old son to sing his song "Halfway to Jackson."

In 2001, in Justin's first official billing on a commercially released recording, father and son duetted on a cover of Mississippi John Hurt's "Candy Man" for a tribute album. Around then, Steve started having his son open shows for him, by far the biggest stage of Justin's young career.

"They started talking to us about opening acts, and I told them that I had my own," Steve Earle told a German crowd in 2002, introducing Justin. "I kind of grew my own hydroponically."[5]

Opening for his dad, a twenty-year-old kid performing for hundreds of adults who'd paid to see his father, Justin was reserved onstage. He seemed nervous, saying almost nothing in between Mance Lipscomb covers and originals like "Down on the Lower East Side" and "Cold Hearted Kisses."

As Steve boosted his son's career, Justin felt unmoored and out of control. "I was a wreck, a total wreck," he later said, reflecting on his turbulent time touring with the Dukes. "I was falling asleep with cigarettes, burning holes in mattresses in hotel rooms. . . . I'd go downstairs and drink my whole per diem on top-shelf bourbon and get thrown out of the bar."[6]

In May 2001, Justin and several roadies took advantage of a day off in San Diego. "We thought it'd be an amazing idea to rent a car, drive down to the border, and walk over to Tijuana," said Svobodny, who remembered purchasing every drug they could find—Benzedrine, Percocet, Xanax, hydrocodone—and embarking on a several-day bender.

"Evidently I had a three-day blackout that resulted in some kind of hysterics," Justin recalled. "I thought I was doing good because I wasn't doing any heroin, but I was eating like twenty-five hydrocodones a day and drinking like a fiend."[7]

Justin's behavior eventually resulted in his father temporarily kicking him off tour. "I deserved to be fired," Justin said during an interview with a Chicago local news station several years later.[8] Reflecting on that period, Justin acknowledged that his substance use had become a problem. "It's kind of one of those things you just grow to expect when you have that lifestyle," he said. "You get fired. You lose things. You go to jail. You just kind of get used to it."[9]

Throughout his yearslong tenure as a Steve Earle roadie, Justin remained the lead singer and primary songwriter in the Swindlers. Whenever he returned home to Nashville, he resumed gigging, recording, and writing with his band. After a few years, they started to gain momentum.

"Justin Earle and Dustin Welch (yes their daddies are Steve and Kevin) perform tonight . . . as part of a combo called The Swindlers," read the *Tennessean*'s first write-up of the band, previewing a Springwater show on January 3, 2002, the night before Justin's twentieth birthday. "Earle has played around Nashville for years, but most clubgoers haven't yet heard Welch, who plays guitar and clackety banjo and combines a love for blues and old-time sounds with a whisper-to-howl vocal style reminiscent of his father."[10]

The Swindlers had been anonymously busking around town since around 1998, but by 2002, the strange old American music they played didn't seem quite as strange.

At that year's Grammys, the type of music they were perfecting was honored with the biggest award of the night: Album of the Year. To present it, Janet Jackson, Gloria Estefan, and Matthew McConaughey stood onstage in LA and announced the contenders for the category, which was full of heavy hitters. Bob Dylan's critically acclaimed *Love and Theft* was pitted up against Outkast's *Stankonia*, a blockbuster and critics' favorite, as well as India Arie's album *Acoustic Soul*, a platinum-selling promising debut. Most predictions had the award going to U2 for their comeback hit *All That You Can't Leave Behind*.

McConaughey's face lit up with shock when Jackson named none of those four albums. The winner was the soundtrack to the 2000 Coen brothers' film *O Brother, Where Art Thou*?

The film, a southern Odyssey parable starring George Clooney, had jump-started a roots music revival that was as unexpected as it was popular. The soundtrack was produced by T Bone Burnett and was filled with spirituals, a 1920s Jimmie Rodgers tune, and childhood standards like "You Are My Sunshine."

In the two years after the film's release, seven million Americans purchased the soundtrack, which featured nineties Nashville traditionalists like Alison Krauss and Gillian Welch as well as forebears like the eccentric fiddler and singer-songwriter John Hartford and bluegrass legend Ralph Stanley.

The fervor may have been accelerated by a profound cultural shift. During this multiyear phenomenon, the Twin Towers and the Pentagon were attacked on 9/11, killing nearly three thousand Americans and ushering in a new political and social moment in the United States. Commercial country music changed overnight, shifting from the boy-band pop of Lonestar to the jingoistic patriotism of songs like Brooks & Dunn's "Only in America," which was released prior to 9/11 but became a number-one country song in October 2001.

Suddenly, it seemed, Americans also couldn't get enough of bluegrass and Depression-era roots music. Eighteen months after its release, the *O Brother* soundtrack was the best-selling album of *any* genre in the country, the first bluegrass record to reach those heights in nearly thirty years.[11] The industry took notice. The soundtrack opened the doors in Nashville to country music that was less obviously commercial than Tim McGraw and Toby Keith. "If it's roots, bluegrass, string, acoustic folk music," said one industry executive years later, "it very quickly brought it to the mainstream."[12] Much of this music was categorized and marketed as "Americana," an industry term for roots music that started getting used in the midnineties.

A new crop of rootsy singer-songwriters hit their commercial and critical strides: Gillian Welch (no relation to Dustin Welch's family) and David Rawlings released their 2001 breakthrough, *Time (The Revelator)*; singer-songwriter Patty Griffin turned heads with 2002's *1000 Kisses*. Griffin's album was released by Dave Matthews's ATO Records, one of several independent, commercially viable roots-oriented labels that sprouted up in the early 2000s. The label Lost Highway also formed in 2000. (Its first release? The *O Brother* soundtrack.) Part-time Swindler Andy Moore started working at the label, helping oversee releases including Drive-By Truckers' career-defining *Southern Rock Opera*. The label established upstart songwriters like Tift Merritt and Kim Richey and cemented Ryan Adams as a star.

Justin Earle and the Swindlers were paying attention.

"It was strange that it happened," one of the Swindlers, Travis Nicholson, said of the post–*O Brother* roots boom, "and it wasn't lost on us." Nicholson had a front-row seat: He'd started pursuing film and managed to score an internship on the *O Brother* set in Mississippi. He'd bring back trinkets from the Delta—flour sacks, tins of "Dapper Dan" pomade—as souvenirs for the Swindlers. On the movie set, everyone called Nicholson "Tex" due to his oversize cowboy hat. The hat was a gift from Justin.

A 2002 Associated Press story on the "'O Brother' phenomenon" showed increased radio airtime for bluegrass, and bumps in album sales for anyone with the loosest associations with the soundtrack and its subsequent series of associated tours. "Attendance is up at the more than five hundred bluegrass festivals held across the country each year, and instrument manufacturers report backlogged orders for banjos, mandolins, and guitars," the report claimed.[13]

Two young Nashville bands besides the Swindlers that were making ragged jug-band and blues-inspired roots music that existed outside the strictly defined bluegrass and old-time scenes were Old Crow Medicine Show and the Hackensaw Boys. The three groups overlapped and befriended one another in this proto-Americana scene, busking on Second Avenue and showing up to each other's gigs around town: When the sound guy didn't show up for a Hackensaw Boys show at the historic bluegrass club the Station Inn, Justin and Dustin Welch helped run sound for the night. Both Old Crow and the Swindlers regularly covered the traditional tune "Hesitation Blues," and the Swindlers often opened for Old Crow.

Old Crow's lead singer, Ketch Secor, recalled meeting Justin—"really gangly, really acne-scarred, and taller than everybody else"—around this time. "He had this deep-voiced timbre, and he had a nonchalance to him—sucking on a toothpick, smoking on a cigarette—that was almost like he was trying to figure out what character he was going to play," said Secor.

Secor saw his band and the Swindlers as engaged in the same fundamental project. "The New Lost City Ramblers, Pete Seeger, that's who me and Justin were all following the trail of: the other white boys that walked the Black music highway and the hillbilly highway," said Secor. Old American music provided young men like Secor and Justin a "cloak we want to get wrapped up in because it feels more rock and roll than being ourselves," he said.

In the midst of this blooming scene, the Swindlers started playing larger venues and got written up in the local press, attracting industry attention.

At the Chicken Shack, Dustin Welch set up a makeshift recording studio so he could press *record* whenever the banjo jams turned from drunken noise into something sublime. Sometimes that meant recording at 7:15 in the morning, when Justin, likely having stayed up all night, would be ready to lay down a take.

Welch began preserving dozens of the first-rate songs Justin was writing. He recorded the Swindlers backing up Justin on their standard repertoire, future Justin album cuts like "Halfway to Jackson," "Down on the Lower East Side," and Justin's signature tune "Ain't Glad I'm Leaving," with the band chiming in with fifties-sounding country backup vocals ("*oughta be, know you oughta be*") after Justin sang the chorus.

Welch also recorded Justin running through in-progress songs that he'd soon discard: the rock-leaning "Cry for a Fool," the yearning come-on "Girl in My Dreams," the fingerpicked murder ballad "Where the Redbirds Sing," the heartbroken honky-tonker "Cold Hearted Kisses," and the noir travelogue "Zapatista Gold."

Welch had conjured a community by transforming his bedroom into a teen's dream of a folk-music Shangri-la. Now, in that same bedroom, he was capturing early recordings of one of that scene's most promising talents, assembling the songs that would push him to stardom.

One day at the Chicken Shack, Justin introduced a brand-new song. The Swindlers sat in silence as Justin shouted this latest tune as if he were performing in an arena.

Did you ever get the feeling you'd die in the streets you were
raised in?
Doing the same things your daddy done
Like you've been set up, you're plain out of luck
Now you're waiting for your time to come
See, I get that feeling from time to time
And it puts cold chills down the back of my neck
Because nobody wants to grow up to be their parents
And you know why? Because nobody shows their parents no respect

Justin kept going. He sang about the corner of Fifty-First Avenue and Charlotte Pike, a nondescript part of town he sometimes wandered around, alone, in the middle of the night. He sang about standing at that intersection and staring at the statue of Mary above the doors of St. Ann Catholic Church, seeing the reflection of his mama's eyes staring back at him.

You gotta ask yourself what kinda beast would roam these streets?
In the wee hours looking for another desperate hit

The song was called "Decimation of a Southern Gentleman," and it soon became a regular in the Swindlers' repertoire. When Justin set out on his own in 2007, he screamed the song to sparse crowds in dive bars and barbecue restaurants. Then he discarded it.[14] His bandmates and friends—some of whom consider it among Justin's best work—can only speculate why: It was too intense, never quite finished, too diaristic, too revealing, too painful for public consumption. Months before Justin died, an old friend of his asked him to play "Decimation" for them in private, as a favor. Justin obliged, with a caveat: "Don't tell people about that song," he said.

"I said, '*papa*,'" he sang in its refrain, often screaming that word—"papa"—so loud his voice strained, "your little boy is falling down."

In May 2002, the Swindlers went on their first tour, crisscrossing Oklahoma and Texas in a passenger van. The trip's premise was practical: They were driving bandmate Cory Younts to a job at Philmont, the Boy Scout wilderness ranch in New Mexico where Younts, an Eagle Scout, spent summers. They figured they'd play some shows along the way.

The resulting tour was comically ramshackle. The Swindlers accidentally camping in a cemetery in Oklahoma. The Swindlers frantically phoning their dads, having convinced themselves it was Father's Day. ("Dumbass," Welch remembered Steve telling Justin on the phone. "That's next month."[15]) The Swindlers driving six hours from Oklahoma to Spicewood, Texas, for a gig at a biker joint, owned by Willie Nelson's former stage manager, called Poodie's Hilltop Bar & Grill.

Eager for attention and in need of cash, the Swindlers said yes to every opportunity, happy to charm anyone tickled by their Depression-era presentation, their lead singer playing up the act in his signature pork-pie hat, vest, and goatee. Back home, the band played a benefit for the Atlanta-based Southern Center for Human Rights, a fundraiser for Nashville public schools, and a celebration marking the opening of a condo complex.[16] They played weddings, where, under their alternative moniker the New Lazy Swing, they covered "Ode to Joy," "Bittersweet Symphony," and Madonna.

At a private event at the Belle Meade Plantation, the former home of one of Nashville's largest slaveholding families, part-time Swindler Derek Pell recalled, the organizers enjoyed them so much that Justin talked them into letting the band play an extra hour for more cash.

"We *swindled* them again," Pell remembered Justin telling them. Each Swindler walked away with about $300, one of their biggest paydays.

The Swindlers also played private parties hosted by the novelist-scholar-songwriter Alice Randall. In 1994, Randall became the first Black woman in Nashville to ever cowrite a country number one when Trisha Yearwood's "XXX's and OOO's (An American Girl)" topped the charts. Randall was also an old friend of Steve's, and she'd become one of the Swindlers' foremost supporters. She often hosted dinners at her well-appointed home. Political figures and intelligentsia, authors, reporters, artists, and professors mingled while waiters in white tuxedos served cocktails. In the corner of the dining room, the Swindlers, wearing their best suits, performed Memphis Jug Band covers for the guests.

Mostly, the Swindlers gigged at Springwater, where the shows remained raucous. Steve relished telling an anecdote about watching Justin and the Swindlers, the sons of *his* friends, play at the bar: Someone elbowed him, pointed at the boys onstage, and said, "I wonder how many of them were conceived right out here in this parking lot?"[17]

When Springwater closed for the night, Justin and Cory Younts sometimes followed Old Crow member Willie Watson to his apartment around the corner to keep the party going. The trio would stay up all night playing songs, singing rounds, and listening to Gus Cannon records. Watson, who'd grown up in upstate New York, reveled in the Nashville romance of it all: eager young men singing songs until the sun rose.

When it did rise, Watson and Justin would wander down the street to the Kwik Sak gas station, buy a couple of tallboys, go back to Watson's, pop a valium or Xanax, then fall asleep for twelve hours. Justin often passed out in Watson's closet.

None of this running from responsibility toward a life devoted to art was unique to Justin Earle and his cohort. In cities across the country, entire subcultures of outsider musicians were doing the same thing. At Springwater, those various scenes—the punks, the indie rockers, the heavy-metal kids, scrappy roots bands like the Swindlers—all collided. At that bar, the goal was not to become famous but the opposite. The space was for the songwriters, stand-up comedians, poets, rappers, and noise guitarists who believed so much in the art they made they were willing to perform it to sparse drunk crowds for little to no money. The dark underside to the community provided by spots like Springwater was the fealty so many of those musicians had toward *the myth*, the belief that self-destruction should be valorized, that true art required self-sacrifice. Listening to a loud band, picking a guitar until your cuticles bled, drinking until you couldn't feel your feelings, any of that felt easier than dealing with whatever was really ailing you.

"It was the reason we were all hanging out," said Watson years later. He recalled:

> If there was too much silence, we'd have to acknowledge our reality and the pain that a twenty-two-year-old might be feeling. . . . When the guitars were out and the voices were singing or the speakers were on, that's where the bonding was. But in those in-between moments after you sing the song and you didn't have a record playing, and you just sat there in between songs or lines of cocaine, everything in-between wasn't great. . . . We were all killing something, running away from something, or finding solace in those old jug bands, or sitting around my record player. But a lot of it was fucking dark. Everything between the guitars was dark.

By 2002, Justin had spent years trying to bury everything between the guitars. He'd established an ever-expanding, constantly rotating list of coconspirators—anyone willing to follow him halfway to the sunrises he insisted on staying up for.

Those who became part of Justin's inner circle grew accustomed to late-night calls from pay phones and knocks at their door at all hours of the evening: "Want to party like rock stars?" he'd ask. (If they missed out on the shenanigans, he might tell them after the fact that he'd gotten "high enough to chase ducks with a rake.")

"There was always a progression of desperation," said Jenn Ramsey, Justin's sisterly close friend and Steve's goddaughter, "a progression of realizing your friends are not going to come with you to the next level, and the intense feeling of abandonment that he had over that."

It became a familiar ritual when he was back in town from touring with his dad: Justin would call up old friends he hadn't seen in months and see if they wanted to get back to their old behavior.

That's what happened to Ramsey in October 2002, shortly before she got sober. Justin, then twenty, arrived at her home at an ungodly hour with a mischievous question: "Do you want to do some serious adult drugs?"

It's a memory Ramsey can't forget, in part because, like so many others who once used with Justin, it's a moment that later became part of her own path toward recovery: the way they placed the large mirror on a table; the way they dumped out the cocaine and sorted it into lines; the way it had felt, for Ramsey, like they needed to finish all the drugs so that they wouldn't be tempted by having them in their possession anymore; the way, at one point, Justin stopped, looked at her, and said, "We're going to have to get clean one day."

CHAPTER 6

IN EARLY 2003, JUSTIN WAS BACK ON THE ROAD WITH STEVE, WHO WAS touring his latest album, *Jerusalem*. In the hysteria of the post-9/11 years, where just months earlier Toby Keith topped the country charts with his "we'll put a boot in your ass" anthem "Courtesy of the Red, White and Blue (The Angry American)," one of Steve Earle's new songs had garnered controversy. "John Walker's Blues" was a first-person portrayal of the American-born Taliban fighter named John Walker Lindh who had been captured by US forces in Afghanistan. Steve wrote the song, in part, because when he saw news coverage of Lindh, he was reminded of Justin.

"What I saw was a 20-year-old kid that looked like he hadn't eaten in a long time," Steve said at the time. "My kid is 20, and he always looks like he hadn't eaten in a long time."[1]

As Steve took the stage each night in front of a drum kit that read NO IRAQ WAR, Justin often joined him onstage on guitar, sporting a patchy goatee and wearing overalls, a white T-shirt, and a kaffiyeh wrapped around his head.[2]

Justin was now causing near weekly disruptions on Steve's tours. In March 2003, he returned to his fancy hotel room in Germany with a package of bright-red hair dye, put it in his hair, and then passed out. When he came to, he realized the room was destroyed.

"I stood up and saw red handprints, footprints," he said. "All over the room. All over the walls. All over everything. . . . I evidently put the hair dye in and got high, nodded out and didn't rinse it out."[3]

"It looked like a murder scene," said Brian Willis, Justin's roommate in Germany. "I mean, it really looked like somebody had been killed."

On that same 2003 European tour, Justin ran wild during an extended break in Amsterdam, disappearing for several days. Svobodny captured a photo of Justin from the tour, a moment of peace amid the disorder: He's climbed on top of the parked tour bus wearing his newsboy cap and denim overalls. Sporting a scraggly goatee and pencil mustache, Justin squints into the midday sun; in one hand, he's holding a lit cigarette and half-empty bottle of beer. In the other, he'd folded over a book he's reading.

That winter, Justin's recklessness came to a head. It was a day off in Portland, Maine, and Justin got drunk at a lobster boil for the crew and band. Shortly after 11:00 p.m., he charged into the Eastland Park Hotel, where everyone was staying, and asked the front desk for a new room key. "This hotel fucking sucks," Justin shouted. "The fucking service here sucks."[4]

He disappeared and then returned to the lobby a few minutes later, smoking a cigarette. Indoor smoking in bars and public places had recently been banned. "Fuck you," Justin said when he was asked to put out the cigarette, before stamping it out on the carpet. A hotel security guard told him to leave.

"I'll kick your ass and *her* ass," Justin responded, pointing to the woman behind the desk. He shuffled outside, but when he reentered, claiming he was going upstairs to retrieve his belongings, the hotel called the police.

Justin knocked on the hotel room where his fellow roadies were relaxing and smoking weed. When he entered, his knuckles were bloody from having punched a glass frame in the elevator. Minutes later, police officers knocked on the door, looking for the man causing the disruption. They asked Justin to sit on the bed and recount what had taken place.

"Get that fucking flashlight out of my face," he told an officer.

Justin then swung his left hand at a cop and resisted being placed in handcuffs. At one point, Steve came into the hotel room. Brian Willis, one of the roadies present for the arrest, remembered Steve looking as angry as he'd ever seen him.

Justin was arrested and taken to the police station, where he answered some basic questions: Education? Ninth grade. Occupation? Musician. Employer? Exit Zero, Inc., his father's touring company. Address? His father's home in Fairview, Tennessee. Officers took his weight and height (six foot six, so he claimed; 160 pounds) and charged him with misdemeanor assault and criminal threatening. Justin spent the night in jail, pleaded guilty to a lesser charge of disorderly conduct, paid a fine, and rejoined the tour shortly thereafter.

Steve's sound engineer, Gerry Diaz, coined a nickname for Justin behind his back: "Where's the Prince of Darkness today?" he'd ask fellow roadies when Justin went out at night and couldn't be found the next morning.

To the crew, he seemed feral and disheveled, carrying his belongings in a plastic bag and wearing the same pair of overalls for weeks at a time. Toothbrush? Showers? Not a priority for Justin, who trashed hotel rooms within minutes of checking in, ripping covers off the bed, throwing towels on the floor, and tossing cigarette butts into the toilet.

On tour, hijinks and pranks were commonplace, and Justin was an easy target. One day, sharing a hotel room in Ireland, Steve's longtime roadie Svobodny grew irritated after Justin threw his fried-chicken bones out the hotel window onto the tour bus below. When Justin went out alone that night, Svobodny flipped his mattress below the box spring, turned the hard box spring upside down, and then remade Justin's bed.

"He came back hammered at two in the morning, jumped in the air, and plopped his back on the bed," said Svobodny. "It was a hard landing."

Back home, Justin's substance use started to scare the Chicken Shack's more innocent bystanders. The only bandmate he was spending extended periods of time with was Younts, with whom he'd grown close after first meeting at an open mic years earlier.

"I went to his apartment the next day; he'd been living with his girlfriend at the time on the West Side," said Younts. "It'd been snowing, and he had this Ovation guitar in his room, but it was broken, the back of it was missing. I was like, 'What happened there?' And Justin said, 'Oh, I got into a fight with my girlfriend the other day, so I broke the guitar, took the back off it, and went sledding.'"[5]

By 2003, Justin and Younts were isolating themselves from the Swindlers and spending much of their time around people, places, and scenes that revolved around hardcore drug use, which for Justin now included smoking crack and injecting opioids like heroin, mixing speed and opiates, "everything he could get his hands on," said friend and cowriter Scotty Melton.

His bandmates didn't know what to do. "It just wasn't in our wheelhouse," said the Swindlers' Travis Nicholson. "I remember a moment when he was showing us the holes in his arms. He was almost bragging, but I wonder if it was also a subconscious cry for help."

Younts and Justin began going to a derelict club called the Shirley Street Station, where musicians and sex workers squatted for days at a time.

For a place described by those who spent time there as a functioning crack den, Shirley Street Station had a surprisingly professional setup, with a high-grade sound system and a raised stage. It hosted shows throughout 2003 and 2004 and was owned by a sound engineer and club owner who sold drugs but also had world-class amps. One show flier from 2003 described the chaos of Shirley Street Station in euphemism, calling it a "slightly out of tune music venue."

"A portal to hell" is how musician-producer Mark Nevers remembered it.

The club was a relic, misaligned with the city's plans for revitalizing downtown, located just blocks from new tourist attractions like the arena and the Country Music Hall of Fame and Museum. Like a degenerate photo negative of the Chicken Shack scene, it hosted singer-songwriter showcases, blues bands, and avant-garde performance artists in an anarchic, DIY atmosphere.

On November 15, 2003, Shirley Street Station hosted the proper live Nashville debut of David Berman, thirty-six, the lead singer of an indie-rock band with a devout cult following called the Silver Jews. Berman had been persuaded to play his songs in front of a live audience, something he rarely did at that time, as he was suffering from severe mental health and addiction issues. But he'd grown comfortable in the lawless atmosphere at Shirley Street Station, a place he later referred to as his home for the better part of eighteen months. Earlier in 2003, he'd hosted a singer-songwriter night at the venue called "D. C. Berman's Burn Down." ("Bless David Berman," wrote the *Nashville Scene*, "for giving Nashville night owls something to do after 1 a.m. besides downing coffee at the Waffle House.")[6]

On this November evening, Berman was one of four acts performing, alongside outsider folksinger Tom House and Patty Lemay, who performed under the moniker Spiritual Family Reunion and who had organized the entire evening. The other act was Justin Earle.

It was the type of evening where half of the fifty-some people in attendance were artists themselves: filmmaker Harmony Korine, Dustin Welch (who joined Justin during his set), Duane Denison from the noise-rock band Jesus Lizard, Lambchop's Mark Nevers, and future Silver Jews drummer Brian Kotzur.

Justin was out of his element, performing for an indie-rock crowd suspicious of his earnest folk songs. But the entire show, some of which was filmed by an audience member, ended up being a drug-den debacle. When Berman finally took the stage in the middle of the night, he staggered his way through an off-the-rails set, while the few fans still standing yelled slurs and nonsense at him from the crowd.

"Justin, who started out the show, he's like twenty-one going on eighty-nine," Berman mumbled into the microphone.[7]

Berman's drummer, Bob Nastanovich, had driven down from Louisville for the gig.

"When I got there, I fell asleep on a couch, which I later discovered had been used for years by hookers and their clients," Nastanovich remembered. "During this time, many of the other musicians indulged themselves with narcotics. . . . [Justin] was messed up and people seemed concerned about his well-being. . . . I was in my car and headed back to Louisville less than a minute after I hit the snare for the last time."

Patty Lemay, who'd also played in Berman's band that evening, was onstage gathering her belongings as soon as Berman finished. The very long night was finally over. Lemay leaned over and addressed the man filming Berman's set. "That was the hardest thing I've ever done," she said with a laugh, then walked offstage.

Lemay had something of a caretaker role in Nashville's indie-rock scene. She was often the only woman musician in a room of men who rarely took her songs seriously.

And more often than not, Lemay, sober and devoted to twelve-step recovery, was the only person in a room not drinking or using. She had grown up in Murfreesboro, a half-hour outside of town, in a household she described as volatile and traumatic. Lemay had always been drawn to fellow broken souls. She believed deeply, and spiritually, that compassionate caregiving was what someone in the throes of addiction most needed, flaunting twelve-step orthodoxy and stupefying others by growing close to wounded musicians like Berman and Justin, frequently cooking and taking care of them when they were strung out.

"Anybody's going to think, 'That's crazy for a sober person to do that,' but I felt like God wanted me to," she said. "It sounds stupid, or naive, I understand that. But that's why I did it: I felt it in my heart."

In 2003, Berman's next-door neighbor on Fairfax Avenue was Kevin Welch, Dustin's father. When Kevin wasn't around, Dustin and Justin sometimes squatted at the house. Eventually, they befriended Berman, who was fifteen years older, to the day, than Justin.

One day, Lemay got a call from Berman. "Get over here," Lemay remembered him telling her over the phone. "You've got to hear this kid. He's *way better* than his father!"

Lemay went over and Justin sang her "Rogers Park." She was blown away by the way this young man sang about "punching holes in the dark," by the way his guitar picking sounded, to her, like chimes. And she remembered what Justin later told her about *her* music: "You can write the *goat piss* out of a song."

Justin, Lemay, and Berman started spending a lot of time together.

Lemay found herself pleading with Berman, begging him to not be a bad influence on Justin, whom she saw as a fragile young man. She was afraid Justin would die before he ever put out a record.

Berman and Justin, nevertheless, congregated at Shirley Street Station. For Berman, the venue was a place to escape from reality. So much so that it was also where he decided, that fall, he would die: Days after his erratic November Shirley Street debut performance, Berman took too much Xanax, scribbled a suicide note, and headed to the club.

When Berman arrived at Shirley Street Station,[8] he caught part of a show by the obscene French performance artist Jean-Louis Costes, who was staging his "trash opera" *The Holy Virgin Sex Cult*. (One of the few others in attendance was critic Jim Ridley, who raved about the show in the *Nashville Scene*. "While the rest of the city slept," wrote Ridley, "thirty people sat in a David Lynch psycho-lounge watching two naked men smear each other with chocolate syrup."[9]) Berman was rescued, at the club, by his wife, who'd found his note.

In the fall of 2003, the Swindlers played the biggest gig of their career at San Francisco's Hardly Strictly Bluegrass festival, on the same bill as Willie Nelson, Emmylou Harris, and, naturally, Steve Earle.

The set, by several bandmates' accounts, was a mess.

"I got so drunk the night before I was drunk onstage the next day at 11:00 a.m.," Justin said of the show.[10]

Justin and Younts were alienating themselves from the rest of the band. They started squatting at Shirley Street Station, living with unhoused men and sex workers in the semiabandoned club. They pawned anything they could find, including Justin's prized '46 Martin guitar, for drug money. The club didn't have proper heating, so its inhabitants—all living in disparate offices, closets, and curtained-off corners—got by with a few space heaters.

Younts remembered him and Justin serving as unofficial janitors and bouncers at Shirley Street, working the door and cleaning up after johns. They spent the rest of their time shivering on couches and playing chess or the guitars they hadn't yet pawned.

In January 2004, Justin's Johnson City collaborator Scotty Melton was deputized to try to retrieve Justin from Shirley Street Station. When Melton arrived, Justin greeted him wearing dark sunglasses. He refused to leave.

When, on February 1, 2004, the rest of the country watched Janet Jackson and Justin Timberlake's infamous Super Bowl halftime show, Justin and Younts were holed up at Shirley Street Station and heard about it only days later.

"The darkest of our days," as Younts remembered of that time.

Justin concurred. "One of these days, when I make enough money," Younts remembered Justin once telling him in the club, "I'm going to buy this place and then buy a bulldozer so I can drive over it."

A few years later, the entire street on which Shirley Street Station once stood would be razed to make room for Nashville's half-billion-dollar convention center, its memory obliterated from future maps of the city.[11]

David Berman would go on to cement his legend as a sardonic, troubled genius who inspired future generations of songwriters with his songs that mixed wistful surrealism and black humor. Berman spent years in reclusion, but in 2019 returned with an album that opened with a song alluding to his self-destructive past: "I spent a decade playing chicken with oblivion," he sang. In August 2019, a few days before embarking on tour to support his new album, Berman died by suicide at age fifty-two.

Patty Lemay would continue to write songs, record albums, and collaborate with a who's who of underground Nashville musicians under the moniker Spiritual Family Reunion. In 2008, she released her debut record, *Goodbye Ceremony*, a title her friend Berman came up with. One of its songs, "Ferris Wheel," would memorialize the pitch-black darkness of Shirley Street Station:

A Ferris wheel going round and round just stunned me
'Cause all the people on it were just screaming to get out of town

CHAPTER 7

JUST AN AMERICAN BOY, A DOCUMENTARY ABOUT STEVE EARLE'S 2002 *Jerusalem* tour that focused on the singer's outspoken opposition to the Iraq War and the death penalty, captured Steve's tender, tense working relationship with Justin. By that point, Justin was not merely a roadie but a full-fledged member of Steve's band.

"Try it again, Justin?" Steve calls out to Justin during rehearsals. "Do you remember your part at the end, or did you completely forget and get flustered?"

"I haven't gotten flustered about shit," Justin replies.[1]

Accompanying the documentary was a live album. At the end of the collection, immediately following Steve calling out his "oldest and tallest son" during band introductions, is a song that was neither a live recording nor by Steve Earle. The final track on *Just an American Boy* is "Time You Waste," a song written and sung by Justin Earle, his first to be commercially released.

The ballad is sentimental, a series of lonesome childhood vignettes—returning to his empty home after school, waiting for his dad, "someone I didn't even know," to pick him up from his mom's.

It illustrated the father and son's unusual closeness and dynamic: Son writes song about his father's original sin of abandonment. Father releases song on *his* album, not only providing a platform for his son's emotional truth but claiming it as part of the Steve Earle story, too.

As his son sank deeper into his addiction, Steve developed a tough-love approach, doing his best to draw necessary boundaries as he maintained his *own* sobriety. Justin, for his part, seemed to have made little progress working through the river of resentments he still harbored toward his dad. As an aspiring artist, he seemed desperate for his father's approval. When they both performed at Hardly Strictly Bluegrass in 2003, Justin did something he often did when his dad was watching, arms crossed and stone-faced, from side-stage: he repeatedly looked over his left shoulder at Steve, searching for any sign of approval.

"I'm really, really proud of him," Steve, speaking about Justin years later, told a journalist. "But . . . it's really hard. . . . Because I'm an addict, most addicts are also codependent as hell. And it's painful for somebody like me to watch him perform. . . . You're terrified that he's gonna fuck up."[2]

Throughout the early 2000s, Steve largely refrained from commenting as his son's struggle with substance use intensified. But in 2002, Steve took an acting role in a new HBO show called *The Wire*, a police drama that centered on local politics and drug trafficking in Baltimore. Steve's character is a drug counselor named Walon who first appears on the show speaking at a Narcotics Anonymous (NA) meeting. "It didn't require any acting ability from me because he's a redneck recovering addict," Earle said of his character, in 2008.[3] In one episode, Walon explains to his sponsor in recovery that he is trying to help his "little nephew," who is suffering from a drug problem.

"He ain't anywhere near his bottom. Gotta see that bottom coming up at him," Walon says. "Hard, too, 'cause he's young, twenty-four."[4] When the episode aired, Justin was a few months shy of twenty-three.

Sometime around 2003, a journalist Justin befriended named Lisa Marie Turner was sitting with him in a Taco Bell drive-through, pouring out her heart about her childhood: how she'd spent forever on the front porch waiting for her dad to arrive before getting dragged inside by her mom.

Justin looked Turner in the eye. "I have a song about that," he said.

The song was "Time You Waste," and the story it told—being a little boy waiting for dad to show up on his mom's front steps—was one of several haunted childhood memories Justin shared with friends: Justin outside with his bags packed, ignoring his mom's pleas to come back inside, holding out hope Dad might arrive; Justin wandering down the street and standing by a lonesome streetlight, waiting for Dad in the dark. "Justin had so many of what I call 'soul wounds' that had not been healed, and they were still just surfacing," recalled Dustin Welch's mom, Jennifer Patten, one of the people Justin would share these memories with. "He had this sweet, tender, loving, caring, beautiful side to him that was so clouded by these wounds."

After they connected at the drive-though, Justin and Turner swapped lyrics and poetry and soon moved in together. Turner began vaguely managing Justin, helping him book and promote shows. Both were writers and were blunt, quick to blurt out what they were thinking. Both were also tangled in overlapping mental illnesses and addiction struggles, and their romantic relationship, like most of Justin's up to this point, quickly grew turbulent.

Turner's mother wasn't pleased to discover who her daughter was dating, so much so that Turner stills remembered a tense and revealing exchange:

"How do y'all even pay the bills?" Turner's mom once asked the young couple.

"She books me shows," Justin responded, "and I play them."

"What do you do with the money?" she asked.

"It goes into a bank account," said Justin.

"For what?" she asked.

"Guitar strings," said Justin, "and bail."

Steve and his producer Ray Kennedy tried to professionally record the Swindlers. They were finally being taken seriously: Lost Highway, the label that released the *O Brother* soundtrack, had expressed interest in the group, so much so that the band set up a showcase at the venue the Basement for the label to attend. To further show the band off to the label, Kennedy recorded the Swindlers playing Justin's songs like "Ain't Glad I'm Leaving," "Maria," and "Decimation of a Southern Gentleman."

The sessions, however, were a mess. Before recording the EP, the Swindlers had persuaded Justin to go to rehab, to which he'd consented. When he got out, however, sobriety didn't stick. The Swindlers never knew exactly what happened with the recordings or Lost Highway's interest, but they were never signed by any label.

It was a difficult, devastating experience, and Justin blamed himself. "I got more interested again in getting high than making music," he said.[5]

He fell even further into despairing drug use in early 2004, living, sometimes with sex workers, between Shirley Street Station and, as he later recounted, a series of budget motels. Justin later spoke about the experience of coming to a stark realization while staring at himself in a motel-room mirror somewhere off Brick Church Pike in North Nashville. "My hair was singed from smoking crack," he said. "I was missing my front tooth. I weighed about 125, 130 pounds. My arms look like somebody had been throwing darts at them. I remember just standing there and looking at myself and having no clue who it was I was looking at. I did not recognize that person, and I think that's where I realized the drugs and alcohol and life I'd been living, and the people I'd been around, had fooled me into thinking I was this really tough, really mean street kid. But I wasn't."[6]

Yet, as Justin nose-dived, the Swindlers received glowing local media attention.

"After absorbing the blues in his teens, Earle has matured into a songwriter who draws on all manner of modern and traditional styles to create something uniquely powerful and personal," Michael McCall wrote in the *Scene* in March 2004. "Backed by his young band, the multifaceted Swindlers, Earle has been drawing fervent record company interest of late. . . . He's clearly come into his own."[7]

"Call it roots-country or old-time informed or whatever," the *Tennessean*'s Peter Cooper claimed that spring, "but it's a cool thing."[8]

This attention came as no relief to the Swindlers, who were, by then, barely functioning. Nicholson was going to move to Los Angeles to pursue film. Newer members, like Derek Pell, were frustrated by the band's lack of professionalism: When they were hired to play an upscale wedding, Pell was forced to pull an all-nighter writing out charts for the music.

After they recorded with Kennedy and Steve, the Swindlers told Justin they were having a band meeting. When he showed up, he realized it was an intervention. Dustin Welch, the Swindlers' founder, told Justin he couldn't be in a band with him while he watched him die. Nicholson agreed: If Justin couldn't seek help, they were leaving the Swindlers. They'd begged him to get clean, leaning on what little they understood of addiction and disease.

"Your dad was a millionaire before he was a junkie," Nicholson told him. "What have you done?"

Justin disregarded and resented his friends' concern. He thought they were hypocrites: They drank constantly and used drugs; who were they to tell him what to do?

Justin's bandmates tried a zero-tolerance, tough-love approach they'd internalized, in part, from their dads, specifically Justin's. By this point, both Carol and Steve had become paralyzed by their inability to help their child, who was now in his early twenties. They felt terrified, out of options, and backed into a corner of projecting inflexibility in the face of his continued flailing.

Looking back, Swindlers bassist Willie Domann, who later had a falling-out with both Justin and his former bandmates largely over publishing credits,[9] believed that the intervention, and the way his bandmates dealt with Justin, did more harm than good. "By the end of it, Justin was more heartbroken," said Domann. "He was betrayed by everything and everyone he was relying on as a support system."

Justin began seeking refuge at Patty Lemay's South Nashville apartment, where she bristled at the hard-line approach she thought Justin was receiving from everyone else. She fed and took care of Justin as they sat around listening to Tom Waits's first record (especially "Ol' 55") and Neil Young's *On the Beach* (Justin's favorite line: "I need a crowd of people / But I can't face them day to day").

But Lemay was deeply worried. "Please pray and send any energy to

Justin Earle," she wrote to David Berman in a March 2004 email. "Last night he stayed at my place and we shared songs. He is very delicate and I am afraid for his life. He did call the methadone hotline around 7am, and also his momma."

"Justin is so ill, he doesn't eat, ever," Lemay continued in the email. "I had to tell him how scary it was to see him that way."

Lemay could see there was a much deeper hurt behind Justin's drug use. "We had a serious talk, and I asked him, 'Why?' Why have you decided to do the drugs that your dad did, and mimic the behavior that caused you so much pain?" she said. "He had said to me that no one had ever asked him why."

Justin shared his foremost fears with Lemay, oftentimes while coming down from or in the midst of a high. "Justin told me that he was afraid to go to sleep alone," she said. "He said, 'When I lay down if I'm by myself, I just know my heart's going to stop, and I'm just going to die and I'll lie there for days and no one will find me.'"

Through all the self-obliteration, Lemay saw a beautiful young man striving toward a light that was becoming harder to see, and she told him as much.

"Do you know why God made you so tall?" Lemay remembered asking him one day.

"No," Justin said. "Tell me why."

"So you don't have to stand in anyone's shadow," she said.

Still, there were fewer and fewer people Justin felt he could turn to. "I have to watch myself around people like Justin," one acquaintance wrote to another of Justin's friends in the summer of 2004. "It seems like his troubles are a lot worse than any of ours."

With the Swindlers on the rocks, Justin formed a short-lived band with bassist Willie Domann, adding local singer-guitarist Steve Poulton on guitar and part-time Swindler Ben Martin on drums. Justin decided the group would be called Khadafi.

Khadafi rehearsed several times a week for a month or two. Domann's memory of the quartet was that they "didn't flow correctly," but Poulton remembered them sounding "definitely rocking and at times surprisingly soulful," especially with Domann's bass playing.

"I do recall repeatedly insisting that the tempos allow the words to be heard," said Poulton. "Certain practices by certain players influenced the volume and pace of the delivery."

Khadafi booked one gig on June 24, 2004, opening for Oklahoma singer-songwriter Mike Hosty, which earned Justin yet another *Tennessean* write-up teasing the "new band" he'd been rehearsing "for months."[10]

Khadafi never played the show, or any other gig. But Justin did show up.

The headliner, Mike Hosty, had seen Justin perform a year earlier, and he'd been moved by Justin's dedication to songcraft and showmanship. As far as Hosty was concerned, none of the professional songwriters playing the Bluebird had anything on Justin, whom he'd seen pouring his heart out to a couple of audience members in a tiny club as if he were headlining a sold-out football stadium.

But now, observing Justin just one year later, in June 2004, Hosty was alarmed by his level of dysfunction. Justin passed out after his opening set. After the gig, Hosty jotted down impressions from the night in his diary: "New Nashville wildman was drunk under the table."

After Justin came to, he took Hosty to Springwater, where he drank some more, then explained to him that he was living in a treehouse with another man across the street in Centennial Park. The two kept drinking, and then Justin disappeared. "He was wandering through the park into some trees, and then he was gone," said Hosty.

The bullet point under the page labeled "Justin Earle" in Hosty's diary was four words long: "Lives in a tree?"

Justin's self-destruction had become so pronounced that even his most reliable coconspirators were backing away.

On one afternoon, circa early 2004, one of those friends, Justin's former roommate Sean Locke, sat in his black Chevy Impala across the street from Springwater watching his friend walk farther and farther away from him until he disappeared into the bar. It was daytime, just past noon or so, too early to be anywhere near such a place. Locke can't quite remember what month it was. Those were fuzzy years.

Locke had fallen for Justin's radiant charm when he'd first seen Justin playing "So Different Blues" outside his dad's record label's office across the parking lot from Locke's apartment. That was years ago. Now, Locke was sitting in his car watching Justin walk away, perhaps for the last time.

Locke was thirty-two. He was trying to straighten out his life after years of traversing the city's bars and parties. But Justin had a knack for persuading friends to follow him at least partway through whatever dark portal he would descend into on any given evening.

That's what had happened the previous night, and it had been a wake-up call—even though it'd started off the way most nights started with Justin: the two friends staying up late snorting cocaine and singing songs. But Justin had seemed like he'd been awake for days, and that night, he kept going, and going, and going, ingesting what to Locke seemed like a "monstrous" amount of cocaine. Locke, who was no stranger to the drug, was scared.

It unsettled Locke how easily he'd slid back into old habits with Justin. It disturbed him further when he realized Justin was *not* the same, that his friend was freefalling in a way he'd never before seen. As Locke tried to fall asleep as the sun rose, he heard a noise from outside: Justin was wandering around the apartment complex, acting paranoid, talking to himself, "talking to the trees," remembered Locke. In that moment, Locke was flooded with a dreadful image: having to call Steve Earle to tell him that Justin had died in his apartment.

The next day, Justin woke up and announced he had nowhere else to go, but he knew a Springwater bartender was opening up early: Could Locke please give him a ride to the bar?

As Locke drove Justin to the bar they'd once frequented, he came to a painful realization: Their time together was over. Alone in his car, he watched his friend wander into Springwater.

"There goes a guy that I love, but I can't do it, I can't be around for the demise," he thought to himself.

After that day, Justin left Locke a few late-night voicemails, but Locke never picked up or called back. Then, a few months later, Locke received some news.

In July 2004, Justin was hospitalized at Vanderbilt's ICU. Following months of nonstop crack smoking and heavy drug use, he'd gone to the emergency room after waking up one morning with what he later described as a burning in his lungs. He had been unable to breathe.[11]

Now, Locke heard, Justin was living in St. Paul, Minnesota. He'd been sent to the world-class inpatient drug-treatment program at Hazelden, and had then transitioned to a halfway house nearby. Justin had nearly died. His only hope was to try, as hard as he possibly could, to face his illness. He had agreed, reluctantly, to give rehab a real shot.

PART II

Anywhere at All

CHAPTER 8

IN JANUARY 2005, A TWENTY-THREE-YEAR-OLD NAMED MOLLY MCCLARY saw a *Nashville Scene* concert listing that caught her eye. McClary was back home living in the Nashville area after recently graduating from college in North Carolina. Like so many young people around her, she was taking full advantage of the burgeoning roots music scene in the city. She'd recently seen Old Crow Medicine Show play, and some old-timey band called the Swindlers had opened. Now the Swindlers' lead singer, Justin Earle, was performing solo at Bongo After Hours Theatre, a performance space above the café Bongo Java. It cost five dollars. She figured she'd check it out.

The show, it turned out, was Justin's first billed performance in more than six months, his live debut after returning from rehab in Minnesota. The choice of venue wasn't coincidental; Bongo Java After Hours didn't sell alcohol.

Fliers were printed with a photo of Justin Earle messy haired and passed out on the floor—seemingly a darkly humorous commentary on the show's postrehab premise. His return was greeted warmly: "Anyone who hasn't heard Justin Earle lately would do well to head to Bongo After Hours," said the *Tennessean*. "Earle's fingerpicking is deft, his voice is authentic and convincing, and his songwriting has grown more powerful. A few years ago, he was getting good. Now, he's good."[1]

McClary knew nothing about Justin Earle when she heard him play that night, but she enjoyed his set enough to see him perform again the following month. That time, something clicked. McClary was entranced. She stuck around after the show to give Justin her number on a matchbook.

Justin called the next day. They talked for an hour. Justin was extremely direct: He'd recently gotten out of rehab, he told her. McClary told him she was surprised he was sharing such intimate information so readily.

"You gotta know what you're getting into," Justin responded.

Justin tried to impress McClary for their first date, taking her to a fancy restaurant downtown. That evening, Justin didn't talk about his troublesome past. "Only song lyrics and laughs and plans for the future," she said.

The two connected, first and foremost, over songwriting. They got goose bumps over the same lines in songs. On their first date, Justin recited, verbatim, the entire word-crammed first verse to Bruce Springsteen's "It's Hard to Be a Saint in the City," unable to contain his enthusiasm for Springsteen's use of rhythm and alliteration.

"He was charming and confident," McClary recalled, "and had me hook, line, and sinker."

McClary's upbringing was nothing like Justin's. She'd grown up in a stable family in the Nashville suburbs. But the two liked each other immediately, both feeling they had found someone else who somehow saw the world in much the same way.

Justin started buying McClary antique jewelry and stopping by Otter's Chicken Tenders, the restaurant where she worked, to put flowers and Marlboros in her car. Soon, McClary moved into Justin's basement bedroom at Steve's Fairview home outside the city—the same room Justin had lived in as an out-of-control thirteen-year-old. Justin, now twenty-three, was house-sitting for his father, who was either touring or spending his spare time with Allison Moorer, the singer-songwriter he'd fallen in love with and married (his seventh marriage) in 2005. Sometimes, McClary and Justin went outside and stargazed.

After Justin got sober, Steve found new ways to be supportive: At one point Justin was being paid around $400 a month to house-sit and write songs for J-Trane Publishing, a company Steve set up for the sole purpose of providing a regular income for his son.

Justin confided in McClary. He told her about his several months in rehab at Hazelden the previous year. It hadn't been his first rehab stint, he explained, but this most recent treatment had stuck in a new way. He told her about the month or so he'd spent at a halfway house in St. Paul, Minnesota, how he'd worked at a gift shop, he joked, because he didn't have the skills for anything else. He told her about how his life as a sober person looked, how he now spent his time attending Narcotics Anonymous meetings in Hillsboro Village.

That this latest round of sobriety had taken hold surprised everyone in Justin's life, nobody more than Justin.

"When I went to treatment that last time, it wasn't with any intention of staying clean," he told a magazine in 2008. "Rehab was like vacation: You knew that first hit was gonna be so good. But I ended up listening, heeding the advice of people, which is so unlike me."[2]

He seemed comfortable in his skin. When McClary got anxious at the industry parties Steve took her and Justin to, Justin "always took my hand and introduced me with a compliment," she recalled. He introduced her to Guy Clark as "my Susanna" and told Lyle Lovett she had the prettiest voice he'd ever heard.

"He had a charm that just wrapped up me and anyone in his orbit," McClary said.

Justin challenged himself to confront his past, making amends and coming to terms with both the damage of his childhood and the damage he'd inflicted on others. In his journal, he listed ten things he was grateful for, a common practice in twelve-step programs:

1. Sober
2. Alive
3. Pesonally stable
4. Sheltered
5. Sleep
6. Family
7. Liveing now
8. Serenity
9. Self respect
10. The program

He wrote, in his journals, that he needed to unburden himself of past transgressions: "I have several haunting memories that need to get out in order for me to grow and move on," he wrote.

He processed, in verse, his emotional past and present:

See I have always been a loner
Since I was young
I had it all figured I didn't
Need no help from anyone
But now I'm older and I'm
Fallin to Pieces and
I don't know what I
Believe in
And I still can't bring myself
To reach out for help

And he reflected, in his journal, on the effects his illness had on his life and how much he'd overcome: "My disease has taken me to many places that youre so called normal would find unfathemable," he wrote. He continued:

> I sought comfort in such places a abandoned houses and cheap motel room in parts of town where only hooker junkies and hillers hang out and I found these places very welcoming after everyone I knew had turned there back on me and I had turned my back on life.
>
> My powerlessness was very aparent to me for many years. . . . I thought . . . that it was cool to be as screwed up as I was and my unmanagability was just as aparent for the mere fact that I couldn't do any thing with out the obsession of drugs and alchole ruling my every thought.

"Coming to meetings I don't have to be powerless anymore," he continued. "So I will just keep coming back."

The night McClary met Justin, he was playing the first of several fundraising benefit shows for a soon-to-be-opening nonprofit community arts space in a gentrifying neighborhood north of downtown known as Germantown.

"Community arts center is a very important thing," Justin said onstage during one of these benefits. "A place where broke-dick musicians and other artists can get together."

It was at one of these benefit shows, a blowout event at the Belcourt Theatre on April 1, 2005, that the Swindlers played—and headlined—their last big show. It was billed as their "farewell performance."

At least fifteen different young men had played onstage in the Swindlers throughout its seven-plus-year existence. Band members came and went; when Cory Younts left each summer for Boy Scout camp, Elliot Currie filled in to sing Younts's high harmonies. Sometimes they called in an extra musician, including the young fiddle prodigy Joshua Hedley.

But by 2005, the amorphous collective of Chicken Shack boys had grown apart. Too many scares from Justin, too much self-sabotage and sloppy shenanigans, too many clashing egos. Welch was ready to leave Nashville and tour the country in a band. Nicholson had moved to Los Angeles. Justin wanted more autonomy over his musical decisions.

Despite never having officially released any music, the Swindlers threw themselves a formal farewell, conceiving of their Belcourt gig as their own *Last Waltz*, the famous star-studded 1976 farewell concert from the Band filmed by Martin Scorsese.

And like the Band in *The Last Waltz*, the Swindlers tried to tell their story through its set list. They started without Justin, playing old Chicken Shack classics including Django Reinhardt's "Blue Drag," Bob Wills's "Old Fashioned Love," Gus Cannon's "Walk Right In."

Forty minutes later, their lead singer strutted onstage. "Now," Justin announced, "we gon' make it *real* ruckus."

The previous documented gig Justin had performed with the Swindlers had been a full year prior. The Belcourt show was, in reality, as much a reunion as a farewell. But the Swindlers sounded slick and rehearsed. Justin, eight or so months sober, led them through Chicken Shack–era standbys like "Hard Livin'," "Ain't Glad I'm Leaving," and their classic country ballad "Cold Hearted Kisses."

"If you've ever been walking down Charlotte Pike at five o'clock in the morning," Justin said, introducing his next song, "then you'll know what this feels like."

Justin then launched into "Decimation of a Southern Gentleman," screaming his way through the pitch-black musical memoir. "I said '*Mama*,'" he shouted at the top of his lungs. "I'm so far away from you right now."

"That's a real happy song, innit," Younts cracked when they finished the song.

"Makes you feel good on the inside," Justin replied.

For the finale, a throng of Swindlers past or present hopped onstage. Dustin Welch sang lead on the band's signature rendition of "Chittlin' Cookin' Time in Cheatham County," then introduced each Swindler, all ten of them: Skylar Wilson, Josh Graham, Travis Nicholson, Ben Martin, Willie Domann, Andy Moore, Derek Pell, Cory Younts, Justin Earle, and himself.

"The Swindlers, ladies and gentlemen!" said the emcee, the crowd still shouting. "They might be calling it quits as a band for right now, but we ain't heard the last of any of those boys."

The Swindlers ended before the band could capitalize on a musical moment and cultural boom in their hometown that they had helped kick-start. The same year they broke up, Loretta Lynn won Best Country Album at the 2005 Grammys, beating stars like Tim McGraw and Keith Urban, with *Van Lear Rose*, a spare, defiantly lo-fi album produced by Jack White that presented Lynn as a rock-leaning country risk-taker and rejuvenated her career.

The album had been recorded in East Nashville in the home of a man who loved tinkering with recording equipment named Eric McConnell. Industry executives took notice: How did an album recorded in a house across the river beat out their big-budget Music Row blockbusters?

In 2005, East Nashville wasn't yet an unaffordable neighborhood populated by transplants from Los Angeles and New York drawn to the high-end restaurants and coffee shops on every corner. It was still a transitional neighborhood experiencing a much earlier wave of gentrification. Struggling artists were fomenting an underground roots music scene.

That this tree-lined part of town, with Victorian homes, public housing, and historic neighborhoods, was undergoing a renaissance was hardly unique. As in many cities across the United States, in the second half of the twentieth century, a mix of updated zoning laws and white and middle-class flight had transformed the area into a neglected, under-resourced neighborhood. Slumlords had subdivided old homes as rentals, and federal urban renewal programs had razed many of the neighborhood's historic homes.

But as early as 1983, the *Tennessean* used the word "gentrification" to describe "hundreds of residents" moving into East Nashville's historic districts. In 1990, twenty-plus years before the neighborhood became a nationally recognized avatar of cultural cool, the newspaper outlined a series of city policies and rezoning efforts that positioned East Nashville for growth. "Neighborhood rising like a phoenix," the *Tennessean* declared that year.[3]

Its music scene kick-started in 1995, when a small club called Radio Cafe opened in the building of a former pharmacy. The club seated only a few dozen patrons and was lined with old pharmacy cabinets. In the back of the room, behind the soundboard, was a weed-dealing, motorcycle-driving, walrus-mustache-sporting former Marine named Skip Litz, who quickly became the unofficial mayor of the slow-budding community of pot-smoking, day-job-avoiding, Music Row–averse songwriters who flocked to the area for cheap rents.

Radio Cafe was one of few spaces for musicians on the east side of the Cumberland River, which separated East Nashville from the city's corporate music industry. On any given night, you might hear Lucinda Williams, Gillian Welch and David Rawlings, Emmylou Harris, Elizabeth Cook, Todd Snider, Jason Ringenberg, or Rosie Flores play there.

Litz worked the soundboard and was known for yelling "play a fucking train song!" whenever he got bored, which was often.[4]

In 2001, Gillian Welch and David Rawlings purchased the historic Woodland Studios in East Nashville and started recording their albums in the legendary space located in the center of the Five Points neighborhood. When they purchased the studio, it was abandoned, having been damaged in a 1998 tornado that destroyed much of the neighborhood. But the studio had a long history: It's where the Nitty Gritty Dirt Band recorded their 1972 album, *Will the Circle Be Unbroken*, and where Charlie Daniels recorded "The Devil Went Down to Georgia." Having the studio under the new stewardship of revered local transplants Rawlings and Welch was a sign of the neighborhood's shifting tides.[5]

Shortly after *Van Lear Rose* came out, Todd Snider released his breakthrough album, *East Nashville Skyline*, also recorded at McConnell's home studio. *East Nashville Skyline* established Snider as a sardonic folk storyteller, its title nodding to the neighborhood and its centerpiece paying tribute to the man, Skip Litz, who'd helped start it all. That song was called "Play a Train Song."

All of Nashville seemed to be surging with creative energy in 2005. "It was a city that was waking up," said Christine Hall, a poet, Springwater regular, and behind-the-scenes arts organizer who booked the Swindlers' final show at the Belcourt, "and I could smell it."[6]

Over on Music Row, two young singers named Miranda Lambert and Carrie Underwood both released instant-hit debut albums (the melody of Lambert's title track sounded so similar to Steve Earle's "Feel Alright" that she gave Steve a writing credit).[7] Meanwhile, an eighth grade Nashville transplant named Taylor Swift was prepping her debut LP.

West of downtown, Springwater, the bar where Steve and Carol spent much of their courtship and Justin spent much of his late adolescence, was flooded with a new mix of teenagers and indie rockers congregating to listen to a mix of alternative rock, freak-country, experimental folk, and stand-up comedy, PBRs in hand.

The crowd included Caitlin Rose, Tristen Gaspadarek, and Jonny

Fritz, who soon began performing their own songs on the red-streamer-adorned stage. A Nashville teenager named Kesha Sebert started sneaking into the bar and eventually got onstage to sing country covers before she dropped her last name, and later shot to global fame. The Springwater scene was nonhierarchical; there was little difference between the stranger sitting at the bar and the singer onstage. The man who presided over it was the iconoclast cult comedian-singer Dave Cloud, who performed obscene stand-up routines and songs with titles like "School of Hard Knoxville."[8]

Not far from the honky-tonks, a weekly Sunday showcase called Lovenoise provided a much-needed space for the city's perpetually marginalized underground R&B, hip-hop, and jazz scenes. The showcase highlighted local acts like the rapper Crisis and the soul duo Descendants of Reality. Nashville hip-hop was flooded with excitement after local rapper Young Buck released *Straight Outta Ca$hville*, which debuted as the third-best-selling album in the country in 2004.[9]

South of downtown, clubs like the Basement and Mercy Lounge were fostering a flourishing rock scene featuring bands like indie rockers Glossary, pop-rockers the Features, garage-rock revivalists Those Darlins' and Jeff the Brotherhood, and the alt-punks Be Your Own Pet and Pink Spiders. "Now is a better time for local rock bands than any in recent memory," declared the *Scene*'s Tracy Moore, noting the recent major-label signing of a local band called Kings of Leon.[10]

East Nashville was undergoing a boom in popularity among artist types that mirrored what was happening in parts of Portland, Oregon, and in Brooklyn's Williamsburg neighborhood at the time. As young adults increasingly moved to cities in the aughts, rents started climbing, as did displacement of the nonwhite population. Some longtime residents could already see the writing on the wall.

In 2003, the *Tennessean* ran a story about the owners of Edgefield Restaurant, a local Black-owned eatery, who'd noticed a disturbing trend: Younger white East Nashville denizens had stopped patronizing their restaurant. "The restaurant noticed a drop in its white clientele," noted reporter Alison Miller, "shortly after the other restaurants began popping up."[11]

This was just the early beginning of a process that would accelerate in the coming decades. The wave of artists, bohemians, and queer people who moved into the neighborhood in the '80s, '90s, and early '00s gradually gave way to later waves of increasingly affluent, white gentrifiers, eager to live in what had become, by the mid-2010s, the most desirable neighborhood in the city.

Although Justin was artistically aligned with much of what was happening in East Nashville in 2005, his sobriety had changed his relationship with the city. He was no longer staying up all night or crashing on couches or sleeping in trees. In 2005, he'd essentially stopped going to bars.

Instead, for the first time, perhaps ever, Justin had a steady home and a daily routine. He and McClary eventually got their own place: a house on Stewart Place, south of downtown, far from the bustling new scene in East Nashville.

Each morning was the same: Justin drove the 1999 black Ford F-150 his father had lent him two miles toward Hillsboro Village, where he stopped into the café Fido for coffee, then walked to a Narcotics Anonymous meeting.

When he wasn't at meetings, Justin was at home writing songs. He decorated his home office with musical ephemera: the sleeve of Bruce Springsteen's *The River*, a 1985 Townes Van Zandt concert poster, Loretta Lynn 45s, and a 78 record of the 1919 vaudeville singer Billy Murray's Prohibition-era lament "How Are You Goin' to Wet Your Whistle? (When the Whole Darn World's Gone Dry)."

Sitting under these musical talismans, Justin would scribble lyrics and pick his guitar. He mumbled his new songs into his tape recorder and handed them in to J-Trane, the publishing company his father had set up to employ him (by 2005, he'd submitted forty songs). Some, like "Black Eyed Suzy," were songs that would end up on his first few records. Countless others were rarely, if ever, even sung in public: He wrote a catchy folk-pop tune called "Gloria." He wrote a lovesick harmonica ballad called "That's Me Without You." He wrote a melodramatic tale about New York City called "My Manhattan" (sample lyric: "I got me a Brooklyn girl / She's from Bensonhurst / Works over in the Alphabets").

At night, Justin and McClary watched PBS documentaries and *The Simpsons*, saw music together at clubs like the Station Inn and the Basement, and went out to eat: Athens for Greek food, Siam Cafe for Thai, Las Cazuelas down on Nolensville Pike for Mexican. Justin drank coffee, chain-smoked cigarettes, avoided bars, got french fries at Hot Diggity Dog, or went on ice-cream runs with McClary, sometimes bumping into the fellow sweet-toothed singer-songwriter John Prine.

The songs Justin was writing were often inspired by whatever he was learning about: McClary remembered that after watching Ken Burns's *Civil War*, Justin escaped into his office and appeared thirty minutes later singing "Lone Pine Hill," a freshly written tale of a disillusioned Confederate soldier. After watching a Chet Baker documentary called *Let's Get Lost*, he wrote a song with the same title.

Other times, the songs were inspired by his new sobriety, and they gestured at the difficult work of self-reflection.

"Travelled down a thousand lonesome roads / Lost and found," he scribbled in his journal, "I'm ready now."

When McClary had a job opportunity in Washington, DC, Justin was supportive, insisting he was ready to move with her for the job.

"It was his quiet years," said McClary, "and they were great."

As he was instructed in recovery, Justin attempted to take accountability for his past few years in his journals. He wrote he was "way to fucked up to drive but did anyway and totaled my car." He wrote that he'd "insisting on useing while liveing with a girlfriend until I began stealing and ended up on the streets." He wrote that he'd lost a friendship because he "insisted on seeing my friends girlfriend." He wrote about the time he "went to a bar loaded and acted an ass even though the owner of my record lable was there." He described being abandoned by his band because of his drug use, of rejecting the help and concern of friends and family, "insisting I was okay," as he wrote, "and wereing a mask so no one really could get to know me."

Justin scribbled aphorisms he absorbed in recovery meetings. "The power to end resentment," he jotted down, "is in the hands of the one who resents."

And though he had previously resisted spirituality, Justin grappled with and took seriously a core tenet of twelve-step recovery: the idea of a higher power. He wrote:

Wanted higher power
for lost soul seeking
salvation Requirment are
ability to forgive for life
of sining . . . ability to
be available at all hours
of the day including the
wee hours of the morning
as far as stipulations there
is only one that you
can provide me with love
I need that I cant get
anywhere else includeing from
myself
Sincerely
Lost and Lonely

McClary remembered Steve accompanying his son to a milestone NA meeting in July 2005 celebrating Justin's first full year of sobriety. Justin spoke openly about it too. "He would call a lot, making sure I was going to meetings and whatnot," he told a newspaper in 2011. "It was his idea to send me to rehab the first time. He knew what I had to do."[12]

In 2005, Justin started rehearsing a brand-new band called the

Distributors. Sonically, the band was a far cry from the Swindlers, even though all its members had played in that acoustic group, too.

The Distributors were a loud rock band. Justin had been listening to the Replacements and Elvis Costello and Bruce Springsteen. For the first time since his preteen punk years, the twenty-three-year-old strapped on a Telecaster and turned up his amp.

On bass was Willie Domann, who'd accompanied Justin on a series of transitional post-Swindlers projects. On drums, Skylar Wilson. For lead guitar, Justin recruited Wilson's roommate Josh Graham.

The Distributors repurposed Justin's older songs ("Rogers Park," "Far Away in Another Town") as fast-paced full-band rockers or power ballads. But he also started writing original songs for the band, like "Enough Is Enough," a thrashing lament that bordered on pop-punk.

As Justin processed his past and concentrated on his sobriety, the loud noise of the Distributors provided a helpful toughness to hide behind. "The rock [band] was a good front for him," said McClary. But behind his new formulaic pop-rock love songs, she said, was something else. "They're all about heroin," said McClary. "You think they're about a lover, but they're not."

The group started playing shows at the Basement and lasted for only about six months. But during that period, they had at least one big gig, a set at Exit/In, a cavernous club that served as a milestone for aspiring Nashville rock bands. They opened with "The City Tonight," a catchy number that channeled eighties rock revivalism and ended with two covers, one of which was the Replacements' "Can't Hardly Wait."

In interviews, Justin traced his love of the Replacements—the scrappy and notoriously self-destructive Minneapolis punk band—to his mother. He fell for "Can't Hardly Wait" as an eighteen-year-old touring with his dad, when the Philly rock band Marah closed their set opening for Steve Earle with a raucous rendition of the song each night. "It just sunk in deeply," Justin explained.[13]

The song held a special significance for Justin, a portrait of stumbling and addiction that withheld judgment and resisted cliché. In the lyrics, the band's songwriter Paul Westerberg offers a depiction of recklessness and self-obliteration that nevertheless, with help from its cheery nursery-rhyme riff, communicates tenderness, even hope. Justin nerded out over the song's backstory, oftentimes singing Westerberg's dark alternative lyrics that more directly hinted at suicide, depending on his mood. "Can't Hardly Wait" would eventually become one of the most important songs of Justin Townes Earle's career, often serving as his final song of his shows. But he first started performing it in the Distributors.

In the fall of 2006, after they'd played their final gig, the Distributors recorded nearly an album's worth of their hard-edged, tough-sounding material with local producer Brad Jones. "For about six months," said the band's guitarist, Josh Graham, "we had a pretty good little rock band."

But writing upbeat rock songs, Justin later said, felt unnatural. The Distributors were declared over, their recordings relegated to what Justin called a "limbo of the mind."[14]

As was often the case after he moved on to his next artistic period or project, Justin promptly dismissed his recent past.[15] "When I got sober, I came back to town and I did this freak thing: I wanted a rock band," he said. "It turned out to be a really bad idea."

CHAPTER 9

JUSTIN NEVER STOPPED WRITING QUIET FOLK SONGS, EVEN DURING HIS short-lived tenure in a loud rock band. After being pulled in several artistic directions, he eventually began focusing on the types of character-driven stories he wanted to tell.

Around this time, he also settled on some useful imagery to tell some of those stories: rushing water. He'd become interested, obsessed, even, with the concept of the rising river: "biblical floods," as McClary put it.

The country was still reeling from Hurricane Katrina, which had resurfaced one of Justin's favorite songs about rushing water: "Louisiana 1927," Randy Newman's 1974 lament about the historic Mississippi River flood. Justin would soon start singing it at shows.[1]

He'd composed several songs about water as a metaphor for mortal release. "A Desolate Angels Blues," written years prior,[2] was about returning to earth's heavenly river. "Let the Waters Rise," inspired by old-time murder ballads, was about being delivered to the afterlife by a flood. These songs initiated what McClary believed was a recurring theme in Justin's work: "When he's talking about the water rising, he's talking about relapse, he's talking about how his troubles are coming," she said. "He always represented his death with the [imagery of] the waters rising."

Justin started gathering songs he'd written about death and deliverance, release and redemption. One of them was a spare, tender ballad that tells the tale of a young man's final moments before taking his own life at age twenty-three. The disheveled protagonist puts on his father's old suit, heads to a bar for a quick shot of liquor, walks outside to bum a cigarette, then winds up calling his mom from a pay phone to confess how desolate his young life had become: "There ain't nothing I fear," he tells his mama, "so much as being alone."

Partway through the song, a mysterious first-person narrator appears, offering perspective on the tale being told, before disappearing entirely: "Looking back I'd say, it wasn't so much the girl," the narrator opines, "as it was the booze, and the dope, and the way he took the weight of the world upon his shoulders."

Justin sang the fingerpicked folk ballad gently, voicing his character's decision with matter-of-fact respect. "It was his weary heart that pushed him to the edge," Justin sang.

Justin called the song "Yuma," or, as he also may have been singing when describing the farewell postcard his protagonist sends back to the titular city where his mother lives, *you, ma*.

"Yuma was the dark side of my imagination," Justin said of the song. "It was the 'What if?'"[3]

Justin decided these musically cheery, lyrically dark folk songs should constitute his first release, an EP. He titled the six-song collection for the unforgivingly dark song he'd written: *Yuma*. Justin had been motivated to put the EP together when, in late 2006, he and his friend, fellow singer-songwriter Joshua Black Wilkins, cooked up an idea to self-book a joint tour for the following year.

Justin had played one-off regional shows throughout the years, but he'd never properly hit the road without Steve. Justin and Wilkins booked the two-week tour themselves, calling up cafés and clubs in the eastern United States. Justin had wanted a reason to record the acoustic songs he'd written at Stewart Place over the past year. Now, he also needed something to sell at shows.

Comprising only Justin's voice and an acoustic guitar, *Yuma* was clearly informed by the twentieth-century American folk music and history Justin studied: "The Ghost of Virginia" was the story of an imaginary Civil War–era freight train with a melody that conjured Woody Guthrie. "A

Desolate Angels Blues," initially inspired by a Jack Kerouac book, was a country-gospel hymn Justin imagined one day being played at his funeral. "I Don't Care" was a fast-paced ramblin'-man travelogue Justin wrote after reading Joe Klein's 1980 biography of Guthrie.[4]

As much as the title track, "Yuma," marked a songwriting breakthrough, it was "I Don't Care" that served as Justin's mission statement. Cloaked in old-time train-hopping tropes, the bouncy three-verse, three-chord folk tune was an ode to past and future roaming. It was striking in its simplicity—"like it was unearthed rather than created," as songwriter Allison Moorer put it—but Justin sang the song so fast it buzzed. The tempo of the two-minute tune tumbled with restlessness and excitement. Singing and picking his ode to rambling as fast as he did wasn't merely some showbiz trick (though it was also that): It showed how fast Justin's mind moved, how ready he was to begin this next phase of his journey, how eager he'd become—after these past two years of stability—to start running. He rattled off cities he'd once wandered (Chicago, Johnson City) and towns to which his destiny would surely bring him: Miami, Tucumcari,[5] Amarillo, Saskatoon, Baton Rouge. "Anywhere but here," he sang, "anywhere at all."

Justin recorded the songs with musician Steve Poulton and punk drummer Tony Read serving as producer and engineer, respectively. *Yuma* began and ended with the only sound on the album other than Justin's voice and acoustic guitar: a toy music-box recording of the left-wing anthem "The Internationale" he stole from his dad.[6]

The collection showed the twenty-four-year-old singer-songwriter had made titanic leaps as a songwriter.

"I needed to start from the ground," Justin said of his stripped-down approach, "the most bare form of it."[7]

To make the record real, he called in favors: Ray Kennedy, his father's producer, mastered *Yuma*. McClary loaned him a thousand dollars to have CDs made.

The first review of the EP—the first review of any solo Justin Townes Earle record—was positive, if cautious, about its anachronistic sound.

Writing in the *Nashville Scene*, a journalist and future friend of Justin named Jason Wilkins (no relation to Joshua) remarked that the recording showed Justin "has more than a little in common with the man who gave him his middle name, Townes Van Zandt." But, he added, "the danger with aiming for the kind of timelessness Earle strives for is that you just might end up sounding not only out of step, but out of touch."[8]

The *Tennessean* was more effusive, singling out the title track: "It sure is affecting, and it sure works."[9]

Yuma so impressed an agent named June Lehman, who represented older songwriters Justin admired, that she started booking him shows.

Touring the country for the first time throughout 2007, Justin was confronted by the expectations of crowds who'd shown up to see some singer whose name ended in *Townes Earle*. Audiences demanded to hear his father's music, particularly "Copperhead Road." But they went further, barking requests for songs by not merely Steve but also his contemporaries. When someone called out for a Guy Clark tune, Justin snapped back: "I don't play God's music."[10]

In bookings, Lehman downplayed the Steve connection, turning down unusually high-paying offers Justin received solely because of his surname.

That's what Justin wanted. Yes, he was desperate to work, eager for any gig, no matter how rough or low paying. But he refused to be his father's sideshow.

"There's always one drunk who wants to tell me a story about how he got drunk with my dad in 1983," Justin said, "about how he's the greatest guy on earth and blah-blah-blah."[11]

When a radio promoter named Joe Swank saw Justin perform around this time, he was struck by how deftly Justin handled this delicate dynamic with strangers. "Every other person that came up to him asked him something about his dad," said Swank. "He'd already worked out these answers that weren't pissy, or condescending, but that cut the conversation short."

Justin neutralized crowds by performing one—and only one—song by each of his two namesakes: typically, Townes Van Zandt's "Mr. Mudd and Mr. Gold" and Steve Earle's "Tom Ames' Prayer."

"I used to not play my dad's songs at all," he told one audience. "And somebody said, 'What if you went to see Arlo Guthrie and he didn't play any fucking Woody Guthrie songs.' . . . I was like, 'Well, I'd be pretty pissed off.'"[12]

Still refining his stage persona, Justin was more forthcoming about his career indebtedness to his father than he'd later be. "We don't write together because we'd kill each other," Justin said of Steve in the summer of 2007, "but we have a publishing deal together. . . . All of my songs go through him."[13]

When he wasn't on the road, Justin played around Nashville at mainstays like the Basement and Mercy Lounge, or farther-flung rooms like Norm's River Roadhouse or the Pond, a strip-mall dive outside of town where he tested out new material every Wednesday.

Copies of *Yuma* flew off the merch table. Justin was quickly able to repay McClary the $1,000 she'd loaned him.

But the relationship between the two of them was fraying. Though Justin was committed to sobriety, a series of erratic habits and compulsions had replaced his chemical dependencies. Foremost among them was speeding in his F-150, which Justin drove with a reckless abandon he once applied to pills and powder.

If Justin became angry about something while driving, he pressed down on the gas in a rage, accelerating to a hundred miles an hour as McClary would sit, terrified, in the passenger seat.

"Do you feel better now?" McClary would ask him afterward.

"Yes," Justin would reply. "I do."

Sobriety had saved Justin Townes Earle's life, but it had not made his problems vanish, no more than it had for his father. He was volatile and easily irritable, prone to mood swings and outbursts.

Serving as Justin's main support system, and the main recipient of such outbursts, started taking its toll on McClary.

Justin was now also breaking his routine, heading out on tours that sent him away for weeks at a time. The peaceful isolation of Justin and McClary's time on Stewart Place came to an end. Their private world had grounded Justin in the shaky early years of his sobriety, but, McClary said, "I knew he had to go be Justin Townes Earle."

While on the road, Justin got jealous and upset when he learned McClary was out at night with friends back home. They broke up in the summer of 2007, with McClary saying goodbye "to the biggest-hearted asshole [she'd] ever met."

Around the same time, Justin joined a two-week tour opening for a brash, baby-faced singer-guitarist named Jason Isbell. Isbell was also embarking on a brand-new solo career and touring his first solo record, but unlike Justin, he'd spend the past half-dozen years playing large, rowdy shows as the third singer-guitarist for the punk-leaning southern rock band Drive-By Truckers. Isbell and Justin knew each other from Nashville and hit it off, despite the fact that Isbell was, at the time, drinking heavily and Justin was completely sober.

"Few people know who Justin is besides that Steve is his dad," Jason told a journalist before their 2007 tour. "But he's a great songwriter."[14]

Justin drove his truck on the Isbell tour and made only a couple hundred dollars per gig (splitting the cash with his guitarist, Steve Poulton), but he was thrilled to be on what felt like his first real-deal tour.

"I'd been in . . . coffee shop hell before that," said Justin. Playing proper rock clubs "gave me a chance to prove myself live, which made a world of difference."[15]

The Isbell tour exposed Justin to rock fans outside of Nashville who didn't know his music and didn't care who his father was. The crowd had never seen anyone produce so full a sound out of their guitar—the charging rhythm, the fingerpicking, the high melody—to the point that people started asking Justin if he wasn't employing some sort of trickery.

"I call it a sleight-of-hand guitar playing," Justin said, "because every time I play a show somebody accuses me of having a sampler."[16]

Justin was road-testing his act, trying out stories, witty quips, and unusually unguarded disclosures.

"I don't know anybody alive who doesn't have a problem with their parents," he told a crowd that fall. "None!" Justin then performed the suite of Carol-and-Steve-inspired songs he often sang back to back: the talk-screaming "Decimation of a Southern Gentleman," followed by "Time You Waste," a tenderhearted ballad.

The songs displayed Justin's emotional and musical range: the first, a stormy excavation of rage; the second, a sensitive reflection on childhood abandonment. Both presented Justin Townes Earle exactly how he thought of himself: as a victim of his upbringing.

"We're going to get angry, and we're going to yell, and then we're going to be pitiful," he told the crowd. "This one goes out to mom and dad."

After screaming through a particularly angsty rendition of "Decimation," Justin reminded the crowd what was next: "You get upset, and you yell, you say what you mean to say, and you say a bunch of things you don't," he said. "You play it all over in your head, probably one too many times. And the only thing left to do is cry."[17]

That stage banter came in London, on a tour in the fall of 2007 where Justin was forced to think about his family name more than usual. He toured Europe alongside aspiring singer-songwriter Jubal Lee Young, son of another seventies outlaw pioneer singer, Steve Young. Steve Young began releasing albums in the late sixties and had his songs covered by Waylon Jennings and Hank Williams Jr. But his breakthrough came when his song "Seven Bridges Road" was covered by the Eagles and eventually included on their megablockbuster 1980 live album.

The two sons of successful musicians traversed the European continent on a billing branded, much to Justin's chagrin, as "The Sons of the Guns" tour.

"It doesn't take a rocket scientist to figure out that I'm Steve Earle's son," Justin said of the tour's name. "So I don't see the point in telling anybody."[18]

With their fathers' images looming over them, the two young men settled on a rule: "We don't do the 'Road' songs."

For Justin, that meant steering clear of his father's signature tune,

"Copperhead Road." For Young, it was "Seven Bridges Road." Each night, Justin played his father's "Tom Ames' Prayer" along with Townes Van Zandt and Gram Parsons covers, and Young played several of his dad's songs. They negotiated the balancing act of being children of stars: Young was barely more inclined to play his dad's songs than Justin, so the tour's premise presented a problem for fans who'd shown up to hear a next-gen reincarnation of *Heartworn Highways*, the much-romanticized documentary of Guy Clark and Townes Van Zandt's seventies Nashville in which both elder Steves had appeared.

When Justin returned from Europe that fall, he immediately headed back out for another unglamorous run of playing southeastern dives and barbecue joints.

Justin remained completely sober on the road. His strategy was simple: keep busy with activities during downtimes—grabbing coffee, eating at IHOP, taking long drives—in order to keep his mind occupied.

He was also careful to spend as little time as he could at the venues he played, where he'd be tempted by drugs or alcohol. He arrived to gigs as late as possible and left the moment he walked offstage.

At a show in Macon, Georgia, it became clear why Justin minimized his time in venues. During sound check, a stranger beelined to Justin and started chatting him up. When Justin left the club afterward to grab dinner, he was livid.

"That guy is a dealer. He heard I was in town and came looking for me," Justin explained to his friend accompanying him. "I'm really pissed at the bar owner." Local promoters, club owners, and bartenders still thought of Justin as the degenerate drug-gobbling son of Steve Earle, the kid who'd caused havoc every time he passed through. They had no reservations about alerting local drug dealers when Justin was back in town.

Justin's friend asked him how often he was approached by such dealers in venues on the road. "Everywhere I go," Justin said.

CHAPTER 10

THE TRAPDOOR WAS MEANT FOR ELVIS.

That was the idea in 1972, anyway, when the musician-producer David Briggs purchased a former boardinghouse on Nashville's Music Row. Briggs converted the home into a studio, hoping to record his boss, Elvis Presley, there; he'd been playing keyboards in Presley's band for years.

Briggs knew Presley needed a place where he could record unbothered. "Girls would chase him, and pull his hair, as well as his clothes off," Briggs said. "It got to be a pain in the ass."[1]

He rigged an elaborate setup in the studio that would ensure Presley's privacy: Underneath the building, there was a hidden subterranean garage where Presley could park, open a custom-built trapdoor to the basement, then ascend a staircase to a professional recording studio, all without taking a single step outside.

Too late: Presley died in 1977, a year after construction ended. He never stepped foot through the trapdoor. Still, Briggs had a brand-new recording studio. He moved in upstairs and named the place House of David.

By the time Justin Townes Earle strutted into the studio in 2007, it'd amassed a fair bit of history. B.B. King, Neil Young, Willie Nelson, George Jones, and Roy Orbison all recorded there. This was the studio where an undiscovered Garth Brooks recorded a beer jingle in his first session in town, the studio where Tennessee transplant Count Bass D cut his 1995 debut, *Pre-Life Crisis*, likely the first major-label rap album ever recorded on Music Row.[2]

Artists were drawn to the studio's homey feel; the old wallpaper, creaky floors, dark wood, high ceilings, and fireplaces made the studio feel like a grandparent's home.

Justin came to House of David to record his first proper full-length studio album. It would be released by Bloodshot Records, a scrappy independent label based in Chicago that had been releasing off-kilter roots-punk records since 1994. Over its first dozen years, the label earned a venerated reputation as the home of Alejandro Escovedo, Old 97's, Neko Case, and Ryan Adams, whose 2000 blockbuster, *Heartbreaker*, solidified the label's "insurgent country" descriptor.

The label's cohead, Rob Miller, had taken a chance on Justin, even though he was wary of solicitations from Nashville next of kin. "We would get the occasional pitch by somebody who was like, 'Hey, I'm Waylon Jennings' second cousin,' or, 'Hey, I'm Little Jimmy Dickens' grandson,'" Miller recalled.

So Miller was skeptical when twentysomething Justin Earle crashed on his couch in March 2007 while in Chicago for a gig. But when Miller went to see Justin perform, he was entranced. It wasn't so much what Justin sang, but the conviction with which he sang that captivated him: the way he stared into the middle distance, forcing eye contact with an uninterested crowd. Back home, Miller scribbled down two words: "Very compelling."

Throughout 2007, Justin had taken steps to solidify his solo career. He'd self-released *Yuma*. He'd connected with industry professionals he knew through his dad, including a publicist named Traci Thomas, who was now looking to get into artist management, as well as Andrew Colvin, who'd interned with Thomas years prior and now worked as an agent. Colvin took over from Justin's old agent, and Justin began working with Thomas as his manager.

The final step was securing a record label. Rob Miller had been so smitten with Justin that he'd practically offered him a deal on the spot after seeing him perform. Justin and his new team bristled at the one-off handshake agreement Bloodshot initially offered. They negotiated a four-record deal that ensured Justin's complete creative freedom. Justin would make the exact records he wanted. Bloodshot would pay for their recording and use its limited resources and trusted brand to sell, market, promote, and distribute them in the transitional post-Napster, prestreaming MP3-blog era of the late 2000s.

Signing with a hip, small label outside of Nashville positioned Justin as a country-roots outsider who could appeal to college-radio and indie audiences. It also helped reinforce the narrative that Justin would soon cultivate: that of an independent artist who not only refused help and support from his famous father—but never needed it, either.

When Justin entered House of David to record demos in June 2007, he had spent the first half of the year touring. On the demos, he sounds confident, like he already knew exactly the album he intended to make later that fall.

It would be a mix of songs from his time living at Stewart Place (the Civil War folk ballad "Lone Pine Hill," the self-probing confessional "Who Am I to Say"), his best traditional country tunes from the Swindlers ("Lonesome and You"), and some of his most accomplished teenage material ("South Georgia Sugar Babe"). He'd open with "Hard Livin'," his honky-tonk tale of teenage mishap, and end the record with "Far Away in Another Town."

Justin viewed his first full album as an opportunity to exorcise his troubled past. "This record dealt with a whole lot of things," he said, that "I don't ever want to deal with again."[3]

He enlisted Steve Poulton, who'd helmed *Yuma*, to produce. At the last minute, R.S. Field, a Mississippi-based producer who'd worked on records by Billy Joe Shaver and Justin's stepmother, Allison Moorer, was enlisted to coproduce. The musicians who played on the record were either former Swindlers (Skylar Wilson, Cory Younts, Josh Hedley) or session pros (drummer Bryan Owings, bassist Bryn Davies, Chicken Shack regular Chris Scruggs).

Justin was interested in the sounds and styles of midcentury country music that had been long out of fashion by the time his father arrived in

Nashville in the seventies and hadn't been cool since. He drew from classic country influences like Ernest Tubb, George Jones, Johnny Paycheck, and Porter Wagoner. "What Do You Do When You're Lonesome" was an up-tempo lament with a chorus that cribbed the melody of Kitty Wells's 1952 hit "It Wasn't God Who Made Honky Tonk Angels." But the song's throwback sound disguised an agonizing isolation in its lyrics: "Do you stay out late nights drinking / Trying to smile through," he sang over Wilson's bouncy piano. "A pain that everybody knows / Is tearing you in two."

Sprinkled in were two opiate odes cowritten with Scotty Melton ("Turn Out My Lights," "Far Away in Another Town") from his time in Johnson City.

The process was lightning quick. Justin established the unfussy recording approach that he stuck to the rest of his career: bang out two or three focused takes, choose the one that best communicates the song, then move on. "I don't like going to the same space every day," Justin once said of recording. "The studio can turn into that."[4]

After a few days, Justin Townes Earle completed his first full-length album.[5] For its title, he turned to one of his newer tunes, a sarcastic portrayal of newfound fame with a music video that contrasted boasting verses ("All the fancy restaurants won't let me wait inside") with grainy shots of Justin haplessly roaming around Nashville and New York by himself. For a record that documented a decade of devastation and whose cheerful country arrangements masked tales of loneliness and isolation, there was no joke more fitting, no motto more aspirational, than what Justin conjured as his debut album's title: *The Good Life*.

On November 21, 2007, Joshua Black Wilkins (Justin's friend, fellow songwriter, and aspiring photographer) shot the album cover. They'd cooked up a visual concept, one Justin stuck with for his first four albums: Justin would be photographed with a different woman on each cover, each with a different hair color. The idea, at least, was for Justin to never be romantically involved with any of his album cover models; putting a woman you were dating on the cover of your record, he liked to say, was bad luck.

For *The Good Life*, Justin posed with a new fiddle-playing friend who'd recently moved to town to start writing songs of her own. Justin called her by her middle name, Pearl, but most knew her as Amanda Shires.

"My first impression was that Justin was tall and smiley, engaging, and charming," said Shires. "He was straight-up sober, drove a truck, and was fun to go shopping with." But Justin, she said, wasted zero time trying to violate his rule about not dating his album-cover models. Shires believed she was asked to appear on *The Good Life* cover because Justin had a crush on her, something Justin also admitted to at least one friend at the time.

One evening that fall, Shires invited her friend Bonnie Whitmore to join her, Wilkins, and Justin at the Pond, the strip-mall dive outside Nashville where they often played. Like Shires, Whitmore was a Texas singer-songwriter new to town. Justin and Whitmore immediately connected over music and songwriting, and before long, they were staying up until four in the morning strumming songs in Justin's apartment. At a certain point, Whitmore looked at Justin. "So," she asked him. "Are you going to kiss me?"

Whitmore was infatuated with Justin's giant personality and even bigger smile. As a shy songwriter in a new city, she quickly felt welcomed into his enormous web of friends and artists.

She couldn't believe how tall and skinny Justin was, almost like a string bean, so she gave him a nickname: *Bean*.

The Justin that Whitmore began dating in late 2007 was sober, surrounded by close friends, and feeling confident after having just recorded his first full-length album for Bloodshot. Yet he remained fixated on his wounds. He freely shared, with Whitmore, tales about the time his father refused to lend him a guitar, the time his mother gave him an alarm clock as a young child so he'd be able to wake himself up, stories that were uniformly sad and brimming with resentment.

Within a few months, Whitmore had moved into Justin's apartment, a cramped attic space in the East Nashville neighborhood of Inglewood. (Justin rented from his downstairs landlord, singer Bobby Bare Jr.) The ceilings were sloped, low enough in places that Justin had to crouch. His scattered possessions filled the space: guitar straps, Townes Van Zandt ephemera, a picture of *The Last Supper*, a photo of Martin Luther King Jr., a toy keyboard with a *BUSH bin-Lyin'* sticker, CDs, DVDs, VHS tapes, and books, so many books: Tom Robbins and Michael Chabon novels, obscure Civil War history, Truman Capote, Flannery O'Connor, the compiled writings of Samuel Taylor Coleridge and Oscar Wilde.[6]

The two musicians spent nearly all their time reading, writing, and working on songs.

"It's kinda perfect for us right now," Justin said of their shared home that summer when speaking with the *Chicago Tribune*. Shortly after Whitmore moved in, about three months into their relationship, Justin proposed, offering Whitmore a spoon ring with a turquoise falcon that he had gotten from his mother.

They barely knew each other, and Whitmore could sense the dark undercurrents beneath the surface of Justin's charm. But she felt protected by him. More important, he made her laugh every day. She said yes.

One day, Whitmore split open her finger while washing dishes. Shocked by the sight of her own blood, she started screaming right as Justin was arriving home.

Justin charged into their apartment brandishing a Derringer pistol and shouting, "Where is he?"

They both burst into laughter after realizing that Justin had noticed a man downstairs installing DirectTV and thought he had done something to her. Then he drove Whitmore to the ER for stitches.

But Whitmore sometimes questioned the foundation of their bond. When she asked Justin what it was about her that he loved, she was unsettled by his answer.

"How much you love *me*," he said.

Whitmore wasn't alone in falling for Justin. Most everyone who encountered him around this time was drawn in by his sly, sweet magnetism and devilish charm.

"That *goddamned* smile," an old friend Travis Stephens called it, the smile that revealed as much as it concealed. It was a smile that made anyone Justin directed it toward feel close to him.

Justin Townes Earle tended not to smile in press photos. Those were occasions to communicate he was a serious man making serious art. But without cameras around, he constantly flashed his goofy grin. He smiled to communicate privately in public: In the middle of a song or a solo onstage, he'd turn his back to the crowd and sneak his bandmates a half-smile, thanking them, in a glance, for everything they'd put up with the previous twenty-three hours.

When Allison Moorer collected her memories of Justin in writing after his death, she focused on his smile and laughter: "Sometimes," she wrote, "it's the memory of his laugh that makes me miss him most. I'd never heard one like it before and we used to laugh and giggle together a lot—about our country-ness, things that were obvious that no one else would mention—he was always in on the joke and was often telling it. He laughed like he couldn't control it. And maybe he couldn't."

In late March 2008, Justin's smile was on full display all over his hometown. He'd landed on the cover of the *Nashville Scene*, wearing a cowboy hat and flannel shirt, flashing his mischievous grin with green-blue eyes and dimples that made him look like both a young child and a wise sage.

THE GOOD LIFE FROM NOW ON, read the headline.

"Steve Earle's son Justin struggled with addiction in the shadows of giants," it said on the cover, teasing the story written by journalist Michael McCall, "and came out swinging."[7]

The Good Life, Justin's first LP, was released March 25, 2008, the same week his face stared out from the cover of the *Scene*. But that week, the actual Justin Townes Earle was far away, driving around the country playing shows, astounding audiences everywhere he went.

"All I had to do was line people up in front of him," said Justin's publicist Heather West, "and they'll be fucking fans for life."

The musician accompanying Justin on tour was his close friend with whom he'd already lived several lifetimes of misadventure and music:

his old Swindlers bandmate and former Shirley Street Station roommate Cory Younts.

The two quickly developed a stage act that was part vaudeville-comedy duo, part glimmering Grand Ole Opry salesmen, and part Hank Williams troubadour performance art.

This act was one way to distinguish Justin from his father, whose stage presence was a gruff, self-serious exercise in southern, Springsteenian working-man authenticity. Justin's show was playful and less cool, modeled after the showbiz camp and country glitz of old-fashioned acts like Porter Wagoner.

"I wear a suit with rhinestones around the pockets and a cowboy hat," said Justin of his stage outfit, before moving on to his hair routine. "I grease it up, parted on the side and flipped back, like Ray Price. . . . Those people knew they were working an existing form. . . . There was a certain amount of showmanship too: those suits . . . talking in nasal voices and telling jokes. They wanted to entertain people."[8]

Onstage, Justin fashioned himself after old-world performers, cracking jokes, forging constant eye contact with front-row fans, toe-tapping in half-circles around the stage in between verses. "He was *so* different from his father," said Rosemary Carroll, both Steve's and Justin's attorney. "His father is all about the sensitive singer-songwriter talking about himself, love, and politics, and Justin was all about, '*Ladies and gentlemen: Let me entertain you!*'"

"Lanky and hyperactive," *The New York Times* wrote after seeing Justin perform that year, "Mr. Earle was the picture of extroversion."[9]

When he played by himself, his intensity radiated. "He was either hunched like a Dickensian villain over the microphone," read one review of a 2008 solo gig, "or shuffling and dipping his way across the stage."[10]

When he played with Younts, they dressed in sharp suits and hollered one-liners back and forth:

"We're going to play you a song now for a girl," Justin said while introducing a number. "I met her when I was about fifteen years old, and she ran the counter at the methadone clinic in Asheville, North Carolina."

"Pick of the litter, folks," Cory chimed in.[11]

The two men sprinkled their set with inside jokes and nonsense non sequiturs. They sold T-shirts and buttons that said "Who the Fuck Is Cory Younts?" In between songs, they called each other "Charlie," a bit they stole from Old Crow Medicine Show ("We didn't really know why they did it," said Younts. "But it made us laugh").

"Ain't that right, Charlie?" Justin asked Younts in between songs.

"I think that's right, Charlie!" Younts responded.[12]

Underground enthusiasm started forming around Justin's first album the moment it was released. Justin Townes Earle found himself, for the first time, with a prominent platform to tell the tale he'd been sculpting since childhood: the story of a young man who'd seen it all, who'd almost drugged and drank himself to death by twenty-two and then overcame his addictions, daddy issues, and cursed country namesake.

Justin relished the opportunity to burnish and spread his tale. Journalists—taken off guard by the unusually forthcoming, unguarded fast-talking kid with a famous name—relished the opportunity to print it.

"I wasn't ready before," he explained. "I'm ready now."[13]

He told journalists he'd been sober for nearly four years (true). He told them he once spent six months in jail (false). He told them he'd been arrested more times than his famously frequently arrested father (not true). He told them he had been banned by several hotel chains around the world (a wild exaggeration, but based on the fallout from his 2003 red-hair-dye incident). He told them he'd already performed at Madison Square Garden (true, but as part of his dad's band). He told them he'd spent two years living with prostitutes in a Nashville motel (overstated, but partially true).[14]

All those experiences, Justin explained, informed the artist he'd become. "I'm grateful for everything that's happened in my life," he said, "even the bad stuff."[15]

There was one legend Justin took pains to *dispel* in this first flurry of interviews. None of the self-destruction he'd subjected himself to as a younger man had made him a *better* songwriter, even if he'd once believed it had. "There's enough torture in life without you inflicting anything on yourself," he said.[16]

Weeks after releasing *The Good Life*, Justin received the most meaningful opportunity of his career: an invitation to perform on the Grand Ole Opry. The Opry, a country variety show that began broadcasting in 1925, was considered the most sacred institution in country music, something Justin's grandparents listened to their whole lives. Playing the same stage that Johnny Cash and Roy Acuff once graced was, as Justin put it, "every Nashville boy's dream."

Justin made his Opry debut on May 2, 2008, sharing a bill with Brad Paisley and eighty-seven-year-old country legend Little Jimmy Dickens. Backstage, Justin was exhilarated, pointing out plaques and photos of assorted heroes framed on the wall. Justin's mom, Carol, showed up for the occasion, both of them beaming with excitement.

Justin was introduced onstage by Jeannie Seely, a sixties country singer and Opry stalwart.

"We got a special guest at the Grand Ole Opry, a very talented young man," Seely told the crowd. "He's got a brand-new CD out called *The Good Life*. . . . I don't think he'd mind if I let you in on a little secret: He is the son of Grammy Award–winning singer-songwriter Steve Earle."

Justin jumped onstage sporting a two-piece suit, a "JTE" rhinestone-studded guitar strap, and a western bow tie. He'd invited two friends to accompany him: Younts on mandolin and Josh Hedley on fiddle, also making their Opry debut. Hedley, a twenty-three-year-old fiddle virtuoso, rented a jacket for the occasion and spent the day searching for matching pants. He was so nervous that when he started the intro to Justin's first song, "Hard Livin'," he played a flat note, grimacing to himself.[17]

Justin's mom, Carol, sat in the Opry's VIP side-stage church pews, nervous and thrilled. She had been seeing her son perform for years: When she started attending his concerts before he had become a proper showman, she'd gotten incensed if the crowd wasn't paying attention.

"Being the mom in the audience, I'd be like, 'Will y'all shut up so you can hear him?'" she remembered.

That night at the Opry, Justin's publicist Heather West sat next to Carol in the church pews, holding her hand. When Justin walked onstage, Carol clenched West's hand so tight West thought Carol might break a bone.

But Justin projected a calm confidence, smirking and cracking jokes for the tourists and fans who'd congregated from all over the country to catch country music's most hallowed show.

"We had to go to Chicago to release a country record, if you can believe that," Justin said after "Hard Livin'," referring to his non-Nashville record label, Bloodshot.

Then he launched into a breakneck-paced rendition of "I Don't Care," bursting alive during the song. He was working extra hard to sell his folk anthem of restless wandering as he sang about booking a one-way ticket out of the city that raised him.

The crowd lapped it up, clapping along as Justin sang the chorus of the Woody Guthrie–inspired ode. When he arrived at the last line, he bounced his head, his right thumb moving around his guitar so fast it looked like a blur, listing the cities the song's narrator yearned to travel to.

"I don't want to see the sun rising up on this dirty little town again," he sang to the hometown audience.

Justin bowed, saluted with his left hand, and winked at the crowd as if he were Roy Rogers.

"Good time," he said, before vanishing.

"Remember that name: Justin Townes Earle," Seely announced. "Gonna go far."

Justin was elated by the experience. "It was a magic moment," he said shortly after. "I grew up in Nashville with the Grand Ole Opry as the end-all and be-all. . . . It's everything you strive for."[18]

The Good Life entered the *Billboard* country chart in April 2008, just below pop-country singers like Joe Nichols and Trisha Yearwood. It peaked at seventy on the chart, an impressive feat for a honky-tonk traditionalist on an indie label competing with Rascal Flatts and Taylor Swift.

In the fall of 2008, Justin shared a bill with Swift, Gretchen Wilson, Lady Antebellum, and Luke Bryan at the Chicago Country Music Festival, a country-music megafestival outside Soldier Field.

(The week before that festival, the American stock market suffered the largest weekly loss in its history.[19] Signs of economic calamity had already surfaced: Wall Street firms that had invested in subprime mortgages were either collapsing or declaring bankruptcy. The financial crisis was fully underway. "We're in a recession," Justin said that autumn, "and people are starting to get rowdy again."[20])

But, almost overnight, despite or perhaps because of the success he was experiencing, Justin grew disenchanted with being labeled a country singer. He changed course on the Opry: "It gave me a sense that I'd finally made it," he said less than a year after gracing its stage. "But I wasn't quite sure where I'd made it to."[21] He wanted nothing to do with the country-music industry, which, to him, represented crass commerce. In commercial country music, professional songwriters clocked in each day to write the hits for the stars. Justin wanted to be known as a singer-songwriter—an artist who can carry a crowd with only themselves, a guitar, and the songs they wrote, not unlike his dad.

If Justin disdained the pop-leaning sounds of contemporary country, he also started to resent the stodginess of the niche but rabid audience that actively sought out his brand of old-fashioned country.

"Country is a very narrow thought," he said years later, reflecting on this period. "After I saw where that was taking me, it was not the direction I wanted to go in. I didn't want that fan base. I didn't want to play the Grand Ole Opry. I did once and I don't want to ever again."[22]

The month after the Opry, Justin played a much more humble gig for about $200: the backyard of songwriter Liz Rose.

The occasion was the twenty-first birthday of Liz's daughter, an aspiring singer-songwriter named Caitlin Rose. Caitlin adored Justin's music and, just like Justin, had spent her adolescence sneaking into Springwater to see shows. Justin, like most artists, had started earning extra money by playing assorted private gigs (one offer Justin turned down: an invitation to play a show for Nashville's Church of Scientology).

Rose and her friends idolized Justin, this ancient-seeming twenty-six-year-old writing the type of classic country songs they, too, wanted to one day perform. To them, Justin was the hometown boy made good. Rose and her friend Tristen Gaspadarek, performing as the Garland Sisters, served as Justin's opening act.

In a photo from that evening, Justin has his arm around Caitlin Rose. She's wearing Justin's cowboy hat, dangling a cigarette from her mouth. It was a muggy summer night in Nashville, one Justin spent surrounded by college-age kids drinking without care. He was used to being the only sober person in a backyard or bar: That July, he'd celebrate four years without a drink. In the photo, he is smiling, his mouth open just enough to let his two front teeth poke through. Justin looks sweaty, a curl of hair falling over his eyebrow, in jeans and a low-cut white tank top, his *Townes* tattoo poking through his frame.

CHAPTER 11

Justin was desperate for saltwater. Not because it was June and ninety degrees in Alabama, or because he finally had a day off after spending the past month touring the South.

The reason: Justin had purchased a pair of raw denim jeans. He was convinced the only way to break them in was to soak them in saltwater, then scrub them with sand.

He and Whitmore were at Callaghan's, a bar in the Gulf Coast city of Mobile, Alabama, for a gig. He asked the club's owner, John Thompson, where he might be able to find a place to swim.

Thompson directed the couple to Dauphin Island, a nearby barrier island. When they arrived at the beach, Justin jumped out of the car, sprinted into the sea wearing his pants, then proceeded to furiously rub them with sand.

Moments like these deepened Whitmore's love. She loved how downright *odd* and childlike Justin was. She remembered how his ringtone was "Only the Lonely" by Roy Orbison, how he'd insisted on planting a palm tree outside their home.

But she also gradually realized that Justin was combustible, prone to tantrums. When a soundman on tour that summer accidentally dropped an expensive microphone, Whitmore watched Justin pick it up and hurl it across the bar.

"If he was in a good mood, there may as well have been fireworks going off around him, because there was just so much celebration and jubilation," she said. "But if things were not [happy], it was more like gunshots."

Still, Whitmore began wedding planning: They'd be married at her parents' home in Denton, Texas, with Shires serving as Whitmore's maid of honor. There was one detail they kept debating: Should they serve alcohol?

Such a decision came at a tentative time. Justin had gone years without drinking. But at some point in 2008 he changed his definition of sobriety and, for the first time in years, quietly began smoking weed.

It's not clear exactly when he began, though he once referred to "relapsing" with marijuana at a festival in Portland, Oregon (he played the Pickathon festival in August 2008).

"I started smoking reefer and managed for about eight or nine months and I was doing OK," Justin later recounted.[1]

A less romantic account comes from several friends and acquaintances who hung out around the Pond, Justin's favored dive bar in Franklin. After gigs, Justin would retire to one of the bartender's houses to play *Grand Theft Auto* and hang out with a different group he'd recently met, guys far removed from Nashville's cloistered roots-music scene who refrained from judging once Justin started taking hits from the joint being passed around.

Being the only sober person in the room over the past few years hadn't been easy. When Justin had played a New Year's Eve show at the Pond, he'd grown increasingly frustrated at his friends' drunken antics as he chauffeured them each home as the designated driver. When a slew of wasted fans and friends rushed the stage for a messy beer-spilling encore at a Felice Brothers concert in New York in April 2008, Justin clapped along uncomfortably in the back of the onstage scrum, a solitary sober man in a sea of sloppy revelry.

He'd also been recently rattled by loss: In late 2007, Justin's grandfather Jack Dublin Earle, Steve's father, died. Justin began closing every show by dedicating "A Desolate Angels Blues" to the Earle patriarch. He'd idolized his grandpa.

Much of Justin's self-conception—his storytelling, the way he dressed, the old-fashioned country music he favored—he credited to grandpa.[2]

"My only goal," he said years later, "is to make sure if my grandfather, who has been gone for about a decade now, can see me he's proud of me."[3]

Shires, who was close with Justin at the time, believed that Jack Dublin Earle's death had a profound, underacknowledged effect on her friend. "He'd always tell me when he was going to visit him, he'd be so excited," said Shires.

Between Justin's grief, the pressure of managing his surging career, and the accumulated toll of spending years as the only sober person in the room, Whitmore thought, at first, weed might be harmless, a way for Justin to unwind.

But to those who'd known Justin earlier in his twenties, that he was smoking weed again felt like a red flag.

When Sean Locke, Justin's old songwriter friend who'd cut ties because their relationship had gotten too dark, was told by one of Justin's friends that Justin was now smoking pot, Locke expressed his concern. "I'm telling you right now," Locke remembered telling the friend, "if he's doing *anything*, he's going to be doing *everything* within weeks."

It didn't take long for Whitmore to realize Justin's weed use was compulsive, too.

Like his growing penchant for clothes, antiques, or the golf arcade game Golden Tee, which he sometimes spent $500 a week playing at the East Nashville sports bar Beyond the Edge, Justin dove into smoking weed with an obsessive fervor. As he spread his narrative of the sober man who'd conquered his darknesses and addictions, he also began storing different strains of marijuana in assorted mason jars. By the fall of 2008, he was smoking weed openly on the road with fans and promoters.

One of several pressures Justin was numbing himself to was the increased scrutiny and fixation surrounding his relationship to his father. He'd perfected the art of deflecting the topic, but the sheer quantity of questions he now fielded about his dad was overwhelming.

Justin established a black-and-white narrative: As alike as they were, Justin Townes Earle was his own artist who hadn't ridden Daddy's coat-tails. Carol had raised him, *not* Steve. Justin emphasized their musical differences. "It would be kind of foolish for anyone to compare us," he said, "because what we do is so different."[4]

He mostly stopped covering his dad's songs. When he did occasionally play one, he reached into his dad's back catalog, avoiding the hits.

Still, the presence of Steve Earle, by then a beloved country-folk elder, loomed large in interviews and at shows, where Justin remained inundated with Steve Earle fervor. "I don't need some lunatic girl telling me what a great man my father was," he said in 2008. "I know."[5]

One evening, a fan shouted out for a "Steve Earle song" seconds after Justin finished covering Steve Earle's "South Nashville Blues."

"That's what I just did," Justin calmly responded.[6]

When Justin's face graced the cover of the *Scene*, the article closed with a not entirely complimentary quote from Steve, giving Justin's father the last word in his son's cover story: "Justin . . . can't fucking do anything else," Steve said of his son's career choice, "so he knew he better make it work."[7]

When father and son appeared on NPR's *Morning Edition*, the reporter pressed Justin on whether he lifted a specific line in his Civil War song "Lone Pine Hill" ("I just can't tell you what the hell I've been fighting for") from his dad's Civil War tune "Ben McCulloch" ("I don't even know what I'm fighting for").

"That's what we do, is to pay tribute to the great songwriters," Justin said. "And it just so happens that my father is one of the best that there's been."

It was a tense moment. The idea that Justin would be so influenced by his father's music that he'd be lifting lines from his songs directly clashed with the narrative Justin had sculpted for himself. But as the interview wrapped up, father and son exchanged jokes on air. "Hey, Justin, call your grandmother please," Steve reminded his son.[8]

That joint NPR interview was one of the topics Steve later pondered in a series of conversations about fatherhood and parenting with the writer Joe Hagan. "I could tell Justin was pissed off," Steve said of the NPR conversation. "He's so preoccupied with just trying to figure out how to be him. It's hard. It's hard for him, it was hard for [Steve's singer-songwriter sister] Stacey."

Because of you? Because he's got the name Townes?

"Both of those things. Yeah."

That's heavy.

"It's way heavy. Especially when you do what he does."

Do you feel like the more you try, the less you're helping? Do you feel like you have to be a brother to [Justin]?

"I think he's not going to listen anyway, so even if I got lucky and gave him the right advice, he'd reject it. So I'm trying not to give him any advice at all, and just sort of be supportive. I failed the other day because I said 'I told you so.' . . . He called me freaking out the other day because his van broke down again. And it's a van I told him not to buy, and it's a piece of shit, and I said, 'I told you so.' . . . Then he hung up on me."[9]

Steve continued to plead his case with Hagan. "Since I got sober I've saved it up and showed up as a parent," he said. "I'm absolutely positive of that. I haven't been the best parent in the world but I haven't been the worst parent in the world, since I got sober. I'm there and I'm willing to do whatever, but I can't make him, you know, not be mad at me. He gets to do that. That's his to deal with. And it isn't good for him to stay mad at me, but I can't make him not be mad anymore for *my* convenience. It's hard enough for him to live with."

One person who observed the unusual relationship between Justin and Steve up close was Allison Moorer, Steve's wife at the time. Moorer remembered:

> I know Steve loved Justin fiercely. Steve likes to tell a story about trying to get a young Justin in the car to go to a wilderness camp or something that he thought might straighten him out a little. He likened the experience with trying to get a live deer in the trunk of a car. I don't think there's any

better way to describe the head butting they did. I don't think there's any way I can describe the massive love between the two of them either. It was so big that most rooms couldn't hold it—the energy tended to vibrate when they were together.

Still, Steve couldn't begin to understand what it meant for his son to jump-start his career so fully in his shadow. In the summer of 2008, Justin played a few shows with James McMurtry, a singer-songwriter who'd spent his career shaking off attention surrounding his own famous father, Texas novelist Larry McMurtry. One evening, Justin and McMurtry were having a conversation when Justin was approached by a fan who said they loved his music, then handed him a Steve Earle CD to sign. Justin did so reluctantly.

A few minutes later, a fan approached McMurtry, asking him to sign one of his father's books.

"No," McMurtry replied.

Whitmore watched the scene unfold: "You could see the joy in Justin's eyes at that response."

As Justin continued to be asked about his famous dad, he settled on a five-word truism that summed up their relationship, gave the press what it wanted, and ended the conversation. It encapsulated the whole story: the child who adored his father yet inherited his flaws, repeated his mistakes, and ended up more like him than he cared to admit: "I am my father's son."

That was the phrase Justin repeated when speaking to reporters throughout 2008. Sometimes, he changed tenses: "I was my father's son," he said, laughing, while explaining how he'd squandered opportunities earlier in his career.[10]

One day, Whitmore was in their little attic apartment when Justin called her over to his writing nook. Justin had a new song he wanted to show her.

It began with those words Justin was using in interviews: *I am my father's son.* The song had no traditional chorus, but it used Justin's complex inheritances as a narrative device to tell his story honestly and intimately: "I was a young man when," he sings, "I *first* found the pleasure and the feel of a sin / I went down the same road as my old man." By the time Justin finished the soft-spoken ballad, tears filled Whitmore's eyes.

He worked on the song for a long time, removing one verse entirely and moving around the placement of the song's revelation: That despite the troubled inheritance he got from his father, his "mama's eyes" kept him on the straight and narrow. The song, he later explained, was "a very surgical, exact, put-the-point-across exercise to say that I will always be my father's son, but first and foremost I'm my mother's boy."[11]

The song was called "Mama's Eyes," its title a phrase Justin had used years earlier in "Decimation of a Southern Gentleman," the raw Swindlers-era confessional about his parents he never released. In that song, he'd sung of haunted visions of his "mama's eyes in that statue of Mary" while stumbling past a Catholic church.

"After the first record I got asked about my father so much, which I don't mind," Justin said. "I would actually be kind of appalled if people didn't ask me about it. But the one thing that needs to be made clear is that people always say, 'What's it like growing up with Steve Earle?' and I don't fucking know. You have just as good of an idea of what it's like growing up with Steve Earle as I do. I grew up with Carol Ann Earle."[12]

"Mama's Eyes" solidified Justin's narrative that cast his father as villain and his mother as hero. In this narrative, Justin established Steve as his punching bag, downplaying their intimacy, amplifying their tension. Accordingly, he rarely, if ever, vocalized his resentments toward his mother. Carol Ann was a sensitive, easily flustered woman who hadn't been able to be fully present for Justin as a child due to her own private struggles. But in public, Justin did not blame Carol for her part in his feral childhood; instead, he remained incredibly protective.

With the help of "Mama's Eyes," he developed a careful, considered public depiction of his mom—*mama*—as a mythical avatar of fortitude. As he'd explain when introducing "Mama's Eyes" most nights for the remainder of his career, Carol Ann Earle was a model of strength, a tough-as-nails single mom whose absence was due to the three jobs she worked to support him. She was the woman, Justin would boast, who'd once detached his father's retina with her left hook.

The reality, per both Carol's own telling as well as the rare moments when Justin punctured the bulletproof image he'd crafted of his mom, was much more complicated.

"Here's to my mother, who's always I think managed to end up on the losing end of things," Justin once said, revealing more than usual, when introducing the song at a show. "But she's the toughest human being I know, and I'll always look up to my mama."[13]

One of the reasons Justin often spoke of feeling like he couldn't risk burdening his mother with his own fears and needs as a child was because Carol found herself relying on her son for support. "As Justin grew older and grew up, he was not only a son but a confidant," Carol said, reflecting, several years after his death, on her unique closeness and profound love for her son.

Thinking back on her countless memories of the many years they lived together, one rose to the surface: Driving on the highway with Justin, age nine or ten or so, sitting beside her in the passenger seat. Carol couldn't forget what happened when, at some point, somehow, she lost control of the steering wheel.

"Justin grabbed it," she said, "and he straightened it out."

As a song, "Mama's Eyes" was a breathtaking display of Justin's maturation as a songwriter. His simple lyric style allowed for layers of meaning: When he sang "I've got my mama's eyes," it could mean that his blue-green eyes came from his mom, that he'd inherited her way of seeing the world, that her sweet kindness counterbalanced his father's rough-edged temper, or that he feels his mom's casting her eyes on him wherever he goes.

The song was an "honest portrayal of who [Justin] was scared he was," said Whitmore, "and who he wanted to be."

Alternatively, as Justin once put it, it's a song about all the kids who grow up "hating their father and are scared of turning into their mothers."[14]

Whitmore, too, was writing songs, several of them about Justin. One of them, "Cowboy Lullaby," expressed the loneliness and increasing distance she felt from her fiancé—this "smoking, gun-toting boy of mine"—as their relationship progressed. "I need more than a ring," she sang.

She started writing another song called "Embers to Ashes," but had only a first verse about a couple going through a hard time. *How should the song proceed?* she asked Justin.

"He was saying maybe it could be like *Married with Children*, Al Bundy and Peggy, where they sort of loved each other but were still together," Whitmore recalled. "I was not quite sold on that idea, and that's not what ended up happening [in the song]: The guy cheats on her, and she sets fire to his house."

By the fall of 2008, Justin and Whitmore's relationship had soured. As they had throughout his life, the dynamics Justin outlined in "Mama's Eyes" played out in real life: During their relationship, Justin expressed to Whitmore his disdain for his father having cheated on his mother during their brief marriage. So Whitmore was surprised when she learned Justin had cheated on *her*. "Embers to Ashes" would become the title track of her 2011 album.

About a year after meeting, Justin and Whitmore broke off their engagement. "There was not going to be enough love that I could give him," she said, "to make him love himself."

As soon as Justin broke up with Whitmore, he began dating Rachel Keesecker, a very young aspiring stylist from Nashville who met Justin in New York. Justin was twenty-six. Keesecker had just turned nineteen.

Justin let the breakneck pace of his life and career propel him forward: That October alone, he toured the country, appeared at several festivals, traversed California with Keesecker, and traveled to New York, where he opened for his hero Charlie Louvin (one half of the Louvin Brothers).

The same month, during a five-day break from tour, he also recorded his second album.

In Justin's case, the music-industry adage "ten years to write your first album; ten months to write your second" turned out to be true.

Momentum was growing, Justin wanted to keep touring, and he wanted to release more music while the iron was hot.

The songs Justin brought to the sessions for his second album, *Midnight at the Movies*, conveyed his desire to position himself less as a country throwback and more as a serious songwriter. To signal his new direction, Justin opened the record with a line in the title track ("the couple in the corner have been going at it all night long") that nodded to one of his singer-songwriter heroes: Paul Simon. The lines echoed the opening lines of Simon's 1972 song "Duncan," a song that represented the type of character-based literary storytelling Justin was trying to move toward. It was his way of warning his audience, he explained, that his follow-up to *The Good Life* "was not going to be a honky-tonk record."[15]

"They Killed John Henry" showed off his unique picking style and command of traditional form. Older songs "Black Eyed Suzy" and "Halfway to Jackson" showed he still wanted to entertain crowds with fast-paced numbers. But it was the more contemplative ballads that made *Midnight at the Movies* feel like a determined next step. Songs like "Someday I'll Be Forgiven for This," "Here We Go Again," and, most of all, "Mama's Eyes" opened up Justin to an audience that was younger, more indie-leaning, and wasn't necessarily interested in straight country or roots music.

Justin's collaborators (the same basic crew from his first record) helped broaden his sound. On the title track, newly appointed bandleader Skylar Wilson and engineer Adam Bednarik mimicked the sound of a movie theater's pulsing projector on an electronic keyboard. Producer R.S. Field, unsure if the singer's ten-month time span had produced enough original songs, suggested Justin include a cover; everyone figured he'd pull out some old Mance Lipscomb song or country-blues standard.

Justin's choice, however, was a mandolin-driven version of one of his all-time favorite songs: the Replacements' "Can't Hardly Wait," which he'd started singing in the Distributors. In the context of Nashville, it was a daring choice for a cover. In the context of his label, Bloodshot

Records, which relied on college radio, it was promotional catnip, a way to win over country-music skeptics and expand Justin's appeal with a younger crowd.

Most of Justin's newly written tunes reflected the cycle of romantic turbulence and commotion of his cresting career. "I had come to a crossroads in my life," Justin said of these songs. "I had to make some major decisions in order to make myself happy. . . . I was writing it while all the turmoil was going on."[16]

At the center of Justin's quarter-life crisis in late 2008 was his decision—after assorted temporary stints elsewhere—to fully flee his hometown. Except for brief periods in Chicago, Fairview, and the wilderness camp he was sent to as a teenager, Justin had never lived anywhere else. But he'd grown wary of Nashville, haunted by the way it contained his past and alienated by his inability to see himself in its rapidly changing future.

"My ghosts," he said, "have taken my town from me."[17]

Justin was convinced he needed a permanent change of scenery. He felt like the Justin Townes Earle story needed a new setting. He settled on New York.

"I was in a bad relationship where I wasn't happy," he told a journalist from the alt-weekly the *Memphis Flyer* in late 2008. "I was coming home to the town where I was born, watching people I grew up with go to jail and die of drug addiction and shit like that. I was just in a real weird place. I got out of that relationship. Must admit, [I] ran away with another girl, very happy with that situation. I decided to move on to New York, and I made some personal changes in my life that had to be done. It was a spiritual experience for me in that it got rid of a lot of weight that was ready to go."[18]

The abrupt break with his hometown (and with Whitmore) was the latest example of Justin's pattern of torching his life—and starting anew—whenever he pleased. He'd grown confident in his ability to charm new love interests and comfortable cutting them out of his life as soon as they began to sense what his charm concealed.

The dark running joke among his friends, as Justin's romantic history turned into a dizzying cycle of short-term serious relationships that resulted in proposals (but never weddings), is that Justin treated engagements the way his father treated marriages (his friend musician Dawn Landes once tried writing a song about this: "five little fingers ain't enough").

Justin's new girlfriend, Rachel Keesecker, lived in Brooklyn with a friend who dated Cory Younts. In late 2008, Justin and Younts stayed at Keesecker's apartment when they weren't touring. (The two-man band spent every waking minute together on the road; they figured they might as well live together off the road as well.)

Just like that, Justin Townes Earle had suddenly moved to Brooklyn. Keesecker's place, where he crashed, was a run-down apartment—leaky faucet, peeling drywall, caving ceilings, a temperamental boiler—on the first floor of a six-story brick building in a then barely gentrified section of a neighborhood called Crown Heights. The majority-Black neighborhood was known for an uneasy coexistence between its Hasidic Jewish community and its West Indian–descended population. Those tensions, which boiled over during the 1991 Crown Heights riots, had resurfaced by 2008.

"Crown Heights is flaring up again," *The New York Times* reported, following a series of violent altercations in the neighborhood, a few months before Justin landed in Brooklyn.[19]

As with much of Brooklyn, Crown Heights would soon fall prey to an intense wave of gentrification and displacement in the 2010s. But in early 2009, with the Great Recession halting real estate speculation, that wave had not reached the far-flung pocket of the neighborhood Justin had landed in.

Justin despised the griminess of his girlfriend's apartment at 1730 Carroll Street but was thrilled to have left home. Crown Heights was merely where he'd landed. *Anywhere at all, anywhere but Nashville.*

He wasted no time declaring his New York era, folding his arrival into his mythology. It was, he said, what Woody Guthrie and countless other musicians and strivers did before him: "He showed that southern men can come to the big city and have just as good a chance as anybody else."[20] Justin began espousing the virtues of his new hometown in nearly every public utterance.

"I'm twenty-seven-years old, living in New York City with my girlfriend who is doing a lot of good things with her life. I'm making music for a living," he told a newspaper in Knoxville, Tennessee. "That sounds pretty good to me!"[21]

Left unspoken in Justin's Big Apple boasting was the other role model for his move: Steve Earle, who'd first decamped to New York City four years prior, in 2004, and had similarly not shut up about it since.

It didn't take long for Justin to incorporate his time in Crown Heights into the tale of his hardscrabble life. He even wrote a song about it: "One More Night in Brooklyn."

"There was a crackhead coming in every day, smoking crack at our dining table, just jumping through the window," he later claimed. "He never touched anything. . . . He'd go in there and shoot his dope and smoke his crack, so we'd come home to burnt up tinfoil and shit all over the table" ("Almost true," said Keesecker years later).[22]

It was an idyllic, romantic period for the four aimless Tennesseans in Brooklyn, though none of them necessarily saw it that way at the time. When everyone else went out at night, Justin stayed in and wrote songs. He wasn't drinking and didn't want to spend time in bars when he wasn't touring.

Ultimately, Justin's time in Brooklyn was brief. He claimed 1730 Carroll Street as his residence for just a few months, during which he was primarily on the road.

In March 2009, Justin embarked on an extensive tour, again opening for Jason Isbell. After one of the first shows, in Oklahoma City, heavy snowfall blanketed the region. Six thousand people lost power, and Oklahoma's governor declared a state of emergency.[23] By nightfall, when Justin and Younts were just a few hours into their eight-hundred-plus-mile drive to the next gig in Colorado, so much snow had fallen that Interstate 40 shut down in both directions. The Colorado show was canceled.

Stuck in the panhandle, Justin and Younts pulled into the nearest Love's truck stop outside Amarillo, Texas, to wait out the storm.

Justin went into the rest stop and purchased every blanket they sold. For the next day or two, Younts and Justin lived inside their van at the truck stop, watching movies on their laptop, wrapped up in sleeping bags and blankets. When they got hungry, they walked into Love's and grabbed food from Subway. At one point, a truck driver gifted the two derelict-looking musicians a box of cereal out of pity. When their vehicle, which they ran 24/7 for heat, ran low on gas, they drove a few feet to the pump, filled it up, then drove back to their parking spot.

Justin didn't mind the pause.

"It was actually one of the most relaxing times I've had in the past two years of touring," he told Isbell a few days later. "Nobody could call me because my phone died, and I just sat there watching *The Simpsons* all day."[24]

Over the previous year, Justin and Younts had crisscrossed the country from Hoboken, New Jersey, to Bryan, Texas; to Boise, Idaho; to Richmond, Virginia. In one typical stretch that spring, they played eleven shows in eleven nights, logging thirty-two hundred miles along the way.

Back in Crown Heights, Justin had written a tune that he started playing live every night, though he never released it. It was called "Boy Keep Movin'," and it spoke to his life's new pace.

"Boy, keep movin'," went the chorus, "and you'll never get caught."

Justin and Younts had grown inseparable, finishing each other's sentences in the van and unable to disentangle their art from one another. Modeling their act after classic harmony-brother duos like the Louvin Brothers and Delmore Brothers, their camaraderie and collaboration *became* the live act of Justin Townes Earle.

In Younts, Justin found his ideal onstage partner, an ace high-harmony singer who could switch from mandolin to harmonica to banjo and serve as Justin's comedic stage foil.

Much in the same way that "Gillian Welch" was the name of the two-piece band of Welch and her partner, David Rawlings, to see Justin Townes Earle in 2008 and 2009 was to see Younts and Justin. They called each other "Soul Mole," a reference to the matching moles they each had on their Adam's apple. That shared mole, they joked, was the reason they sounded so great when they sang together.[25]

With Younts's help, Justin Townes Earle presented himself as a time-traveling carnival barker. Whipping through wisecracks, he'd greet the crowd as if they'd gathered in a Depression-era barroom, introducing songs as "this here number."

"All right, thank you folks, now, ladies and gentlemen, it's Saturday night, ain't it?" he greeted one such audience. "Saturday night in Knoxville, Tennessee, ladies and gentlemen, it's good to be back in East Tennessee, *by God*. We're going to have us a good old time!"[26]

Even if Justin was ambivalent about being labeled a country singer, he still seized on the novelty of Nashville's most affected showbiz vernacular. He combined that Opry showmanship with a dose of medicine-show salesmanship and *Hee Haw* humor, delivering down-home one-liners.

"Boy, this ain't hillbilly music," he'd say while introducing his cover of "Can't Hardly Wait," "but the boys who wrote and recorded this here song sure as shit did act like hillbillies."[27]

The whole act was profoundly anachronistic. Locally, in New York, much of the industry attention was centered around disaffected indie rock from bands like Grizzly Bear and TV on the Radio. Nationally, dark-tinged electronic acts like xx, a duo from England, were ascendant. The year 2009's most critically acclaimed record was the psychedelic abstraction of Animal Collective's *Merriweather Post Pavilion*, which topped that year's *Village Voice* Pazz & Jop poll, a survey of music critics across the country.[28]

To Justin, the anachronism was the point. "We don't need another guy looking at the floor through his bangs," he told *American Songwriter* at the time. "We have Morrissey already."[29]

What's more, Justin's Depression-era presence started connecting with a growing audience of millennial and Gen X fans who found themselves, in the early years of the Great Recession, either underemployed, plagued with student loans, or unable to secure mortgages—oftentimes all of the above—and looking for some relief or distraction in music that sounded like it came from another time.

"We slick our hair back and dress nice," Justin said of his act. "We tell stories and goof around and make sure people have a good time. Songwriters take themselves too seriously sometimes. . . . It *isn't* that serious, it just isn't."[30]

Justin Townes Earle was defining himself through opposition and in contradictions: He was eager to entertain yet quick to disassociate with any genre that wanted to claim him. He was anxious to be taken more seriously as a songwriter while doubling down on a campy stage presence that could overshadow that talent. He was desperate for recognition yet quick to discount his own dreams—like playing the Opry—when he achieved them. He was hungry for stardom yet deeply resistant of anything that looked like a conventional path to success.

By 2009, he'd already largely abandoned the earnest folk tunes from his 2007 EP. When a fan requested "Yuma" one night that spring, Justin fired back: "We're not going to play that, that's depressing," he said. "Not now. Hey baby, it's a recession, it's already depressing enough."[31]

Midnight at the Movies was released on March 3, 2009. Justin's label, Bloodshot, was thrilled by how the album refuted the idea that Justin Townes Earle was some retro revivalist, widening his appeal in a way that spoke to the moment. *Rolling Stone* ran a four-star review.[32]

Justin had a record deal, manager, and booking agent. But in 2009, Justin and Younts still handled everything themselves on the road—the local morning radio appearances, driving, selling merch, tour managing and coordinating logistics, phone interviews while driving between gigs, setting up and breaking down and sound checking and gear hauling before and after each show. At first, they did all of this in Justin's F-150, showering and sleeping at truck stops to save money. Eventually, they splurged on motels.

Younts and Justin ran out of stories to tell each other. They started getting on each other's nerves. At one point in Arizona, Younts remembered him and Justin getting so fed up with one another that they pulled over on the side of a deserted highway, swung their fists at each other for a few moments, got back in the van, and kept driving.[33]

Younts was the consummate country professional, a multi-instrumentalist so focused on his parts and perfect harmony that he didn't always even pay attention to the words his boss sang. One of the high points in their set in 2009 was "Poor Fool," a classic country pastiche about someone urging their hapless friend to cheer up after a bad breakup.

One day, after months of playing and singing harmony on "Poor Fool," Justin revealed the song's backstory. "Dumbass," Justin told Younts, "I wrote that song about you!"

CHAPTER 12

TOWNES VAN ZANDT HAD BEEN DEAD FOR LITTLE MORE THAN A decade before he was discovered by a new generation of fans. In the ten years between his 1997 death and the late '00s, a flurry of documentaries, tribute concerts, magazine articles, and biographies chronicling his tragic life and underappreciated-in-its-time body of work grew Van Zandt's legend. The man who spent his final years playing to tiny, half-empty clubs was now the subject of headlines like "Was Townes Van Zandt Better than Dylan?"[1]

That 2008 headline, which ran in the *Guardian*, was thanks, in large part, to Steve Earle, whose shock-value promotional quote to that effect in the eighties had taken on an air of prophecy since Van Zandt's death. Steve continued to pay tribute to his late mentor, beginning with "Ft. Worth Blues," a song he wrote in the wake of his death in 1997. In public, he told Townes stories and sang his songs. "I'm part of a cult," Steve explained.[2]

Eventually, Steve decided he'd release a full tribute album to his mentor. For one song, he enlisted Justin. It was the first time father and son had sung together on record in nearly a decade.[3]

On a December day in 2008, they spent the day arguing about Van Zandt in a recording studio, trying to nail the arrangement of a song by their shared hero.

The song in question was "Mr. Mudd and Mr. Gold." As a wily teenager, Justin would sit on front porches playing it for friends, claiming, sometimes, that he'd written it. Singing the fast-paced, tongue-twisting tale of a five-card-stud game was his parlor trick.

"I'd drink as much as I possibly could and I'd take all the drugs that you could give me, and then I could still remember the words," he once told a crowd.[4]

But at the studio, father and son spent the day bickering.

When Justin tried recording his part, Steve picked apart his performance.

"Hey," Joshua Black Wilkins, who was there, remembered Steve telling Justin. "You're playing it wrong!"

"That's how *you* taught me how to play it," Justin countered.

Had it been a bonding experience? Justin wasn't sure.

"Yeah, I think," he said afterward, before describing the session as "fucking war."[5]

Steve and Justin rarely, if ever, collaborated. But they competed with one another, envied each other's songs and successes, then played it up in the press.

When Justin wrote his version of the steel-driving folk legend John Henry ("They Killed John Henry"), Steve was jealous. Justin, in turn, claimed he gave his father a copy of *Midnight at the Movies* and Steve hadn't listened to it.[6]

"Whatever bad can be said about our relationship, one thing about it is it's always been pretty honest," Justin said. "We've never tried to be the fucking Cleavers."[7]

In interviews, Justin couldn't avoid questions about his dad. "Some people just aren't cut out to be fathers," he told the *Green Bay Press-Gazette* in 2009. "They're better buddies or something, but unfortunately, they go through life and they have kids. That's the chink in their chain. . . . I fully understand the mistakes my father made, because I've made them myself."[8]

It could be hard, for Justin, to disentangle questions about his father from questions about sobriety. He had overcome his past attempts at obliteration. And he associated the earlier self-destruction with the world he had been force-fed as the son of Steve Earle.

"I had come to a conclusion that Gram Parsons wasn't cool because he was a drug addict. Neither was Townes Van Zandt," Justin proclaimed. "They hurt a lot of people. I've already done all that."[9]

By 2009, Parsons and Van Zandt were seen as forbearers of country-folk cool as roots music began to spike in popularity. Singers Ray LaMontagne and Hayes Carll each covered Van Zandt's song "Loretta" that year ("a beautiful song written by a very fucked-up man," LaMontagne said of the song).[10] The bluegrass-pop group the Avett Brothers started covering Van Zandt's songs "Greensboro Woman" and "Highway Kind."

Another artist singing Van Zandt was Jason Isbell, who covered his most famous song, "Pancho and Lefty." In early 2009, Isbell and Justin cemented their friendship when Justin joined Isbell for their second tour together, a grueling trek, twenty shows in twenty-five days.

Jason and Justin had a lot in common: They were southern and stubborn, quick-witted, prone to dark humor. Each struggled with addiction and was devoted to songwriting. They developed a mutual admiration for each other's work and, at one point, even considered starting a music-production company together.

"I feel like Justin's more devoted to the craft of songwriting than just about anybody else," said Isbell.[11]

They also enjoyed each other's company. "We both love good music, and we don't like talking about it much," Justin said of their friendship. "We're just good ol' boys hanging out."[12]

Instead, Isbell and Justin talked about billiards, *SNL*, the pitfalls of technology, their respective childhoods in Muscle Shoals and Nashville, how to eat healthier on the road, fatherhood.

"What's your take on having kids yourself?" Isbell asked Justin that spring, during a conversation between the two artists published in the blog *Aquarium Drunkard*. "Would you do it while you're still touring, or would you want to wait until all that was over with?"

"It's completely doable to have kids and be a touring musician and still be a good father," Justin responded. "Because I know people that have done it. But they seem to be extraordinary people and I don't think I'm one of them."

"I'm one of those people who . . . feel like I'm living on borrowed time due to the way I've treated myself," Justin told Isbell. "But I don't feel any rush, I'm trying not to set any timelines. . . . I have enough time keeping up with my manic mind, let alone trying to plan what my manic mind is gonna do."

Isbell asked Justin if he was feeling healthy. A few months prior, one of their shared musical heroes, fifty-six-year-old singer-guitarist Buddy Miller, had a heart attack onstage and underwent emergency triple-bypass surgery. The event scared both young men. "Doing as many shows as we do, health is a relative term," Justin told Isbell. "There's only so many fucking Frito chili pies and Waffle Houses you can go to before you know you're probably not gonna be healthy ever again."[13]

The truth was Justin was very focused on dealing with his mental health and maintaining his version of sobriety, which now included marijuana. He'd been smoking weed for the past year or so but steered clear of boozy partying and late nights after shows.

The plan was to tour so relentlessly that his mind never had time to wander: "I'm working myself almost to the point of exhaustion," Justin said in 2009, "on purpose."[14]

Justin's old-fashioned act may have been out of sync with some contemporary notions of hipsterdom, but his come-up was happening at an opportune time. Justin's years of constant couch-hopping and rambling through Nashville in the 2000s had prepared him for the moment he found himself in. Who better to speak to the greatest economic collapse since the Great Depression than a young singer who fashioned himself after Woody Guthrie?

The year Justin released his debut album, 2008, had been a particular watershed for folk-leaning music: Jenny Lewis and Conor Oberst had both abandoned indie/emo and released rootsy solo records. Two of 2008's critical favorites were a folk group from Seattle named Fleet Foxes and a newly rereleased record from a solemnly strumming Wisconsin singer-songwriter who called himself Bon Iver. Another folk band from the Pacific Northwest, Blitzen Trapper, broke through with their underground hit "Furr." On the East Coast, in Rhode Island, folk-rock bands like Deer Tick and the Low Anthem were making a splash. The upstate New York roots collective the Felice Brothers had become critical darlings with their cult-classic 2008 self-titled LP. In Europe, songwriters Laura Marling and Tallest Man on Earth were releasing records that absorbed and repurposed American folk traditions.

Singer-songwriters like Kathleen Edwards and Hayes Carll and Ray LaMontagne all released their most acclaimed works at this time. Veterans from the nineties alt-country scene—Lucinda Williams, James McMurtry, Alejandro Escovedo—put out celebrated records.

In 2009, Alison Krauss and Robert Plant took home Grammys for Album and Record of the Year for their Nashville roots record *Raising Sand*, beating out acts like Adele, Coldplay, M.I.A., and Lil Wayne.

A decade or so after *O Brother*, roots music was having another moment. In the wake of Krauss and Plant's domination, and after lobbying from the Americana Music Association, the Grammys announced that their Americana/Folk Album category would split into two: There would now be a Grammy album award solely devoted to Americana.[15]

That category became a catchall term describing roots music—often Nashville based—with blues, folk, country, and R&B influences. It was more traditional and less commercial than contemporary country. Unlike commercial country music, artists were expected to write their own material. The music often featured instruments (fiddles, banjos, pedal steel) and southern working-class signifiers (freight trains, dusty roads, rushing rivers) that defined country music before it was suburbanized during the eighties and nineties.

As an industry term, "Americana" had been around since 1995, when the trade publication *Gavin* established it as a radio format with a corresponding chart. From its onset, the label was associated with reverence:

The chart's first number one was a tribute album to Merle Haggard. In the beginning, the music defined itself in opposition to Music Row: skeptical of modern sonic innovation, musically conservative, a home for midcareer country singers like Robert Earl Keen, Emmylou Harris, and Lucinda Williams, who had been unable to find radio airplay in the era of Garth Brooks, Shania Twain, and "Achy Breaky Heart."

"It's high time for new and old trailblazers alike to band together and rekindle that torch of twang we'll now call Americana," read a 1995 *Gavin* essay accompanying its new chart. "It's steel guitars, mandolins, and acoustics rather than synthesizers and line dance remixes."[16]

Four years later, in 1999, the Americana Music Association formed its trade organization (modeled after Nashville's Country Music Association, or CMA), which lobbied to transform the niche radio format into a consumer-facing "genre." In 2011, *Merriam-Webster* added the word's oft-debated musical meaning to its dictionary, defining "Americana" as a "genre of American music having roots in early folk and country music."[17]

Having a famous father who'd been a nineties proto-Americana star made Justin Townes Earle the perfectly marketable rising musician in this little corner of the industry. Americana had struggled, in its first decade, to resonate with younger audiences.

But here was a handsome, charismatic young singer with a sexy backstory of regret and redemption, who covered the Replacements in one song and then sang about nineteenth-century folk hero John Henry in the next. Like his father, Justin branded himself as outside and above the crass commercial confines of popular country music. His ambivalence about his own success—he wanted to entertain crowds like an old Opry star while playing music so out of time it felt anticommercial—was the perfect balance for an Americana audience that demanded its entertainers scan as authentic.

On May 21, 2009, amid the dinging and clanking of slot machines at a Lake Tahoe casino where Justin was covering John Prine, Buck Owens, and Merle Haggard tunes, he received big news: Justin Townes Earle was nominated for Album of the Year, Artist of the Year, and Emerging Artist of the Year at that year's Americana Awards ceremony. That fall, he won the Emerging Artist award.[18]

That summer, Justin joined the Felice Brothers, Gillian Welch and David Rawlings, and headliners Old Crow Medicine Show for a barnstorming tour.

Old Crow Medicine Show had made their stamp on modern roots music with their 2004 hit "Wagon Wheel," a repurposed Bob Dylan song snippet that, by 2009, had been steadily growing in its campfire-jam ubiquity. The romantic tale of American wandering, written largely while lead singer Ketch Secor attended boarding school in New Hampshire, was the rare twenty-first-century song to become a bona fide standard, performed at bluegrass festivals, high school talent shows, coffee shops, and street corners, even punk clubs, where singer Laura Jane Grace of the band Against Me! covered it. In 2009, *American Songwriter* named it one of the best songs of the past quarter century.[19]

Old Crow Medicine Show collected their favorite artists—three acts who all, as Justin put it, shared "a firm belief that rock 'n' roll predated Elvis"[20]—for their traveling roots-music revue that August. It was called the Big Surprise Tour.

Justin initially grumbled about having to perform first, but he seized the opportunity to perform at venues like the twenty-nine-hundred-capacity Beacon Theatre in New York for the first time on his own. Wearing a bow tie and plaid jacket, Justin opened the show each night, thrilling crowds with a compact, compressed version of his act with Younts. They were followed by the Felice Brothers, who were soaring largely based on the success of their cult sing-along accordion hit "Frankie's Gun."

After an intermission, Rawlings and Welch performed as Dave Rawlings Machine, with Rawlings singing lead on mesmerizing covers of Bob Dylan and Neil Young songs. Then Old Crow would treat crowds to their ragtag blend of bluegrass, blues, and folk rock, heavy on harmonica and hoedowns.

At the end of each night, the dozen or so musicians performed an encore of ensemble renditions, including the Replacements' "Can't Hardly

Wait" (with Justin singing lead), Welch's "Look at Miss Ohio," AC/DC's "It's a Long Way to the Top (If You Wanna Rock 'n' Roll)," and, naturally, "Wagon Wheel."

The Big Surprise Tour lasted less than two weeks, but it captured a cultural moment teeming with so much energy that it felt ready to explode.[21] And that's exactly what happened.

In late 2009, a series of records crystallized the bursting bubble: *Sigh No More*, the debut from an English band called Mumford & Sons, brought banjos to the Top 40; the Rick Rubin–produced major-label debut from the Avett Brothers, *I and Love and You*, catapulted the hard-gigging bluegrass punks to arena-level headliners. *Monsters of Folk*, the self-titled album from a supergroup featuring M. Ward, Jim James, and Bright Eyes' Conor Oberst and Mike Mogis, proved that rootsy folk now had indie credibility.

It all meant more attention, money, and interest on the type of banjo- and mandolin-driven music Old Crow, Gillian Welch, and the Swindlers once played in Nashville cafés to varying degrees of local uninterest. For Old Crow lead singer Ketch Secor, the Big Surprise Tour was a final moment of community before everything felt different. Now, for better or worse, the secret was out; Americana had found a contemporary audience.

The Big Surprise Tour crystallized Justin's standing as one of Americana's up-and-coming stars. But in classic Justin fashion, it also marked the beginning of the end of the very live act that had gotten him to that point.

Justin hinted as much when he noted he and Younts's unusual travel arrangements for the Big Surprise Tour. After spending the first half of 2009 driving each other mad on the road, on this tour Justin and Younts would be traveling separately. "He's actually riding on the bus with the Old Crow boys," Justin remarked. "He's taking notes."[22]

By 2009, Cory Younts and Justin Townes Earle had been playing together in one form or another for a decade. They'd spent the past two years as each other's only real company on the road. But Younts had always idolized Old Crow Medicine Show, for whom he and Justin had frequently opened. So when Old Crow invited Younts to ride with them on their bus for the Big Surprise Tour, he eagerly accepted.

Shortly after the tour, Younts approached Justin with a nervous question. If Justin felt any jealousy or betrayal when Younts asked it, he didn't show it: Old Crow had asked Younts if he'd join them for a short West Coast run that October while Justin was touring Australia by himself. What did he think?

"I know how much you love that band," Younts remembered Justin telling him.

But both men saw what was coming. In October, Younts told Justin that he was going to continue touring with Old Crow Medicine Show. He planned to play a few shows he'd already committed to with Justin—opening a pair of concerts for Justin's heroes the Pogues—then wrap up his time as one half of "Justin Townes Earle."

Justin decided the split would be determined on his own terms. When he returned from New Zealand and Australia, he called Younts and told him he was fired.

"Cory will no longer be playing with me," Justin announced to the public the next day. "He's moved on to bigger and better things and we wish him luck."[23]

CHAPTER 13

Were it not for the glow of the neon, the darkness would've been pitch-black.

It was late at night, and Justin was holed up, alone and in a bad way, in someone's apartment on East 11th Street in New York City, when he noticed through a drug-induced haze that a single bright light was emanating from across the street, shining through the windows and flooding the walls and floors of the room.

It came from a sign outside Father's Heart Ministries, a church that had tended to underserved East Village communities for more than a century. Affixed to its facade was an illuminated cross, adorned with blue and red neon letters that spelled:

JESUS
A
V
E
S

When Justin, still publicly sober, arrived in New York in 2008, he shared this mythological tale from his strung-out past as if it were proof of his salvation. The details were fuzzy, but the story he told of seeing the neon church sign had likely taken place on a long-ago trip to New York, before he got sober, while touring or traveling with his father as a teenager or young adult. Those trips had shaped Justin's image of New York, and had left him enamored with East 11th Street, specifically. Nestled between the heart of the East Village and Alphabet City, the block was rich with punk lore and music history, full of locals who shared stories of its changes over the years.

This hyperspecific slice of New York came to Justin via his father's social world, which revolved around a six-story apartment building at 516 East 11th Street.

That's where Steve's former guitarist Eric Ambel, the musician Justin once guitar-teched for, lived for years, along with Jim "the Hound" Marshall, a legendary deejay at the fiercely noncommercial community radio station WFMU. It's where Jack Smead, the teenage guitarist of the sixties garage-rock group the Banshees, lived for years in an apartment known, to his acolytes, as "Tiny Pines," which hosted after-hours jam sessions. Three doors over was the 11th Street Bar, an inviting and unpretentious Irish-style pub with creaky floors, a long bar, and a cozy back room for live music. The bartender was Kenny O'Connor, Steve's friend and former merch guy.

Justin had determined his ramshackle tenure in Brooklyn was over.[1] It was time to bathe in the faint neon glow of the *Jesus Saves* sign. It was time to move to 11th Street.

Using his connections to the block, Justin moved into 516 East 11th Street with his girlfriend, Rachel Keesecker, in the spring of 2009, taking over the lease on a $400-per-month tenement-style apartment. The bathtub was in the kitchen.

There was a dose of irony in Justin fleeing the fast-spreading gentrification of East Nashville for Manhattan's East Village. By that point, the New York neighborhood was well on its way to being a real estate developer's fantasy version of the rough-edged neighborhood for punks and poets it had been during New York's AIDS-crisis and crack-epidemic eighties and nineties.

By the time Justin Townes Earle moved in, the fabled artist's haven had been largely repaved by high-end restaurants, designer boutiques, and

New York University (NYU) dorms. While the legendary appeal of the neighborhood still lingered, and survived in small pockets, many of the music venues that had nurtured the neighborhood's storied past—CBGB, the Mudd Club, Sin-é, Luna Lounge—had shuttered or rebranded for millennial young professionals.

Still, it being New York, downtown strivers, musicians, and actors continued to flock to the neighborhood in search of bohemia. Many of them found it at 11th Street Bar, which catered to loyal locals—"old men who drink out of desperation, not for fun," as Justin put it[2]—and younger artists (like Justin) who preferred being with old-timers over the many bars and clubs catering to the NYU students.

It was a heavy-drinking bar—a former guitar luthier shop that had opened as an Irish pub in 1997—where regulars had been occupying bar stools with shots of Jameson for years, but also where Scarlett Johansson might drop in to see her friend Julia Haltigan sing on Tuesdays, or where Norah Jones might play an unannounced set, or where Steve Earle and Benmont Tench might sit in with the Punch Brothers for a secret show. Veteran musicians interacted with artists decades younger: The guitarist from the Counting Crows, or the trombone player for Levon Helm and Bruce Springsteen, or Lukas Nelson (Willie's son), or Ian Hunter (of Mott the Hoople), or the singer-songwriters Leslie Mendelson and James Maddock, or Justin's friend and fellow Nashvillian Chris Feinstein, the guitarist for Ryan Adams, or Eric Ambel (who owned Lakeside Lounge, another one of Justin's haunts, just around the corner), or Chris Masterson and his partner Eleanor Whitmore (the sister of Justin's ex-fiancée), or the band the Madison Square Gardeners, might be either drinking, performing, or both.[3]

Planting himself at the center of the scene was Justin Townes Earle, new to town and eager to fit in. Landing in Manhattan solidified his transformation, and he subsumed his move into his larger story: the country-bluesman blooming into a southern-influenced singer-songwriter who transcends the insularity of Nashville. Justin Townes Earle was ready to share this story with the entire world. The 11th Street Bar would be his staging ground.

Much like his father, who'd also recently moved to Manhattan, the younger Earle wasted no time sounding off about his new hometown as if he'd lived there his whole life. He immediately disparaged Brooklyn as bullshit, a place either for phony hipsters or boring parents with strollers. "None of those things I particularly liked being around," he told New York's alt-weekly, the *Village Voice*.[4]

Justin's relationship with Keesecker quickly grew serious. At some point in 2009 (Keesecker remembered it being summertime), Justin's touring van stopped in a parking lot. Everyone else departed the vehicle, leaving Justin alone with Keesecker, who was not yet old enough to legally drink. In the back of the van, Justin surprised Keesecker by proposing to her with a diamond ring from Walmart.

Keesecker said yes. At age twenty-seven, and for the second time in the span of little more than a year, Justin was engaged. He boasted that he left his former fiancée for Keesecker and referred to her casually in conversation as his wife, even though she had made one thing clear when she said yes: She wanted to wait a full year before getting married.

When a journalist pointed out the eerie similarities between his serial engagements and his father's seven marriages, Justin shrugged off the comparison.

"This time," he said, "we actually have plans."[5]

One of the first friends Justin made in New York was Josiah Early, an actor and aspiring musician from Virginia. Early met Justin after he responded to a public Myspace post Justin made looking for someone selling cheap weed in New York. When Justin showed up to Early's apartment to buy some, they struck up a conversation and bonded over music.

A few days after Early gave Justin a recording of one of his first gigs, he woke up to an early-morning voicemail.

"This is Justin Townes Earle," he remembered it saying. "I wanted to call you yesterday, but as a Tennessean I knew better than to call a Virginian on the Sabbath. . . . By god, I want to make you a record."

Justin was enthusiastic about producing Early, and before long, the two southern singers started spending time together in Early's Greenwich Village apartment. Early remembered their precise routine whenever Justin—almost always wearing tight jeans and a red-checkered shirt—would show up. "We had this greeting where I'd answer a door, and like a dog wagging his tail, Justin would be like, 'Where's your *terlet*? I'm *firsty*!' . . . It never changed," said Early. "When you heard the buzzer ring, and you'd know he's coming over, you'd already be presmiling."

At first, Justin told Early to not offer him any drugs or alcohol: He was sober, he explained, and wanted to keep it that way.

Early suspected Justin wasn't being truthful. Eventually, he gave Justin a heart-to-heart. If they were really going to truly collaborate, there shouldn't be any secrets; Early would never judge Justin for his substance use so long as it didn't get in the way of work. Justin changed course, as Early recalled, admitting that he was, indeed, drinking and doing cocaine.

"By the time I met him," Early said of Justin's tenuous public sobriety, "I think it was more of an act."

It'd been five or so years since Justin had gotten sober. He'd reintroduced weed into his life in 2008. He believed he was in a good-enough place that he should be able to have a beer without it being a problem.

In September 2009, right after the Big Surprise Tour, Justin headed to Australia and New Zealand for a tour. At the end of that run of shows, he confessed to his opening act, Australian singer-songwriter Henry Wagons, that he'd started sneaking a few of his beers backstage.

This surprised Wagons, who'd been under the impression that sobriety was all-important to Justin. After all, he'd been giving interviews to New Zealand journalists about the day-to-day reality of avoiding alcohol on the road.[6]

In reality, Justin was navigating a shaky balance between his public-facing sobriety and his gradual, private slipping. Sobriety *was* crucial to the way he wanted to be understood and seen: as a man redeemed, a man who'd faced his demons, conquered them, and had benefited from the advice he now shared with fans, friends, and fellow musicians who struggled as he once had.

"I'll only hang out until people start getting drunk, and then I leave to get some sleep," he said that August, crediting a strong support system—namely his fiancée—for keeping him centered. "I guess I'm starting to enjoy being at home for the first time in my life."[7]

But he also hinted at a new feeling, a different kind of liberation. "Nobody cares in New York what you're doing," he said. "Because they're too absorbed in what they're doing."[8] The idea that Justin could act how he pleased without having others overly concerned, without Nashville friends and family casting their judgment, was its own form of intoxication.

So nobody cared, or at least that's how it might've felt, when Justin started sipping on a few beers on tour, "barley-pops" with the boys in Early's band, or Guinnesses when he slid into 11th Street Bar. Those who understood Justin's past weren't around to sound any alarm bells; his manager, Traci Thomas, a maternal presence, was in Nashville, as was his mom. Steve lived nearby, a mile or two across town, but toured constantly and was starting a family with his wife, Allison Moorer. None of the Swindlers saw much of Justin. His two-person band had been cut in half; Cory Younts was now with Old Crow.

Justin's home slowly became the 11th Street Bar. He stopped in nearly every time he left his apartment. He liked the bar stools near the door; he could step outside easily to smoke his American Spirits.

Several years later, Justin reflected on the unrelenting pace of his relapse during this period. As late as October 2009, he was sheepishly sneaking a few beers on tour. Two months later, by New Year's Eve, he was staying up all night mixing coke and opiates.

"I started drinking and I was doing okay with that, just having a couple of beers a day," he confided to Associated Press journalist Chris Talbott. "One night I stayed out and I got drunk and as soon as I got drunk, the coke came out. And as soon as I started waking up with hangovers, pain pills came into play because I love opioid pain pills."[9]

Artistically, Younts's sudden departure had prompted Justin to reconsider his very identity as a performer.

"He was the best sideman I will ever have," he said after Younts left. "I will never try to replace Cory, it can't be done. And my stage show will have to change."[10]

In the last few months of 2009, Justin road-tested a new live act, presenting in a more solemn and less affected fashion as he toured solo.

On the road with Black Keys singer Dan Auerbach that December, he bonded with the other opening act, Jessica Lea Mayfield. Mayfield was only twenty, but she was a fellow fire starter, one who liked to crack jokes and court trouble as much as he did. They goofed off at roadside gas stations and developed a sibling-like intimacy. Justin called Mayfield "Big Bird" when she wore a yellow coat and told her that she was "so skinny she could hang glide on a Dorito."[11]

They also took drugs together, so much so that people close to Justin began to regard Mayfield, despite her being barely old enough to vote, as a negative presence in his life. Their relationship involved a complex closeness, one that riled up each of them in ways that created excitement, art, and harm. That tangled relationship would provide Mayfield with material for what would eventually become her breakout song: 2011's "Our Hearts Are Wrong."

"I know how you work," she sings in the song's heartsick chorus. "I am just like you."

"There was like a portal that opened up and aligned when we were both hell-bent on destruction," Mayfield said of Justin, reflecting on their relationship years later. "There were definitely times when we were bad influences on each other."

Throughout it all, Justin was writing his next record, his fourth in as many years. He'd been scribbling scraps of lyrics and phrases on his iPhone, taking in the sounds and sights and smells of his new Manhattan surroundings. He'd written a song called "One More Night in Brooklyn," transforming his brief Crown Heights period into myth. He'd begun performing a new song about meeting an alluring lady Down Under called "Christchurch Woman."

On December 14, he used his favorite new form of public communication, a fledgling social media site called Twitter, to inform his few followers of his progress: "Almost done writing the new record."[12]

On January 2, 2010, Justin performed at the home of Levon Helm, the legendary drummer and vocalist of the Band.

Helm had taken to hosting intimate concerts he called Midnight Rambles in the converted barn-studio on his Woodstock property, a few hours north of New York City, in part to help fend off foreclosure and pay off staggering medical bills from cancer treatments. There were fewer gigs more prestigious. When Justin was asked to open for Helm, he was ecstatic: He'd be filling a slot that'd recently been occupied by his heroes like Elvis Costello, Emmylou Harris, Dr. John, and Allen Toussaint.

A crew from the 11th Street Bar braved the below-freezing January temperatures and drove to Woodstock to be there for Justin. Steve Earle also showed up for his son's big evening.

Before the show, Justin entered a dream state: He sat with Helm, watching football with his hero. Onstage, he seemed calm and at peace, having somewhat discarded, or at least tamed, his frenetic honky-tonk throwback persona that had been his trademark for the past few years.

Josiah Early watched from the crowd, impressed with the work his friend was doing to slowly redefine himself as a performer. The proudest moment—for Justin's friends—came during the end of Helm's main set, when he brought out Justin to sing a verse of "The Weight." At the song's conclusion, Early remembered Helm grabbing Justin's hand and raising it above his drum kit, as if Helm was formally anointing the twenty-seven-year-old. What struck Early most, in that moment, was the look on Justin's face.

"He was so proud of himself," said Early. "And I had never seen that."

What Early remembered happening next is equally vivid. As Justin, still beaming, received booming applause, his hand held high by his hero, Early noticed Steve Earle pushing through the crowd, ambling toward the front of the stage. After "The Weight" ended, Steve Earle was suddenly onstage singing "Sweet Virginia" by the Rolling Stones with Helm's band. The moment Steve jumped onstage, Early watched Justin sink into himself.

After the show, Justin and Early drove back to Early's upstate house, where they were hosting a celebratory gathering with the 11th Street crew.

As they drove through the dark, cold night, Justin talked a mile a minute, filling in his friend on the whole night: how he'd asked Levon about the late Band bassist Rick Danko, how he couldn't believe any of it happened. He'd been thrilled, firing off a tweet while still at Helm's: "This is the coolest thing I have ever had the pleasure of being a part of!"[13]

But Justin was also fixated on the one moment that'd tempered his joy: his dad jumping onstage, stealing his spotlight.

"He's going through the night, all the great stuff," said Early. "And then he just lets it out: 'My dad can't even fucking just be my dad.'"

When they arrived at Early's house, Justin seemed ready to forget all of it. He wanted to celebrate, he wanted to keep going, he wanted to rage. He stayed up all night, snorting lines and drinking Guinness. His friends were amazed by the sheer quantity of drugs and drinks their friend consumed, but no one seemed too alarmed. Justin's rock-star dreams were coming true. He encouraged the small crew to stick with him, to keep partying, though no one could keep up. No one ever could.

When Justin woke up to a house of hungover friends the next morning, the day before his twenty-eighth birthday, a stark truth presented itself: No matter what he claimed in interviews, he was going to have a hard time pretending—especially to *himself*—that he was, in fact, still sober. Just two nights before he played at Levon's, on New Year's Eve, Justin and a few friends had taken enough drugs that the friends he'd been partying with thought they might not wake up on New Year's Day.

It's a common problem shared by artists who make their sobriety and ongoing recovery part of their public narrative. By leaning heavily into the redemptive arc of sobriety, a narrative that was initially completely truthful, Justin now had the misfortune of navigating his sobriety in public for the remainder of his career. Onlookers, gossiping fans, industry peers, anyone curious for a peek behind the surface, a crack in the veneer, would ask: Was he still sober? Were his drinking and drugging days behind him? Had he slipped?

"How's your sobriety?" one such journalist asked him in early 2010.

"I smoke my weed," Justin said, "but I'm good."[14]

The already intense pace of Justin's life was only getting faster: 2010 would be another action-packed year of touring, recording, and promoting yet another new record.

That January, Justin popped into a recording studio in Brooklyn to cut a duet with singer Dawn Landes to promote their upcoming tour. Landes suggested "Do I Ever Cross Your Mind" by Dolly Parton and rehearsed a guitar part before the session. When Justin showed up to the studio in Brooklyn, he picked up a guitar, started fingerpicking, recorded the song with Landes, and left the studio not much more than an hour or so later. Landes never even picked up her guitar. That's the speed at which Justin was operating. Blink, and he was on to the next task.

"Justin Townes Earle" transitioned into an acoustic power trio. Fiddle virtuoso Joshua Hedley started playing with Justin, as did bluegrass go-to Bryn Davies, on stand-up bass. Justin met Hedley in the Swindlers; Davies had played on his first two studio albums. She was excited to finally tour with musicians her own age, so she put up with significantly lower pay (about $100 per show, at first) and acquiesced to Justin's demand that she wear a dress onstage.

Several-hundred-person clubs were becoming too small to contain the excitement surrounding Justin. Fans waited after shows for autographs, lined up to buy CDs, desperate for a picture or word with this star in the making. "People *could not believe* it when they came to the show," the singer Joe Pug, who opened for Justin that winter, later said on a podcast, reflecting on this period. "This was a special artist at a special time."[15]

Once his career took off in earnest, Justin changed his look every few months: One day he'd appear onstage in a linen suit, the next with a bow tie, or corduroy jacket, or seersucker pants, or suspenders, or a flannel shirt with a neatly tied red bandanna around his neck. He'd wear his hair shaggy, then slicked back, then with a crew cut. He began discussing style as much as songwriting in the press: "I'm not afraid of patterns"; "No white shoes after Labor Day"; "It's always good to have a guy who knows your inside leg measurement."[16] To some old friends, his new focus on how he looked was proof of his New York snobbishness; to others, it was evidence of how well he understood how closely he was now being observed. "A lot of musicians know the difference between being onstage and offstage," said Matt Eddmenson, cofounder of one of Justin's favorite clothing brands, Imogene + Willie. "I don't think Justin saw it that way. I think he always was onstage."

The show starts, as Justin once explained to a fellow songwriter, the minute you pull up to the venue.

That February, *GQ* published its list of the 25 Most Stylish Men in the World. Sandwiched between Brad Pitt, Jude Law, and Jay-Z was Justin Townes Earle, standing with his head tilted to the side, wearing a Stetson hat, a white Urban Outfitters shirt, a flea-market leather belt, and a humble set of blazer and slacks from Uniqlo.[17]

Justin was booked to make his acting debut, appearing on David Simon's *Treme* alongside his father. Justin was set to appear on a tribute album to John Prine, alongside My Morning Jacket, Justin Vernon, and the Avett Brothers. One journalist at the *Minneapolis Star-Tribune* added it all up in a blog post that spring: "Suddenly," the headline read, "Justin Townes Earle Is Everywhere."[18]

When Justin was in New York, which was less and less often, he was at the 11th Street Bar. The pub became the common space his apartment with Keesecker lacked.

It was also somewhere to hide. Justin started buying drugs—weed, cocaine, Vicodin, Percocet—from a friend he knew through the scene at the bar. Beneath the pub's cheery bohemian surface was an undercurrent of darkness. It was a bar that could feel like "a swimming pool of booze," as one former patron and drinking mate of Justin's, Stephen Thorne, put it.

For Justin, destroying himself looked and felt different in the East Village—more glamorous, more anonymous, sexier than the Springwater bathroom. Walking down Avenue A, buzzed, as the rain hit the sidewalk, Justin must've felt like he was starring in a story he'd been writing in his mind since adolescence, when he wrote a tune called "Down on the Lower East Side" with Dustin Welch.

But when some of those who survived the scene looked back at that time, their memories were no longer imbued with romance so much as grief for the ones they lost: the staying up all night shooting shots and sharing pints and stories and songs—then waking up, grabbing a Guinness, and starting again—belied the addiction that haunted so many regulars.

It didn't take long for Justin to recognize what was happening. "Everybody has these small apartments, so everybody's living room is usually a bar," he said soon after his relapse came to a head. "I won't even call it partying, because I wasn't having much fun."[19]

But that didn't mean he could stop. And for a while, it *did* feel like fun—at least for everyone around Justin, and this was part of the problem. On tour, Justin and his band stayed up drinking and carousing in hotel rooms, the type of clichéd rock-and-roll life a young singer dreams about. The shows were electric, the crowds were screaming for more, and Justin was reveling in a moment he knew might not last. When his bassist, Bryn Davies, got a JTE-inspired tattoo on her own stomach, Justin told her it was bad luck. Getting a band tattoo, he said, was like asking for that band to break up.

The cracks in the surface were starting to appear: a forgotten lyric, a smashed guitar, a fleeting onstage mention of having had "a little too much of one thing or another."[20]

Justin kept writing songs through it all. It was what he understood to be his purpose, how he derived self-worth and meaning, what he cared about most. No matter where he was—pacing backstage, plopped on an 11th Street Bar stool, sobering up in his apartment, crunched together in the back of a van on the road—Justin continued to write.

He had grand aspirations for album number three. He envisioned a record that swept from the mountain music of East Tennessee to the blues of the Mississippi Delta to the gritty soul of Muscle Shoals and Memphis. At its center were twin influences: the Carter Family and the Staple Singers.

"Gram Parsons looked at where soul had arrived at," Justin said. "I'm looking at where it came from."[21]

Justin Townes Earle was finished with his self-conscious Porter Wagoner act. Now, there were many retro-presenting, cutesy throwback singers sporting vintage clothing and a phony working-class affectation, several of whom had taken more than a few cues from Justin. No, Justin would not be lumped in with his imitators.

He was, so he proclaimed, a southern artist "chasing the ghost of Woody Guthrie up the New Jersey Turnpike," as he put it.[22] He knew he was the umpteenth folksinger who'd arrived in New York eager for stardom. It was something singer-songwriters had done ever since Bob Dylan arrived in town chasing the same ghost fifty years prior.

In the late 2000s, the idea of journeying to Manhattan to chase folk-music dreams felt as absurd as it was antiquated.

Yet that's exactly what Justin was doing: taking inspiration for his folk music from the modern city. The songs—about subway conductors and chance encounters and suicide and sobriety and cramped Crown Heights apartments—told a bold story. It was the story of an old soul confronted with the temptations of contemporary city life, a story of rural southern music colliding with the electrified R&B of the North, a story of what happens when a young man who can't stop moving starts to slip and slide. What fused the songs, musically, was the church. It was gospel that Justin Townes Earle had turned toward, and it was neon light and salvation he saw shining down 11th Street just as he started to lose control.

That loss of control ramped up in April 2010, when Justin Townes

Earle and Jason Isbell landed in Australia. Isbell, like Justin, had released two acclaimed solo albums by then and was also being positioned as a next-generation inheritor of southern roots traditions. A year earlier, Justin was opening for Isbell. In Australia, where Justin was fast becoming a cult phenomenon, Isbell opened for Justin.

Now they were both using at the time, and they began chasing vices the moment the airplane touched down.

"All kinds of mischief" were Justin's words.[23] It started druggy and got druggier. They kicked things off at Boogie, a new festival outside Melbourne that operated on the premise that Australians who wore cowboy hats and camped out at semirural music festivals also wanted to party. There was electronic music, a "shot bar," and festival-branded motorcycles adorned with the words "*Shake It Loose Together.*"

A photo from Boogie captured Isbell and Justin, surely still jet-lagged, each holding what looks like a margarita. Isbell's wearing a black button-down shirt and a newsboy cap. Justin is unshaven, wearing a vest, tie, and tight jeans. Both flash sweet southern smiles with an almost guilty innocence.

"Me and Jason are two hillbillies far from home," Justin tweeted shortly after arriving on the continent. "But I dig this shit!"[24]

Australia was a blur of chaos: Justin and Isbell performing at a blues festival. Justin and Isbell, surrounded by "a bunch of pretty girls and [a] lot of whiskey," watching Taj Mahal perform. Justin and Isbell getting their hands on cocaine and tequila and over-the-counter cold and flu tablets that contained codeine. Justin and Isbell getting so messed up in a coastal village in New South Wales that it became visible onstage.

Justin live-tweeted the PG-13 version: Here he was, craving comfort food in the midst of the madness: "its gotta be pho for lunch!" and witnessing nature: "seen a dolphin today too!" and complaining about the price of breakfast in Brisbane: "have you ever paid 18 dollars for yogurt and fruit? fuck me!" Here he was, declaring he'd learned of the birth of his younger half brother, John Henry Earle, via the roots-music magazine *No Depression*. ("I'm not sure Justin found out about John Henry's arrival through news from *No Depression*," said Moorer, John Henry's mother. "But I am sure he inherited his father's ability to create a snappy headline.")[25]

And yet, even in his public tweets, Justin started hinting at something much darker: "I think I was born this fucked up," he tweeted in Australia. "Its got nothing to do with the drugs."[26]

A few years later, after Isbell got sober, he went on Terry Gross's *Fresh Air*. He'd written a song called "New South Wales," and Gross wanted to know what inspired it.

The song tells a tale of two men trying to find themselves through stories and substances. It's about the thrills of road life, the stumbling through chemical highs in an attempt to replicate the adrenaline rush of standing onstage each night feeling, finally, understood by a crowd.

Isbell told Gross about touring in 2010 with Justin. "Debaucherous in a whole lot of ways" is how he put it. The tour was a hell of a good time, Isbell admitted. It was the coming home that was the problem.[27]

On May 1, two days after ending his tour Down Under, Justin stood onstage next to Garrison Keillor at a taping for *A Prairie Home Companion* at New York's Town Hall.

"You never stop when you're this age, do you?" Keillor asked Justin, who was running on four hours of sleep after having just arrived home from the other side of the world.

"No, no," Justin said, "and I come from the future."[28]

Then Justin explained he had a wedding to attend in the East Village and needed to run.

Two days later, on May 3, still jet-lagged, Justin woke up earlier than expected on a rainy Sunday morning in his apartment at 516 East 11th Street. With Keesecker still asleep in their tiny apartment, he got up, made frozen waffles, and spent the morning watching old westerns and *The Simpsons*.[29]

Keesecker had been excited to get married, but her goals and dreams far exceeded becoming Justin Townes Earle's wife: She attended the Fashion Institute of Technology, served as a fashion assistant for magazine photo shoots, worked part-time at a boutique in Soho, and had her own life.

Justin's peaceful Sunday morning came amid an upsetting reunion for the two of them. The man who came home from Australia was unrecognizable to Keesecker, not someone she wanted to spend the rest of her life with. Justin no longer seemed able to hide his drinking from her. It was becoming impossible to keep his story straight.

Though he'd started drinking months earlier, in Keesecker's memory, it was Australia where Justin fell off the wagon. And it was his drinking in Australia she credited as the reason for their breakup. Shortly after he returned, she left the apartment for good.

Justin, Keesecker said, "got really violent when he was drunk." She didn't go into any further detail.

CHAPTER 14

In May 2010, a devastating flood struck Nashville. DeFord Bailey Jr., the son of DeFord Bailey Sr.—the harmonica virtuoso who'd helped popularize the Grand Ole Opry as its first (and, for decades, only) Black star—was one of thousands of Nashvillians who found himself in its dire straits.

Like his dad, Bailey Jr. was a musician. On Sunday, May 2, he'd set out for downtown early in the morning to perform at Greater Bethel AME Church. Leaving home, he hadn't thought much of the downpour. It had rained quite a bit the previous day, but the roads seemed fine.

Bailey Jr. drove down Jefferson Street, the once bustling, long-neglected, and now rapidly gentrifying historic Black business district and cultural center of North Nashville where his old bandmate Jimi Hendrix once gigged.[1]

After turning onto Fifth Avenue North, Bailey Jr. realized something was wrong. Not only were the streets no longer clear, but they'd become so flooded he couldn't budge. Water poured into his car.

"Everything just covered," he later recalled, "except the top."

There was too much water, too much pressure bearing down, for the seventy-eight-year-old to even open his door. A police officer arrived on the scene, smashing his window and extricating both Bailey Jr. and his guitar.

The officer still dropped Bailey Jr. off at his destination. But on arriving at the Greater Bethel AME, normally bustling on a Sunday morning, the musician realized it was virtually empty.[2]

Steve Earle holding baby Justin in Nashville, 1982. *Courtesy of Judy Hilton*

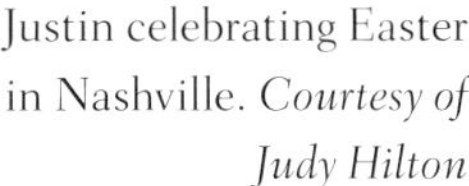

Justin celebrating Easter in Nashville. *Courtesy of Judy Hilton*

Justin at the Elliston Place Street Festival in Nashville, September 1986. *Alan L. Mayor Photography Collection, owner Theresa Mayor-Smith*

Justin celebrating his birthday at Chuck E. Cheese. *Courtesy of Judy Hilton*

Justin and his mom, Carol, at Justin's grandmother's house in Nashville. *Courtesy of Judy Hilton*

Willie Domann, Cory Younts, Dustin Welch, and Justin Earle (*left to right*) in the Chicken Shack. *Courtesy of Dustin Welch*

Justin at a rehearsal for his band Lubbock in Ravenswood, Chicago, 2000. *Courtesy of October Crifasi*

The Swindlers at Springwater: Willie Domann, Justin Earle, Dustin Welch, and Travis Nicholson (*left to right*). *Courtesy of Dustin Welch*

Justin and Dustin. *Courtesy of Dustin Welch*

Justin on tour with Steve Earle and the Dukes, 2003 European tour. *Courtesy of Matt Svobodny*

Patrick Earle, Gerry Diaz, Justin Earle, and Eric Ambel (*left to right*) on the Steve Earle tour bus in Europe, 2003. *Courtesy of Matt Svobodny*

The Swindlers: Travis Nicholson, Skylar Wilson, Willie Domann, Dustin Welch, Justin Earle, Elliot Currie, and Boscoe France (*left to right*), circa 2002. *Photo by Lawson Little, courtesy of Dustin Welch*

Justin and Steve shortly after Justin got home from the hospital and just before going to rehab in Minnesota. Fairview, Tennessee, July 2004. *Photo by Elizabeth DeRamus*

The Distributors at The Basement: Justin Earle, Willie Domann, Skylar Wilson, and Josh Graham (*left to right*), 2006. *Courtesy of Molly Jones*

Justin onstage with Amanda Shires and Joshua Black Wilkins at the Pond in Franklin, Tennessee. *Courtesy of Molly Jones*

Justin Townes Earle and Carol Ann Earle backstage at the Grand Ole Opry, the night of Justin's Opry debut, May 2008. *Photo by Joshua Black Wilkins*

Justin Townes Earle performing with Cory Younts (right) and Josh Hedley (left) in Murray, Kentucky, February 2009. *Photo by Nathan Doyle*

In an East Village apartment, circa 2009. *Courtesy of Angela Schmidt*

Performing at Bonnaroo, June 2009. *Photo by Joshua Black Wilkins*

Justin and Cory Younts rehearsing with members of the Felice Brothers, Old Crow Medicine Show, and Dave Rawlings Machine backstage on the Big Surprise Tour, August 2009. *Photo by Justin Borucki*

At the Sellersville Theater in Sellersville, Pennsylvania, June 2010. *Photo by Doug Seymour*

Outside the F. M. Kirby Center for the Performing Arts in Wilkes-Barre, Pennsylvania, March 2015. *Photo by Doug Seymour*

Justin with his half-brother John Henry Earle as their dad looks on, Hardly Strictly Bluegrass, October 2017. *Photo by Ken Friedman*

Backstage at the Ryman Auditorium, August 2018. *Photo by Joshua Black Wilkins*

At Sound Emporium in Nashville during the recording of *The Saint of Lost Causes*, 2018. *Photo by Joshua Black Wilkins, courtesy of New West Records*

The forecast had predicted up to five inches of rain, but the weekend brought more than thirteen inches, the most rain within forty-eight hours the city had ever seen. Nashville experienced what was soon referred to as a "thousand-year" flood, which left in its brown, muddy wake eleven deaths in the Nashville area and ten thousand displaced residents and ruined homes.[3]

"The common denominator is water," wrote journalist Peter Cooper, describing the flood's particular toll on the city's musical community. "Water bending hundreds of wooden instruments at Soundcheck Nashville rehearsal studio, and halting production of Gibson guitars. Water destroying historical documents at the Grand Ole Opry House."

"For musical Nashville," wrote Cooper, "much—no one is sure how much—has been lost to this water."[4]

When the Grand Ole Opry, which had flooded, held its first broadcast at an alternate location days later, Opry star Jeannie Seely borrowed shoes for the occasion; she'd lost her home.

"Somebody said, 'I can't believe you're going to play the Grand Ole Opry tonight,' Seely said onstage. "I said, 'Well, it's not like I can stay at home and watch T.V.'"[5]

"Nashville is hurtin!" Justin Townes Earle proclaimed after arriving in town, surveying the damage.[6]

He'd landed in Nashville just days after the flood to cut his third record, *Harlem River Blues*, an album of gospel tunes for dark times, whose centerpiece was the tale of a young man submitting to the rushing water rising up around him.

It made some kind of prophetic sense that Justin's arrival to document his new songs coincided with a real-life flood. The Cumberland River was too flooded to allow for his first meaningful task in town to go as planned: a photo shoot for the cover of an album he hadn't yet recorded.

For the shoot, then, Justin ventured south to North Alabama. He stood on the Tennessee River riverbank in a soaked white dress shirt and black tie looking stern and solemn, the river's murky water out of focus behind him.

Harlem River Blues would eventually become Justin's biggest album; it flew off the shelves of record stores from Portland to Atlanta, earned him his first indie radio hit, and delivered him scores of new fans in increasingly large clubs across the country. The album was the culmination of Justin's development as a songwriter and a testament to his past few years of sobriety, even as it documented that sobriety collapsing. Some songs were peppy odes to fried chicken, full of church organs and sloppy sing-along choirs and handclaps and raucous harmonica. Others were downcast tales of isolation and loneliness delivered as sparse, pedal-steel ballads or piano rockers. The breakout song, the title track, was a little bit of both.

"Harlem River Blues" is a fast, cheerful-sounding song with a chorus catchy enough to conceal its grim tale. The song tells the story of a man in New York City traveling to the northern tip of Manhattan to drown himself. "Dirty water gonna cover me over," the narrator sings in the gleeful refrain, "and I'm not gonna make a sound."

The narrator sounds jubilant as he outlines an informal will in the second verse: "Tell my mama I loved her, tell my father I tried," Justin sings, "give my money to my baby to spend."

It took one listen to realize Justin had, at long last, written a *hit*, one with layers of meaning and interpretation and an internal rhyme scheme that displayed the seriousness with which he took his craft. "I'm on a *roll*, mama, I've gotta *go*," Justin's narrator announces as he kicks off his journey uptown. In his quest to modernize gospel, Justin struck gold with "Harlem River Blues." The song was an urban hymn—"I'll Fly Away" but with NYC traffic—that applied the tried-and-true gospel formula of setting songs about death to cheery melodies. Justin took the premise further: Why wait until the end of life to carry over? Why not go while you're already in His good grace?

"Even though I enjoy life pretty thoroughly, I'm of the opinion that it's a pretty tough thing," Justin once said when discussing the song. "People who say they're going to kill themselves generally aren't going to. People who make the decision to take their own lives usually don't talk about it. They're looking for a release."

Justin laughed a dark laugh, then kept going: "I just decided to take that to a newer, sicker level. Make it a celebration."[7]

There goes the song's narrator, skipping and singing up the FDR Drive, a parkway that carries several hundred thousand cars daily and isn't generally known for leisure strolls. Is it a flight of fancy? A surrealist daydream? A manic episode? Or the calm confidence of someone who's already made their final decision?[8]

It wasn't the first time Justin had written about suicide: He'd done it, to great effect, on the title track of *Yuma*, but that song hadn't been a hit. He'd never had to answer questions about it in the same way.

Inevitably, the inspiration for "Harlem River Blues" changed depending on to whom Justin was talking.

"I have friends with fairly miserable lives and a few who actually took their own lives," he said in 2011. "I talked with one friend about eight hours before he did it. And as he told me his plan, I saw a look of ease on his face I'd never seen. It was what he wanted to do, and [it's] why the song has a celebratory feeling."[9]

But when a journalist asked about the album when it came out, Justin struck a different tone.

Interviewer: "There's an undercurrent of depression to [*Harlem River Blues*]. Are you depressed?"

Justin: "Not in any way I haven't been all my life."[10]

As for where the idea for the song actually came from, Justin's story never changed: "Harlem River Blues" was inspired by a book, *The Basketball Diaries*, by Jim Carroll. Justin had read it as a teenager.

The 1978 cult memoir—a collection of drug-fueled diary entries pulled from the punk poet's preteen years—was a totem of romanticized New York nonconformity. Justin zeroed in on a passage about a juvenile jinx Carroll and his friends dared each other to do in the sixties.

"Every crowd of young guys has its little games to prove if you're punk or not," Carroll writes. "Here in Upper Manhattan, guys jump off cliffs into the Harlem River, where the water is literally shitty because right nearby are the giant sewer deposits where about half a million toilets empty their goods daily."

Carroll details the site of these jumps: a "series of minor cliffs" overlooking the polluted river at the northern tip of Manhattan, the highest one eighty-five feet tall. Then he, himself, makes the jump.

"I didn't really think, I didn't even take my sneakers off," he writes. "I just jumped into this herky dream that lasted all the way down until I hit bottom. The feeling isn't movement anyway, but rather being suspended in front of the sheer cliff, mid-air, with the waters rising up sharp and fast at you."[11]

Years after Justin first read the book, he had a vision. As he told it, it came while stuck in a hellscape of New York traffic. Driving into Manhattan one evening, Justin was stopped to a halt on the FDR Drive. Not knowing what to do, Justin called 11th Street bartender Kenny O'Connor for advice. O'Connor had a tip: get off the highway, and take the Third Avenue bridge into Harlem.

Justin took the suggestion, but traffic wasn't much better. Stuck on the Third Avenue bridge, he peered into the black muck of the river Jim Carroll and his friends once jumped into.[12]

The gospel music that informed "Harlem River Blues" would serve as the underpinning for the whole new album. These were the familiar sounds Justin claimed he'd heard walking past the neighborhood AME church as a kid.[13] They were also the sounds that the album's coproducer, and former Swindler, Skylar Wilson, honed during his year as the Sunday-morning church organist at a Black Baptist church in Murfreesboro.

Justin began recording *Harlem River Blues* at the studio House of David on May 17, as Nashville continued to recover from the flood.[14]

This time, it was Justin and Skylar Wilson serving as producers. The atmosphere was loose, built on years of trust the two had developed. Wilson had played on Justin's past two albums and had become his de facto studio bandleader and primary sounding board, the man entrusted with the execution of his vision. "He always knew the movie he wanted to make," said Wilson, whose job was to manifest that movie.

The new album Justin was making—a sweeping millennial take on southern gospel prompted by the sights, sounds, and smells of New York City—felt fresh. Justin mixed in dispatches from his new hometown ("Workin' for the MTA," "One More Night in Brooklyn") with tales from his worldly travels ("Christchurch Woman") and songs that conveyed a new level of introspection and self-probing ("Learning to Cry," "Slippin' and Slidin'").

To close the record, Justin reached back for one older composition, "Rogers Park," a nearly decade-old song Justin had written after his brief stint in Chicago as an eighteen-year-old. Its premise—the tale of a young man lost and alone in a big city far from home—had become newly resonant.

The *Harlem River Blues* sessions pulled from the energy surging through Nashville: Jason Isbell and Old Crow's Ketch Secor showed up to add guitar and harmonica on a few songs. When Justin and Wilson wanted the sound of a ramshackle choir for the chorus of "Harlem River Blues," Wilson summoned some musician friends—"every hipster we knew"—to the studio.

Those musicians who appeared on short notice—Caitlin Rose, Rayland Baxter, Jordan and Alex Caress—were part of a budding community of early 2010s East Nashville songwriters who idolized Justin Townes Earle. They viewed *Yuma*, *The Good Life*, and *Midnight at the Movies* as gold standards of the type of music they strove to make.

"I didn't think anyone was really doing it well until *Yuma*," said Andrew Combs, one of Nashville's many young and impressionable artists at the time. "We definitely held it on a pedestal."

To many of them, Justin was a born-and-bred Nashville superhero. "We saw him in a way he never saw himself," said Rayland Baxter, one of several singers who sang on *Harlem River Blues*.

As the 2000s turned into the 2010s, these artists started garnering attention for their own music. Baxter also sang on *Own Side Now*, the breakthrough debut from Caitlin Rose, which was also coproduced by Skylar Wilson.

Tristen Gaspadarek, a young songwriter who'd played alongside Rose at her twenty-first-birthday party that Justin had also played, was prepping her label debut, *Charlatans at the Garden Gate*. *Rolling Stone* would deem her "an artist worth watching."[15]

It was still several years before *The New York Times* infamously declared Nashville's "it city" status.[16] But the press was taking stock of this crop of millennial songwriters planting their flag in East Nashville, many of whom were influenced by Justin. They wrote their own songs and shared a lack of interest in, if not outright contempt for, the idea of writing for country radio. They preferred older stuff: Guy Clark, Mickey Newbury, "Dead Flowers."

Acoustic music in East Nashville wasn't new, but this crop of artists was a generation younger than neighborhood stalwarts like Gillian Welch, Todd Snider, and Elizabeth Cook, and they made for a sexier story. Many of them arrived on the east side ready to carve out their own spaces, make their own friends, and find new rooms to occupy. Baxter, Rose, and Gaspadarek were locals. Most were not; there was Combs, who'd arrived from Dallas eager to re-create *Heartworn Highways*; Jeremy Fetzer, a guitarist from Ohio; Nikki Lane, a fashion-forward South Carolina transplant; Jonny Fritz, an oddball Virginia songwriter who adopted the surname Corndawg; Brian Ritchey, an Indiana-bred friend of Justin's who formed the talented yet unfortunately named trio Korean Is Asian with Jordan and Alex Caress; and Derek Hoke, a Georgia songwriter who worked at the Belcourt Theatre.

Most of these artists revered Justin, and he returned the praise. He was quick to shower local songwriters with encouragement and kindness, to let them know he'd been listening, that the songs they were writing mattered. When he was back in town, Justin would show up to old coffee-shop haunts, chat up the baristas, find out what band they were in, then go see that band play a show on a night off. "It was the first time we had someone in our corner," said Jordan Caress. "And it was cool that it was him."

On May 25, Justin headlined a flood-benefit show with various local musicians at the 5 Spot, the dimly lit East Nashville dive where his disciples congregated. Justin presided over the proceedings, likely proud as he beheld the singer-songwriter scene blooming, once again, out of his hometown: These songwriters, just a few years younger, had carved out their own space that was being appreciated much more than the Swindlers ever were. Justin wanted to do what he could to support it, and he told the artists as much.

But behind the scenes, throughout recording and mixing *Harlem River Blues* that May, Justin was struggling. He continued to relapse.

He'd spent the month crashing in the spare room of his friend and photographer Joshua Black Wilkins. At night, alone in his hometown, Justin sat in the dark quiet of the guest room and gulped down cans of cheap beer by himself. Wilkins knew, by then, that Justin had started drinking: They'd been to bars together, and every so often, when Justin was out, Wilkins came into the guest room to sweep out the wreckage of empty beer cans Justin had stuffed underneath the bed.

But Justin avoided any outright communication with his old friends about what was going on. Instead, one night in Nashville, he tweeted into the void: "There's nothin wrong with warm beer."[17]

A year later, Justin would claim that he recorded *Harlem River Blues* while "doing an eightball of cocaine a day and choking down pain pills, you know, just loaded."[18]

Over the past year, he'd written the songs, so he said, during the day, while he was still pacing his vodka intake and hadn't yet started on cocaine, finishing his writing by five in the afternoon.

"Usually by that time I was what most people call drunk," he said, "then I'd go out and get what *I* consider drunk."[19]

It was a dark and abrupt change in narrative to hear Justin talk about writing and recording his most acclaimed body of work in the height of a relapse. Was *the myth* haunting him again? He'd spent the past three years preaching that great art wasn't contingent on getting fucked up—or on fucking up one's life. But as much as he'd once worked to dispel *the myth*, he propagated it anew in the story he told about *Harlem River Blues*.

Anyone watching Justin in the studio could appreciate that he was creating brilliant art *despite* the drugs and alcohol. At one point in recording, when Justin seemed possibly too intoxicated to credibly play his instrument, Wilson politely suggested that maybe *Harlem River Blues* didn't actually need acoustic guitar. Justin trusted Wilson's instincts.

After *Harlem River Blues* was finished, Justin flew back to New York, this time to an empty apartment: He'd given Keesecker thirty days to find a new place while he was out of town. For the first time, he was living in New York City by himself. There wasn't much use in sitting around alone. Within twenty-four hours of landing in New York, Justin was back at the 11th Street Bar.

CHAPTER 15

THE COHEAD OF JUSTIN'S LABEL, ROB MILLER, SPENT THE SUMMER OF 2010 in Chicago preparing for Bloodshot Records' biggest release in years. "Don't let me fuck this up," he remembered thinking to himself. Bloodshot was a small, nimble operation, effective at selling a couple of thousand records of a critically acclaimed niche act to a specific targeted audience.

Now, it had on its roster a bona fide emerging star, a cultural figure, if everything turned out right. The calls and emails Bloodshot started receiving about *Harlem River Blues* months before it was out—from glossy magazines, eager journalists, distributors, folks in Europe—were telling them as much.

Bloodshot printed a half-dozen times more CDs than they normally would, spending money they only sort of had. They hired a fancy publicity firm to promote the album's September release. They spent tens of thousands on retail marketing (nothing for a major label, but quite a bit for Bloodshot). The small staff spent the summer preparing for a release they hoped and believed would take off.

When Justin returned to New York after recording in Nashville that May, his Twitter dispatches made it seem as though he had a hard time adjusting. "I am going insaine!" he tweeted in early June, a sentiment that turned darker a day later: "I'm not sure of anything anymore."[1]

Justin was now living alone and far away from home. "I am in a strange place," he posted.[2]

He headed back on the road where he felt more comfortable, more himself. "Ya'll feeling good tonight?" he shouted to a crowd in Wisconsin that summer. "All right! Because I'm feeling damn fine."[3]

Justin accelerated his already crazed pace in the months leading up to the release of *Harlem River Blues*. He went out to see shows when Nashville friends—Brian Ritchey, Dave Rawlings and Gillian Welch—had New York gigs. He played a Brooklyn food-and-music party hosted by Rachael Ray. He sang his new songs in a sweltering Iowa barn full of rabid fans. He drove past his former halfway house in St. Paul, Minnesota ("Good times!" he tweeted),[4] a flashback to his earliest days of a sobriety long broken. He immediately dove into yet another new relationship, this time with a chef who worked at an East Village wine bar.

At some point that summer, Justin gashed his hand open in a violent outburst that landed him in the ER for stitches in the middle of the night and forced him to cancel several gigs, including a high-profile appearance at the Newport Folk Festival.[5]

It's not clear what exactly happened. One friend heard he'd smashed a vase in his new girlfriend's apartment. When *Stereophile* magazine interviewed Justin that summer, its description of the incident, presumably a paraphrase of the account Justin provided, was disturbing: "a mishap with a female and a broken bowl."[6]

Pressed further, Justin refused to explain. "It was an unfortunate incident of grave stupidity," he told another reporter. "We'll just leave it at that."[7]

As Justin's substance use increased, so too, seemingly, did the chance he'd erupt in violence: bar fights, heated altercations, moments of uncontrolled rage.

In an effort, perhaps, to maintain anything resembling control, Justin's manager, Traci Thomas, hired Justin a tour manager, a twenty-two-year-old recent college grad named Lauren Spratlin. She'd already interned for Thomas, helped as an assistant running errands during the *Harlem River Blues* sessions, and was eager to land her first real job in the music industry.

Being Justin Townes Earle's tour manager in the summer of 2010 was quite an introduction. Spratlin was tasked with keeping Justin and his hard-partying band alive and on time. That first summer, Spratlin remembered Justin sitting in the van, as nervous and excited as a kid before the first day of kindergarten, playing "The Weight" on repeat as he tried to memorize his lines after being invited to sing the song, again, with Levon Helm. She also remembered narrowly avoiding a moose while driving a sedan full of drunk band members on a foggy, dark night in Maine.

Spratlin was an innocent newcomer into Justin's touring life, which had become a cyclone of dysfunction and merriment. She quickly found herself in over her head.

"At first it was like, 'This is really fun,'" Spratlin said of that summer. "Then it was like, 'Oh, wait . . . I don't know how to do this.'"

Early on in her tour-managing tenure, she called Steve Earle, told him his son needed help, and asked if Steve would intervene.

In August, Joshua Black Wilkins flew to New York to see his old friend. The trip's official purpose was to open for and accompany Justin at a few solo gigs. The trip's actual purpose, as Wilkins saw it, was a wellness check. Justin was no longer communicating with anyone back in Nashville.

Wilkins was taken aback by the sheer pace and intensity of the cyclone he encountered: In the span of two days, he broke up three fights Justin got into. He accompanied Justin to a bar that Justin insisted on going to within a half hour of waking up. He sat in a car headed to Massachusetts that Justin insisted on driving, as fast as possible, while drinking. He watched side-stage as Justin sang Randy Newman's song about six feet of water rushing into the streets of Evangeline. And he stood on the street in Manhattan as Justin paced up and down the block, yelling, over the phone, at his manager, Traci Thomas, who'd presided over and aided every element of his career since *The Good Life*.

By the end of the call, Justin was no longer being managed by Traci Thomas. Thomas told Justin she was done. She quit; Justin then told Thomas she was fired. "She was calling him on his bullshit, and he didn't like that," said Wilkins. "Like his dad, if you told Justin Earle what to do, not only would he say 'no,' he'd get mad at you."

It wasn't the greatest time to lose one's longtime manager. *Harlem River Blues* was out in two weeks.

As soon as Wilkins left, Justin and his band headed to Seattle for a festival alongside Bob Dylan and Mary J. Blige. After appearing at the festival, they played a secret gig under the name Alabama Finger Bang at Seattle's Tractor Tavern.

The tightrope walk was now a dance.

"Ladies and gentlemen, I am *drunk*," he told the rowdy Seattle crowd. "I'm not usually this wasted."

Before the set ended, Justin laughed. "I should be in bed," he said.

Justin was performing his own self-destruction now. One part of the problem was that the crowd couldn't get enough of it. The showbiz son of a showbiz star, Justin surely sensed it.

"You'd go out onstage and all these people were cheering," Justin told an Australian television show in 2015. "It was in the back of your head, 'Well, they don't care about me as a person.' That *is* partially true."[8]

Everyone, even fellow artists for whom partying and pills were normalized, sensed something was really wrong. There was now an uncontrolled frenzy to Justin's daily movements. If Bryn Davies, Justin's bassist and the responsible figure in the band, told Justin they had a long drive the next morning and perhaps should call it a night, Justin would lash out. If Justin overheard someone mention Arby's, he'd respond with a fifteen-minute monologue expounding on every experience he'd ever allegedly had inside an Arby's.

Onward to Atlanta, where the latest bystander was singer-songwriter Derek Hoke, who was now opening for Justin. "Help yourself to anything backstage," Justin told Hoke when he arrived at the venue, before pointing to his bottle of vodka, "but just don't touch this." Hoke watched Justin and the band sweat through their gig: packed bar, fans screaming for their favorite songs. The next morning, he remembered waiting to drive to Birmingham for the next gig; Justin had gone missing.

"I'm watching this guy, almost at the peak of his powers, but killing himself," said Hoke. "It was like, 'Dude, we are not in Guns N' Roses.'"

Meanwhile, rave reviews for *Harlem River Blues* started to pour in.

"Earle has never been one to do what he's told," read one astute observation in *Slant*, "and the formalism of traditional blues gives him a set of confines to fight against."[9] The *Observer* gushed that "there are echoes of Guthrie and Springsteen, but at twenty-eight, Earle's clear, considered voice is clearly his own."[10]

The blog *Line of Best Fit* called it "the record that finally causes all of us to quit focusing on Justin Townes Earle's famous father."[11]

But on September 10, 2010, the day *Harlem River Blues* was released, Justin didn't have the luxury of forgetting about his dad. Both of his parents—Carol and Steve—stood next to one another as Justin performed an intimate in-store set at Grimey's, the record store located a mile up the street from the first house the three of them had shared when Justin was born.

Justin was sweating and surrounded by loved ones: his parents, aunt, old bandmates, and god sister all showed up to celebrate the release of an album poised to change Justin's life.

Playing to the packed record store, Justin seemed drunk, his voice rough and raw. He occasionally slurred his speech between songs. Still, as he performed the new album in front of friends and family for the first time, it was clear the bumbling local singer they'd once known had transformed into a profound artist.

Throughout the set, Justin seemed acutely aware of his parents' presence. Steve stood to the side, arms crossed and expressionless, as Justin sang about his family's original sin on a new gospel tune:

Now my father was a traveler and my mama stayed at home
And she cried the day that he walked out and left us on our own
Now I'm older than he was when I was born and I don't know
Which way is home so I'm wanderin'

Then Justin introduced the next number, "Slippin' and Slidin'":

"This here song is about knowing your limits, and it's about knowing where you should and where you shouldn't and not giving a fuck."

Justin stopped himself. "Sorry about my language," he said, breaking into a nervous laugh and pointing at his dad. "That's *his* fault."

Four songs later, Justin was introducing his new song "Christchurch Woman" when a cell phone started ringing.

Justin identified the culprit: Steve.

"HA, HA," Justin shouted, pointing at his dad, who'd answered his phone. Some crowd members, recognizing the psychodrama unfolding before them, started groaning.

"We'll just wait 'till he's done," Justin announced.

Steve Earle spoke with his wife for a few seconds and then held up his phone to the crowd: "Say hey to Allison," Steve announced, having commanded the room's full attention.

Justin played along, leading the crowd in greeting his stepmom.

Steve brought the phone back to his ear, said goodbye, then hung up.

Justin attempted to defuse the moment. "That was awesome!" he said as he took a sip of his drink.

As Justin started the riff of "Christchurch Woman," he looked over, again, at his parents, who were now engaged in some stern-seeming exchange, Carol leaning over and talking to her ex-husband, who now appeared to be texting.

"Mom, leave him alone!" Justin barked. Steve, seemingly amused by the familial drama he'd instigated, started grinning and said something back to his son as Justin continued to play the song's riff.

Justin let out a loose smile to his dad. Then he started to sing.[12]

One of the many people in the Grimey's crowd was Jenn Ramsey, his old friend, someone he'd known since childhood and referred to as his sister. After the show, she headed around back to say hi to Justin, whom she hadn't seen in years. Ramsey wondered how Justin might greet her. So much had changed. They'd both gotten sober. Now, Justin wasn't. "Is he going to be weird and aloof?" she wondered.

"Oh, my God," Ramsey remembered Justin shouting when she sneaked up behind him and tapped him on the shoulder. He picked her up and swung her around in a hug.

Ramsey, Justin, and a few old friends headed to their late-night haunt, Athens Family Restaurant. It wasn't until Justin suggested to Ramsey that they should get matching tattoos that she realized just how drunk he was.

After the meal, everyone stood around the parking lot, prolonging the overdue catch-up, saying their extended goodbyes, consecrating the informal reunion that had taken place to celebrate Justin Earle. He went by his full name now, but they all wanted him to know that, should he ever return to his old stomping grounds between Belmont Boulevard and Eighth Avenue South, they'd be waiting for his call. Eventually, everyone said goodbye. "I hated to leave that parking lot," Ramsey said.

The next morning, Justin was setting out on the biggest tour of his career, a six-week headlining run in major clubs promoting his new record. The album was out for less than twenty-four hours, but radio stations across the country—in Santa Rosa, California; and Norfolk, Virginia; and Canton, Ohio; and Hanalei, Hawaii—were already playing "Harlem River Blues." The next few weeks would bring him to some of the most important venues for a young blooming star: Minneapolis's First Avenue, Toronto's Horseshoe Tavern, DC's 9:30 Club.

So as they said their goodbyes that night in the Athens parking lot, Jenn Ramsey had no idea that, in just a few weeks, she'd see her old friend right back in Nashville, at an inpatient rehab facility called the Cumberland Heights Treatment Center.

Two days after the record release show in Nashville, Justin showed up for another afternoon promotional gig at LUNA Music, a record store in Indianapolis. A friend who spoke to him outside the store could tell that the Justin who'd arrived in Indianapolis that day was in a much different place than he normally was when he rolled into town. He seemed frustrated and inebriated, asking how to find "adult drugs," as he called them.

At Radio Radio, the small club where he was playing that evening, Justin's frustration morphed into agitation. It was the third time in little more than a year that Radio Radio was hosting Justin Townes Earle, but members of Justin's party (tour manager Lauren Spratlin, opening act Jessica Lea Mayfield, bandmate Bryn Davies) remembered something feeling off about the evening from the start. This included the foul mood their boss seemed to be in.

First, there was a tense exchange over exactly which space inside the club could be used as the band's dressing room.

Next, there was an unpleasant back-and-forth between the musicians and the sound engineer during a sound check that left Mayfield in tears. Sometime around that point, said Spratlin, Justin went into "maniacal drinking mode."

Then, a rough gig. Sound issues, a pissed-off singer unafraid to show it, and a crowd, perhaps feeding off Justin's energy, that was rowdy and mildly combative. "The crowd is loud, people are buzzed and taunting and it all hits the stage wrong," one show review noted.[13]

Nothing out of the ordinary for a Thursday night in a rock club, but enough to unravel an intoxicated and infuriated singer. When a fan threw a T-shirt that landed on Justin's guitar toward the end of his set, Justin walked offstage and didn't return.

Unwise, drug-fueled decision-making continued from there. Justin and Mayfield proceeded to the dressing room to "start breaking things," as Mayfield remembered it. They wrecked a table, lamp, and mirror.

And then there was the altercation that would forever alter Justin's image.

How it happened, exactly, varies slightly depending on who's asked, but pretty much everyone, including Justin, club owner David "Tufty" Clough, and the Indianapolis police officers who soon arrived on the scene, agree on most of the following broad strokes:

The club owner, Tufty, was livid after the show. Justin had treated his club like shit. The damage to his dressing room, however minor, was the final straw. So, when settling up afterward, Tufty said he and

Spratlin agreed to dock Justin's pay a few hundred dollars to account for the damage.

Justin and his bandmate Joshua Hedley left the club after the show and left Spratlin and Davies to load up the van with gear. Both women vividly remembered Tufty and another Radio Radio employee approaching them, determined to smash Justin's guitar in retribution for his dressing-room escapades. Spratlin remembered Tufty throwing instruments; Davies remembered being threatened as they tried to pack up. (Tufty denied any such exchange took place: "We would have never done that.")

However unpleasant the load-out, Spratlin and Davies assumed the storm had blown over. The tense and unpleasant evening seemed to be behind them. But when they picked up Justin and Hedley to leave, Spratlin told Justin about her and Davies's interaction with Tufty and the club employee during the load-out. This, Spratlin remembered, set off Justin, who declared he was going back to the club to have a word with the owner.

As Radio Radio began to lock up for the night, Tufty remembered hearing a banging on the door. Justin Townes Earle wanted to talk. (Spratlin remembered Tufty meeting Justin outside the club as Justin approached: "I wouldn't say Justin instigated the fight," she said. "It was mutual.") Either way, the two men ended up outside, screaming at each other. At some point, someone at Radio Radio called the cops. Justin was incensed his pay was docked after having been mistreated all night. Tufty was outraged by the damage to his club, outraged Justin was arguing about money when, in Tufty's opinion, their financial arrangement—the artist taking all the money from the door, the club taking bar sales—was generous.[14]

As Justin continued to shout, Tufty countered with an insult he knew would sting. "Everybody just came to the show because of your famous dad," he later remembered yelling back at Justin. "That's the only reason people were here."

At this point, Tufty recalled, Justin began "swinging wildly," throwing punches that didn't quite land. Tufty's twenty-three-year-old daughter, who'd been working at the club that night, got in the middle of the two men, later telling police that she "attempted to stop Mr. Earle's assault on her father and was struck by Mr. Earle with a closed fist one time in the shoulder/neck area." Justin later denied striking Tufty's daughter, and neither Spratlin nor Mayfield remembered such a thing happening.

When police arrived, Justin refused to cooperate.

"What did I do?" he repeated from inside their Sprinter van, according to the incident report.

After police removed him from the car, Justin, now slurring his words, pleaded his innocence. "I didn't do anything," he told officers, who described Justin in their arrest report as "surly and agitated and [refusing] to follow basic directions." Eventually, an officer struck Justin "with an open hand" twice and placed him in handcuffs. Justin was arrested and charged with two counts of battery, public intoxication, and resisting law enforcement.

Within twenty-four hours, Justin was out of jail, having posted bond. But the story was already everywhere.

Everyone at Radio Radio that night agreed that the drunken altercation ended up getting blown out of proportion in the press and the public's imagination. But in the days after Indianapolis, blogs across the internet covered the incident, and after a local newspaper obtained the police report, coverage zeroed in on the allegation of Justin assaulting a club owner's daughter: "Belligerent Justin Townes Earle Arrested in Indianapolis;" "Justin Townes Earle Arrested for Battery," read several headlines.[15]

The firestorm was fueled further by Justin's own free-flowing narrativizing of the evening, on Twitter and onstage, in the following days.

He offered his account to an eager crowd the very next night, in Louisville, Kentucky. A local journalist, Selena Frye, was in the crowd. She recounted Justin's loose set, which included his unfiltered memory of Indianapolis, in her review of the show.[16]

Now that he was a free man, he told the Louisville crowd, he'd do whatever the hell he wanted onstage. Accounting for the fact that his band had shrunk by a third, he explained that Davies had gone AWOL. (The morning after Indianapolis, Davies left the tour and drove back to Nashville.) Justin seized on the opportunity to brandish his bad-boy credentials. He began freely sharing his arrest tale, tweeting that he was "Free Again!!!" and that Radio Radio "and all its staff can kiss my fucking ass!"[17]

Eventually, through his label, Justin released a more legally advisable statement, which denied all allegations and, crucially, condemned violence against women.[18]

But it was horrible press for a budding star, and Justin couldn't keep from spinning his desperation into dark humor. He later opened a show by dedicating his song "Who Am I to Say" "with love, to the city of Indianapolis."[19] He transformed his mug shot into his backstage tour laminate. In the liner notes to his next record, he thanked his defense attorney as well as "the state of Indiana for the free press."

Justin tried to keep up good spirits for a couple of days. During a stopover in Chicago for a show, Justin, Spratlin, and Mayfield pranked a stranger they met in a hotel hot tub, convincing him that Justin was the father of the two women.

But there was little humor to be found at Justin's show in Chicago. Watching him sweat his way through that set was like witnessing "a man in agony," said Rob Miller, the cohead of Justin's label, who was in the crowd. Miller had seen Justin at his best many times over the past few years. The contrast he was witnessing further drove home all the money his label now stood to lose. Their long-planned campaign was blowing up in their faces, thanks to Justin's arrest, not forty-eight hours after *Harlem River Blues* was released. Those losses were "heartbreaking," said Miller, "but it didn't touch how heartbreaking it was to have seen the obvious pain [Justin] was in that night."

Then Justin flew home to New York. He had five days off before the next gig.

Suddenly off the road, Justin had to sit with what had transpired over the past few weeks. His bass player had seemingly quit. His tour manager, Spratlin, not wanting to see Justin die, also resigned. He'd lost his longtime manager. His mother was a thousand miles away. His father lived across town and was worried sick, without question, but was wary of interfering and further pushing his son further away when he was using.

Brimming with shame and self-hatred, Justin threw himself into a multiday bender like he hadn't since he was twenty-two.

Justin later described his mental state during those few days in New York as a hallucinatory "cocaine psychosis." He believed every person walking down the street had read reports of him hitting a woman and were staring at him as they passed him on the street.

"It absolutely was just crushing me," he told the Associated Press a year later.

"I almost killed myself with drugs and alcohol in the days following that incident because I kept thinking about my grandmother and my mother and all the people that I know reading this article that said I hit a woman," Justin said, repeatedly denying that any altercation had taken place.

But in the same 2011 interview, Justin made a startling confession. First, he explained how tortured he'd been by the idea that anyone would think he would ever hit a woman. Then he admitted there were times when he felt what he believed was a universal violent urge toward women: "I will say that I did not hit a woman. Period. Never have. I've wanted to. I think everybody's wanted to." (What Justin said immediately following this admission didn't provide much further explanation: "I was raised with my mother," he continued. "It was just this idea of that being out there.")[20]

In Nashville, Justin's former manager, Traci Thomas, knew how dire the situation had become. She'd made plans to stage an immediate intervention, enlisting friends like Jason Isbell and Joshua Black Wilkins to write letters.

On the morning of September 22, a small group of people, all of whom Justin in some way employed—including Justin's booking agent, Andrew Colvin; his business manager; and his attorney—joined a professional interventionist to show up to Justin's girlfriend's apartment on 11th Street.

"I was lying in bed shaking and delusional," Justin later recalled. "I was seeing things and hearing things, and I had slipped into delirium tremens in a serious way."[21]

"He looked like he was dying," said Colvin.

The interventionist read Justin the letters.

Wilkins's was a stark cry to his friend. "Over the past several months, you have distanced yourself from me and the people around you," he wrote. "We have all been afraid of what may happen to you if you went 'over the edge,' and we also feel like we have seen you come very close to just that. . . . Your short temper, along with the excesses of drugs and alcohol have not only gotten you in trouble, but pushed away the people that love you the most."

Wilkins ended his letter by reminding Justin that the day of the intervention was Wilkins's birthday. "What I really want," he wrote, "is my friend back."

Steve Earle had been through this process with Justin many times. He was, himself, in recovery. He believed his presence could jeopardize the intervention, that forcing Justin to rehab would be futile unless Justin made the decision for himself. He stayed uninvolved with the intervention.

Justin called his publicist, one of his few professional associates who hadn't quit, been fired, or attended his intervention. He told her, while "hysterically crying," as he remembered, that he wanted to quit music. He wanted to hide. He was angry at everyone who'd participated in the intervention. He was done being Justin Townes Earle.

Later that day, back in Nashville, Wilkins got a phone call. It was Traci Thomas, and she told him, through tears, that Justin had agreed to get on a plane and go to treatment.

Justin was familiar with Cumberland Heights, the Nashville rehab facility he checked into that September. The twelve-step treatment center was founded in 1966.[22] In the eighties, it opened an adolescent wing that Justin had spent time in as a young teenager.

Cumberland Heights was a high-end facility with a game room, chapel, gym, and auditorium. Johnny Cash and Keith Urban were just two of countless country celebrities and famous Nashvillians (including former mayor Beverly Briley) who'd spent time there.

Those who'd seen Justin through various past attempts at getting sober when he was much younger knew how familiar Justin had become with his cycle of addiction. He'd relapse, his substance use would accelerate, there'd be some intervention, he'd agree to short-term rehab, he'd sleep for days and clear the substances from his system, he'd follow the rules and say the right things for a few weeks, he'd check out of rehab, and then he'd appear to be okay for a little while, enough time for his addiction to persuade him to begin the whole process all over again.

Justin also understood that the structures in place to help someone like him were insufficient, that a working musician touring most of the year couldn't address, in three to six weeks, the roots of the suffering that drove his compulsive substance use and self-medication.

Justin engaged in the therapy the center offered. He detoxed; he reflected. "A little hairy to begin with," he said of rehab afterward. "But I definitely feel good now. It usually only takes a few weeks to get the stuff out of your system."[23]

Wilkins was nervous when he showed up to Cumberland Heights to visit Justin, unsure of how Justin might react after his role in the intervention.

But the Justin who greeted him was the one that he'd been so charmed by years prior. "He was full of life," Wilkins remembered. They chain-smoked and talked a bit about what had happened, but mostly just enjoyed each other's company. Wilkins told a story of Justin leading him to the chapel, which had a piano. "Justin sits down, and he starts playing these songs, some of the best stuff I have ever heard from him," Wilkins said. "They were deep, they were dark, they were 'take your guts and twist them around' kind of songs. . . . I didn't even know he played piano."

Justin downplayed whatever he may have written in rehab, once mentioning in passing that he'd written one song in Cumberland Heights.

As far as anyone knows, he discarded the material Wilkins remembered Justin playing for him that day.

The last time Justin had been in rehab, in Minnesota in 2004, sobriety had stuck. He'd spent several months away, living in a halfway house. When he had returned to Nashville in the fall of 2004, he waited months before resuming his schedule of gigging around town.

This time was different. There was too much momentum to grind his career to a halt. No one wanted a break, least of all Justin. There was business to attend to, calls to make, shows to rebook, new management to hire, postrehab interviews to conduct, a damaged image to repair.

The Indianapolis arrest immediately and permanently altered the public's perception of Justin. It became a new line in the story Justin was forced to tell for the rest of his career, and it gave pause to the industry brokers knocking on Justin's door just months prior.

It would have been essentially career ending to put a months-long pause on the *Harlem River Blues* campaign.

So while still in rehab, Justin's team announced his rescheduled tour dates. He'd be back on the road by the end of November. In late October, barely a month after entering rehab, it was announced that Justin had signed with a new manager.[24]

Justin had first met that manager, a young man named Justin Eshak, at the 11th Street Bar sometime that August or September. Eshak worked for Mick Management, a fancy firm started by Dave Matthews's former tour manager that represented John Mayer and Ray LaMontagne, both of whom were playing to fifteen thousand fans a night. Miller, the head of Justin's scrappy Chicago label, remembered a meeting at Mick's Brooklyn office: the wired headsets, the motion-sensor doors, the glass conference rooms. The company was well equipped to help a singer like Justin Townes Earle transcend the world of Nashville-based roots music, which was exactly what Justin wanted.

When Justin emerged from rehab that autumn, he seemed a changed man: quiet, solitary, self-contained. He vacated his apartment on 11th Street. The friends he'd made at that bar, and in Manhattan, were, for the most part, excised from his life, never to hear from or see Justin again. The Josiah Early record Justin planned on producing and had been rehearsing with Early was abandoned.

"It was all pretty sudden," said one friend who'd spent time with Early and Justin. "It was like he was coming out of light speed and showed up, and then coming out of light speed disappeared."

Justin began crashing at the spacious Soho loft of his chiropractor, Dr. Allan Sicignano, who'd become a friend. He began spending more time in Nashville, where those who'd witnessed Justin over the past year couldn't believe how reserved and soft-spoken he now seemed.

"I watched a troubled man come out the other side," said Derek Hoke, who'd seen Justin consume a half bottle of vodka before taking the stage just months prior. Hoke had begun hosting a weekly show called $2 Tuesdays at the East Nashville dive bar the 5 Spot.

That fall, Hoke remembered Justin regularly showing up to $2 Tuesdays by himself, sitting alone at a side table as he spent the evening drinking a soda or a glass of water while watching music from East Nashville newcomers he either knew or had likely, in some way, inspired.

The last time Justin had gotten sober, in 2004, he was an anonymous songwriter. Now he was a nationally known entertainer with a newly bolstered rock-star reputation. When he resumed touring in the fall of 2010, those accompanying Justin on the road could now see how much effort he exerted, each night, to protect himself. No alcohol of any kind was allowed backstage. Justin kept to himself, secluded with Spratlin, who, like Davies, resumed touring with Justin now that he was sober.

Spratlin had gotten close to Justin, and their relationship began to move beyond work. When Justin went to rehab, "both of us realized we cared about each other," she told a journalist soon after. They did their best to ignore their feelings, to be as professional as possible, she explained, but eventually, "we kind of gave in."[25]

Spratlin was drawn in by Justin's wit, by his inappropriate sense of humor and charm. "I was constantly entertained," she said. "I was going to say laughing, but a lot of it would be like, 'Oh my God, Justin, you know you can't say that. What is wrong with your brain? Why did it go *there*?'"

Spratlin's job as tour manager had changed drastically. She was now romantically involved with Justin and simultaneously tasked with insulating him from the realities of touring Florida punk bars and Memphis rock clubs as a newly sober man. Justin went to recovery meetings on the road, but it was infrequent, nothing like his daily commitment to meetings back in 2005.

Spratlin, like everyone else, much preferred sober Justin. Protecting him from substances and fans who wanted to party with the badass singer who'd just gone to jail was exhausting, but it was nothing compared to trying to keep him alive. "Less anger, less weird outbursts, more eating ice cream," she said.

Meanwhile, his team kicked into gear to relaunch the *Harlem River Blues* campaign. Good news quickly arrived: Justin had been booked as the musical guest on the *Late Show with David Letterman*, an enormous platform for an independent singer-songwriter.

On January 5, 2011, the day after his twenty-ninth birthday, Justin arrived at the Ed Sullivan Theater in Manhattan for *Letterman*. He brought a hastily assembled band: Davies, drummer Rob Heath, backup singers Dawn Landes and Julia Haltigan, and Isbell on guitar.

Back in Chicago, the folks at Bloodshot were anxious. No one at his label had so much as spoken to Justin since rehab.

Across the country, friends, family, and admirers stayed up late for Justin's television debut. Steve Earle tuned in. In Nashville, worry vanished into pride as past acquaintances saw Justin transform the *Letterman* stage into the Chicken Shack. In Milwaukee, Justin's first agent, June Lehman, broke into a grin.

In Chicago, Bloodshot employees gathered around a television screen at a bar. Around 11:30 p.m., the bar turned down the music and cranked up the volume on the TV.

"Our next guest is a talented singer-songwriter," announced Letterman, holding up a copy of *Harlem River Blues*.[26]

The organ from Letterman's bandleader, Paul Shaffer, kicked off "Harlem River Blues," and there was Justin, in a tan suit and a black bow tie, craning his neck over the too-short mic stand as he sang his tale of dirty-water deliverance.

It took no more than thirty seconds for the mood at the Chicago bar to turn from unease to ecstasy. The Justin Townes Earle that Rob Miller saw on television was the one who'd so captivated him the first time he'd seen him perform: the determination, the jubilation, the nervous energy that could hardly be contained, the intensity with which Justin stared into the middle distance as he sang about his own absolution.

Justin nodded and shook his head as he sang about the ending he'd avoided, the flood that had risen yet subsided, the fate he'd tempted yet refused. He sang the tale with the clarity and conviction of a man who'd tasted the "carrying over" and didn't like what he'd seen. At the end of the song, he flashed an enormous smile.

After the taping, Landes, one of the backup singers, remembered catching a glance of Justin in the corner of the dressing room. There was something about the way he looked as he placed his guitar back in his case that struck her. Landes had spent weeks on the road opening for Justin, but she'd never seen him carry himself like that. It was something she could barely articulate, but she remembered being able to tell, as he conducted his solitary ritual of putting away his guitar, that, in that moment, Justin Townes Earle was truly proud of himself.

Back in Chicago, after the bar erupted upon the final notes of "Harlem River Blues," Rob Miller stepped outside into the cold and started to cry. He cried tears of relief for his business and tears of happiness for Justin. Maybe his record label would be okay. Maybe this young man he'd grown so fond of would survive.

In his notes from that evening, Miller summed up how it'd felt watching Justin triumph on TV. "FANTASTIC. Much toasting and cheering from the full room," he wrote. "A moment to savor."

PART III

Looking for a Place to Land

CHAPTER 16

IT TOOK THE STOCK MARKET CRASH OF 1929 FOR JIMMIE COX TO FINALLY get a hit record. It was called "Nobody Knows You When You're Down and Out," and it told the story of a once-rich man who loses everything: friends, life savings, a sense of self. The narrator reflects on his past life of merriment and revelry, how he'd once spent his days fraternizing and throwing around money, showering company with "bootleg liquor, champagne and wine."

Now, having squandered his millions, the narrator is abandoned and broke. "In my pocket, not one penny," he decries. "And my friends, I haven't any." Cox's anthem of misfortune would eventually become an American standard, with countless singers across genres, centuries, identities, and circumstances recording the song. One of those singers was Justin Townes Earle, who connected with the song's abject alienation and suffering. This was a knack of Justin's: letting songs others had written that articulated a profound loneliness—the Replacements' "Can't Hardly Wait," Malcolm Holcombe's "Who Carried You"—speak for his own.

Born in 1882 into the horror of post-Reconstruction Richmond, Jimmie Cox began performing at age ten. His debut as an entertainer was traveling in a minstrel show called South Before the War, as one of many Black performers whose job was to demonstrate the "the happy days of slavery."[1]

As he aged, Cox cycled through his own series of acts on the grueling vaudeville circuit: the Georgia Red Hots, the Buddie Austin Players, the Cox Trio, the Jimmie Cox Revue, and "Black Charlie Chaplin," his impersonation of the era's biggest movie star. He traveled the segregated South as a duo with his wife, eventually incorporating a child star—"Baby Cox"—into their show, which was so popular he opened a Baby Cox candy store in Atlanta.

Cox wrote songs to accompany his various acts. About five a month, he claimed. He sang, danced, tapped his feet, cracked jokes, and did whatever he needed to make crowds clap. He'd lived several lives' worth of hustling, entertaining, and indignity when, in 1921, an impostor started stealing his money: Several times that year, Cox arrived at a venue where he was due to perform only to find out that someone posing as him had already collected the promoter's advance payment.

Incensed, Cox wrote to *Billboard*, desperate to distance himself from his fraudulent impersonators. "I have been on the square all my life," he pleaded.

It's impossible to know exactly which combination of injustices and frustrations inspired Cox to write his most famous song. But around this time, Cox wrote "Nobody Knows You When You're Down and Out," copyrighting the composition in 1923, shortly after the impersonator scandal. At first, the song was a modest success, covered in a variety of styles: spoken-word boogie-woogie, maudlin piano ballad, country blues.[2] Then, in 1929, a month before the stock market crashed, Columbia Records released a version by Bessie Smith, the Empress of the Blues. Smith's version embodied a collective mourning for the Roaring Twenties and "quickly became the theme song of the Great Depression," writes Gene Anderson, a musicologist whose writing on Cox provides the most comprehensive account of the singer's life and career.

Over the next century, scores of singers would sing and record the tune: Nina Simone, Sam Cooke, Van Morrison, Otis Redding, Neko Case, Eric Clapton, B.B. King, Duane Allman, Roberta Flack, Janis Joplin, José Feliciano, Rod Stewart, Esquerita, Dave Van Ronk, Bobby Womack.

In the spring of 2011, Justin Townes Earle started singing it, too. Like so many others who'd recorded Cox's ballad, Justin hadn't navigated being a Black entertainer in the era of blackface minstrelsy, nor had he ever experienced a fraction of the violence, hatred, or marginalization that came with being a Black man in the post-Reconstruction South. But he recognized himself in Cox's tale of existential exhaustion and rejection.

"Nobody Knows You When You're Down and Out" became a mainstay in Justin's set list for the following two years. He'd first played it in the Swindlers, and the band had made a slight but meaningful lyrical change: "Nobody *loves* you when you're down and out."[3]

That's one way to put it.

"I am a thirty-one-year-old ex-junkie with abandonment issues" is another. That's what Justin tweeted in the summer of 2013, a period when he was often still singing Cox's song.[4]

Justin turned to the tune during a period of utmost turbulence in his career, a period of personal change, in which he cut ties with many people from his past and, eventually, began one of the most important relationships of his life. These years began with the fallout following Justin's arrest in Indianapolis and subsequent trip to rehab, and they were defined by the immense effort Justin put into climbing back from that setback, as well as the crushing expectations that followed him wherever he now turned.

As 2011 began, Justin's calendar was still filled with promise thanks to the excitement surrounding *Harlem River Blues*. Full of bluster and bravado, yet still nursing his wounds about what had happened in Indianapolis, Justin Townes Earle declared he was moving to London.

"I'm going to take a year to live in Europe and concentrate on that market," he told *Billboard* in February 2011.[5]

Relocating to London would open a world of travel and freedom that made the East Village of New York seem provincial. "It's about being able to go to Marrakesh or Barcelona on the weekend," he explained.[6]

Justin never moved to London. When the same *Billboard* journalist followed up with him about the move, just months later, he'd already reversed course.

"That was before this girl came along," Justin said. "I have to say, me going to England was just gonna be another example of me running to another place, and I'm finally at the point in my life where I have somebody that I love."[7]

That somebody was Lauren Spratlin, who by mid-2011 was in a serious romantic relationship with Justin in addition to being his tour manager. Justin had given up his 11th Street New York apartment after the rent skyrocketed from $400 to $2,400. Though he still sporadically crashed at his chiropractor's Soho loft, he was basically done with New York, little more than two years after uprooting his life to move there.

He started spending more time at Spratlin's home in Nashville. The couple didn't formally discuss moving in together, but they gradually realized Justin no longer lived anywhere else.

In any case, Justin toured so often it didn't make sense to pay rent anywhere. "I am going to be homeless for the next six months," he tweeted. "Gotta get ready to ramble!"[8]

Justin spent 2011 promoting *Harlem River Blues* all over the world: in Europe, where he toured twice; at festivals, which he spent the entire summer playing; and on a high-profile amphitheater run opening for the Decemberists. He appeared on Carson Daly's late-night show and graced the cover of *American Songwriter* magazine.

But by his own account, in the first half of 2011 Justin had a heroin relapse that almost killed him.[9] The trouble started where it often did, in Australia, where Justin once again spent the month of April touring. The six-foot-four singer frequently suffered from back pain, which wasn't improved by his habit of slamming his feet onstage as percussion and craning his neck over microphone stands. In Australia, Justin said, he began taking codeine, which, during this relatively nascent stage of the opioid crisis, was readily available over the counter.

"By the time I came back" to the United States, he told Associated Press reporter Chris Talbott later that year, "I was fucked."[10]

Back on tour in America that spring, Justin's use of heavy narcotics increased. He was now spending thirty minutes at a time in the bathroom, forcing bandmates to wait for him in greenrooms and highway rest stops. When he was using, he could be a commandeering and controlling boss: monitoring where bandmates Bryn Davies and Amanda Shires (who'd replaced Hedley on fiddle) went during nights off, castigating them on the off chance they showed up late for sound check, dictating when the group could and couldn't take bathroom breaks while driving.

Shires tried to keep her friend's behavior in perspective: Behind his attempts at control, mood swings, and trashing of dressing rooms when the slightest thing went wrong, she believed the Justin she knew was still there, somewhere behind his substance use.

Still, Justin was in a new state of crisis and told his band as much.

"He basically said, 'If you guys don't want to see me going down this road, I'm giving you an out right now,'" recalled Bryn Davies, his bassist at the time.

It became difficult for Davies to follow Justin's unpredictable timing onstage. It became even tougher to watch him play. One musician who'd seen Justin perform throughout 2010 was alarmed when he caught his set that spring. "It was like all the pieces of the music were happening," he said, "but they weren't synced up."

With support from Spratlin and medical professionals, Justin eventually confronted his intertwining mental health and addiction struggles with a series of prescribed medications. Chief among them was Suboxone. Like methadone, Suboxone's active ingredient is a synthetic low-grade opioid called buprenorphine used to treat opioid-use disorders. Unlike methadone, typically administered at a clinic, Suboxone can be taken via oral strips, making it well suited for a constantly touring musician.

The drug helped Justin make it through each day. But he eventually started mixing Suboxone with large quantities of marijuana, and those around him noticed that his day-to-day demeanor seemed to be affected, his speech slowing dramatically. Suboxone also wasn't the only serious prescribed medication he was taking.

When a journalist asked Justin what his favorite medication was in 2011, Justin didn't hesitate. "My Seroquel," he responded, referring to the antipsychotic prescribed for conditions including bipolar disorder, depression, and schizophrenia.[11]

That question came during a rapid-style Q&A with *New York Magazine*, the type of mainstream press he was now receiving. Justin injected his dark seriousness into the interview's lightweight, rapid-fire Q&A premise, mixing local restaurant recommendations (he loved Cafe Mogador in the East Village) with confessions about his mental state.

Who is your mortal enemy?

"Heroin," he responded.

In one sentence, what do you actually do all day in your job?

"Hurry up and wait. But my mind is constantly bent around my songs and whirling around my songs. It actually does get in the way of my life sometimes."[12]

The Q&A was published before a big-deal performance Justin had booked at Carnegie Hall.

Performing there in December 2011, Justin told the crowd that everyone had spent the day of the show asking him if he was nervous. "Nope," he said he told them.[13] Justin Townes Earle didn't get nervous unless he was jumping onstage with Levon Helm.

But, in fact, on this evening, something was very off. His mom flew up for the show. Seeing her son perform always instilled a mix of emotions in Carol: excitement, nervousness, and, most of all, pride. But she was also apprehensive, said Michael O'Brien, her longtime boyfriend who accompanied her to many of Justin's shows, "because I'm not sure she really approved of the life he was living."

With his mom watching him up front, Justin froze. He stumbled over songs he sang every night. He forgot the lyrics to "Mama's Eyes" several times. ("One of my medications can make me fairly cloudy," he later explained. "Backstage was just full of people. I was flustered.")[14]

Spratlin watched in horror. For her, Carnegie Hall was a wake-up call, a realization of the profound effect Justin's various medications were having on his daily existence. "I was starting to think, 'Okay, you might not be drinking a case of Bud Light a day, then switching to vodka, but you're hardly sober.'"

Unlike his publicized breakdown following his altercation at the Indianapolis bar, Justin's 2011 relapse happened out of view of the press. The public narrative was that Justin's sobriety had slipped the year prior, culminating in Indianapolis and rehab, but that he was okay now. It was the same publicity playbook Justin's team had followed during his first two album cycles: Yes, Justin had relapsed, but he was now sober and in better shape than ever.

There *were* long periods when it seemed like Justin found a manageable state of mental and chemical equilibrium. And there were periods of genuine abstention from alcohol and drugs other than weed, periods when Justin's reliance on chemicals was limited to prescribed medication.

But the reality is that, after emerging from rehab in 2010, Justin spent the next decade in an unceasing struggle with his illness. Justin admitted in interviews that his month of treatment that fall hadn't miraculously cured him, that he'd contend with his illness for the remainder of his life, that he refused to promise he'd never relapse. But he withheld just as much.

It was an illness he could conceal from new friends, girlfriends, and bandmates. Regardless of how Justin was actually managing his addiction at any given time, a common narrative, from those who came to know him, is that Justin seemed to be in a really good place when they first met him: healthy, mostly sober, on top of things. When newcomers eventually saw past the well-constructed facade Justin had built around his inner life, Justin often found ways—a new phone number, an abrupt firing, a swift breakup—to cast those people out or create distance in the relationship.

With *Harlem River Blues* still taking off, Justin also started plotting his next album. He'd secured his biggest recording budget yet from Bloodshot to execute three ideas he was hell-bent on: recording outside of Nashville, recording fully live, and incorporating a full horn section.

Justin settled on a church-turned-studio called Echo Mountain in Asheville, North Carolina.

Before entering the studio, Justin tried to articulate his vision to collaborators. "The record that I kind of want y'all to listen to for, like, the idea of what I'm shooting for . . . is that first Ray LaMontagne record," he explained. "He has this acoustic soul band kind of thing, but he has this weird fiddle player that it seems like he just turned her loose and let her snake her way through the songs, and it's really cool."

Like *Harlem River Blues*, his fourth album would be coproduced by Justin and Skylar Wilson. To help with horn arrangements, Wilson enlisted his friend Jordan Lehning.

Lehning was tickled by Justin's eccentricities. There were the tall tales (Justin regaled Lehning with a story about an acid trip in Amsterdam that resulted in him seeing a fifty-foot-tall Abraham Lincoln walk across a river). Then there was the baffling behavior: When Justin came to Lehning's house to work, he sprinted from his car to the front door, claiming he didn't want his "cousins" to see him.

"He had this nervous energy: excitable, happy, talked a lot, interrupted himself all the time, would go off on these long tangents," said Lehning, before detailing a night they spent demoing songs. "But when he went into the booth and we started tracking the first song, I could just see him completely relax. I remembered thinking, '*That* is his natural habitat.' All that other shit is not normal for him."

If *Harlem River Blues* was Justin's country-gospel synthesis, his fourth album would be his first full-on foray into rhythm and blues. He'd become obsessed with Stax Records and had been thinking about Charlie Rich's 1973 country-soul hit "Behind Closed Doors." He wanted to make a record that sounded like *that*.

Retro soul had, over the past few years, become en vogue, from Amy Winehouse to Sharon Jones to Raphael Saadiq. By 2011, white soul revivalists like Eli "Paperboy" Reed and Mayer Hawthorne were receiving major-label deals. The biggest pop breakthrough of the year had been a twenty-two-year-old British soul balladeer named Adele.

It's unclear how much Justin paid attention to this soul-revivalist craze, but he was aware enough of the phenomenon to offer a caveat when teasing his forthcoming record that fall. "Don't worry," he said, "it's not a white boy soul explosion."[15]

Several years before contemporaries like Chris Stapleton, Sturgill

Simpson, and Margo Price had similar ideas, Justin viewed soul and R&B as natural roots-music reference points.

"We had the alt-country nineties thing where everybody did every kind of music in the world with a little bit of twang," Justin said. "I thought, 'Why is that the only roots music that people have gone into and tried to innovate?' I wondered why soul hadn't been tried."[16]

The resulting record, *Nothing's Gonna Change the Way You Feel About Me Now,* was a moody, midnight soul-jazz statement, more Tom Waits than Tom T. Hall. It mixed wounded pleas that pointed fingers at both parents ("Movin' On," "Look the Other Way," "Am I That Lonely Tonight?"), R&B raves ("Baby's Got a Bad Idea"), and a bitter title track, which Justin said was influenced by heroin use.[17]

As he'd done on each album to date, Justin also reached back to his Swindlers-era songbook. It had been a long, difficult year, and he didn't have a full record of new material: "Maria" and "Down on the Lower East Side" were both Swindlers regulars. One song, "Memphis in the Rain," lifted the melody and chord progression from a Swindlers tune called "Back Home in Tennessee." He even considered including a Distributors-era rocker called "The City Tonight."

But the album—somber, slow, and serious—shared little in common with his previous records. Several covers recorded during the sessions—"Hang Down Your Head" by Tom Waits, "Nobody Knows You When You're Down and Out"—represented his new headspace.[18] Justin sang with a pronounced weariness, slowing down his phrasing and singing, almost woozily, behind the beat, something several of those involved with the record felt was influenced by his new Suboxone prescription.

The song that best represented the moodiness of Justin's fourth LP was "Down on the Lower East Side," with its almost Sinatra-esque arrangement. Singing over a muted trumpet, Justin tells the story of a dejected narrator walking down the streets of downtown Manhattan alone in the rain. "The city is unforgiving," he sings, "when you've got no one to love."

When he wrote it with Dustin Welch a decade prior, the song was their take on the "country boy in the big city" trope: two Nashville teens' romanticization of Manhattan malaise, written, Justin said, after his first trip to New York.

The version on *Nothing's Gonna Change* is a much different song from what Justin sang with the Swindlers: less rootsy, wearier. Now that Justin had lived out the one-act play of East Village ennui he'd written for himself years ago, wandering around 11th Street alone at three in the morning no longer seemed so glamorous. In reality, it almost killed him.

Justin had survived 11th Street, but *Nothing's Gonna Change* was a testament to the toll the past two years had taken.

His latest songs were personal to the point of confrontation, taking specific aim at his parents. Before the album came out, Justin claimed he gave his dad's wife, Allison Moorer, a heads-up "because this fucking record's really heavy with daddy issues."[19]

On the upbeat soulful single "Look the Other Way," Justin pleads with "mama": "you're never gonna notice / if you always look the other way." Justin's maternal aunt, Judy Hilton, could sense the autobiographical pain lurking beneath the catchy tune. "The first time I heard that song, I thought, 'Wow, he's talking about Carol,'" she said.

When Carol was brought up in an interview, in relation to "Look the Other Way," Justin barely sidestepped the question. "I think everyone at some point has been disappointed by their mother," he said.[20]

Justin's relationship to his father, at least as Justin portrayed it in public, hadn't become easier. He told one journalist that when he went to his dad's place, he saw the same shrink-wrapped copy of his album on his dad's countertop. "I don't know if he ever listened to *Harlem River Blues*," Justin said. "My dad means well, but he gets all over the place sometimes. He's just like me, scattered as shit."[21]

Steve, for his part, could be ornery when asked about Justin in interviews. "I wish he could come see his brother more, but he's doing what I was doing," Steve told a reporter in 2011. "He has a record out and things are going pretty well and he's touring."[22]

CHAPTER 17

When they were not touring, Justin and Spratlin were building their life in a home on Blair Boulevard in Nashville, not far from where Justin grew up. They enjoyed quiet Scrabble nights with couple friends Jason Isbell and Amanda Shires as well as singer-songwriter Cory Branan and his then-wife, Rebecca. Isbell tended to win. Justin tended to get so much loose weed and tobacco from the spliffs he rolled all over the place that Isbell would spend the rest of the evening vacuuming.

Justin had already known Shires for years, as both friend and bandmate, but he and Isbell grew very close. When Isbell and Shires got married in February 2013, Justin purchased Isbell a three-piece Billy Reid suit for his big day. Their relationship was rooted in mutual admiration and the shared struggle of staying sober. Justin talked about Isbell at his concerts[1] and listened to advance copies of his music while on tour.

When *The New York Times Magazine* prepared a feature on Isbell on the verge of his next album, *Southeastern*, his 2013 breakthrough that chronicled his newfound sobriety, Justin granted a rare interview about his friend, cracking jokes with the biggest newspaper in the country.

"When I sit around and talk with Jason, he can sound, just as I can, like a dumb redneck," Justin said. "But put him on paper, or behind a guitar, and he can fly."[2]

Isbell returned the favor, boasting about Justin in advance of 2013's Newport Folk Festival. "Justin Townes Earle writes songs that appeal to the uncontrollable parts of me," he wrote. "He's unafraid to shed light on his mistakes . . . and unburdened by the constraints of outside expectations. . . . I may be biased; Justin and I are good friends. Still, I doubt we'd be so close if I wasn't such a fan."[3]

Justin had released his fourth album, *Nothing's Gonna Change*, to great reviews. He'd produced a record for another artist—a longtime goal—rockabilly legend Wanda Jackson's *Unfinished Business*. He'd also made a life-changing upgrade to touring on a bus after years of traveling in Sprinter vans. His cell phone's ringtone had once been "Only the Lonely"; now it was Al Green's "Love and Happiness." Justin would spend hours writing, simultaneously watching Ken Burns's *Baseball* in his basement full of antique knickknacks. Outside, in his front yard, he would often prune rose bushes with an enormous joint in his mouth.

In December of 2012, Justin and Spratlin drove up and down the California coast—on what he called a "Christmas-money tour"—playing club gigs, opening for John Prine, and stopping at the beach in between shows.

Spratlin remembered these times as carefree and adventurous. She also recalled moments when Justin would throw a wrench into their moments of peace—or lash out in a way that recalled his past. In November 2012, a few friends of theirs rented an Airbnb in East Tennessee for a few days.

The trip went well, even after Justin got horribly lost driving alone, having ignored the directions Spratlin gave him to the location. (He was convinced that years of visiting Scotty Melton in the mountains had taught him how to get anywhere in Tennessee east of Knoxville.)

They ate tacos, smoked weed, wandered into shops selling gold in downtown Gatlinburg, and relaxed. But when they were leaving the next day, the morning of Thanksgiving, Justin was set off when someone wished him a happy holiday.

"I don't celebrate that!" he snapped. He launched into a diatribe about how he hated Thanksgiving and how he refused to celebrate the slaughter of Native Americans.

The outburst came as no surprise to Spratlin. Even if she agreed with Justin's political reasoning, she knew he was having an emotional response to something else—in this case, the reaction was a reflection of Justin's discomfort with holidays. Whenever Spratlin's parents were around for gatherings, Justin withdrew. Suddenly, there was work he needed to take care of.

"He was so afraid of opening himself up to normal, open, close relationships," she said. "Justin was so scarred by his childhood that when things started to look normal, like, 'Oh, cool, we have a house, and a dog, and we're happy,' he would be like, 'Better hit the "Shit" button.'"

"I think I thrive on chaos," Justin tweeted in 2011. "Fuck that cant be good."[4]

In January 2013, Justin was driving himself and Spratlin to the airport when he tossed an engagement ring into her lap.

Spratlin was surprised and, at first, confused. It hadn't helped that Justin barely said anything when he tossed a ring at her. When he explained that he was, indeed, asking Spratlin if she wanted to get married, it didn't go well. Spratlin said no without saying much of anything else, and the two continued to the airport for an uncomfortable few weeks of touring in Australia.

The proposal helped Spratlin realize their relationship had run its course. As Justin's live-in girlfriend and road manager, she'd become his entire support system. He relied on her to manage his daily existence: helping him stay on top of his meds, getting him from one place to the next, dealing with his business affairs, managing his moods after furious outbursts. Justin's desire to provide emotional support to Spratlin, in return, had outrun his ability to actually do so. All of it was taking a toll.

They broke up that spring, but their professional and personal lives had become intertwined. They shared friends and colleagues. After their split, Spratlin immediately stopped working with Justin, who lashed out, attempting to wield power over Spratlin, who was several years younger, by threatening her future job prospects as a tour manager.

"He was really trying to do the whole 'You're not going to work in this town again' thing," she said.

Publicly, he weaponized his spite and self-pity, tweeting through his postbreakup loneliness. Privately, his actions started isolating him from his peers, forcing them to take sides. Justin resented those who didn't side with him. It was something he remained fixated on for years, sussing out whether one future opening act was friends with his ex-girlfriend before hiring them.

Shortly after the breakup, Isbell hired Spratlin to be *his* tour manager. The two friends stopped speaking. "'You're not a loyal friend,'" Isbell claimed Justin yelled at him, explaining the rift on Marc Maron's podcast the following year. "He just got really mad about it. . . . He was pissed off that we took her out on the road. . . . He'll get over it."[5]

Justin Townes Earle never did get over it. He viewed Isbell's hiring of Spratlin, and his seeming siding with her after their ugly breakup, as the ultimate betrayal. There were certainly other complicating factors that impacted their abrupt split: the difficulty of maintaining a relationship between two friends with histories of addiction when one person (Isbell) gets completely sober; the competition between two headstrong entertainers as Isbell, whose breakthrough, *Southeastern*, was released during this exact period, became far more successful than Justin; the complex industry ties in the tight-knit town of Nashville (Isbell's manager was Traci Thomas, who'd had an acrimonious split with Justin).

But their fight over Spratlin cemented a permanent rupture.

When Justin appeared at the Newport Folk Festival that July, he took the stage directly after Isbell, who was at the festival with Spratlin. Had Newport taken place only two months earlier, the back-to-back booking could've felt like a reunion of two old friends.

Much had changed. While at Newport, Justin fired off a vile tweet that further alienated him from everyone who'd known him and Spratlin as a couple.

"Any fans see my ex at Newport today?" he wrote in a soon-to-be-deleted tweet. "Spit on her and get tickets for life."[6]

Justin's breakup with Spratlin came as he was grieving his beloved maternal grandmother, Norma, who'd introduced him to baseball as a child by taking him to Nashville Sounds games. She'd died at age seventy-three in March 2013.

Justin was also attempting to assume a more hands-on role looking after his mother, now that he was back in Nashville. He'd helped Carol buy a two-bedroom house in West Nashville and kept in close communication with her boyfriend. "I would do anything for her," he explained.[7] Still, Justin worried constantly about his mom. If Carol didn't respond to his calls, he'd leave his house to check up on her.

The responsibilities of caring for his mother sometimes overwhelmed him so much he'd puncture the protective public image he typically painted of her. One day in May 2013, Justin pleaded, on Twitter, for anyone who worked in the Middle Tennessee mental health system to please contact him. "I have a situation at home," he explained.[8]

That night, onstage, he told a crowd his mom had been "kind of losing her mind" over the past few years and, just the night before, had been temporarily held for observation. "They better get ready for a battle with the lawyers," Justin told the audience, "because I ain't letting them keep my fucking mother." Then he launched into "Mama's Eyes."[9]

Two months later, he posted a photo of his latest tattoo: a rose adorned with the word *Mother*.[10]

Justin's family turmoil, nasty breakup, and largely self-induced isolation in the wake of that breakup all made it hard for him to write songs. When his new touring manager, Kevin Morrow, moved in with Justin for a short period, he was struck by the level of creative block his boss seemed to be experiencing. Justin spent the first half of 2013 writing songs for what would be his next record; it had been a year and a half since recording *Nothing's Gonna Change*, his longest break between recording sessions.

But for the first time in his career, he was having difficulty identifying a concept that would bring those songs together. He planned on making an album in May 2013, but that never happened. He told a reporter he was planning on making a "post-doo-wop, rock 'n' roll record."[11] He was adjusting to writing while taking his variety of prescribed medications. He was distracted. He scribbled songs in his office and then threw away much of what he wrote. "Justin felt he didn't have enough material," said Morrow. "But what I saw was that he had so much material that he couldn't put it together."

Justin tasked Morrow with reaching out to his management when he needed a cash advance or to help stonewall them when they inquired about the next record.

At some point, Justin and his longtime collaborator Skylar Wilson, who'd coproduced Justin's last two records and had become Justin's go-to creative partner in the studio, went into Nashville's RCA Studio A to record a new song. It was called "Farther from Me," and Justin cut the song in a horn-heavy soul arrangement reminiscent of *Nothing's Gonna Change*. But, as Wilson recalled, the results seemed to give Justin's team pause.

Shortly thereafter, Wilson and Justin went to a Nashville Sounds baseball game. At the stadium, Wilson broached an awkward conversation: He told Justin, as delicately as he could, that some of the new material he'd been writing was, perhaps, not his best work. "It was an odd rest of the game," Wilson recalled.

Justin never worked with Wilson again.

CHAPTER 18

JENNIFER MARIE MAYNARD HAD AN ITINERANT CHILDHOOD. GROWING up, she and her brother moved between various family homes—in Park City, Utah; in Kawaii, Hawaii; in Southern California—from season to season. Sometimes she stayed with relatives in Arkansas and Virginia. Maynard loved the outdoors and from a young age took to whatever outdoor sport—downhill skiing, horseback riding, surfing, waterskiing—was popular in the various environments she constantly moved between. Her father was an enigmatic businessman always traveling for work. Her parents divorced when she was in grade school, after which she didn't see much of her mother.

In high school in Los Angeles, she found refuge in music, sneaking into Cat Power and Social Distortion shows at the Knitting Factory with her fake ID. She got a job at a record store in Long Beach. She started teaching Pilates as a teenager. She moved back and forth between California and the tiny town of Pangburn, Arkansas, where she became part of the country-punk music scene in nearby Memphis, befriending musicians and songwriters.

In her twenties, Jenn Marie moved to Salt Lake City, bought a house, and started her own business: a Pilates and Gyrotonic studio called En Route Movement. The free-spirited wanderer who'd spent much of her young adulthood seeking extreme adventure and constant change was ready to stop racing around the country. "I'd moved so much that I wanted to prove to myself I can stay somewhere: 'How deep can I sink my roots?'" she said.

All the while, Jenn Marie stayed connected with the group of musicians and bands she'd befriended in Memphis. Some of them, like the band Lucero, got bigger and started touring. When they passed through town, Jenn Marie loved providing these smelly musicians with a home-cooked meal, fresh-baked cookies, and a floor to crash on. On weekends, she hosted brunch gatherings for the group of Salt Lake musicians, tattoo artists, and painters she'd befriended. Growing up primarily with her brother and father, caretaking and cooking were familiar roles for Jenn Marie. "I was a housewife, essentially," she said of her childhood.

At some point back in Arkansas, Jenn Marie had crossed paths with a rabble-rousing young songwriter named Justin Earle. "I remember seeing him and thinking, 'He's tall, he's interesting,'" she remembered. "He wore baggy pants and was definitely a different version of himself." In those adolescent days, she remembered a friend's warning: "He's great," the friend said. "But he's trouble." This, unfortunately, only intrigued Jenn Marie more: "I was always pushing the limits, keeping up with the boys," she said, "so I was always drawn to the harsher ones that were a challenge."

Jenn Marie and Justin met again at one of Justin's shows in Salt Lake City in December 2012, but it was a platonic encounter: Justin was dating Spratlin at the time, and the two hung out in a larger group after Justin's show. They really hit it off the following summer, in July 2013, when Justin returned to Salt Lake City to perform at a festival.

"We were just enthralled with one another, in a 'I really want to get to know you deeply' [way]," she said.

Their connection progressed so quickly that when Jenn Marie mentioned to Justin that she had an upcoming shoulder surgery, Justin asked if she'd move the date of the operation: He had time off in late September and wanted to return to Utah to help take care of her as she recovered.

Justin and Jenn Marie spent the next two months flying across the country visiting one another. On one early trip, Jenn visited Justin in Denton, Texas, where Justin was rehearsing with his new touring band: guitarist Paul Niehaus, plus bassist Mark Hedman and drummer Matt Pence, the rhythm section from Centro-Matic, a cult indie-roots band Justin adored.

In Texas, Justin and Jenn went swimming at a lake, bought kolaches from a roadside bakery, and drove around as Justin sang Jenn Marie a new tune he'd written called "Worried Bout the Weather." They talked about their complicated, confusing childhoods; their love for finding the best off-the-beaten-path antique shop wherever they went. During one of those early conversations, Justin told Jenn Marie he wanted an old-fashioned rocking chair.

One morning in Nashville that September, Justin awoke to a vintage rocking chair outside on his front porch. Justin posted a photo of the chair, proud as ever: "Antique angels must be around."[1]

Affixed to the chair, which Jenn Marie had delivered after scouring Craigslist, was a note. *A place for you to land*, it said.

Jenn Marie rescheduled her surgery. She was skeptical of this musician's romantic promise to help her recover, so she made contingency plans with friends, in case he bailed.

When Justin showed up after driving sixteen hundred miles from Nashville, Jenn Marie knew she was deeply, irreversibly in love. "I am fucking *toast*," she thought as he walked through her front gate with a fresh haircut. Justin spent the week taking care of her. "I wasn't used to that," she said.

In October 2013, three months after they started dating, Justin Townes Earle and Jennifer Marie Maynard were married in the woods above Lake Tahoe in California. They'd planned their elopement a few days prior, in San Francisco, where Justin performed at the Hardly Strictly Bluegrass festival. On the way from San Francisco to Lake Tahoe, they stopped into a store in the town of Vacaville and picked out an engagement ring. They wore jeans and flannel as they pledged their vows in a private ceremony, just the two of them and an officiant, in the pine trees above the lake late at night. A scarf of Justin's had torn in two, and the couple each wore one half of it during the ceremony.

They left their parents out of their wedding. "Our families tend to complicate our lives," Justin said. "We thought this is our day and has nothing to do with anybody else, and we shouldn't have to run around on our wedding day and take care of people."[2]

Justin even kept his wedding plans from his then-roommate and tour manager, Kevin Morrow. "He said this girl was a good friend, that's all he would call her," said Morrow. Justin went dark, ignoring texts and calls for days, as Morrow tried coordinating Justin's upcoming touring. Then, Morrow said, "I get a call from him one day, and he's like, 'You're never gonna guess.' I'm like, 'Guess what?' And he's like, 'I'm a married man.'"

Justin was smitten with Jenn Marie; he loved how different yet relatable their lives had been, like they'd existed on a parallel plane. In interviews, he talked her up, rarely revealing anything too intimate. He loved how outdoorsy she was, referring to her in the press as a professional downhill skier. He loved how she'd exposed him to the beauty of the West: Guardsman Pass in Utah, Pagosa Springs in Colorado. He loved that she was nearly as tall as him. He felt flooded by the warmth and kindness she radiated. "Every time I look at her," he said, "I absolutely adore the woman."[3]

They'd met during one of the lowest times in Justin's life. "I was expecting the wheels to come off," said his friend Andy Moore. "And quite the opposite happened."[4]

Before he met Jenn Marie, Justin said he'd "lost complete faith in [the idea] . . . that I could sustain a positive relationship."[5]

In Jenn Marie, he found someone who felt like home. Justin declared that their lifelong commitment had lifted his fears and doubts. "I have somebody who has promised to take care of me and I believe will, which is a massive, massive change," he said. "Before I met my wife, I had lost faith in women and love and life wasn't far behind. . . . But the feeling that comes from that person that you know is going to be there for you is the most overwhelming thing on the face of the earth."[6]

"I went west stopped short of the coast and got lost in the mountains of Utah," he wrote in his journals. "I've really never known what to look for but I got lucky, I was found."

Even in private, Justin was particular about word choice. He realized there was a better way to describe what happened. He scribbled out a word: "I got lucky," he wrote, "I ~~was~~ got found."

A few days after they got married, Jenn Marie said her first goodbye to her husband. They were back in Utah, and Justin needed to resume his busy fall of touring. He set out for the long drive back to Nashville. A day or so later, Jenn received some disturbing news: Justin was in jail.

He had stopped off a highway to sleep in his car, which resulted in the Aurora, Nebraska, police department charging him with several misdemeanors for possession of marijuana and a concealed firearm.

Jenn Marie immediately got on a plane to bail out her husband. "I ended up having to fly to Lincoln, Nebraska, with my arm in a sling, newly married, and totally confused," she said. Justin paid a fine and was released from jail.

Justin's dishevelment had always been a part of his life as a touring musician. "There was many a time when a panic-stricken promoter would come running in, literally minutes before showtime, going 'Where is he?'" said Simon Gardner, one of Justin's longtime European tour managers. "And then he would literally walk through the door five minutes before showtime."

But his unpredictability, lack of communication, and penchant for going AWOL were starting to hurt his career. By late 2013, Justin's affiliation with his high-powered management firm had grown strained. His managers were frustrated by the lack of progress on his next album. He was ignoring their phone calls and emails. In November, a month after getting married, Justin was informed that Mick Management would be dropping him as a client.

That same fall, with his Bloodshot Records deal having expired, Justin was in talks with a prospective label, Communion Music, cofounded by Mumford & Sons' Ben Lovett. For a musician making acoustic music in the first few years of the 2010s, there was no bigger name to be associated with than Mumford & Sons. The British quartet's kick-drum catharsis in songs like 2009's "Little Lion Man" and 2012's "I Will Wait" had smuggled banjo onto pop radio and helped usher in an unexpected moment as acoustic-based acts like the Lumineers and Of Monsters and Men scored Top 40 hits.

By 2013, music branded and marketed as Americana/folk had an outsize mainstream appeal. Someone like Justin, who'd fashioned himself after obscure, anticommercial musicians like Mance Lipscomb and Malcolm Holcombe, was receiving mainstream opportunities simply by association.

When Mumford & Sons organized their own traveling festival, they invited groups harvesting the retro-roots-boom enthusiasm of the moment—Old Crow Medicine Show, Dawes, Simone Felice (who'd recently left the Felice Brothers), Alabama Shakes—to join them. They also invited Justin Townes Earle, who they viewed as a real-deal representation of the Americana music Mumford was exposing to mass audiences. "JTE is the coolest man in the game and that is why we are so nervous about having him play the Stopover fest," read a statement from the band around this time. "Everyone will realize (if they haven't already) what frauds we are."[7]

When Justin began searching for a new record label to elevate his career, the Mumford-associated Communion Music seemed like a smart fit. But after a series of negotiations with the label, Justin's deal fell apart. Sources involved differed on exactly who, or what, was to blame for the breakdown between parties. But at the heart of the dispute, according to most, was creative control. Justin was hell-bent on being the sole arbiter of his work. Unlike at Bloodshot, which let Justin operate with complete autonomy, Communion wanted a say in which of Justin's songs best fitted his next record, which songs worked as singles—typical label feedback Justin wasn't interested in receiving. "He was really insulted that they thought he should have his material vetted," said Mark Hedman, Justin's bassist at the time. "He thought of them as *his* protégés."

Justin went public with his grievances. "I have now learned that you can never trust a bunch of babies that ain't worked a day in their lives," he tweeted.[8] The deal was dead.

Justin ended 2013 in professional limbo. He had no label and no manager, and he had severed ties with his producer. He'd developed a reputation as a difficult artist who was hard to manage.

Justin later described this period of career crisis in essayistic reflections in his journal, one of the only known times he wrote about his life in prose. "Music has an ugly side," he wrote, "and it is the business."

He felt completely burned out. "I went off the map," he wrote. "Spent days reading, driving in the country and feeding my lust for antiques. I was in a down place. I never answard the phone, never called anybody, spent days in my basement office."

And he wrote about how he was being perceived, how his actions impacted others. "My friend[s] all worried, as they always do," he wrote. "It was not the first time."

CHAPTER 19

In Utah, Justin's career troubles felt far away. At least that's how Jenn Marie mostly remembered their first few months of marriage: as a sweet and short-lived period in which Justin moved into her tiny seven-hundred-square-foot home in Salt Lake City. "We just made it super-cozy," she said.

The couple took walks around the city and went on road trips around the West. Justin eventually graduated from writing songs in Jenn Marie's bathroom to taking over a rolltop desk in the house, where he sat with his scattered belongings and scribbled lyrics.

After a year or more of stumbling, Justin finally wrote a song that made him proud. He was prouder of this one, in fact, than anything he'd ever written. The composition, which he toiled over in his journals, honored one of his heroes, Billie Holiday. The jazz singer was on Justin's mind; he'd watched a Holiday documentary and listened to her music constantly. He identified with the way Holiday's agency was stripped from her as she'd transformed from Eleanora Fagan to Billie Holiday, from person to myth, from young girl to heroin-addicted tragic legend. He sought out the Holiday "who was not always, and certainly not only, a victim," as scholar Farah Jasmine Griffin writes.[1]

Justin's goal was to write something that told Holiday's tale without mentioning drugs. "I'm done glorifying the junk," he said.[2]

The result was "White Gardenias," a warm ballad with a lazy jazz strut and a title cribbed from Holiday's memoir. The song, like much of the material Justin was now writing, was laid-back and direct.

Justin went deep into Holiday's story in drafts of the song. He wrote, endlessly tinkered with, then discarded, a line that resembled the song's emotional thesis, a line he might've felt was too on the nose: "So if she tells you that it hurts," he wrote, "Boy, you best believe her."

Justin had always found ways to create distance between his innermost feelings and the semifictional characters about which he sang: a cheery melody, an ambiguous second-person *mama*, an arrangement so retro it obfuscated its subject matter.

In Billie Holiday, he'd found another new way to safely sing about himself. "I didn't write that song for the Billie Holiday that everybody knows," he said. "I wrote that song for the little girl from Baltimore that never had a chance."[3]

"White Gardenias" gave Justin new energy and became the focal point of his new material.

He'd been so discouraged by recording delays and label woes that, at one point, he considered completely shelving ten songs he'd written. "In my mind," he wrote, those songs "lay at the bottom of the dust bin." But "White Gardenias" gave those songs a new meaning. He resuscitated old drafts, and felt energy to compose new tunes, amassing twenty songs in total. He envisioned recording them as a double album.

Shortly after his label deal with Communion fell through, Justin invited a music manager named Nick Bobetsky to Salt Lake City for a meeting. Bobetsky worked at Red Light Management, a high-powered firm that represented acts like My Morning Jacket and Alicia Keys. As they talked in Jenn Marie's home, Bobetsky noticed, on the table, a handgun, which remained unremarked upon, even as Justin fidgeted with it during their conversation.

Bobetsky passed whatever test Justin had seemingly given him. "You've got good eyes," he remembered Justin telling him before leaving. "Let's get to work."

Their first order of business was getting Justin into the studio.

Justin enlisted his live band—Niehaus, Pence, and Hedman—to emulate their free-flowing live show on record.[4] No horns, fiddle, banjo, or backup vocalists. "Less of the honky-tonk," as Justin put it, "and more of the blues."[5]

The sessions, which began April 27, 2014, were full of uncertain beginnings. Justin was in a new studio with his longtime studio engineer Adam Bednarik, who was making his debut as Justin's coproducer. But it was also the first time Justin ever made an LP without his studio collaborator Skylar Wilson or the group of seasoned Nashville session musicians he was used to. It was the first time he'd be recording twenty songs instead of ten and the first time he wasn't recording a single old song from his back catalog.

The recording sessions at Nashville's Quad Studios (also a first) were, thus, more chaotic than usual. The quartet hadn't rehearsed all the material beforehand, and Justin spent quite a bit of studio time finishing up lyrics at the last minute.

It'd been two and a half years since recording his last album, a source of anxiety for an artist accustomed to recording one album every year. But Justin remained outwardly relaxed, scribbling down lyrical rewrites, talking baseball—intent, as always, on keeping the session loose, in not belaboring any one song. To his new rhythm section, Hedman and Pence, everything felt rushed, almost like they were recording demos rather than making an album.

After the big-band soul expanse of *Nothing's Gonna Change*, Justin wanted a pared-down, less arranged record, almost reminiscent of *Yuma*, something his four-piece touring band could easily re-create live.

"White Gardenias," with its behind-the-beat blues phrasing inspired by Holiday, provided the musical foundation. Justin's timing as a guitarist and singer had always been off-kilter. He began further imitating the way Holiday turned her distinctive timing into a narrative tool on songs like "When the One You Love Loses Faith."

In some ways, the slow tempos and offbeat time signatures of his new material felt like a continuation of the leisurely R&B Justin explored on *Nothing's Gonna Change*. (What both sessions had in common, as some collaborators later surmised, was Suboxone and weed, which slowed down Justin's tempos.)

Both sessions also prominently featured Paul Niehaus, the Nashville guitarist who'd played on several Justin albums and whose mournful pedal steel set the tone for Justin's new slowed-down songs.

But one major difference was Justin's voice. It now quivered and floated, hovering over certain syllables as long as possible and barely enunciating others. The onetime honky-tonker now nearly sounded like a jazz vocalist. On "Today and a Lonely Night," one of the sessions' overlooked masterpieces, Justin delivered a haunting farewell-to-New York tale with a shaky resignation that accentuated his protagonist's isolation.

"Moaning, sighing and singing in gentle tones," read a 2014 *Chicago Tribune* concert review by Bob Gendron, "he elongated syllables and rolled vowels, shaping words on the fly and emphasizing certain passages."[6]

The songs were intimate and intense, even if the struggle they contained was often masked by retro-blues arrangements. And, as always, at the center of Justin's lyrical dartboard were Mom and Dad.

"Just like all my records momma plays a big role mommy and daddy issues being a reacurring theme in my records," Justin wrote of the albums in a journal. "They had more time to fuck me up than I've had to get better and its a long way to go."

His new songs also spoke to upheaval and change, including a peace he'd discovered with Jenn Marie. Justin kept revising the order for his new group of songs, but the one near constant, in his endless track-listing drafts, was the final song: "Looking for a Place to Land." The acoustic ballad is the story of a pilot, who after a lifetime of traveling the world, searches for a way to end his roaming.

He wrote it after meeting Jenn Marie.

Justin had always bristled at the idea that being in love meant happy songs. He detested the very existence of such music: One of his go-to diatribes was how much he hated the song "Walking on Sunshine." It's not surprising, then, that he excised the most heartfelt verses he wrote for "Looking for a Place to Land." Still, they represent Justin at his most uncharacteristically tender. In his journal, he wrote:

I touch down
And steped out into your arms
You held me up Till I could
Stand
You looked me in the eyes
And I knew I'd never look away again

Another couplet that he cut read:

And I still feel the thrill of flight
Simply from a touch of your hand

The finished version is less about the character aiding in the landing and more about a lost soul trying to touch down. In its own way, "Looking for a Place to Land" is a refutation of Townes Van Zandt's signature song, "To Live Is to Fly." Perhaps, Justin's song suggests, to live, or at least to survive, is not to soar, but to land.

The ballad was "not so much a resignation," Justin said, "but a realization that I don't have to run for the rest of my life."[7]

Justin's new management had gotten him a deal with Vagrant Records, a punk label that released records by one of Justin's heroes, Paul Westerberg of the Replacements. It had more recently found success with the Mumford-era collective Edward Sharpe and the Magnetic Zeros.

Justin's team debated how exactly to release these twenty songs. It was determined, with some disappointment from Justin, that what he'd conceived of as a double album would be two separate, related records with staggered releases a few months apart.

The first album was called *Single Mothers*.

The second: *Absent Fathers.*

When the collections came out in the fall of 2014 and winter of 2015, respectively, they failed to garner much buzz. When Justin set out on a tour in the fall of 2014, he struggled, for the first time in his career, to fill seats in some cities.

Much had changed in just the two years between 2012's *Nothing's Gonna Change* and 2014's *Single Mothers.* The entire network and infrastructure of blogs and independent music media that supported and spread the word about artists like Justin Townes Earle in the late 2000s and early 2010s had all but dried up or vanished. Not coincidentally, those two years marked the rise of streaming services like Spotify, which went from six hundred thousand paying subscribers in 2012 to fifteen million in 2014.[8]

Justin was working with a new label on a one-off deal, a more transactional arrangement than his career-oriented relationship with Bloodshot. He'd tried to secure a big-name duet for "Worried Bout the Weather," the opening track to *Single Mothers,* but nobody came through. His breakneck pace of record making and touring had also, seemingly, left him vulnerable to old-fashioned market saturation. Even with the delay of these two albums, by the time Justin released *Absent Fathers,* he'd released six records in an eight-year span, touring nonstop the whole time. Only his most diehard fans could keep up.

And if his casual *Harlem River Blues*–era fans checked out either of the two new records, what they heard felt different. This was laid-back roots music suited to a listening room or jazz club, not a rowdy rock hall. If *Harlem River Blues* carried an aura of sexy mishap and will-this-go-off-the-rails-or-not intrigue, *Single Mothers* and *Absent Fathers* were determinedly grown-up records devoid of obvious singles to play on the independent radio stations—Seattle's KEXP, Minneapolis–St. Paul's the Current, New York's WFUV—that had supported Justin and contributed to his radio play. When his label commissioned music videos for two new songs, "Time Shows Fools" and "Call Ya Momma," they failed to resonate.

Single Mothers and *Absent Fathers* also sounded out of step with the retro seventies-country momentum gaining steam. The new rising star of Americana in the mid-2010s was a Kentucky country singer named Sturgill Simpson, whose Waylon Jennings–reincarnate tales of rowdy times and druggy revelations on his 2014 album, *Metamodern Sounds in Country Music*, caught fire with the type of crossover indie crowd Justin had captured only a few years prior. But Simpson's fast tempos and hard-charging, hard-living anthems were exactly what Justin was running away from. Given Justin's contempt for the artistic pressure to follow the commercial trends of the day, it was likely no coincidence that his determined pivot away from rowdy honky-tonk-inspired music occurred right as those sounds spiked in popularity in the mid-2010s.

Justin grew more and more paranoid about the music industry, convinced its power brokers were conspiring to subjugate his career. He'd become combative with his competitors, like Jack White, who had a petty rivalry with Justin that escalated in 2014 when Justin tweeted "Jack White is such a pussy."[9] White had hired several of Justin's former bandmates (Cory Younts and Bryn Davies), but some of the hostility was also because White was publicly at odds with Justin's friend Dan Auerbach. White also likely represented, to Justin, a carpetbagging presence in Nashville, someone receiving credit for revitalizing Justin's hometown after White opened Third Man Records there in 2009.

The only constant in Justin's career had become his own insistence on self-reinvention. The moment his latest sound caught on—the old-time country of *The Good Life*, the rowdy gospel-folk of *Harlem River Blues*, the sixties soul of *Nothing's Gonna Change*—was the moment Justin pivoted. Was it his own stubbornness, his refusal to conform, his need to provoke his audience, his difficulty accepting adulation, or just the innate instinct of an artist who couldn't stop searching for the sound he heard inside his head?

"I hope if I ever get stuck I hope I have the good sense to quit," Justin wrote in his journals around this time. "I hope I never stop learnin and moving," he continued. "I would rather get lost."

Justin was working through this creative restlessness, once again, back in his hometown. In 2014, he'd moved with Jenn Marie to Nashville, eventually settling in an apartment in the Stahlman building, a historic high-rise downtown blocks from the tourist bustle of Lower Broadway. The city of Nashville had spent enormous amounts of money promoting its modern image to a new generation of tourists. Bachelorette parties, pedal pub enthusiasts, and young revelers flocked to town in the wake of ABC's prime-time country-music soap opera *Nashville*. The state of Tennessee viewed the show as an invaluable promotional vehicle, spending millions of public dollars to ensure it would be filmed in the city.[10]

The TV show had simply accelerated a plan—to rapidly develop the city's downtown—that had been in motion since the nineties. When, in 1997, the Opryland theme park, which drew millions of guests each year, closed, the city was left with an economic hypothetical: What if Nashville's very own downtown became, essentially, a country-music amusement park?

Justin grew embittered witnessing the aggressive development. He began bemoaning what was happening to his beloved, booming city. "What Nashville means to me isn't here anymore," he told the British magazine *Songwriting*. "It's buried under a bunch of crap and trampled under the feet of a whole new population that has moved here from L.A."[11]

To Justin, the musical and cultural transformation of the tourist honky-tonks that occupied Lower Broadway represented everything wrong about Nashville. What was once a street of bars where traditional live country music emanated from every stage was transforming into a frat row for young adults who'd traveled to the city in order to party in destination nightclubs with contemporary country stars' names stamped on them: Florida Georgia Line, Kid Rock, Jason Aldean, Miranda Lambert, Luke Bryan. Justin viewed the Guns N' Roses, Pitbull, and Bon Jovi covers that now emanated from these clubs as evidence of a larger cultural rot.

"Do you know how pissed off Tootsie would be if she knew that was happening?" Justin said, referring to Tootsie Bess, the original proprietor and namesake of Tootsie's, one of Lower Broadway's most famous honky-tonks.[12]

Around this time, Justin worked on a surprising piece of writing, almost dreamlike in tone, about a Nashville native listening to classic country music on an unexpectedly charming trip to Lower Broadway: "Hits of Paycheck, Pride and Strait / Music from the good old days."[13]

He could at least find comfort in his apartment building's old history. When it opened as one of Nashville's first skyscrapers in 1907, the building housed a bank in what the *Nashville Banner* called "the largest and handsomest banking room to be found in any city with the possible exception of Chicago or New York."[14]

The refurbished Stahlman building was not where a kid who'd grown up bouncing from one working-class apartment complex to another usually ended up living. Looking down at the city from his eleventh-floor view represented its own form of achievement.

In his home office, Justin began writing long-form fiction and nonfiction. He wanted to leave his comfort zone and experiment with poetry or books. He wrote what seemed to be a prose poem about baseball, capturing his beloved sport's rhythm and sensory splendor:

A clean crack of the bat
Drowns them out
A holy
Unmistakable sound.

Much of his writing around this time, in both unpublished lyrics and several long-form ideas he was exploring, was concerned with the concept of American decline. He scribbled down lyrics about children of the eighties ("the lost generation," he wrote). He explored, in a draft of a never-completed book titled "Baseball, Blues and LSD," the idea that the labor strikes and ballooning wealth that defined Major League Baseball in the eighties and nineties mirrored the societal decay of Reaganomics.

Late-twentieth-century American decline also served as the backdrop for an early draft of a novel with two protagonists: Slocumb, a star high school baseball player who enlists in the military during the first Gulf War in the nineties and ends up homeless, living by the banks of Nashville's Cumberland River; and Miss Marigold, the daughter of a Chinese scientist who left home at fourteen after getting addicted to the opioid Dilaudid at age twelve. "A warmth she had never felt," Justin wrote of his character's first time taking Dilaudid at a young age, "filled the void left by her hard hearted family and years of being misunderstood by class mates and teachers felt far away."

Around this time, Justin also toyed with a radio show, compiling notes for a Stax-themed episode (Carla Thomas, William Bell, Barbara Stephens, the Canes), a country-oriented episode (Tom T. Hall, "Amarillo by Morning," Roger Miller's "My Pillow"), as well as a more seventies-leaning playlist with Springsteen's "Thunder Road" and Fleetwood Mac's "Dreams," the latter of which Justin began covering around this time. As he wrote in his journal, it always reminded him of Carol. On the notebook's cover were the words:

A JOURNAL
OF THE LIFE AND TIMES OF

____

Justin filled in the blank space:

A worried man.

Justin would look outside his office window and see the Cumberland River, the old redbrick warehouses between First and Second Avenue South, even the AT&T Tower, which had been the tallest building in Nashville for as long as Justin could remember. From this vantage point, Nashville still sometimes looked like the town Justin remembered.[15]

In the early 2010s major labels zeroed in on the independent, songwriter-focused music being made in East Nashville. The traditional divide between those two sides of town, between Music Row country and East-side Americana, got blurrier than ever: In 2013 and 2014, country singers like Kacey Musgraves, Brandy Clark, Lee Ann Womack, Ashley Monroe, and Angaleena Presley all released forward-thinking songwriter-driven records that were unabashedly country yet sounded more at home on the Americana charts than country radio.

In 2015, a bearded country songwriter named Chris Stapleton found mainstream success with his Americana-oriented 2015 debut, *Traveller.* The year after *that,* Margo Price debuted her Jack White–approved *Midwest Farmer's Daughter.* Seventies country-rock-leaning Americana was now both culturally cool *and* commercially successful.

"It feels like there's a twangy riot going on," *GQ* gushed in 2016 underneath the headline "Meet Three Country Badasses Who Are Shaking Up the Nashville Establishment." Those three badasses were Chris Stapleton, Jason Isbell, and Sturgill Simpson. The only Justin mentioned in that *GQ* piece was Timberlake, who'd jump-started Stapleton's career with a viral CMA Awards duet.[16]

Americana had become big business. Just a few years prior, it seemed like Justin Townes Earle would be at the forefront of its modern commercial moment; he'd won the Americana Music Association's Emerging Act of the Year award in 2009 and Song of the Year in 2011, for "Harlem River Blues." But he'd largely removed himself from the retro-roots boom in his own hometown.

Like many artists, Justin Townes Earle had always been cagey when asked to label his music. He'd never considered himself strictly country, or folk, or blues. The Americana tag had been a fine way to sell records, and the validation he'd received from that subset of the industry had been meaningful to him earlier in his career. "When you get a thumbs-up from the AMA [Americana Music Association] you're getting it from people like Buddy Miller and Robert Plant," he'd said after winning his second Americana award. "It's something we do amongst ourselves that I think is a beautiful thing."[17]

But Justin was also dismissive of so-called Americana, even as he should have been the face of it. "It's starting to collect a specific sound, and it's not good a lot of the time," he said in 2014. Sometimes, he argued, the type of music he'd helped usher into the twenty-first century was becoming too specific, and sometimes it was becoming too broad.[18]

It didn't help that one of its newly anointed stars was Isbell, with whom Justin was still not speaking. In September 2014, they both appeared at a festival in Cincinnati. With their buses parked next to one another, Justin's bandmates, who were friends with both Justin and Isbell, spent the day going from one bus to the other trying to negotiate a truce, or at least persuade the former friends to talk. Their efforts failed.

As Isbell's career skyrocketed in 2014, Justin's business as a live act began to falter. He could still sell out big clubs in Chicago or Minneapolis, but at other venues on his 2014 tour, like a thousand-person theater in Chattanooga, Justin struggled to sell even a fraction of the available tickets.

When Justin played Nashville's Ryman Auditorium that fall, he couldn't fill the hallowed room. Was it because he'd just played the venue two years earlier? Because it was the week before Thanksgiving? No one was sure, but the show was so undersold that when a local blog offered a free ticket giveaway, the promoter gave the blog tickets to distribute to all the hundred-plus fans who'd entered the contest.

Due to his prior success, Justin was still coasting on high road guarantees, the fixed amount of money an artist is paid by promoters, regardless of ticket sales. But not being able to sell tickets, even in his hometown, was a bad sign. "That was a hard record cycle," said Andrew Colvin, Justin's agent. "We wanted him to do the business he'd done before, and the venues and guarantees were based on that. And it just didn't happen."

If any of this affected Justin, he showed it to no one. He never asked his team for sales figures or ticket counts. "Whether it was a full house or a big theater with one hundred people in it, he didn't change a fucking thing," said Gill Landry, a songwriter and former member of Old Crow Medicine Show who opened for Justin in 2015.

Outwardly, it seemed like Justin was in a stable place. His band—Paul Niehaus, Matt Pence, and Mark Hedman—finally had new music to promote. He was now touring with Jenn Marie and Gunnar, their German shepherd, creating their own home-within-a-home in the tour-bus back lounge. He was still playing some of the largest venues of his career.

"I was dealing with an excited kid who was at the height of his career and had just married the love of his life," said BJ Barham, whose band American Aquarium opened for Justin. "I got to see a perfect cocktail of how happy that dude could be, or at least how happy that dude could show everybody else he was."

Days before joining Justin's 2014 tour, Barham got sober after years of alcohol and drug use. Spending time around Justin at this point in Barham's life was enlightening, a beacon toward a better future. Justin relished his role as sober elder, sharing stories from rehab and recovery, offering tricks to maintaining sobriety on the road, lending wisdom, advice, and hard lessons that he had a hard time internalizing himself.

Even if Justin smoked ungodly amounts of weed, seeing a fellow artist with prior addiction issues abstain from booze and cocaine helped Barham conceptualize how life as a touring musician might look without alcohol. "I had a lot of questions about sobriety and recovery," said Barham, "and Justin answered them."

If Justin didn't directly express frustration with his flailing album and touring cycle, in conversations with his wife, he began questioning the sustainability of his career, of indefinitely living his life primarily on tour buses and in hotels all over the world. He started scheming up exit routes and escape plans from the music business. He told friends and associates he was considering quitting the road to become a sportswriter or a novelist. Steve Earle started publishing short stories later in his career; why couldn't Justin? He began spending what little downtime he had on tour with his fiction, sneaking off before shows to write alone.

Given how long it'd taken to write and record *Single Mothers* and

Absent Fathers, the commercial failure of those records seemed to privately flood Justin with self-doubt.

"He was really feeling like a failure," Jenn Marie said of this period. "And he wanted to do something else."

There was one metric, however, that could make Justin feel successful. He let everyone around him know if he ever was playing a bigger venue in a given city than Steve, who often toured at the same time as Justin.

Jenn Marie encouraged Justin to work on his relationship with his father. Instead of trying to persuade him to call his dad, she said she'd sometimes dial Steve herself and then chat with Steve alongside Justin, on speakerphone.

Jenn Marie came to understand that the reality of Justin and Steve's relationship was much more nuanced than how they portrayed it in the press. They saw each other—during holidays, on the road, whenever Justin was in New York—more frequently than either of them made it seem in interviews. Both son and father played up their psychodrama, criticizing and critiquing one another in public, seemingly as a form of competitive closeness and perverse intimacy. There were moments earlier in Justin's career when Justin would slag off on his dad in a phone interview, end the call, and then immediately ring his dad to say hello.

Still, their relationship remained loaded. It didn't help that, after years of "daddy-issues" songs, as Justin called them, Justin named his sixth record *Absent Fathers*.

When a journalist asked Steve what he made of his son's new album's title, Steve cut him off. "If you want to get into a thing about Justin, just forget it," he said, before explaining he hadn't listened to the record.[19] When Justin previewed his new song about "absent fathers" and "broken homes" at a show in New York in 2014, Steve sat in the crowd, seemingly unfazed, staring at his phone as Justin sang.

It was becoming apparent to Jenn Marie that Justin was suffering in regards to his mental health. She noticed how he could become completely unraveled by something as minor as misplacing his luggage or a tiny amount of weed. Her loving, gentle husband could transform, from one moment to another, into a destructive person with no command of his rage.

It was apparent to fellow singer-songwriters touring with Justin who also had mental health struggles. And it was apparent to his bandmates, who viewed Justin's bluster as a shield for his own struggles, and sometimes worried about his mental state.

Justin was easily agitated and prone to fast-shifting moods. On tour, he sometimes disappeared alone without explanation for hours on end, only to return with a fanciful tale about, say, a fistfight with a weed dealer he met on the street.

To label Justin Townes Earle with a simple mental health condition would be foolish at best and harmfully reductive at worst, especially given the ever-shifting series of diagnoses he received from counselors, therapists, psychiatrists, and mental health professionals throughout his life.

But through the early and mid-2010s, Justin thanked prescribed psychiatric medications for improving everything. "It's really changed my life for the better," he said in 2012. "I started calming down a lot."[20]

In 2014, Justin tweeted a photo of his cocktail of prescription pills, which included Lamotrigine, a drug that can be used to treat bipolar disorder, Vyvanse, prescribed for ADHD, and Escitalopram, which treats depression and anxiety. "Sweet mental stability," Justin wrote as a caption.[21]

On top of those medications, Justin was usually high.

Anyone who spent any time with Justin during these years remembered him smoking an exorbitant amount of weed. He devoured potent edibles. A tour manager might provide Justin with what they thought was enough weed for several weeks, only for Justin to go through it in a few days. If he ran out of marijuana and had a hard time obtaining it before a show, he could become agitated, even inconsolable.

It affected his performance. Halfway through his song "Call Ya Momma" at a show in 2015, Justin suddenly began singing "Christchurch

Woman." He hadn't even realized what he'd done until Niehaus told him during the encore break.

And his short fuse and impulsivity could result in combustible situations. After a show in Lincoln, Nebraska, in September 2014, a group of bugged-out teens or college kids began banging on the band's tour bus, which was parked in a back alley. Hearing the commotion, Justin stormed to the front of the bus and whipped out a pistol. He waved his gun at the teens outside the bus while yelling at them through the glass.

"What, are you going to shoot us?" someone yelled through the glass.

"That's right, motherfucker!" Justin shouted.

The kids eventually ran away.

That altercation in Nebraska stood out during a time when life on the road with Justin was relatively calm. The presence of Jenn Marie, who typically accompanied Justin on tour in the mid-2010s, was stabilizing.

One of the couple's favorite shared hobbies was clothes shopping and scouring for antiques. Justin started collecting vintage knickknacks and dusty doodads, offbeat items he'd find at junk shops and roadside yard sales. After years of touring, he'd developed a mental inventory of these places. "I mapped out hundreds, possibly thousands, of antique stores all across the country," he once said. "I go down to Florence, Alabama, where they dump ancient hotel furniture."[22]

When Justin and Jenn Marie rolled into a new city on tour, they often spent the day perusing these shops.

The items Justin scoured and collected became an extension of his quirky taste and off-kilter vintage aesthetic: a nineteenth-century French barometer, a brass diaper pin, a trout-fishing wading belt, Spanish gold doubloons, buffalo nickels, early-twentieth-century baseballs, an antique gold lighter, cigar-store Indian figurines, pre–World War I baseball bats, early maps of Nashville, shark teeth, rare coins, offbeat jewelry, vintage belt buckles. They were also a point of connection. One day, in his early thirties, Justin stormed into the backyard of Imogene + Willie, a Nashville-based high-end jeans shop he loved, in a state of frazzled agitation.

"I've lost my marbles," Justin declared. The person working at the store was named Erin McAnally, an old acquaintance of Justin's from the Chicken Shack. It took her a moment to realize what was going on. But as he explained the situation, it dawned on her: Justin was talking about having misplaced a literal bag of marbles.

These activities started as a healthy replacement for Justin's self-destructive fixations, but shopping and antiquing soon became similarly compulsive.

Justin accumulated a dizzying and destructively expensive array of fancy belongings: aluminum Rimowa luggage; multithousand-dollar leather jackets, of which he had several; designer pencils he could buy only in Australia; high-end cameras; handmade leather boots; antique quilts; designer shoes; and, most of all, vintage Rolexes. His love for high-end clothing, he once said, came from wearing his cousin's hand-me-down shoes as a child. "White trash kind of like nice things," he explained, "if they can get their hands on it."[23]

But the items also piled up to the point of chaos. Eventually, his shopping became so compulsive that Jenn Marie stopped going into antique stores with him. He filled several storage spaces with his purchases.

"I tend to be a bit of a collector," Justin once said. "I get into the weirdest things for periods of time and kind of blow through them and leave them behind."[24]

CHAPTER 20

When they returned home from the road, Jenn Marie and Justin thought about leaving Nashville. "I have many times seeked geographic change," Justin wrote in his journals, "as a cure for what aled me."

Jenn Marie had long-standing ties to rural Northern California, a part of the state—Humboldt and northern Mendocino County—full of outlaw weed growers and roughneck libertarians. It was a dangerous part of the country, with scarce law enforcement, a deeply entrenched distrust of authority, and commonplace violence because of the deeply rooted black market for marijuana grown there (Humboldt County once had the highest per capita rate of missing persons of any county in California).[1]

It was also gorgeous, green, remote, and quiet.

In 2015, Justin and Jenn Marie rented a house in the tiny coast-side village of Westport, California, "a town of skittish hillbillies that all grow marijuana," as Justin described it.[2] It was a quirky community—each Mother's Day, Westport held town-wide rubber-ducky races—so small that the hours and menu of its lone pub was a front-page story in the village newsletter. In 2010, its population was sixty.[3]

Cell service was spotty. If Justin had a phone interview, he and Jenn drove thirty-plus minutes down the coast to the nearest town. If he wanted human interaction, he walked to the local convenience store to chat up whoever was working.

Life in Westport was, for a while, exactly what Justin and Jenn Marie dreamed of.

"Between the music business and nashville I became very bitter," Justin tweeted in 2015. "So I left nashville and I found out it was mostly nashville."

A fan responded to the tweet, wishing Justin peace and beauty with his family.

"A lot of peace," Justin responded. "Thankful finally."[4]

Each morning, Justin woke up, drank coffee, sat on the porch reading his iPad, then retreated into his office to write. Their house was so close to the ocean that it shook when a big wave rolled in. He took walks on the beach collecting driftwood alongside their dog, Gunnar. He fixed up a red Jeep Jenn Marie bought him. He read books. He painted cabinets.

"He was learning how to be home," said Jenn Marie, "and he liked it."

Justin's yearning for rootedness was remembered by many of those close to him after he was gone. "Justin had such a sweetness, softness, and an inclination toward domesticity," remembered Allison Moorer, who divorced Steve Earle around this time. "He wanted a home more than anything in the world."

Justin had always been hard to get in touch with: He lost phones constantly and ignored texts and calls for days. But in California, he became virtually impossible to reach. "I love that the wife and I got a place where there is no phone service," he tweeted in September 2015. "Nobody knows where it is."[5]

Like many eighties and nineties kids growing up without a local Major League Baseball team, Justin became a Chicago Cubs fan. His fandom was thanks to WGN, the Chicago station that broadcast nationwide. As a child, when Justin returned to an empty home after school, he'd watch afternoon Cubs games. That the team was the longest-standing lovable loser in professional sports fitted Justin's underdog disposition. "Purgatory" is how he—and so many others—described Cubs fandom. He made his backstage tour laminates the Cubs logo and got so worked up when they lost that one friend refrained from attending games with him at Wrigley Field when he rolled into Chicago. "Cubs baseball has been one of few constants in my life!" Justin once tweeted.[6]

In his greenroom before shows, he'd often be watching vintage St. Louis Cardinals or Baltimore Orioles World Series games on his iPad, games he'd already watched dozens of times.

But his heart belonged to the Cubbies. After his team lost an unimportant game in 2013, Justin invoked Saint Jude, the apostle of the desperate and downtrodden. "The patron saint of lost causes must intervene!" he tweeted. "She must be a cubs fan!"[7]

A few years later, something strange happened: The Cubs started doing well. When the 2016 regular season ended, they had 103 wins, the most in the league.

"I can't focus on anything but the Cubs right now," Justin tweeted that October. He flew to Chicago to attend two World Series games. He was wired, shooing off collaborators when they called about work matters. "Couldn't sing right now if I tried," he tweeted at four in the morning after the Cubs won Game Six, bringing the series to a do-or-die Game Seven.[8]

Then, finally, the Cubs won it all.

"It was so incredible" is how Justin described being in Chicago for the World Series. He hated "Go Cubs Go," the team's feel-good anthem written by Steve Goodman. But after the World Series, he found himself shouting it out loud.[9]

Everything was changing. The Cubs were no longer losers. Justin was singing happy songs.

That same fall, in California, Justin received the most joyful news of his life: Jenn Marie was pregnant. He was going to become a father.

Years before meeting Jenn Marie, Justin admitted he wasn't ready for a kid, but that if he had one, he would "do the opposite of anything my parents ever did." Marrying Jenn Marie, he said, opened him up to having a child, with the same caveat. Two years before she got pregnant, he told a reporter that "me and my wife both have very strong intentions of being better parents than we had examples of."[10]

Sitting with this life-changing news, Justin changed his behavior in another way: He started calling his dad.

"It's kind of weird," Steve told Justin a few months into Jenn Marie's pregnancy. "You started calling me, all of a sudden."

Steve said this to Justin on air, where father and son were playing music and telling stories on Steve's satellite radio show. The conversation was its own performance, father and son displaying their fraught, tender closeness to their shared fans who'd always taken an interest in their relationship.

They laughed together, laughed at each other, and bonded over all they had in common.

> *Steve:* *Things are changing at your house.*
>
> Justin: Yeah, I got a daughter on the way.
>
> *Steve:* *You're so fucked. I can't ever imagine, I had all boys and I didn't have to worry about that side of it, but you're so fucked.*
>
> Justin: Well, I think I got off good, because you got three boys that are all bigger than you. I get a sweet little girl . . . and little girls love daddy, like Homer Simpson says, and then can marry sports stars and get daddy tickets.
>
> *Steve:* *Homer Simpson is a role model . . . yikes.*[11]

Secluded in California, Justin filled notebooks with verses. He wrote about the thrilling romance of jumping into a crowded car as a teenager for a spontaneous road trip. He wrote an eighties Nashville version of the myth of Stagger Lee, a fictionalized St. Louis pimp who became the subject of hundreds of folk songs and murder ballads in the first half of the twentieth century. He wrote a song about Jenn Marie called "Short Hair Woman" that embarrassed and delighted her. He wrote a mythologized tale of rambling to Chicago and East Tennessee. He wrote about surviving his youthful mischief, and about aging and memory—what Justin called "the unstoppable tide of time."[12]

In Europe, his longtime tour manager Simon Gardner marveled at how Justin carved out time in his daily touring schedule for songwriting. Justin scribbled notes in transit. Then, as Gardner did paperwork or conducted his tour-manager duties in greenrooms before shows, he'd listen to his boss work through whatever ideas he'd been working on.

"He was always playing new song ideas," said Gardner. "His method was to write in sequence, so you'd hear a chord sequence, and sometimes a snatch of melody. He'd say, 'This is going to be the first song on the new album.' Then he'd play a version and interject with things like, 'There's a keys part here' or 'there's a harmony there.' . . . I was taken aback several times when I heard the final version on an album and it sounded just as he'd described it in the writing process."

When one fellow singer-songwriter toured with Justin in 2014, he was struck by how seriously Justin took his volunteer role as guest judge for a songwriting competition. On the tour bus, Justin methodically considered each entry, scribbling down notes on his legal pad, devoting all his attention and spare time to the task. "It was a glimpse," said Justin's touring partner, Cory Branan, "into what mattered to him."

He particularly labored over one song he'd started years earlier, when he was with the Swindlers. It was an impressionist montage of memories from his preteen wandering years called "Kids in the Street." This Proustian paean to Justin's aimless youth originally included tales of a sweet old woman named Miss Phyliss and her mean old man Marcus, an elderly woman who walked the streets talking to herself, a car whose subwoofer filled the neighborhood with booming bass, a woman who provides the young narrator with their first romantic experience, and a neighborhood kid whose loaded gun lands them in prison.

There were entire verses—some bitter, some humorous—about gentrification and neighborhood change. At one point, Justin rhymed the song's title with "What the hell is a lifestyle boutique?"

Justin often claimed he wrote no more than ten to twelve songs a year, never more than what was required for an upcoming album. But his notebooks from his time in California show that in addition to what Justin may have considered finished songs were a trove of abandoned ideas, half-written verses, and seemingly nearly completed tunes that never made it to a recording studio. He reworked a socially minded song set in the 1980s Bronx ("And for a new generation coming up / In the land of plenty, there just weren't enough"). He worked on a song seemingly titled "Killers on This Road." He worked tirelessly on a song that began with the line, "You're older than you ever thought you'd be," but couldn't seem to finish it.

"I like the tune," he wrote after its umpteenth draft, in a seeming rare note to himself, "but I hate the song."

In December 2016, Justin headed to Omaha, Nebraska, to record his latest batch of tunes with producer and longtime Bright Eyes band member Mike Mogis. It was his first record with New West, a Nashville-based roots label that released records by many of Justin's heroes, including Kris Kristofferson and Justin's father. Justin balked when New West recommended he work with an outside producer. "I'm making my eighth record," he remembered telling the label. "What do I need a producer for?"[13] But Justin had known the label's head of A&R, Kim Buie, since he was a teenager, and unlike his attitude toward just about everyone else in the industry, he respected her opinion.

After the lukewarm reaction to *Single Mothers* and *Absent Fathers*, the idea was to shake it up creatively. Justin insisted on being accompanied by his longtime guitarist Paul Niehaus, but the rest of the musicians who'd be playing on his next record were a group of Omaha locals whom Justin had never even met before arriving in town.

At Mogis's studio, Justin was stoned and chatty. He had two large bins of medical-grade marijuana (labeled "AM" and "PM") shipped to the studio. He seized on his new captive audience, lecturing about the history of stride piano and Professor Longhair, the New Orleans keyboardist Justin viewed as a reference point for the sound of several new songs.

The man who could hold forth about any given subject—Civil War battles, the intricacies of selvedge denim, the trick to making the best steak, the 1973 St. Louis Cardinals, where to find the best shark-tooth dealer in St. Petersburg, Abraham Lincoln's 1838 speech as junior Illinois state congressman, the proper way to pronounce Nashville's "Demonbreun Street"—was in his element. After long days in the studio, he spun stories and tall tales about his self-professed criminal past with the band at night. At one point, the studio assistant drove Justin into town to shop for boots at Omaha's famous Dehner Company as Justin blasted "Werewolves of London" in the car and told stories—perhaps true, perhaps not—about how he'd known Warren Zevon.

The Omaha musicians were delighted and mystified by this larger-than-life songwriter who simply would not stop talking. "It was instantly apparent to me that he seemed like someone who was, kind of, a know-it-all," said drummer Scott Seiver. "But then he *did* sort of know it all."

Justin finished his new album after a few days. He called it *Kids in the Street*, after the song about his youth. It was, in a way, his first record that didn't forefront the hurt he felt toward his parents as its explicit emotional core.

This time, there were a few credible singles: "Champagne Corolla," a raw blues rocker that recalled Justin's rowdier early records, and "Maybe a Moment," an upbeat, nostalgic ode to teenage mishap, the most sweetly cheerful thing he'd ever written.

"Looking back on life is a bittersweet kind of thing," Justin said, explaining why he'd finally felt ready to deploy nostalgia in his songwriting. "I needed the time," he said, "because before it would have just been bitter, there would have been no sweet."[14]

CHAPTER 21

JUSTIN STARTED TO SLIP AGAIN IN CALIFORNIA. THE REMOTE LIFE Jenn Marie thought was so restorative for her husband had, he later admitted to her, had begun to feel isolating. To complicate matters, Justin stopped taking Suboxone, the medication he'd been relying on since 2011 for his opioid addiction. He didn't like the way the drug made him feel—the way he sang, wrote, and thought—and he'd wanted to get off the medication for some time. Weaning off Suboxone was risky: For someone like Justin, with a multidecade history of addiction and relapse, the drug is often recommended to be taken for the remainder of a patient's life. To make matters even scarier, according to Jenn Marie, Justin stopped taking the medication cold turkey, by himself, without medical guidance from his doctor.

That said, freeing himself from Suboxone, at first, felt like a victory. Jenn Marie could see the color return to his face. He seemed healthier than ever.

Then, after tapering off the medication, Justin's substance use slowly returned. He began microdosing acid. He occasionally had a drink, which scared Jenn Marie, even if Justin wasn't hiding it and even if it was infrequent. When Jenn Marie left town for work or to see family, Justin and a friend started driving an hour into the hills to one of the two small-town bars in nearby Laytonville.

Rolling blunts and smoking weed ruled his daily existence. "It was the first thing he did in the morning," Jenn Marie said, recalling their time in California, "and the last thing he did at night."

He'd projected so much toughness for so long. He'd been so dedicated to getting better. But as much as he'd always talked about heavy substance use in the past tense, Jenn Marie gradually began to acknowledge a painful reality: She shared her husband not only with his artistic craft but also with his addiction. It began to feel like the pane of glass she always found herself staring at Justin through—when he went outside in the early morning to smoke a joint, when he excused himself from a restaurant, midmeal, for a cigarette—represented a much larger distance.

That pane of glass started to warp. Justin found new ways to self-isolate. Jenn Marie had no idea what to do about it. Justin swore everything was fine. Jenn Marie believed him.

It wasn't until years later, after she slowly started picking up the damaged pieces of her own life, that Jenn Marie fully grasped the sheer magnitude and force of her husband's illness. It took time, reflection, and self-education about addiction to realize Justin *had*, in fact, been actively struggling when they'd first started dating in 2013.

When Justin and Jenn Marie had lived in Nashville, they frequently stopped in at Imogene + Willie, Justin's favorite clothing shop in town. "He's being the best version of himself with her," the store's co-owner, Matt Eddmenson, remembered thinking. "Maybe this is the person that allows Justin to come out of the cave he's lived in," he hoped. But, Eddmenson said, "The biggest thing I thought when I would see them was, 'She doesn't know the darker side of him.'"

In Northern California, Justin and Jenn Marie had ingratiated themselves with the outlaw community, traveling into the hills and hollers to socialize with locals. These were the type of people Justin wanted to spend time with: lumber workers, winemakers, weed growers, folks who knew nothing of his career. Justin began visiting them without Jenn Marie, driving into the hills for the night. He also began telling acquaintances in the music industry that he was considering giving up music for good and entering the weed-growing business.

One night right around the 2016 election, Justin went out with a friend. On the way home, he worked himself up railing about Donald Trump while driving, intoxicated, on a dark, windy mountain road. Midrant, he crashed straight into a tree on the side of a cliff. The car was totaled.

Somehow, no one was seriously injured, but the accident was a wake-up call. Jenn Marie was pregnant, and the couple was already in the midst of moving to Portland, Oregon—a pragmatic decision. With a baby on the way, they wanted to be closer to health care infrastructure. The isolation of Westport had tired out Justin, who drove four-plus hours to San Francisco every time he needed to fly to a show.

"Another new town another new home," Justin tweeted after arriving in Portland in late 2016. "Northwest growing on me. I like this rainy motherfucker!"[1]

Justin settled into domestic life in Portland. When he and Jenn Marie attended Thanksgiving with friends in 2016, someone at dinner remarked that they couldn't believe that the larger-than-life Justin Townes Earle they'd seen perform earlier that fall was the same regular guy sitting at the dining room table.

Despite various alarming signs, Jenn Marie's pregnancy brought the couple closer. They talked about what type of parents they hoped to be and joked about how much their daughter might torture her mom when she became a teenager. Justin talked excitedly about how he planned to teach his child important life lessons and anticipated five items that'd soon define his life: diapers, stroller, car seat, crib, changing station.

"We'll baby-proof the electrical outlets and pad any sharp things," he told the *San Francisco Examiner*. "But a kid also needs to understand that if you run into the corner of a table, it hurts."[2]

For the name of their daughter, the couple settled on Etta St. James Earle. It sounded regal; the resemblance to the R&B legend was a bonus. Justin also liked the way Etta St. James drew attention away from her surname. If his daughter ever wanted to be any kind of public person—an artist, a writer, or, god forbid, a musician—a name like Etta St. James could stand on its own. She wouldn't have to be known as an Earle.

"When I have kids, I'm going to have a little girl," Justin had said back in 2008, nearly a decade before becoming a father. "She's going to be, like, completely sensible, and so she probably won't want anything to do with the music industry."[3]

One songwriter who opened a show for Justin in January 2017 was struck by the sweetness of Jenn Marie and Justin's road rapport, which they'd developed after three-plus years of touring together. Justin often performed without a set list when performing solo. That night, when he blanked on what to play next, Jenn Marie fed him song ideas from side-stage. But once Jenn Marie was several months pregnant, she stopped touring with Justin.

Justin wanted to cram in as much work as possible before Etta's birth. He was anxious about money, anxious to promote his new record with a new label after several years of career stagnation, anxious about providing for his expanding family. Even if Justin dreamed of escaping the music business, traveling the country with a guitar remained his best means of earning a livelihood. He scheduled gigs up until a few weeks before Etta's due date.

Justin began conceiving of a life devoted to caring for someone else. As an adult, he'd always relied on others to take care of *him*. Since 2013, Jenn Marie had served that role. She'd kept his business affairs intact, helped him get from one place to the next, kept him on schedule, coordinated phone calls he'd rather not make, helped send emails he'd rather not send. Wherever Justin went, Jenn cleaned up after the literal and proverbial mess he made, organizing the cyclone of weed, clothing, guitars, iPads, and luggage he tossed about backstage or on the tour bus.

But he was ready to be there for the baby. He projected confidence about the future. On walks the couple took around their Portland neighborhood in the spring of 2017, Justin comforted his wife about her fears of motherhood.

"I was the one who was scared, and I was voicing it," remembered Jenn Marie. "I would be crying to him that I was worried I was going to be an awful mother, and he would be like, 'No, we're ready for this; you got everything it takes.'"

Quietly, she was also envisioning what it meant to parent a child whose father would likely be spending months of each year traveling. How would she be able to handle it? Later, Jenn Marie realized her husband was struggling with similar doubts and fears in private. "The pressure was just immense, and halfway through my pregnancy it really crumbled," she said. "Justin didn't want to admit it, so he was hiding it in all the ways he could."

Kids in the Street was released in May 2017. Anchored by a pair of accessible singles, it received mostly positive reviews.

"He's cultivated an easy way of balancing down-home and urban, modern and vintage, role-inhabiting and biographical sensibilities," wrote NPR's Jewly Hight. "Never has Earle sounded more attuned to the spirit and potential of the roots idioms he works with, or freer to play around with them." Critic Glenn Gamboa went further in *Newsday*. The album, he declared, "is one of those rare moments where an entire career falls together all at once."[4]

To promote the record, Justin hit the road that spring, playing several dozen shows with the Canadian rock group the Sadies, who opened for him and served, alongside Niehaus, as his backing band. Justin remained uninterested in, even disdainful of, the idea of commerciality. He was a midcareer artist releasing a record inspired by country blues and fifties New Orleans stride piano in the age of Spotify and Ed Sheeran. If he missed being named one of the most well-dressed people in the world, or appearing on late-night television, or playing in front of thousands at festivals, he kept those feelings to himself.

Justin's press coverage offered only a few indications of cracks in his sobriety. He told some journalists he was sober and told others he was mostly sober but enjoyed an occasional glass of whiskey.[5] On the verge of being a parent, he admitted he struggled to imagine what a stable childhood looked like.

"I'm curious about how it actually works, or how it's *supposed* to work," he said. "What do kids do? 'Cause I don't really know that. I was, unfortunately, put in some terrible situations very early in my life and I grew up very fast. I don't know what it's like to be a twelve- and thirteen-year-old."[6]

CHAPTER 22

When Justin accepted a European tour for late June 2017, he'd discussed with Jenn Marie whether the shows were cutting it too close to Etta's impending birth. She was due in July. Jenn Marie had a feeling her firstborn would arrive early and was apprehensive about the faraway gigs. Justin reassured her. The minute she went into labor, she remembered him telling her, he'd be on a plane home.

Throughout that tour, Justin bubbled with excitement, boasting about the big change on the horizon. "He was so excited to become a father," said one musician who encountered Justin in Europe on June 21. "He kept talking about how Jenn was the only woman who could keep him in line."

About a week later, on June 29, Etta St. James Earle was born, roughly a month earlier than expected. The night of her birth, Justin was forty-five hundred miles away, onstage in Bergen, Norway.

When Justin realized he'd missed Etta's birth, he shut down. He ignored calls and messages from Jenn Marie. Etta had been born so early that there were still five shows left. Justin kept the dates.

Justin told his tour manager, Simon Gardner, that Etta was born when they were in Norway. But when he switched tour managers for his final few European shows, Justin pretended to another of his longtime tour managers, Andy Washington, that Etta had not yet arrived. He was frustrated to be out on the road and not back home with his wife, Justin told him. After the tour finished, Justin missed at least one connecting flight home from London and did not arrive in Portland until a full day after his trip back home began. Where he went remains a mystery, but Jenn Marie remembered evidence on his phone that suggested he'd gone to Amsterdam.

Justin never spoke publicly about missing his daughter's birth. His friend Josh Taylor, who'd accompanied Jenn Marie at the hospital, remembered how hard missing Etta's birth weighed on Justin afterward. But it was a devastation and shame too great to face.

"I had Etta, my dad gets him on the phone, then I don't hear from him for three days, not *once*," Jenn Marie recalled. "That was tough, because I knew how excited he was." Justin's disappearance after his daughter's birth left Jenn Marie hurt and confused and opened her eyes to what Justin might be hiding from her. New fatherhood "made him fearful, it made him scared, it broke him in so many ways," said Jenn Marie, "even though it was the greatest gift we both ever received."

When Justin did finally arrive home, he was happy to be reunited with his wife and even more enthralled and in love with his baby daughter. He held Etta in his arms on the couch, smiled as she slept on his chest, adjusted to his new sleepless routine. He marveled at how much Etta weighed, given how early she'd been, at how her long legs made him convinced she'd be tall, just like her parents.[1]

"Fellas!" Justin posted, "we will never know what a woman goes through during pregnancy. No way no how." Tweeting through the early bleary weeks of fatherhood, Justin congratulated old friends on having baby daughters ("girls are the best!") and ruminated on bringing a kid into the world the summer of the white-supremacist riot in Charlottesville, Virginia. "Whenever I get wound up and worried about the state of America today," he posted that August, "I stop and look at my daughter and it only makes it worse."[2]

Justin kept his schedule light during Etta's first couple of months, but he knew he'd soon have to get back to work. In the subsequent few years, Justin would frequently make offhand, often intoxicated barbs about how he needed to work because his wife was spending all his money. But Jenn Marie, who'd kept working throughout her pregnancy, remembered conversations after Etta's birth in which Justin insisted she shouldn't go back to work. Once Etta was old enough to go to school, she remembered Justin telling her, he wanted Etta to have her mom to be there to greet her when she got home.

In the fall of 2017, Justin headed to Australia and New Zealand. He socialized at night and told everyone how great his wife and kid were. "He was really fucking happy," said Ruby Boots, a musician who crossed paths with him in Australia. "Or at least he said he was. The way he was talking about his family and his partner, I felt a lot of warmth and love. But he was also saying that this is my time where I get to blow off steam, when I'm on the road."

One journalist had a question:

> Q: Hopefully it won't be too hard to leave little Etta behind? I imagine touring is something that has to have a little more thought now?
>
> A: It's definitely harder now. But there is still this burning sense in me that I need to make money, hahaha, you know. More now than ever. There's something that I am working for.[3]

There had been serious warning signs: the car crash, going AWOL after Etta's birth. But what was scariest, for Jenn Marie, was seeing how Justin began to self-isolate even at home during Etta's first year. They lived in a beautiful 1920s three-bedroom home, filled with big windows and light, but Justin started spending more and more time in the house's dark basement, where he'd carved out a space to write. When he went downstairs to his office, he started locking the door.

Justin also now lived in a town that more catered to his addiction. Portland had one of the highest rates of bars per household of any city in the United States.[4] When Justin stepped outside his house on Imperial Avenue, he needed only to walk one-tenth of a mile to find a bar. Chopsticks, a karaoke dive, became his escape of choice. Justin would claim he was heading to the corner store for cigarettes and then return an hour later, loaded.

He tested the wide latitude Jenn Marie had always given him. "Jenn was very good at letting him blow off steam and then bringing him back," said one friend who spent time with the couple in California. "It drove him crazy when he didn't get the reaction to his episodes that he wanted. He wanted to be shamed. He wanted someone to yell at him."

Justin did not want his fans to know he wasn't sober. When he mentioned drinking whiskey during a podcast taping in January 2018, he requested that the interviewer edit out all his references to alcohol.

But by early 2018, Justin was in the throes of a full-fledged relapse. His behavior had become erratic enough that his team started receiving worrisome messages from promoters and bookers, folks who'd known Justin long enough to ring the alarm bell. One of those calls came from a promoter in Winnipeg. An employee at the hotel where Justin was staying while in town for a gig claimed Justin brought a group of seemingly unhoused locals into the hotel and was causing a scene in the lobby late at night.

"You should be aware this is going on," the promoter, Chris Frayer, told Justin's agent. "I'm concerned."

Frayer's worry would soon be shared by just about everyone who spent time with Justin on his lengthy solo tour that spring. Justin was staying up each night on the bus doing coke and drinking, largely by himself. "It was pretty easy to be concerned about him," said Lydia Loveless, one of several opening acts who traveled with Justin on the near-empty tour bus (typically used for full bands and crew) he'd insisted on.

On that 2018 tour, Justin's playfully confrontational stage banter occasionally turned caustic, alienating some fans and yielding even more concerned calls from promoters. But for the most part, the shows were as good as ever. Justin spun stories, chatted with fans, and performed solo acoustic, which was still the way he shone brightest as a live performer and the mode in which many fans most preferred to see him.

Onstage, Justin still commanded the room. His shows had become the part of his life he had most control over. There were occasional stray onstage comments, like the one in Philly, that he was "clean for the first time in three days."[5] But there was otherwise little indication to his audience that he was using again.

"The Earles don't die," he'd say after snorting a line after a show. "We're invincible." Justin was now getting into physical fights with strangers in clubs. He'd mostly stopped communicating with Jenn Marie, leaving his phone on the bus for hours at a time. She was frantic and incensed at her husband, trying to keep tabs on his daily whereabouts by communicating with his tour manager.

Those employed by Justin were placed in a difficult position: say yes to the boss or get fired. It was a position many had found themselves in throughout the years. And many of those employed by Justin believed that once he was already off the wagon, he'd at least be better off surrounded by those who cared for him rather than whomever they imagined he'd replace them with if they told him no.

This, broadly speaking, was how the music industry worked: Artists toured to earn a living for themselves and to keep members of their team employed. If that artist, writhing from the threat of withdrawal, needed cocaine, someone found them cocaine. "Nobody tells the singer no, *nobody*," Jonny Fritz, a singer-songwriter who knew Justin, said shortly after his death. "And when the singer wants to throw fuel on their own fire, everybody suddenly has a budget to help."[6]

Justin's behavior on the tour bus that spring included rampant substance use, outrageous spending, and infidelity, all of which were now being concealed from Jenn Marie, per his orders. His latest tour manager, Paul Horvath, could hardly keep his lies for his boss straight, so thick had Justin's web of deception become. Horvath started worrying he might go into the back of the bus and find Justin dead.

On a rare day off, Lilly Hiatt, one of Justin's opening acts that spring, wrote a song inspired by her bus mate. "The only thing you know how to do," she wrote, "is move."

"It's hard to find something that was crazy, because, shit, every night was crazy with Justin," said Alden Peace, that tour's bus driver. Each night, after everyone else went to sleep, Justin headed to the front of the bus and sat with Peace as he drove from city to city in the pitch black, the two men laughing and telling stories. Justin talked to Peace about his dad, his marriage, baseball, the validation he felt when fans told him how much his songs meant to them. It was nice having someone to talk to in the middle of the night.

Even though the tour bus Justin insisted on was so expensive it canceled out much of his earnings, the idea behind the solo tour had been to bring in some much-needed revenue. How else could Justin earn a living? His fans who spent fourteen dollars on a *Midnight at the Movies* CD in 2009 could now stream *Kids in the Street* for free. Justin Townes Earle no longer sold out massive rock clubs all across the country; the venues were smaller, the margins tighter. Touring solo was a way to keep costs down.

Yet, as much as it provided him a sense of purpose and control, it was also clear that the road actively enabled Justin's disease. It had been the case in 2003, when Justin, twenty-one, caused trouble on his dad's tour. It had been the case in 2010, when he'd spent the year in a Sprinter van loaded on vodka. And it was the case now, in 2018, as Justin was spending much of the money he earned on drugs to numb his feelings.

"Am I feeding into this by having him on the road?" his agent, Andrew Colvin, wondered at the time. "That definitely ate at me."

How to navigate this impossible dynamic—to tour or not, to tour how much and in what manner—became an ongoing difficult debate among Justin's team members and loved ones over the next couple of years. The varying opinions (*he can't be touring in this physical state; he needs to tour to keep food on the table; he will be even worse off if he gets off the road and loses his sense of purpose; we need to find another income source that doesn't involve performing in bars every night*), all of them valid, became a source of loaded disagreement.

At the center of this old-fashioned showbiz conundrum was Justin's own ambivalence. Part of him knew he had no business being on the road. He'd continued to share with Jenn Marie and close friends his dreams of writing about baseball, of getting a house by the water with his wife and kid, somewhere he could sit and write all day in peace, where he could stop getting up onstage to be Justin Townes Earle.

On the other hand, getting up onstage to be Justin Townes Earle was his lifeblood.

"Shit, I'm a criminal," he told one crowd. This was one of his go-to riffs: assuming an outlaw identity as a way of talking about the showbiz treadmill he lacked the confidence to jump off.

"If I wasn't doing this," he said, "I guarantee you, oh man . . ."

The riff usually ended in a neat one-liner: *If I wasn't doing this, I'd be dead or in jail*. But on one night during the previous fall tour in Australia, Justin seemed too tired to tie such a neat bow.

"It's like, I got an eighth grade education; it's this, or . . . I couldn't even get a job at McDonald's."[7]

Each night onstage in 2018, Justin gave a speech about addiction before he sang "White Gardenias," his tale of how the world refused to see Billie Holiday's personhood. Justin talked about the opioid crisis and about how there was no way to solve an epidemic that plagued millions through sheer politics alone. The only way forward, he argued, was through empathy.

One evening he said:

> The problem is, when it comes with anybody who has an addiction problem, no matter what it is, whether they drink too much, do too much blow, shoot heroin, if they fucking cut themselves up, whatever it is, we've always looked at them, throughout time, and we've asked the same question. We say, "What's wrong with you?" All right? Now that's an ignorant, uneducated, dumb-fuck question. . . . Obviously, people with these problems, they hurt. And so maybe you ask 'em, and this ain't gonna solve it, at all, but it'll get you closer to the heart of the matter, and you won't feel like such a dipshit if something happens to one of your friends or your family, but you just ask them, "*Why do you hurt*?" That's it. "*Why do you hurt*?"[8]

One night that spring, Justin's longtime Australian tour manager, Gareth Lindsay, caught up with Justin in San Diego. The two men went out, returned to the bus early in the morning, and then began drunkenly wrestling in the bus's common space. But once Lindsay pinned Justin in a hold, he realized he was, actually, comforting his friend in a tender embrace.

"I could feel all the chaos and stuff inside of him," Lindsay said, "and I remember saying, 'It's going to be okay.'"

Justin put on a strong face, sharing parental revelations he wanted to internalize. "I realized after my daughter was born that I'd been looking at myself as a boy for so long, and that's just not an option anymore," he told one journalist. "I got so much more to learn."[9]

But he was unable to feign control any further when the bus stopped in Portland on June 15, the second-to-last date of the grueling tour. After six weeks away from home, Justin was scared for his family to see him in his current state. His lifestyle on tour had become incompatible with the person he wanted to be to his wife and daughter. After visiting with Jenn Marie and Etta, who was almost a year old, Justin became inconsolable, sobbing in his dressing room before a show. Then, before he went on, he began to cry again as he talked, backstage, about how much he'd missed his daughter.

When Justin finished the tour a few days later, he fought with Jenn Marie. She was terrified by how much alcohol her husband was consuming, by how rapidly he seemed to be unraveling.

On the evening of June 25, 2018, Jenn Marie later told police, the couple got into an argument about Justin's substance use. Justin was drinking a bottle of whiskey each day since returning from touring a week or so earlier, she explained to officers. After her pleading, he'd agreed to limit his daily consumption to six beers. But on this evening, late at night, around one in the morning, Justin left the house to buy cigarettes and returned intoxicated and agitated.

When he got back, Justin was carrying a bag full of alcohol. Jenn Marie took one of the bottles in the bag and smashed it on the front porch, according to a police report. The couple started yelling. When Etta awoke at the commotion and began crying, Jenn Marie implored Justin not to go upstairs to see her. The couple got into a physical altercation on the staircase, at which point Justin "swung his hand and phone back and struck Jennifer in the face," according to the report.

Jenn Marie called 911. When police arrived, they photographed her injuries: a gash down the middle of her nose, cuts on her hand, and a bump above her left eye, which was bruised almost to the point of being swollen shut.

Justin emerged from the basement with his hands raised. He was handcuffed and taken to jail, where he was charged with fourth-degree assault. He pleaded not guilty. The next day, his court-appointed attorney requested his release and asked that he be allowed to travel out of state before trial in order to keep working.

"I was supposed to go to Australia in seven days for five weeks, then I come back, I go to L.A. and work on a movie for eight days, then I come back here for four days," Justin explained in court.[10]

Justin did not go to any of those places. It was decided, after being released from jail, that he would fly to rehab in Texas. Justin was opposed to such a plan, believing it pointless for someone to go to rehab against their will. He didn't want to go, even if rehab was his best chance at making his criminal charge go away.

But before Justin went, he had one more night in Portland. A temporary protective order had been issued; Justin was legally prohibited from going home or seeing his family, so he spent a night at the Hotel Lucia downtown. He was accompanied by his friend Andy Moore, serving as babysitter and chaperone. Moore's job was ensuring Justin made it onto the plane the following day.

Moore had known Justin for nearly twenty years, since the Chicken Shack. He was familiar with how Justin got when his addictions took hold, when he no longer acted like or recognizably was himself. He'd also seen Justin through some of the best, happiest times of his life. Back in Nashville, in 2013, he'd listened to Justin gush about meeting the love of his life. In Portland, as recently as 2017, he and Justin were watching Cubs games and meditating on their futures as Justin prepared to become a first-time father.

So Moore could tell his friend wasn't there at all as he watched Justin blitz through bar after bar that evening, holding court with anyone he thought could procure him drugs.

When they finally returned to their hotel and were smoking cigarettes outside at around three in the morning, Moore suggested they call it a night. Moore went inside the lobby to use the restroom. When he came back outside, Justin was gone.

Moore noticed Justin's shadowy figure down the street. When he caught up with him, several blocks later, he realized Justin was pushing a man he'd met in the intervening few minutes in a wheelchair. The man had a double amputation and, as Moore remembered, Justin seemed to think his new acquaintance could lead him to some drugs, pills, *anything*.

Moore followed Justin farther as he pushed the man through downtown Portland, past Burnside into Old Town, the place to score. When Moore finally caught up with Justin, he gave him a lecture he'd given him many times: Being a *rich* junkie is cool and glamorous, maybe. "But now you're just a junkie in Old Town at four in the morning trying to cop dope from a double amputee."

Moore told Justin he was leaving; Justin could follow him or stay. He stayed.

A few hours later, around dawn, Justin reappeared in their hotel room, crawled into bed with Moore, and rested his head on his friend's chest.

"Oh man, baby," Moore remembered Justin saying aloud. "I'm sorry, I'm sorry."

Later that day, on June 28, Justin flew to Austin for rehab.

The next day, on June 29, Moore joined Jenn Marie and a few close friends to celebrate Etta St. James's first birthday.

CHAPTER 23

Justin was forced to cancel his summer tour in Australia. Instead, despite resisting it as much as he could, he spent much of July 2018 at a high-end rehab facility outside Austin, Texas. During much of his time in rehab, Justin slept. At some point, he sent his friend Josh Taylor a brief letter:

> *Hope all is good and you are hanging in there. This place is fancy way to nice for white trash like me. Everything is good. I have gained fifteen pounds. They did say they want me for sixty days but I said fuck that shit. I got mouths to feed. Plus they said that after four days and that is not enough time to judge. We must keep that in mind that these places are business and I am sure they would love another fifty thousand dollars.*
>
> *I am going straight from here to Nashville to make the record cause I dont get out until the day before rehearsals. I will give you a call soon.*
>
> Love,
> JTE

By the time he left Texas, Justin's assault charge had been dropped. Jenn Marie wanted her husband to continue to receive help. In a dynamic not uncommon in domestic violence cases, after Justin checked into rehab, she requested that her protective order be rescinded. She told the DA's office she wanted to speak openly to the father of her child, that they wanted to stay together. Despite there being photographed documentation of his alleged crime, Portland's deputy district attorney dropped the case.[1]

Justin never spoke in public about his altercation with Jenn Marie, or his assault charge. But at his first show after rehab, a one-off gig in Madison, Wisconsin, on August 9, 2018, Justin slipped in vague allusions to what had happened.

"That's what I do, baby," Justin boasted onstage. "Make music, raise a little hell, manage to get myself locked up about every five years."

During his addiction speech before "White Gardenias" that night, he revealed a bit more. "If you want to know how fragile, you know, people are that have problems with this, I *just* got out of a drug treatment center, *again*," he explained. "I started drinking too much. So just because somebody *solves* it once doesn't mean it's *solved*."[2]

That August, Justin headed to Nashville to record a new album. The songs he'd been writing were big-picture, socially minded originals that pulled from the topical folk song tradition much more than anything he'd ever done before. Avoiding anything remotely political had previously been a cornerstone of Justin's songwriting and showmanship—a way, as he so often pointed out, of differentiating himself from his outspokenly leftist father.

But the 2016 election of Donald Trump had rattled Justin, leaving him paranoid and fearful. Justin believed that the state of the world had gotten so bad that the tide would soon turn, that there would be a mass movement of collective resistance, that violent civil unrest was inevitable. "We have been marginalizing people for such a long time," he said, "that we are going to find out that they are going to strike back at us."[3] As he wrote songs for the album he recorded in Nashville that summer, "the Woody Guthrie came out in me," he said.[4] He wrote songs about the Flint, Michigan, water crisis; the Appalachian opioid epidemic;

the failed political "War on Drugs"; and poverty in South-Central Los Angeles. He also wrote about his wife and daughter and himself. He wrote songs about social issues that were actually about his own life and songs about his own life that were actually about social issues.

And he wrote a powerful song deploying his tried-and-true allegory: the rising tide, the unstoppable flood. This time it was a storm that brought enough rain to drown anyone in its wake. "Frightened by the Sound" might've been about a global uprising, or a slow-rising submission to addiction, or an acknowledgment of each person's slow march toward mortality, or simply a song about bad weather:

Keep an eye on the river
It's already up
There's no need to worry yet
Let us not forget that
Last time rain come
Down like this
So much was lost
We'll never know the true cost

Justin composed these songs throughout 2017 and early 2018, mostly from the dark basement of the Portland home he'd shared with Etta and Jenn Marie. He locked himself in the cramped office for hours at a time, communicating with Jenn through an air vent that led into the kitchen. "If you need me," Justin would shout through the grate that went up to the kitchen, "just stomp your hoof, my little dear."[5]

One song, "Ahi Esta Mi Nina," was the tale of a reunion between a daughter and her father, a Puerto Rican man from Manhattan who had been freed from prison after years of being locked up on drug charges.

The first time Justin played the song for Jenn Marie as she washed dishes in their kitchen, she started to cry. She immediately understood what Justin was trying to communicate, the parts of himself his protagonist was revealing. The song was a confession, an apology, and a prayer for absolution all at once, an "admittance," as Jenn Marie put it, "of choosing the fate of being locked away from what means the most to you."[6]

"I'll just say I'm sorry," the father in the song says to his daughter. "But I know it's not as simple as that."

When Justin arrived in Nashville, fresh from rehab and ready to record, in August 2018, he showed no signs of the ugly turmoil and violence of his past few months. Some of the studio musicians were vaguely aware of what had transpired that summer; others had no idea. To everyone in the studio, he seemed, outwardly, in great spirits: healthier, happier, and more focused than he'd been in a long time.

Before recording, Justin had a series of conversations with Adam Bednarik, his longtime engineer and coproducer. Abner, as Justin called him, had been involved in Justin's recording since his first full-length album and had become far and away his most trusted studio collaborator. This time, Justin wanted to let Bednarik assume more of a hands-on role as the primary producer. Bednarik enlisted members of his local band called Luella and the Sun (guitarist Joe McMahan and Jon Radford, Justin's former touring drummer) to play on the record alongside Paul Niehaus.

When the sessions began, Bednarik realized something special was transpiring. The musicians he'd assembled jelled with Justin. The recordings felt like a new beginning. The songs were strong, the performances dialed in, the concept unified: It quickly became obvious they were recording a profound piece of music. At home at night, Bednarik hesitated telling his wife just how well the sessions were going, for fear of jinxing anything.

After the record was finished, several label employees cried as they listened to the album. When Justin's friends and peers soon heard the record, many agreed: It was his best work, certainly since *Harlem River Blues*, perhaps ever.

After recording ended, Justin made his way back to Portland, where he reunited with Etta and Jenn Marie. Despite everything that had transpired, Justin and Jenn Marie were determined to make things work. To save money, Jenn Marie had moved the family to a less expensive house while Justin had been in rehab. Justin started seeing a therapist. His resentments and wounds were still presiding over his daily existence. He agreed, with Jenn Marie's urging, to try, yet again, to confront them.

Justin and Jenn Marie initially went to therapy together, but after it became clear Justin liked and listened to their therapist, Jenn Marie said he began going by himself. He knew he needed to take his trauma seriously, to face his so-called demons, he told his wife, because they were "nipping at his heels," chasing him wherever he went.

Comments like this gave Jenn Marie glimmers of hope. It was also gratifying to see how fulfilled Justin still was by his work. He was excited to share the album he'd just recorded, playing it for his wife and baby daughter.

"Listen to this!" he'd exclaim right before a line he was particularly proud of.

But even as the family tried their best, Jenn Marie remained scared and worried. As Justin predicted, rehab had put him in good shape to record his album but had little effect on curbing his substance use. He started going to bars as soon as Jenn Marie fell asleep, then slept during the day. He began insisting he needed to fly first class—for the legroom—but started drinking so much first-class free alcohol that he would be kicked off connecting flights.

Those who'd spent time around Justin in his early twenties, during the heights of his cocaine use, recalled disturbing episodes when Justin would be awake for days on end: "He was just walking around talking to the trees, paranoid about something," his old friend Sean Locke said when recounting their all-night bender, circa 2004, that had made him so fearful for Justin's life that he felt forced to cut ties with him the very next day.

No one, back then, had known what to call it—psychosis? a manic episode? paranoid delusions?—but they knew it coincided with his most extreme periods of cocaine consumption.

In Portland, Justin's moments of seeming cocaine-induced psychosis resurfaced.

Jenn Marie began taking regular trips with Etta to visit family in order to get some distance from their increasingly unstable house. When they returned after one trip away, Justin had scrawled alarming messages in red marker in their basement. His paranoia spiraled. He started losing sense of reality. He accidentally misfired a firearm in the house.

Jenn Marie didn't know what to do. "There's a fine line of deciding how you support a person that's struggling with addiction and how you keep yourself safe," she said.

She wanted to help Justin but had no idea how. Desperate for solutions, she grasped for answers: reading books, attending Al-Anon meetings, communicating with Steve, joining another support group for those in a relationship with people who struggle with addiction.

That fall, Justin joined a tour opening for punk legends Social Distortion. Justin's team hoped that spending time with Mike Ness, the band's longtime sober frontman, might be a good influence.

It was wishful thinking. In February 2019, Justin embarked on a cruise ship in Florida for a seven-day trip to the Caribbean. It was his second time on Cayamo, the preeminent Americana music cruise, and this time he was appearing alongside his old friend Amanda Shires and his former friend Jason Isbell.

On board, his peers were alarmed by Justin's disheveled state as he stumbled around the boat. At one point, he ended up in an altercation with Isbell in the ship's casino. "Justin started getting aggressive with me," said Shires. "The pit boss wouldn't help me, and Jason was across the table, and Jason said, 'Do you need help?' And I said, 'Yes.' And then they got into their own thing."

Afterward, Jenn Marie found out that Justin, as she recalled, amassed a five-figure bill on the ship from gambling and alcohol.

Justin shrugged it off, describing the cruise as a "floating hangover."[7] But Justin's team could no longer bear it. Nick Bobetsky, his longest-serving manager, was starting his own management company and told Justin he'd be parting ways. Andrew Colvin, Justin's agent for more than a decade, told Justin in person, later that spring, that he could no longer work with him.

Afterward, Colvin received an obscene voicemail from his former client, one he still recalled years later. "It was *so* Justin," said Colvin. The message began with an extended tirade: *Fuck you for this, fuck you for that, fuck you, motherfucker*—before changing tones as Justin said farewell: "I love you, man."

Justin's team had disintegrated in the months leading up to the May 2019 release of his next album. It was called *The Saint of Lost Causes*, after St. Jude the Apostle, the patron saint of the desperate and uncared for. Justin explained the title by discussing its socially minded focus: These were downtrodden characters he was giving voice to. But he didn't shy away from other layers of meaning.

> Q: "When were you a lost cause?"
> A: "I always have been. I was born a lost cause."[8]

As he promoted the album, Justin laid out his options, as he now saw them: tour forever or wind up in jail. He'd chosen the former.[9]

A journalist at New York's WNYC wanted to know: Could he envision a future where he settled down and quit the road?

"No," Justin snapped. "*Nobody* ever gets to ask me to stop doing this."[10]

By the spring of 2019, on the verge of the album release, Justin's substance use had gotten so out of control that Jenn Marie was certain everyone else around him would finally listen to her desperate pleading: to stage another intervention, to pause the album release, to put a stop to the showbiz hamster wheel, to try, yet again, to get him help, *anything*.

The interviews were getting darker. Justin told the *Broken Record* podcast that he wanted to die on a tour bus. He made unprompted claims in *Rolling Stone* that he had been physically and sexually abused as a child, something he also reiterated in private conversations at the time.

"Nothing will ever change the heart that's inside of me," he told the magazine. "It goes way deeper than my father. I was a kid. I was abandoned. I was molested. I was beaten. . . . There's something that will always be missing inside of me."[11]

On May 24, 2019, the release day for *The Saint of Lost Causes*, Justin showed up out of sorts to a promotional appearance at a Portland record store. He was clearly intoxicated during his brief in-store performance, cursing in Spanish and mumbling about Mark Knopfler. He apologized to the crowd for showing up late.

"Shit happens," he explained. "Such is the life of a sailor man."

Then, during his set, Justin choked up toward the end of "Mama's Eyes." His voice broke on the concluding refrain: *Yeah, I've got my mama's eyes*. He tried to sing it again.

"That happens every now and then," he said, contemplating his next number. "Let's do something non-emotional."

Justin sounded distracted and overwhelmed. He stumbled over the next song, "Lone Pine Hill," despite having performed it hundreds of times.

He muttered into the microphone: "I keep thinking about my fucking family."

After his set, Justin stepped outside and confided in his friend Josh Taylor. "Hoss," Taylor remembered Justin telling him, "I'm really not doing good, at all, in a lot of ways."

Justin knew that his course was untenable, that he needed help, that he needed to face whatever was destroying him. He didn't seem to think he could.

Meanwhile, Justin and Jenn Marie daydreamed about moving to Mexico; to Mobile, Alabama; somewhere in the Caribbean; even back to New York State, where Steve could see more of his granddaughter.[12]

They'd hunted for answers, for anything that could, one day, make their family whole. Jenn Marie said they made plans to move to Nashville, but at the last minute, she changed her mind. Justin's addiction had thrown their life into chaos. The actions and decisions and people he was spending time with when using made Jenn Marie balk at bringing Etta to Justin's hometown. It didn't help that he was repeatedly cheating on her.

Jenn Marie ended up moving, with Etta, somewhere that worked for *them*, somewhere peaceful, somewhere Justin might decompress one day, when he was in a better place. She decided on Montana.

Justin returned to Nashville to stay after four years away, his longest stretch living outside his hometown. He bounced between hotels and homes of old friends, but many of his longest-standing relationships in town had frayed: either Justin had cut ties, or it'd become too hard for his friends to witness Justin destroy himself, or some combination of both.

Using Facebook, Justin reached deep into his Nashville Rolodex, reconnecting with people he hadn't seen, or spoken to, in many years: childhood classmates, neighborhood fixtures, old flames, former friends. He wanted someone to talk to. He wanted to catch up, to reminisce about the nineties Nashville that no longer existed, to trade small-town gossip about classmates who'd wound up in jail. He sought out familiar faces who'd known him as Justin Earle, the name he used on his Facebook profile.

Most everyone was delighted to hear from Justin Earle. Many were surprised. Some were alarmed; many had heard Justin was married with a kid on the West Coast. His being back in Nashville, without his wife and daughter, seemed like a bad sign.

When one ex-girlfriend, Lisa Marie Turner, received a Facebook friend request from someone without a profile picture calling themselves Justin Earle, she assumed it was a scammer or bot.

But in the part of the profile where a user lists their employment, she noticed that this person had written KING KONG as their job title at a company called MUSICIAN. *How Justin*, Turner thought to herself. Once she saw that, she knew it was really him.

Justin's stage banter often included edgy references to past transgressions and substance use. Those references tended to increase when Justin was using. His stage stories became more outlandish. His introduction to "Rogers Park," which always included a recounting of adolescent, drug-induced desperation in Chicago, now concluded with a fanciful tale of Justin fleeing the city after robbing his dope dealer of $30,000 in cash.[13]

There remained a small portion of Justin's fan base that lapped up these outlaw stories. They hollered whenever Justin mentioned cocaine, clamored for him to bleed out further, wanted to party with the singer and leave the club with a story to tell. When Justin told the Wisconsin crowd, in August 2018, that he'd just returned from rehab, he heard scattered "woo's" shouted back at him.[14]

When Justin had gotten married in 2013, he'd started receiving a loaded line of inquiry: Now that you're happily married, what will you write about?

He'd been fucked up for thirty-some years, happy for one or two, Justin usually responded; he had a deep reservoir of fucked-up feelings to draw from for the rest of his life.[15] A diplomatic answer, one that acknowledged the premise of the question without succumbing to its trap.

But now, Justin latched onto a discomforting timeline: Like *Harlem River Blues*, Justin had written and recorded *The Saint of Lost Causes*, an album he and his peers were just as proud of, while sliding far off the wagon. It stopped mattering to him that *Yuma* and *The Good Life*, the records that established his career, were written and recorded when he was stone-cold sober.

The myth had returned.

It was the old lie, "bad information" he'd received growing up, he once called it.[16]

"I'm built for the road," he said in 2019. "I don't know what the hell to do at home."[17]

He told a loved one, around this time, that he had to hit rock bottom before he wrote his most honest songs. He began telling Jenn Marie he believed his fans liked him most when he was using. It broke every part of her to hear it. "He started to try to make himself believe that he was unlikeable unless he was fucked up and struggling," she said.

It'd become impossible for Justin to imagine who he was without his addiction.

That August, Justin headed back to Australia.

"Are you living in Nashville?" one journalist asked. "I thought you were living somewhere else?"

"Life's gotten complicated recently," Justin responded. "It's not really something I want to talk about."[18]

When old acquaintances crossed paths with Justin on that Australian tour, he seemed, on the boozy surface, upbeat and in good spirits: taking acid, waxing poetic about fine wine, enjoying the free-flowing camaraderie of being surrounded by the circuit of casual friends and companions he'd amassed after a decade-plus of touring the country.

But Justin's longtime Australian tour manager, Gareth Lindsay, felt that serving as Justin's day-to-day tour manager had become an impossible task.

If Lindsay left Justin alone for five minutes, he'd return to him having ordered a double shot and a beer at the hotel bar. If an opening act suddenly received an extra fifteen minutes of set time, it sent Lindsay into panic. "I'd mapped out the whole day," he said, "and those fifteen minutes could mean three more drinks, which could mean the difference between him peaking at the right time and him falling off the edge of a cliff."

Justin didn't mind being babysat. He was back on the road, where his needs and desires were paramount, where people catered to his demands. *He* was the baby, he told Lindsay; *he* was the one who needed to be taken care of.

Justin got through the Australian shows, cracking jokes and bantering with the crowd. He sang "Ahi Esta Mi Nina," introducing it with a speech about America's draconian drug-sentencing laws. One night, after finishing the song, he translated its title:

"That means 'my only child,' but specifically to the female, so, 'my only girl,' *eres mi niña*."

Then he abruptly ended his explanation. "Life's a bitch," he said.[19]

Justin started taking his shirt off during encores, singing "Gold Watch and Chain," a 1930s Carter Family song about someone willing to do anything to be told, again, that they're loved. He ranted about racism and discrimination. He chastised Australians for their treatment of Aboriginal people. He told the old stories: about Mama, about his beloved grandpa Jack Dublin Earle, about his hero songwriter Malcolm Holcombe, and he shared one of his aunt's favorite sayings: "Life's a bitch, and then you die."

"When I was a kid, I would just be like, 'What do you mean?'" Justin told one crowd. "Now I get it."[20]

After shows, Justin mingled and held court with onlookers. One night in the small town of Castlemaine, he had a deep chat with one fan—about their childhoods, about Townes Van Zandt, about how Justin loved his wife, but they weren't currently able to be together. That fan, Clare Shamier, was struck by what felt like a profound sorrow in this stranger.

That night, Justin stayed at the venue as long as he could. He didn't want to stop talking, to flee the warm company of strangers. But it was late. He had a plane to catch the next day. When it was time to leave, "I remember him coming out through the doors, and he just looked really, really sad," said Shamier, who'd somehow found herself helping Justin into his car. "He really didn't want to leave."

As Justin was driven away, he flashed a wistful smile, staring back at the venue out of the passenger side. As the car rounded the corner and disappeared, Justin closed the window.

When Justin returned from Australia, he immediately embarked on a nine-week fall US tour with a full band (Niehaus, Bednarik, McMahan, and Radford, the *Saint of Lost Causes* crew). It was a relentless run, forty-one shows with five days off.

Justin's caretaker on that marathon stint was Larry Kusters, who'd started as Justin's road manager the year prior but had taken over as Justin's full-time manager when his last one parted ways. It was unconventional to have one's manager also serve as a day-to-day tour manager, but Kusters had developed a close bond with Justin. He was coordinating with Jenn Marie, who by that point, in a desperate attempt to maintain some semblance of control, was still working for Justin—handling logistics, answering his business affairs—despite being estranged from him.

On tour, Kusters tried reducing Justin's alcohol intake to a minimum, a herculean task now that Justin was reaching for a bottle of liquor the moment he awoke. It was the fall of 2019, and Justin was barely functioning offstage. He was being cared for and treated, indeed, like a young child. Kusters reminded Justin to return his father's phone calls. Kusters fed him crackers with manchego cheese, one of the few things he was willing to eat. Kusters calculated Justin's wake-up time, eventually pushing it back to 7:00 p.m., an hour before he went on, so that he'd be able to drink only so much before performing. Kusters started to sound check for Justin: If he was awake early enough for that, he'd have several hours to drink before he played, too many for him to still be standing come showtime. Kusters switched Justin from Jameson to vodka, because whiskey seemed to make him aggressive.

Nobody on tour had answers. Nobody wanted to quit, to abandon their dear friend in the depths of his suffering. Nobody wanted, either, to give up their one chance to showcase, as a band, the beautiful record they'd made. Rehab was off the table; Justin had made that clear. He'd already been the year before. He was not willing, or able, he told Kusters, to go again.

"Short of giving him an ultimatum, in which case [Justin] probably would have just finished the tour by himself, what are we going to do?" said Niehaus, Justin's longtime guitarist.

The band played on, tried keeping the gigs professional. Often, they succeeded, concealing the barely functioning state of their boss. "Most of the shows were great," Niehaus said. "There was a couple where it was kind of sad."

Sometimes, plenty of the time, Justin kept it together and played a solid show. But he also barked at his band and the crowd, took his shirt off, mumbled and moaned his way through his cover of Fleetwood Mac's "Dreams," and danced around the stage, barely able to stand, while his band vamped on the fifties rock-and-roll classic "Rocket 88."[21]

"If somebody yelled 'Free Bird,' he would fucking lose his mind: 'Say "Free Bird" one more time and I'll come beat you,'" said Kusters. "Is that funny? Yeah, sure. That's fucking funny. Did we have a great laugh about it? Yes, we did. Was it always controlled? No."

At the merch table, a newcomer named Jonathan Buske assumed a heavy role. Buske had been hired to overhaul Justin's merch and was serving, that fall, as the guy selling vinyl and T-shirts after each show. As such, Buske became the unofficial liaison between Justin and the crowd: Fans asked him what was wrong with the artist they'd been seeing live since 2008. Was Justin okay? Some were worried.

So was Buske. Several nights on the bus that fall, Buske went to sleep wondering if Justin would be alive the next morning.

Buske told fans everything was okay. "I kept the mask on for him and led everybody to believe that it was all good," he said. "But it was pretty obvious that he was falling apart."

For those who'd known him for years, the Justin Townes Earle riding the tour bus that fall was unrecognizable.

"It was every rock-and-roll cliché," said Radford. "The carrot that's dangled in front of the horse's mouth to get him to walk, it was dangled at all times. And Justin was running. He was chasing something."

After shows, Justin stayed up all night on the bus. He told stories about Steve, who seemed to be on his mind. "A lot of the conversations always seemed to lead back to his dad," said Buske. Gradually, bandmates retired to their bunks. Oftentimes, Niehaus lasted the longest, staying up until the early morning, but eventually, everyone fell asleep.

Then there was just Justin, the only person still awake, hassling the bus driver or sitting alone in the bus's front lounge. At some point, he'd pass out on the couch, unable to make it to bed.

One day on tour, Justin went for a walk with his drummer, Jon Radford. It was daytime, before Justin had revved up. Radford doesn't remember how it came up in conversation—perhaps they were joking around, perhaps Radford was trying to address Justin's pain, perhaps they noticed a roadside sign that prompted this exchange—but, at some point, Radford, a religious man (Justin called him "Churchy"), turned to his friend.

"Jesus saves," said the drummer.

"From what?" Justin snapped back.

Radford looked at Justin and smiled. He didn't share with him what he wanted to say: that a full-blown religious awakening might be the only thing, at this point, that could bring Justin back. Instead, he swallowed the two-word answer that popped into his head:

"From yourself."

CHAPTER 24

After years of erratic spending, Justin's business affairs were in disarray. Missing tax payments and debt had amassed in part because of constantly rotating management. His nine-week full-band 2019 American fall tour grossed more than $200,000. After accounting for costs—the tour bus, the cash Justin withdrew every few days—Justin pocketed not much more than $10,000.

Kusters settled on a more profitable arrangement for the first few months of 2020: weekend runs of low-overhead, high-ticket-price solo shows in small, sometimes half-empty clubs in towns that didn't usually draw big-name acts: Wichita, Fresno, Bozeman. One three-show weekend in this format could earn Justin as much take-home money as he'd earned in nine weeks with a band and tour bus.

That January, Justin showed up to one such gig in Billings, Montana, out of sorts: He'd lost his guitar in transit and remained quiet throughout the night. He'd spent the previous night in a San Antonio jail after being arrested for public intoxication at the airport. (Justin was charged with possession of cocaine, but after his dad fronted the bond, Justin was released, the case eventually dismissed.)

Mostly, though, Justin showed up to these shows his gregarious self, connecting with local openers, watching their sets, complimenting their music, chatting with them over beers.

One such opening act was a singer-songwriter named Anna Rose, who joined Justin for a couple of shows in early March 2020. Over barely seventy-two hours, Rose got a profound glimpse into Justin and the anger he harbored at the world, the deep desire he had to be seen as a serious songwriter. She also sensed that Justin seemed uncertain about how long he might be around, that he was, as she put it, "baiting death." This sense came from several offhand comments Justin made to Rose and to others around this time: that he was no longer able to function without vodka; that his body couldn't survive another detox; that everything he worked for or achieved in his life was for his daughter, Etta; that one day everything he owned and earned would be hers.

This sense deepened on the drive home from Nashville after their last gig. Justin sat in the passenger seat smoking cigarettes after having stayed up the entire night, while Rose's friend, who was accompanying the two of them, drove. At one point, he reached over and jerked the steering wheel, laughing as he remarked that they weren't going fast enough.

March 12, 2020, was the very first date of Justin's monthlong tour opening for folk-punk singer-songwriter Brian Fallon. That same day, the country's largest concert promoter announced that it would suspend touring operations due to rising cases of what was then a novel coronavirus.[1]

"By the time we loaded in, they were talking about this thing called COVID," Kusters said of the gig, which was in Wilmington, Delaware. "By the time [Justin] got offstage, the tour was canceled."

"Well," Justin said backstage, after hearing the news, "I guess this is it."

That night Justin performed old standbys like "One More Night in Brooklyn" and "Can't Hardly Wait." He talked about the Brooklyn Dodgers and spouted nonsense. He took out a lighter and cauterized his middle finger. He pulled out a rare cover of "Let Him Roll," Guy Clark's talking-blues tale of a lifelong wino who dies a lonesome death.[2]

"Too many days of not being together," Justin sang, switching up Clark's lyrics. "Too many nights fightin' the weather."

To end his set, Justin, shirtless by that point, played a ragged version of "Ain't Glad I'm Leaving," his sassy country kiss-off, one of the first songs he ever wrote, one he'd been singing for twenty years. It is a song about someone who believes himself to be so much of a scoundrel that those who love him should be grateful anytime he flees.

Justin started the song and then stopped. He'd realized that his profanity-laced set had been witnessed by a young child up front.

"I'm so sorry," he said to the kid. Then he resumed playing.

"I know . . . baby, that it might seem wrong," Justin sang, "But you're gonna wake up in the morning thanking to the heavens that I'm gone."

It was the last song he ever sang in public.

In Tennessee, Governor Bill Lee declared a state of emergency. The SEC college basketball tournament canceled remaining dates at the city's Bridgestone Arena. College kids packed up their dorms at Vanderbilt. The Country Music Hall of Fame closed. By March 17, even Springwater had shut down.[3]

Back in Nashville, Justin crashed where he could: with old friends and acquaintances, at an Extended Stay hotel on West End Avenue. He reestablished connections in his hometown in the early months of the lockdown. He stayed, for a time, in West Nashville, where he befriended a neighboring group of wayward teenagers who lived in a home for young adults who'd graduated out of foster care. He taught them how to make Frito pie and bought them a basketball hoop from Walmart. He went to his mother's for Sunday dinner, bringing her food from the nearby West Nashville institution Wendell Smith's and sitting with her in the house he'd helped her buy. They spent time together watching game shows on her couch.

Later that spring, Justin moved into his own temporary place: a second-floor apartment on Acklen Park Drive, blocks from Springwater. The plan was for Justin to remain in Nashville while he waited out the lockdown—a couple of months, tops—before heading back on tour. The apartment was sparsely furnished, supplied with necessities Jenn Marie had ordered him. Justin slept on a mattress on the floor. Most of his belongings remained in Montana, where his wife and kid lived, in a home he'd never seen.

Stuck with no way to make money, no routine or main event around which to orient his daily schedule of substance use, no ninety-minute window during which he needed to ensure he could function, Justin grew despondent. But he was determined to make something of his downtime. He'd worked up a couple of song ideas, and finished at least one, although nothing close to enough for an album. He cooked up an idea for a low-budget streaming webcast called *Misbehaving*, inspired by the kitschy country variety shows he'd grown up watching on the now-defunct Nashville Network like *Nashville Now* and *The Marty Stuart Show*.

On *Misbehaving*, Justin would interview and perform with fellow musicians and share larger-than-life stories. He made notes on lighting and set design, enlisting friends to help. He floated the idea of having strippers appear in Hazmat suits, but nothing came of the show.

Collaborators, friends, and acquaintances recalled Justin outlining, throughout 2019 and into the first half of 2020, a dizzying number of ideas for what his next project should be. Many of them were barely formed, some were brilliant, some were nonsense, some were dead serious, some were tossed off, and some of them he'd been considering for years.

He wanted to make a record called *Whores and Heroes* at Memphis's famous Ardent Studios, using the *Saint of Lost Causes* backing band. He wanted to make a country-inflected album with the Sadies, comprising unreleased songs he'd written during the *Saint of Lost Causes* era ("Cold Comfort," "All or Nothing"). He wanted to write a record called *The Ghost of Old Nashville*. He wanted to make a duets covers album with artists he admired like Brittany Howard and Mos Def. He wanted to release a down-home blues record with Dan Auerbach. He wanted to cut an album of Billie Holiday songs with the Preservation Hall Jazz Band. He wanted to finish a song cycle he'd begun working on to accompany *Black Bottom Saints*, a novel written by family friend Alice Randall. He had an idea for a collaboration with the Nashville Ballet based around his song "White Gardenias." He wanted, after years of resisting the idea, to record an album with his dad. He talked about making a hip-hop record and producing a local rapper. He wanted to work on a book about the seedy underworld of eighties West Nashville called "The Good Old Boy Network." He wanted to make a documentary about John Prine.[4]

In town, he saw few people. Bars were closed. Restaurants eventually adopted a citywide curfew of 10:00 p.m., which was often when Justin's nights began.[5] Justin reconnected with an old friend named Rosemary Haskins, who lived around the corner. They bonded over their shared circumstances: Justin was estranged from Jenn Marie. Haskins was going through a separation from her wife.

They began spending time in Justin's apartment, watching TV and messing around on guitar. They went out for meals, sometimes with Haskins's mother, at the West Nashville location of Cinco de Mayo, a local Mexican restaurant.

Justin encouraged Haskins, who'd been considering quitting music to become a lawyer, to keep pursuing art. He told her it'd be a huge waste of talent if she gave it up. He confided in Haskins. "He shared the good *and* the bad," she recalled. "He was feeling pretty abandoned, even by some of his friends that he'd known for years."

Justin told Haskins he'd found newfound empathy for his dad after realizing he'd made the same decisions Steve had—putting the stage over family. "He felt terribly about it," she said. "He struggled with feeling like he could never be good enough for what [Jenn Marie] deserved."

Despite having not seen her in a year and having been involved with other women during that period, Justin remained in close contact with Jenn Marie. One day in May 2020, he told her he'd been injured, prompting an exchange about his health insurance.

"Until we are straight don't worry about me. I always fucking survive for some god damn reason," he texted her. "If you and Etta are ok then I'm ok."

"Well, I think you need health insurance," she responded. "You are the money maker and you need to be taken care of, too."

"I am made of spit and barbed wire! Let's worry bout nothing but you and Etta till I get shit right," Justin answered, before following up with an important question: "What is my Apple ID password."

Justin reconnected with another old friend, Steve Poulton. Poulton had produced Justin's first few records, a local who was exactly the type of no-bullshit lifelong musician Justin adored. Poulton relished seeing Justin. Still, he had his boundaries: When Justin called in the middle of the night, Poulton didn't pick up.

Poulton began witnessing what others had also observed: Justin was concerned about his own state, trapped and terrified by his own addiction.

"If you're worried about someone's self-destructive behavior, that's one thing," Poulton later said. "And if, for the first time, you see that person worried about *themself*, you can go ahead and be *real* worried."[6]

Justin's body could no longer keep up. He was thirty-eight, but years of excessive alcohol intake, drug use, and several decades of nonstop smoking had taken a toll. Nearly twenty years before, Justin wrote a song called "I Don't Mind." He never released it, and there's no record of him having ever performed it live, but the ballad speaks to the darkest recesses of the young songwriter's mind.

"If the drugs don't kill the pain," goes the chorus, "then I will."

In July 2020, Justin was hospitalized and admitted to the ICU after coming down with aspirated pneumonia. Doctors shared the grim cause of Justin's condition: He'd been consuming so much alcohol that, when he slept, his lungs would fill with vomit. They'd become infected as a result.

Justin underwent lung surgery. Doctors explained that his body couldn't continue to withstand his current level of substance use.

Still, Justin resumed drinking shortly after he was discharged from the hospital.

One afternoon that August, Steve Earle drove to the house of his ex-wife, Allison Moorer, to drop off their son, John Henry. Justin came along for the ride. It was the first time Moorer had seen Justin in a long while. He looked remarkably frail. His face was hollowed out, his smile gaunt.

"He'd been in intensive care with pneumonia," said Moorer, "and I think had to have some drainage tubes that left insertion marks on his torso. He wasn't wearing a shirt, and he spotted me coming down the sidewalk to meet John Henry, stretched out his arms, and said, 'I got holes in me,' and laughed. I didn't."

Instead, Moorer whispered, "I know, baby."

After leaving the hospital, Justin spent a few days in a hotel before settling back in his apartment. He saw his parents, visited with extended family, went to appointments, slept, spent time at his dad's house in Fairview, and saw Jenn Marie and Etta, who'd flown from Montana to visit him.

When Jenn Marie later remembered the trip, she recalled near-daily walks and their trips with Etta to Dragon Park, where Justin had spent his youth playing soccer, skateboarding, shooting bottle rockets.

And she remembered some of her deep conversations with Justin. He thanked her, she said, for what he felt was her newly gracious, less judgmental tone when talking about his addiction. She sensed Justin's gratitude for all the work she'd done in better understanding how addiction functions. "He said to me, and I was so glad that I was able to hear this, 'My years with you were the best years of my life,'" she said.

She pleaded, once again, for Justin to go to a long-term rehab facility. "He told me he hadn't hit his crescendo yet," she said.

Eventually, Jenn Marie and Etta returned to Montana. Jenn Marie remembered this, too, saying goodbye: After visiting Dragon Park one last time, they got into a car to the airport. When Justin shouted "I love you" to them, they screamed it back at him.

When Justin was hospitalized, Larry Kusters also flew to Nashville. Like Jenn Marie, Kusters believed it was now or never: Justin needed to seek treatment and needed serious help in order to stay alive.

"This is your wake-up call," he said to Justin.

Justin refused. His body couldn't handle rehab, he said, resorting to one of his favorite catchphrases: "The Earles don't die," he said. "We're invincible."

Justin's parents were plagued with fears about losing him. Both knew how impossible it was to know what to do when he was using. Carol struggled to accept the severity of the situation. Steve had relocated to his

Nashville-area home with his son John Henry during the pandemic, and he saw Justin a handful of times that summer. To others, Steve seemed tormented, unable to escape the idea that he'd passed on his howling addiction to his firstborn son.

When one musician went to Steve's house that August to film a project, he asked Steve about his eldest son. Justin was not doing well, Steve told the musician. He was worried sick, referencing another one of his self-destructive songwriting heroes: "I think he's trying to be Jerry Jeff Walker," Steve said of Justin.

Jenn Ramsey, an old family friend, had received similar messages from Steve after Justin was admitted to the hospital. "He's drinking himself to death," Steve said to her.

Steve told Justin he loved him and would support him if he were ever ready to go to recovery.[7] He was one of several friends and family members regularly checking in on Justin, letting him know he was not alone after he settled back in his apartment.

At 4:37 p.m. on Thursday, August 20, Justin responded to one of those messages. Adam Bednarik had been discussing the idea of filming Justin playing music in his backyard, something they could share with fans.

But really, Bednarik wanted to know how his friend was feeling.

"I am good," Justin texted Bednarik. "Damn near fit ta fight!"

That same evening, Justin called Haskins and asked her if she wanted to come over, but she couldn't make it.

"It's all good," she remembered him telling her. "Why don't you come over tomorrow afternoon?"

The following day, on Friday, August 21, Haskins called Justin. He didn't respond.

That weekend, at her father's home in Utah, Jenn Marie woke up in a panic. She'd had a dream that Justin died. She wasn't sure what prompted it. She hadn't heard from Justin and had been trying to reach him. But she'd seen, in their shared online banking records, that he'd taken cash out of an ATM earlier and had ordered food delivery to his apartment in the late evening, none of which was unusual.

Still, something felt wrong. She was sure of it. She tried to keep it together, "just doing normal things, knowing deep inside me that he was gone," and remembered making a series of frantic phone calls to Nashville begging someone, *anyone*, to check up on him, to knock down a door.

At 9:38 a.m. on Sunday, August 23, Jenn Marie called Nashville's Department of Emergency Services, demanding a welfare check.[8]

Later that day, Haskins received a call from an old acquaintance of Justin's, Chloe Green. "Please tell me he's with you," Green said in a panic, at which point Haskins realized the gravity of the situation: No one had spoken to Justin in several days.

Haskins and Green went to Justin's apartment; by that point, it had been nearly seventy-two hours since anyone had heard from him. They banged on the door and tried knocking it down. Haskins tried looking through the peephole but couldn't make out anything other than a shadow.

At 4:47 p.m., Haskins called 911 and requested a welfare check.

Both women were outside Justin's apartment when Nashville police arrived to break down the door. Justin was lying on the floor.

He was declared dead at 6:39 p.m.

An autopsy report eventually determined the cause of death: an accidental overdose after ingesting cocaine laced with fentanyl. He had died on the evening of August 20, it was determined, in an apartment that was little more than a mile from the hospital in which he'd been born.

Despite its endless expanse of glass condos and construction cranes, Nashville was still a small town. In the last few years of his life, back in the city that raised him, Justin reappeared in the lives of old friends and acquaintances. They ran into him in bars, restaurants, and hotels. More often than not, they ran into him strolling around the Nashville of his youth. Walking up and down a sidewalk, smoking a cigarette underneath a streetlamp, or simply at the Mapco gas station on Twenty-First Avenue, the one next to Brown's Diner, down the street from the apartment Justin once shared with his mom.

Songwriter Travis Stephens was an old friend of Justin's from his sober years in the mid-2000s. Like so many, he'd lost touch with Justin once his national career had kicked off.

One night, in late November 2019, Stephens was waiting in line for the bathroom backstage at a club in Nashville. When the door swung open, out walked a tall, lanky figure without a shirt. It had been years: Justin's face had filled out, and he had a goatee. Stephens's hair had gone gray. At first, neither recognized each other. "How's it going, man," Justin said before realizing who it was.

"Then he did that *fucking* smile," said Stephens, "and I just fucking melted."

On June 5, 2018, Dustin Welch, who'd since relocated to Texas, went with his wife to see John Prine perform in downtown Austin. When they got out of the show, they realized Justin Townes Earle was performing at a club downstairs. Dustin's prior reunion with Justin, at a South by Southwest many years before, had ended in tears after Justin rebuked Welch. But this time, when Welch found himself backstage, Justin came sprinting over to his old Swindlers bandmate, jumped on top of him, and wrapped his arms around him.

The reunion was brief. Justin needed to play a show in Houston the next day. He needed to find whoever was accompanying him on his tour bus and get going. When Justin's touring mates thought back on their last few years of traveling with him, one memory that surfaces was a road ritual Justin was adamant about: the family dinner. If Justin was touring with a full band, at least once each tour, he treated his band and crew to a meal at a restaurant.

Part of why this memory stuck out for the merch sellers, tour managers, and drummers who spend their lives on the road is that many of them had never encountered a ritual quite like Justin's family dinner. Everyone would gather around one large table, usually at a steakhouse or local Mexican restaurant. Justin paid for the meal and everyone's first drink. Some folks left right after eating; others stayed out late. The only rule was that everyone showed up. "You had to come to the table," said

Josh Taylor, Justin's friend and occasional tour manager. The point, he said, was to "show up and have a meal together, like a family."

For Justin, the ritual of the road family dinner was deep-seated. He'd inherited the custom, like so much else, from his dad.

On his last few tours, Justin began to discuss, more and more, the epidemic that would eventually kill him. The opioid crisis, he told crowds, was ravaging the country, destroying innocent lives, close to a hundred thousand people per year,[9] and it was a crisis that had been getting scarier each year, thanks to fentanyl.

"All this shit they're putting in heroin these days, it's killing people left and right," he'd told a 2018 audience. "I grew up during the crack cocaine epidemic, which was supposed to be bad, but I've never seen anything like what's going on today. Nobody has."[10]

By 2020, most opioid overdoses were traced back to fentanyl, a synthetic opioid fifty times stronger than heroin that is often cut into other drugs because its lethal strength makes it a cheap way for illegal drug manufacturers to spread a very small quantity of drugs while still maintaining potency. The month before Justin died, the city of Nashville released data showing that opioid overdoses had increased by nearly 50 percent. For several of Justin's friends, Justin was merely one of several Nashvillians they'd known who lost their lives to fentanyl during this period. In 2020 alone, more than three thousand residents of Tennessee died of drug overdoses, the fifth-highest rate in the country. "The majority of victims," noted the *Tennessean*, "are younger men killed by fentanyl."[11]

In his 2019 song "Appalachian Nightmare," Justin narrates a first-person account of a drug dealer turned thief turned murderer. Inspired in part by his time in Johnson City, the song portrays the way the pain-pill epidemic laid waste to a community. Toward its end, the narrator reflects on his life of misfortune, confessing his regrets:

"Wish I could've been better, mama," Justin sings. "Wish I'd never took a shot of dope."

That song was released on Justin's final album, *The Saint of Lost Causes.* When Justin entered the studio to record the LP, he'd shared demos of the material and had already rehearsed the songs with the band. But during the sessions, he pulled out a song he'd written at the last minute in Texas, either during or right after getting out of rehab. No one had heard it.

It was called "Talking to Myself." Even for Justin, it was an unusually stark self-portrait of a haunted man, the type of song Justin used to shelve after realizing he'd written something too exposing.

Not this time. Justin didn't emphasize the track when promoting the album. But he wrote it knowing it'd be its closing statement.[12]

He wanted the world to understand he'd spent his life trying to forgive—and seek forgiveness—but remained too plagued by his past to do so. He wanted to share secrets he'd rarely uttered aloud: that he was scared to fall asleep alone at night, that he felt incapable of true intimacy. He wanted the world to know he knew he needed help.

After his big, beautiful sweep of an album that told stories about Flint, Michigan, and South-Central Los Angeles and Puerto Rican victims of a failed criminal justice system and Kentucky hollers torn apart by opioids, Justin Townes Earle wanted his fans to hear from one more lost cause in need of saving. He wanted everyone to listen to the story of the ten-year-old roaming around Hillsboro Village, the one who'd carved his first name into the playground at Dragon Park, the one who'd spent much of his life wandering the streets of his hometown searching for a place to land. He wanted the world to know that he'd tried hard to find one.

The drinks bring no joy to me,
I just can't remember when
All the drugs began to fail,
Left me only with the lonely child within
So I tried to love and I failed
Put my heart on a shelf
These are things I say only when I'm talking to myself

AFTERWORD

ON JANUARY 5, 2023, ROUGHLY TWO AND A HALF YEARS AFTER HIS DEATH, a few dozen of Justin's friends, former bandmates, and fans gathered underneath the cramped, concert poster–stamped ceiling of the Basement in Nashville. It was exactly twenty-six years to the day since Justin, age fifteen, attended Townes Van Zandt's memorial service a mile and a half away. This evening, it was Justin who was being celebrated: His loved ones had congregated in the same room he'd spent much of his early career.

Gatherings to commemorate Justin's death had been delayed by the pandemic. The night before the Basement celebration, there was a grand public event on what would've been Justin's forty-first birthday: an official memorial concert at the Ryman Auditorium—the "Mother Church of Country Music"—attended by thousands.

Steve Earle had orchestrated that affair, choosing the venue—which had staged public memorials for musical luminaries like Johnny Cash, Tammy Wynette, and John Prine—and choosing which acts would perform covers of his son's songs. He acted as master of ceremonies, introducing each artist, and served as de facto headliner, ending the main set with a mournful tearjerker ballad he wrote days after Justin's death: "Tore my heart apart," Steve sang, "and then you brought me back the piece again."

The aftershock of Justin's death had reverberated through his extended community, causing grief-induced strain in the months and years that followed. One dynamic that survived Justin's tragic death: Anything involving father and firstborn Earle remained complicated. Such had been the case with the star-studded Ryman memorial, which had elevated Steve's friends and contemporaries over many of Justin's closest collaborators.

Yet, like anything involving the father and firstborn Earle, the evening was also full of complex, immense love: Bonnie Whitmore reworked Justin's "Maria" as a fond farewell to her ex-fiancé. Amanda Shires offered up dark country humor by singing, in Justin's trademark raspy shout, the words "If you ain't glad I'm leaving / Girl, you know you oughta be." Folksinger Joe Pug choked up during "Mama's Eyes," unable to make it through the line "I still see wrong from right."

The stately evening at the Ryman had been the main event, but Dustin Welch wanted to host something more informal while everyone was in town. The Swindlers' founder hastily arranged an evening of song swapping and storytelling. The Basement was the perfect spot: It was one of the few remaining Nashville clubs from their youth that hadn't since been bulldozed.

Welch played with songwriters like Justin's old friend and longtime photographer Joshua Black Wilkins and Scotty Melton, Justin's old Johnson City mentor, singing some of their own songs and a few of Justin's. They shared stories onstage. Meanwhile, old acquaintances, family friends, ex-girlfriends, and former Swindlers mulled about, catching up with one another, exchanging glances with faces they hadn't seen in years, transforming the space into a temporary reunion of an artistic community shattered by its star's death.

At night's end, Welch implored the crowd to carry on whatever spirit that had been captured in the tiny club, to keep Justin's legacy alive by honoring his spirit of song, that deep source of creative energy that, for better and for worse, had brought him more meaning, value, and sense of purpose than perhaps anything else.

"It's important that we have to be able to continue on," Welch told the audience. "This isn't some kind of final thing."

In the years following Justin's death, his music found a new life. Tribute shows popped up in Seattle, Washington, and Melbourne, Australia. Artists devoted part of their sets to him. The jam band Widespread Panic covered Justin's song "Don't Drink the Water." Joe Pug started singing "Mama's Eyes" every night. Scottish songwriter Roseanne Reid performed "Ain't Waitin'." The day after news of his death broke, a British singer named Patrick McCallion sang Justin's song "Time You Waste" onstage in the Netherlands.

The song that traveled furthest was "Harlem River Blues." Upstart bluegrass bands around the country added it to their repertoire. Next-generation country-Americana stars like Sierra Ferrell and Charley Crockett sang the song at large festivals and clubs. Legends like David Byrne and Emmylou Harris harmonized on its chorus while sharing the stage with Steve Earle, who released his own tribute album of Justin's songs.

Others wrote songs *about* Justin. A number of songs and albums had been written about him, in all his captivating glory, during his lifetime: In 2011 alone, two records were released—Jessica Lea Mayfield's *Tell Me* and Bonnie Whitmore's *Embers to Ashes*—largely inspired by the singer who couldn't help but leave a lifelong impression on so many of the people he met.

Now, new songs about Justin poured out: the Sadies, Drive-By Truckers, Mary Gauthier, Jason Isbell, Margo Cilker, Andrew Combs, Mark Erelli—some of whom knew Justin intimately, some of whom were merely fans—were just a few who felt moved to write music that reckoned, in some way, with the loss of this immense presence.

Utah songwriter Sammy Brue, whom Justin mentored when Brue was a teenager, embarked on an album-length reimagination of Justin's work, recording a collection based on a trove of half-written and unfinished lyrics Justin left behind.

Others gathered grief in prose. Asked to speak about Justin for this book, author and singer-songwriter Allison Moorer, the mother of Justin's youngest half-brother, John Henry, and ex-wife of Steve Earle, shared thoughts and memories in writing:

> Sometimes it's looking at my son that makes me miss him most. John Henry didn't get to be around him very often, but Justin was so present when he was sober that he delighted his little brother. When I told John

Henry his brother had died, he looked at me like he might've known already. During the summer of 2021, one of Justin's songs came up randomly on a playlist we were listening to in the car and John Henry started pressing buttons on the car stereo—that's what he does when he wants me to change the music. The loss of Justin is a loss for everyone in the family and it will reverberate through our lives forever. One of these days, I hope we'll be able to listen to his records and not feel so sad.

And sometimes I just miss him. We were more than stepmother and stepson—we were also buds. We talked about clothes, architecture, jewelry, design, and objects. He drove me out of my mind with his extravagant nature, his impishness, his adorable sweetness, and his ability to make it seem like he didn't care at all when I know he probably cared more than most about most things he thought were important. He had real empathy.

I feel, believe, and have faith that he is still with us as a powerful spirit, and we can rest in that comfort and know that he is free from his pain. A few short weeks after he died, Labor Day arrived and it was time for John Henry to go back to school in New York after having been home for six months. I wasn't handling it well. I stood on the porch the morning he left after putting him in the car with his father, and as I watched them pull away, a hummingbird flew right up to my face and hovered as if to say—it's all going to be okay.

Others dreamed of Justin.

An old friend and collaborator was visited by a vision of him and Justin running wild around Nashville, just like they used to. When they got to a gig, in the dream, Justin lent him a guitar and sat on the side of the stage, listening to his friend sing.

A past tour mate woke up from a dream in which she encountered Justin shopping in an antique store, dressed fashionably in a beachy outfit.

"We've all been looking for you," she told Justin in the dream.

"I needed to be quiet," Justin responded.

Others, still, expressed their grief through poetry. Chris Crofton, a

Nashville comedian, author, and songwriter, penned a poem about Justin despite having barely known him.

It was about the impossible weight that always seemed to be pressing down on that smiley nineteen-year-old who hung around Springwater in the early 2000s, a poem that pondered what it might've felt like to go through life fighting, yet embracing, a role he'd been cast in—but hadn't, necessarily, signed up for.

"He was a vessel," it read, "and a boy."

A NOTE ON SOURCING

I've tried to incorporate Justin's voice by quoting extensively from the many interviews he gave throughout his career. Beginning in 2009, Justin also expressed his thoughts, feelings, and riffs via Twitter. His tweets are frequently quoted and were used as corroboration of his whereabouts.

Two books written on Steve Earle were indispensable: Lauren St. John's *Hardcore Troubadour* and David McGee's *Fearless Heart, Outlaw Poet*. St. John's 2003 book was particularly essential, containing interviews with Justin, Carol, and much of the Earle family, including Steve.

Justin's story is in many ways a Nashville story, and the archives of both the *Tennessean* and the *Nashville Scene* were invaluable in helping map Justin's life and career onto what was happening in his hometown.

This book draws from assorted primary documents such as unreleased recordings, journal entries, unpublished song lyrics, emails and text messages, letters, notes, photographs, court records, music-industry documents, and concert posters. Where Justin's handwritten lyrics and journals are quoted, I've done my best to preserve his original spelling and punctuation.

Several quotes are pulled from interviews I conducted shortly after Justin's death for a 2021 story in *Rolling Stone*; those quotes are noted as such in an endnote. All other quotations from those other than Justin, unless otherwise noted, are taken from original interviews conducted for this book.

The bulk of the book is based on interviews conducted with Justin's friends, family, loved ones, bandmates, former girlfriends, musical contemporaries, associates, and passing acquaintances. Some of these people knew Justin intimately; some met him once in passing. Some interviews lasted multiple days and included months of correspondence; some were five-minute conversations or brief written exchanges. These interviews were conducted between 2022 and 2024, mostly via telephone, while some took place in person in Nashville, New York, and Montana. In a few cases, interviews were conducted via email or Facebook. In a very small number of cases, sources asked to remain anonymous; their contributions, while not listed below, are much appreciated. Although I spoke to some 250-odd people for the book, many others turned down or never responded to requests to participate, including Steve Earle, who respectfully declined to be interviewed.

LIST OF INTERVIEWEES

Julien Aklei, Ricky Albeck, Eric Ambel, Ian Anderson, Tommy Anderson, PJ Anthony, Melinda Baker, BJ Barham, Michael Batdorf, Scott Baxendale, Rayland Baxter, Adam Bednarik, Adams Bellouis (Rachel Keesecker), Brady Blade, Nick Bobetsky, Ruby Boots, Sonya Kay Boyd, Evan Bradford, Cory Branan, Ben Brodin, Blake Brown, Jonathan Buske, Lee Calvin, Alex Caress, Jordan Caress, Rosemary Carroll, Cory Chisel, Molly Claiborne, David Clough, Andrew Colvin, Shelly Colvin, Andrew Combs, Wilson Compton, Sara Connell, Jim Conway, Darcy Cooke, James Crenshaw, October Crifasi, Chris Crofton, Elliot Currie, Terry Currier, Todd Cyphers, Bryn Davies, Duane Denison, Gerry Diaz, Willie Domann, Geoff Donovan, Bryan Dowling, Murielle Dragness, Nick Dryden, Orsolya Dunai, Marah Eakin, Carol Ann Earle, Jenn Marie Earle, Josiah Early, Matt Eddmenson, Robert Ellis, Justin Eshak, Cole Fain, Jody Faison, Paul Fenn, Boscoe France, Jon-Paul Frappier, Chris Frayer, Irakli Gabriel, Simon Gardner, Tristen Gaspadarek, Lou-Anne Gill, Josh Graham, Chloe Green, James Green, Christine Hall, Julia Haltigan, Nicholas Hardy, Jack Harris, Ward Harrison, Rosemary Haskins, Rob Heath, Mark Hedman, Lilly Hiatt, Judy Hilton, Rich Hinman, Derek Hoke, Cassidy Holden, Andrew Jacob Holm, Patterson Hood, Paul Horvath, Michael Hosty, Vince Ilagan, Robert Jetton, Duquette Johnston, Molly Jones (née McClary), Brigid Kaelin, Sara Jean Kelley, Joie Todd Kerns, Clayton Kidd, Jamie

Kindleyside, Charlie King, Chris Knight, Augusta Koch, Laurens Kusters, Norm Lackey, Dawn Landes, Gill Landry, Jake Lanier, Amy LaVere, Laura Lee, June Lehman, Jordan Lehning, Patty Lemay, Andy Levenberg, Luke Lewis, Gareth Lindsay, Sean Locke, Lydia Loveless, Colby Maddox, James Marshall, Justin Martin, Michael Martin, Jessica Lea Mayfield, Erin McAnally, Richard McBride, Ian McCall, Michael McCall, Dan McCarthy, Jason McIntire, Richard McLaurin, Colin Meloy, Scotty Melton, Gerald Menke, Michael Merenda, Jim Merlis, Ezekiel Miller, Johnny Mark Miller, Rob Miller, Susan Moffett, Andy Moore, Chaz Moore, Allison Moorer, Kevin Morrow, Aaron Mortenson, Bob Nastanovich, Mark Nevers, Shane Nicholson, Travis Nicholson, Paul Niehaus, David Noel, Hunter Nott, Michael O'Brien, Thomas Oliverio, John Orchard, Sam Outlaw, James Overbee, Bryan Owings, Jennifer Patten, Alden Peace, Derek Pell, Matt Pence, Lee Pendarvis, Dorothy Pewitt, Stephen Phillips, Charlie Pierce, Catherine Popper, Steve Poulton, John Purcell, Burhan Qazi, Jon Radford, Jenn Ramsey, Deidre Randall, Billy Reid, Michael Rinne, Ray Rizzo, Adam Roberts, Bryce Roberts, Anna Rose, Caitlin Rose, Viktoria Safarian, Scott Schaefer, Angela Schmidt, Ketch Secor, Scott Seiver, Jacob Sewell, Doug Seymour, Clare Shamier, Brandon Sharp, Amanda Shires, Zach Shoffner, Allan Sicignano, David Sickmen, Trevor Silva, Portia Sipes, Langhorne Slim, Alex Smith, Todd Snider, Ed Snodderly, Kevin So, Lauren Spratlin, Brenton Stanley, Travis Stephens, Matthew Stewart, Neil Stinson, John Stirratt, Matt Svobodny, Joe Swank, Brian Taranto, Josh Taylor, John Thompson, Stephen Thorne, Joe del Tufo, Lisa Marie Turner, Katie Tuten, Tim Tuten, Jared Tyler, James Van Cooper, Henry Wagons, Will Walker, Andy Washington, Willie Watson, Dustin Welch, Savannah Welch, Heather West, Michael West, Bonnie Whitmore, Jason Moon Wilkins, Joshua Black Wilkins, Adam Williams, Jody Williams, Brian Willis, Skylar Wilson, Keith Wood, Scott Woods, Dan Wysuph, Lisa York, David Young, Jubal Lee Young, Cory Younts.

SONG CREDITS

"Frightened by the Sound"
Words and Music by Justin Townes Earle
Copyright © 2019 BMG Platinum Songs
All Rights Administered by BMG Rights Management (US) LLC
All Rights Reserved Used by Permission
Reprinted by Permission of Hal Leonard LLC

"So Different Blues"
Words and Music by Mance Lipscomb
Copyright © 1992 Tradition Music Co.
All Rights Administered by BMG Rights Management (US) LLC
All Rights Reserved Used by Permission
Reprinted by Permission of Hal Leonard LLC

"Wanderin'"
Words and Music by Justin Townes Earle
Copyright © 2010 BMG Platinum Songs
All Rights Administered by BMG Rights Management (US) LLC
All Rights Reserved Used by Permission
Reprinted by Permission of Hal Leonard LLC

"Talking to Myself"
Words and Music by Justin Townes Earle
Copyright © 2019 BMG Platinum Songs
All Rights Administered by BMG Rights Management (US) LLC
All Rights Reserved Used by Permission
Reprinted by Permission of Hal Leonard LLC

ACKNOWLEDGMENTS

I AM INDEBTED TO EVERYONE WHO TRUSTED ME WITH THEIR MEMORIES OF Justin. Several sources, in particular, were remarkably helpful.

Joshua Black Wilkins provided encouragement, wisdom, and several beautiful photographs, including the one on the cover; Larry Kusters offered his support; David Noel and Adam Williams answered endless questions about the Nashville of Justin's childhood; Lauren Spratlin shared invaluable memories; Eric Ambel became a much-welcome friendly neighborhood presence; Adam Bednarik provided detailed recollections of Justin's creative life in the studio; Scotty Melton relayed vivid insights into Justin's early songwriting; Patty Lemay shared profound wisdom; Allison Moorer provided beautiful impressions in writing; Judy Hilton and Michael O'Brien were invaluable resources on less-understood aspects of Justin's life; Jenn Ramsey, BJ Barham, Angela Schmidt, and many others spoke openly about sobriety and addiction in ways that deeply informed this book; Molly Jones shaped my understanding of Justin's "quiet years" and offered deep insights into his songwriting; Carol Ann Earle showed courage and grace in speaking about her late son.

Members of the Swindlers were the first people I interviewed; their willingness to share their band's story propelled this book into existence. Skylar Wilson and Travis Nicholson helped me understand their rascal bandmate; Willie Domann directed me toward forgotten names and shared invaluable unreleased recordings; Andy Moore offered pep talks and old Nashville history lessons; Cory Younts opened up about dark periods and volunteered insights no one else could have provided; Dustin Welch shared his revelatory Chicken Shack recordings and imparted, in our many conversations, endless warmth and wisdom.

Finally, Jenn Marie Earle shared memories both beautiful and painful of her late husband. Her trust and commitment to telling his story in its fullness made this project possible in so many ways.

Thanks to Ralph Martin, JTE's AT&T guy, for accompanying me to the Ryman. Huge thanks to Steve Poulton for introducing me to several nonobvious sources around Nashville and for truly caring about this project. Thanks to everyone who shared with me their precious slice of Justin's hometown.

The first glimmer of feeling like this book could exist came when David Dunton told me he thought it was an idea worth pursuing. Since then, he has provided guidance and calm reassurance as my agent every step of the way.

I am eternally grateful to my editor, Ben Schafer, for patiently answering my questions and, most of all, for believing in me, this book, and Justin's story. Huge thanks to everyone who worked on this book and helped share it with the world: Cassie DeNicola, Fred Francis, Tara Kennedy, Tamara Coleman, Tiffany Porcelli, and Annette Wenda.

Thanks to Jen Larson at the Opry, Glenda Hart at BMI, and Michael McKee at WTTW for digging up footage, and to Christine Hall for preserving audio from the Swindlers' Belcourt show. An enormous dose of gratitude to the Internet Archive, which houses a collection of noncommercially available live recordings spanning Justin's career.

I am deeply thankful to everyone who shared with me unpublished audio recordings or unedited transcripts of their interviews with Justin: Skip Anderson, Stephen Deusner, Selena Frye, Jeff Gage, Gary Graff, Joe Hagan, Brian Hiatt, Jewly Hight, Kirsten Johnstone, Jonathan Miles, Danny R. Phillips, Lauren Streib, Jeff Tamarkin, Joanne Will, and Brian Wise. Thanks, in particular, to Chris Talbott for trusting me with your extensive and revealing transcripts.

John Lingan and Bob Mehr offered much-needed feedback while I was in the book-proposal phase. Ricky Kreitner walked me through many steps in the publishing process. Natasha Martin helped me think about promoting the book and let me daydream about having finished it when that felt very far away. Joe Sivick and John Hendrickson offered brilliant advice. David Browne answered many anxious questions and freely shared his indispensable wisdom.

Eternally thankful to Stephanie Fairyington for taking a chance on me, Coco McPherson for showing me the ropes, and Hannah Murphy for not only teaching me everything I know about journalism but also advising on this book.

Thanks to everyone at *Rolling Stone*, past and present, for their support: Sean Woods offered encouragement; Christian Hoard suggested I write about Justin after his death, an assignment that changed my career; Alison Weinflash welcomed me into the building as an intern; Simon Vozick-Levinson gave me my first real *Rolling Stone* assignment; Tessa Stuart's enthusiasm and interest in this project hugely helped; Elias Leight saved me with cinnamon buns; Jon Freeman taught me everything I know about country music; Jon Blistein provided me with a lifelong doppelgänger—this book may have been written by him.

Huge thanks to Brenna Ehrlich for helming *Rolling Stone*'s mighty research team and gratitude to the two sharpest fact-checkers around: Rick Carp and Meagan Jordan. Enormous thanks to all the hardworking and brilliant colleagues I've learned from at the magazine over the years, including but by no means limited to Ryan Bort, Mankaprr Conteh, Tim Dickinson, EJ Dickson, Jon Dolan, Patrick Doyle, Beville Dunkerley, Suzy Exposito, David Fear, Jason Fine, Maria Fontoura, Toby Fox, Elisabeth Garber-Paul, Andre Gee, Maya Georgi, Andy Greene, Kory Grow, Charles Holmes, Jeff Ihaza, Brendan Klinkenberg, Chris Kobiella, Sacha Lecca, Althea Legaspi, Julyssa Lopez, Andrea Marks, Angie Martoccio, Jason Maxey, Alex Morris, Phoebe Neidl, Jason Newman, Steven Pearl, Jerry Portwood, Joe Rodriguez, Claire Shaffer, Rob Sheffield, Hank Shteamer, Alexis Sottile, Brittany Spanos, Kate Storey, Lisa Tozzi, and Amy Wang.

Thank you to Griffin Lotz for scanning photos; to Chris M. Junior for his invaluable catches and expert first-pass copyedit and proofread; and Corinne Cummings for fact-checking the book, finding many errors I never would have caught, and persuading me to strike the word "pirouette" from the manuscript.

Thanks to Nick Murray and Sarah Grant for your true friendship and country karaoke companionship.

Two people believed in this book before I did: Joseph Hudak humored my incessant rambling about the world of Earle and connected me to various sources, including the barber he and JTE shared. Marissa R. Moss was an indispensable sounding board whose writing and reporting on Justin greatly shaped this project. I'll forever be grateful for their encouragement.

Thanks to my teachers: to Mr. Tucker and Mr. Blum for expanding my mind; to James Dawes, Daylanne English, Dan Gilbert, and Mark Mazullo for showing me how to listen and read carefully; and to Peter Bognanni for assigning music writing from the *Oxford American*. Thanks, especially, to Marlon James for informing me whenever my writing included a line I deserved to be "shot" for having written.

This book's origins can be traced to April 15, 2009, the night I first saw Justin Townes Earle perform, at the Turf Club in St. Paul, Minnesota. Thank you to whoever was working the door that night for letting me in underage.

Thank you to Andrew Berger for your friendship, for the conversations on our yearly Newport walks that helped shape this book in so many ways, but mostly for not being able to see Justin at the Turf Club that night and giving me your ticket.

I'm so lucky to have friends who always pulled me back into the real world while working on this project: Dan, Eddie, James, Jeremiah, Jess, Joe, Lily, Lucas, Mary, Mikey (thanks for that Walon supercut), Nina, Nolan, Oleh, Robbie, Sam, Sarah, Serena, Simon, Steven, and Zoe.

Sam Robertson is the deepest listener I know, and talking with him about this project was truly helpful.

Two friends provided critical feedback on early drafts: Thank you, Cass Saldaña, for encouraging me to think deeper about the book's big-picture themes. Thank you, Kevin Sweeting, for your line-by-line comments and for helping me (hopefully) reduce the number of "Roy Donks."

Thank you to Sharon, Rob, and Virginia for supporting me during this time and offering your home as a much-needed writing reprieve. Endless love to Phyllis, Sarah, Elissa, Tapan, Norah, Sidney, Ellen, Lauren, Julie, Danny, Ilene, Lara, Jillian, Timmy, Mary, and Lila. Thank you, forever, to Laurie Fessler for encouraging me to write.

Anna listened to me talk endlessly through the complicated interpersonal dynamics in this story, and her advice and professional perspective on how to navigate various relationships and more difficult themes in the book were invaluable. I'm so lucky to have her as my sister.

Thanks to my mom, Emma Fessler, my first editor, my most devoted reader, for catching all the typos my editors missed over the years. I never would have written this book, or really done anything, without her lifetime of love and support.

Thank you to my dad, Stuart Bernstein, for always being there, for sharing your passion, for showing me music. This book is for him.

No one supported me more or gave more of themselves to this project than my wife, Natalie Shutler, who often believed in this book far more than I, edited many indecipherable drafts, and reflected back my half-formed thoughts in far more eloquent ways than I could've imagined. I'll forever be thankful not only for her encouragement but also for her playing such a critical role in willing this project into existence. To the degree that this book is remotely readable is entirely thanks to her generous and brilliant work.

NOTES

INTRODUCTION

The introduction draws on interviews with Andrew Colvin, Sean Locke, Amanda Shires, and Joshua Black Wilkins.

1. Justin Townes Earle, interview by Garret K. Woodward, YouTube, May 9, 2018, www.youtube.com/watch?v=gpEZ0fpW2ng&t=226s.

2. Anthony DeCurtis, "Freeing a Mentor from His Mythology," *New York Times*, May 7, 2009.

3. Craig Dodge Lile, "MOKB Interviews Justin Townes Earle," *My Old Kentucky Blog*, March 13, 2008 (emphasis added).

4. Justin began discussing and using the terminology of "the myth" with a series of journalists, namely, Chris Talbott, Lauren Streib, and Brian Hiatt, in 2011 and 2012.

5. Chris Talbott, interview with Justin Townes Earle, 2011 (transcript).

6. Steve Earle's famous quote about Townes was originally included as a promotional sticker on Townes Van Zandt's 1987 album *At My Window*.

7. Lauren St. John, *Hardcore Troubadour: The Life & Near Death of Steve Earle* (New York: HarperCollins, 2003), 83.

8. Interview with Steve Earle, 2001, https://archive.org/details/bpl-earle-steve-2001.

9. Justin Townes Earle, interview by Bob Harris, *The Bob Harris Show*, BBC 2, July 26, 2008.

10. Marissa R. Moss, interview with Justin Townes Earle, 2019 (transcript).

11. David McPherson, "Justin Townes Earle: The Good Life," *Exclaim*, March 23, 2008.

12. Brian Hiatt, interview with Justin Townes Earle, 2012 (transcript).

13. Talbott, interview with Justin Townes Earle.

14. Justin Townes Earle, *Live at the Turf Club on 2009-04-15*, released 2009, streaming audio, https://archive.org/details/jte2009-04-15.adkTLmtrx.flac16.

15. Justin Townes Earle, *Live at the Blue Note on 2013-05-02*, released 2013, streaming audio, https://archive.org/details/jte2013-05-02.mk4mk8.flac16.

16. "The First Time with Justin Townes Earle," *Rolling Stone*, YouTube, May 30, 2019, www.youtube.com/watch?v=5WOJvoBLJMI.

CHAPTER 1

This chapter draws on interviews with Tommy Anderson, Molly Claiborne, Carol Earle, Jenn Marie Earle, Cole Fain, Lou-Anne Gill, James Green, Jack Harris, Judy Hilton,

Robert Jetton, Molly Jones (née McClary), David Noel, Michael O'Brien, Lee Pendarvis, Alex Smith, Adam Williams, Jody Williams, and David Young.

1. Lauren St. John, *Hardcore Troubadour: The Life & Near Death of Steve Earle* (New York: HarperCollins, 2003), 11.

2. Steve Earle most often claimed the soil came from the San Jacinto monument, as he told author Alanna Nash (*Behind Closed Doors: Talking with the Legends of Country Music* [New York: Cooper Square Press, 1988], 147). In later interviews, he's also claimed the dirt came from "his grandfather's farm" (Holly Gleason, "Steve Earle's Low Highway," *Lone Star Music Magazine*, May 1, 2013).

3. A photo of Justin touching Texas soil can be found on the Steve Earle fan site SteveEarle.net: https://steveearle.net/bio/steve&justin.php.

4. The Earle family history is drawn largely from the "History" section of the Friend's of Earle's Chapel website: https://friendsofearleschapel.org/history. Friends of Earle's Chapel is an organization dedicated to preserving the history of Earle's Chapel United Methodist Church and its corresponding cemetery in Jacksonville, Texas, where generations of Earles, including Justin, are buried.

5. St. John, *Hardcore Troubadour*, 95.

6. "Steve Earle—Little Rock 'N' Roller," YouTube, January 25, 2008, www.youtube.com/watch?v=U1IwSXRswvA.

7. Steve Earle has told many versions of the story of calling his father from the hospital as soon as Justin was born: Steve Earle, "Hardcore Troubadour Radio," SiriusXM, May 20, 2017.

8. Holly Gleason, "Steve Earle: A Bad Boy Settles Down," *Rolling Stone*, January 26, 1989.

9. St. John, *Hardcore Troubadour*, 90–91.

10. Ella Sheppard Moore was born enslaved on Andrew Jackson's plantation and was a descendant of Jackson's brother. Dr. Paul Kwami, the former director of the Fisk Jubilee Singers who passed away in 2022, repeatedly refuted the famous story of Nashville becoming "Music City" due to a remark Queen Victoria made upon hearing the Fisk Jubilee Singers: "You people must come from a music city." The year 1979 in Nashville: Ricky Rogers, "Nashville Then: Best of 1979," Tennessean.com, December 30, 2019, www.tennessean.com/picture-gallery/news/local/2019/12/30/nashville-then-best-1979-lamar-alexander-ronald-reagan-billy-graham/2775424001/; Rebekah Gleaves Sanderlin, "Fit for a Country Music King," *Nashville Scene*, August 25, 2005; Kirk Loggins, "Evangelist Preaches Love, Patriotism," *Tennessean*, October 16, 1979; Larry Woody, *Schmittou: A Grand Slam in Baseball, Business, and Life* (Nashville: Eggman, 1996), 90; Alan Carmichael, "Proud Walkers Turn the Page to Century III," *Tennessean*, December 24, 1979; Lia Nower, "Fisk Honors School-Saving Supporters," *Tennessean*, October 7, 1979.

11. St. John, *Hardcore Troubadour*, 94.

12. Both Pat McLaughlin and Don Schlitz were Springwater regulars in the late seventies and early eighties, according to concert listings in the *Tennessean*.

13. St. John, *Hardcore Troubadour*, 92.

14. St. John, *Hardcore Troubadour*, 95.

15. Sandy Neese, "ASCAP Honors Its Own in New Opulent Surroundings," *Tennessean*, October 13, 1983.

16. St. John, *Hardcore Troubadour*, 96.

17. St. John, *Hardcore Troubadour*, 110.

18. Wolfgang Saxon, "L. Clure Morton, 82, Ex-Judge Who Aided Nashville Integration," *New York Times*, April 19, 1998.

19. Carol Ann's 1972 sophomore yearbook photo is preserved online by the Cohn High School Alumni Society, www.cohnhighalumni.net/home.

20. "Vickery, Hunter Vows Said," *Tennessean*, November 28, 1973.

21. St. John, *Hardcore Troubadour*, 103–108.

22. St. John, *Hardcore Troubadour*, 105, 109.

23. Jonathan Miles, interview with Justin Townes Earle, 2010 (transcript).

24. Chris Parker, "Justin Townes Earle Forges Own Name, Identity and Sound," *Oklahoma Gazette*, March 26, 2009.

25. Rob Simbeck, "How Was Your Day, Dad?," *Nashville Scene*, June 13, 2002.

26. Brian Koppelman, "Justin Townes Earle on Loneliness, Songwriting, and Change," *The Moment* (podcast), January 12, 2016, https://slate.com/culture/2016/01/justin-townes-earle-on-loneliness-songwriting-and-change.html.

27. Justin Townes Earle, *Live at Rhythm & Brews on 2009-10-16*, released 2009, streaming audio, https://archive.org/details/jte2009-10-16.flac16/jte2009-10-16t15.flac.

28. "Country Music's Loss of Earle Is Gain for Rock and Roll Fans," *Meriden (CT) Record-Journal*, December 30, 1988.

29. St. John, *Hardcore Troubadour*, 211.

30. Koppelman, "Justin Townes Earle on Loneliness, Songwriting, and Change."

31. Exactly what Justin stuck into the outlet to make his classroom's lights turn off is a matter of debate: Some classmates remembered it being a paper clip; others remembered it being a crumpled-up foil gum wrapper. His aunt, who would have heard the story secondhand, remembered it as a fork.

32. St. John, *Hardcore Troubadour*, 251.

33. Justin Townes Earle, interview by Jane Hutcheon, *One Plus One*, ABC, April 3, 2015. Justin did indeed move with his mother every few years and constantly changed schools, but there's no evidence to suggest that he lived in "over 30 houses" in Nashville, as he once claimed.

34. Chris Talbott, interview with Justin Townes Earle, 2011 (transcript).

35. Talbott, interview with Justin Townes Earle.

36. Paul Bowers, "Even in Good Times, Justin Townes Earle Makes His Sorrows Sing," *Charleston City Paper*, November 12, 2014.

37. Justin Townes Earle, interview by Hutcheon.

38. Chris Parton, "Justin Townes Earle's Second Album Comes from a Different Place," CMT, March 30, 2009.

39. Renee Elder, "Inner-City Crowds Are Thinning Out," *Tennessean*, March 20, 1991.

40. Sierra Rains, "North Nashville Had the Highest Incarceration Rate in the Nation in 2018; What's Changed Since?," WKRN, January 12, 2023.

41. Jerome Moore, *Deep Dish Conversations: Voices of Social Change in Nashville* (Nashville: Vanderbilt University Press, 2023), 10.

42. These are but three examples of the sensational and horrifying stories Justin told about his exposure to drugs at a very young age. There is every reason to believe many of these stories were exaggerated and dramatized just as there's every reason to believe that most of the stories contained grains of truth in them. "Crack at age nine": Skip Anderson, "On *Kids in the Street*, Justin Townes Earle Looks Outward—and Backward," *Nashville Scene*, May 4, 2017. The "crack house" and "Disneyland" stories come from an unreleased recording of Justin's in-store performance at Music Millenium in Portland, Oregon, on May 24, 2019.

43. Brian Hiatt, "Justin Townes Earle: The *Rolling Stone* Interview," *Rolling Stone Music Now* (podcast), June 12, 2019.

44. Many of the interviews in which Justin claimed to inject heroin as a twelve-year-old were conducted during a period when Justin was in the midst of serious substance use. In his more sober periods, he tended to stick to the more nuanced story of discovering his grandmother's Dilaudid prescription. The most detailed description of his introduction to drugs as a child can be found in Chris Talbott, "Justin Townes Earle Looks Back at Year of Recovery," Associated Press, October 15, 2011.

45. Skip Anderson, interview with Justin Townes Earle, 2017 (transcript).

46. Talbott, "Justin Townes Earle Looks Back at Year of Recovery."

CHAPTER 2

This chapter draws on interviews with Sara Connell, Carol Ann Earle, Cole Fain, Lou-Anne Gill, Clayton Kidd, Laura Lee, Chaz Moore, Hunter Nott, Dorothy Pewitt, Stephen Phillips, Brandon Sharp, Adam Williams, and Scott Woods.

1. David McGee, *Steve Earle: Fearless Heart, Outlaw Poet* (San Francisco: Backbeat, 2005), 149.

2. Justin's narrative of his move to Fairview to save his father: Jonathan Miles, interview with Justin Townes Earle, 2010 (transcript); Kenny Berkowitz, "Justin Townes Earle on Songwriting, His Idiosyncratic Fingerpicking Style, and Battling Personal Demons," *Acoustic Guitar*, September 2012; Steve's account of wresting control of his son: Michael McCall, "The Good Life from Now On," *Nashville Scene*, March 27, 2008.

3. Joe Hagan, interview with Steve Earle, 2009 (transcript).

4. Miles, interview with Justin Townes Earle.

5. Jan Botts, "Man Killed as Trailer Crosses Median of I-40," *Tennessean*, April 8, 1994.

6. Chris Talbott, interview with Justin Townes Earle, 2011 (transcript).

7. Justin never mentioned Beck as an early influence, but most of his friends at the time in both Fairview and Nashville in the early to midnineties remembered all of them, Justin included, being enormous fans of the singer. In a 1998 interview with *Bomb Magazine*, Steve Earle explained that Justin turned him on to Beck: "He had the independent single on 'Loser.'"

8. Steve Earle has been consistently telling the story of kicking heroin in jail since

1994, and he recalled it at length in Lauren St. John's biography, *Hardcore Troubadour: The Life & Near Death of Steve Earle* (New York: HarperCollins, 2003). The specific timeline of his arrests and stints in jail and rehab is compiled from various *Tennessean* newspaper accounts throughout 1994, primarily Kirk Loggins, "Judge to Let Singer Earle Trade Jail for Drug Rehab," *Tennessean*, November 2, 1994.

9. Steve Earle, interview by Terry Gross, *Fresh Air*, NPR, July 30, 1996.

10. Robert Hilburn, "Through the Ring of Fire," *Los Angeles Times*, February 18, 1996.

11. Hagan, interview with Steve Earle.

12. St. John, *Hardcore Troubadour*, 304–312.

13. St. John, *Hardcore Troubadour*, 312.

14. Talbott, interview with Justin Townes Earle.

15. Steve and Justin Townes Earle, interview by Steve Inskeep, *Morning Edition*, NPR, December 29, 2008.

16. Steve Earle, interview by George Stroumboulopoulos, *George Stroumboulopoulos Tonight*, CBC, April 23, 2013, www.youtube.com/watch?v=-10JuxewedU&t=111s.

17. Hagan, interview with Steve Earle.

18. An advertisement for a program at Three Springs–Duck River called LEAPS (Letting Experiential Adventure Promise Success) ran in the *Tennessean* several times throughout December 1995, the year before Justin attended.

19. For more information about the troubled-teen industry, see Maia Szalavitz's 2006 book *Help at Any Cost: How the Troubled-Teen Industry Cons Parents and Hurts Kids* (New York: Riverhead, 2006). Information about Three Springs and Three Springs–Duck River is pulled from archived versions of the company's website, as well as reporting from the time: Associated Press, "Juvenile Facility Seeks to Repair Image," May 6, 1998; Mike Salinero, "Youth Center Founder Says Luck Catapulted Him to Top," Associated Press, November 17, 1994.

20. Steve Bell, "On the Confederate Flag, Gun Control and the Constitution," *Music*, February 1, 2016.

21. *Be Here to Love Me*, directed by Margaret Brown (2004; New York: Palm Pictures, 2006), DVD.

22. Eli Petersen, "Justin Townes Earle Talks to Twangville," *Twangville*, November 30, 2009.

23. Michael McCall, "The Song Remains," *Nashville Scene*, January 9, 1997.

24. Justin Townes Earle, interview by Garret K. Woodward, YouTube, May 9, 2018, www.youtube.com/watch?v=gpEZ0fpW2ng&t=226s.

25. In fact, neither Lead Belly nor Kurt Cobain wrote "In the Pines," a song that existed, in various forms, for decades by the time Lead Belly recorded it. Both Steve and Justin extensively told the story of Justin's discovery of the song via Nirvana, but this direct exchange is from Jonathan Miles, "The Trials of Justin Townes Earle," *Garden & Gun*, December 2010–January 2011.

26. For more reading on the thorny relationship between Lead Belly, John Lomax, and Alan Lomax, see Benjamin Filene's book *Romancing the Folk: Public Memory & American Roots Music* (Chapel Hill: University of North Carolina Press, 2000).

27. Miles, interview with Justin Townes Earle.

28. Miles, interview with Justin Townes Earle.

29. Glen Alyn, *I Say Me for a Parable: The Oral Autobiography of Mance Lipscomb, Texas Bluesman* (New York: W. W. Norton, 1993), 17.

30. *Blues Unlimited*, no. 134 (1979).

31. Brian Hiatt, "Justin Townes Earle: The *Rolling Stone* Interview," *Rolling Stone Music Now* (podcast), June 12, 2019.

32. Steve Earle, liner notes for Steve Earle, *J.T.*, 2021, New West, accessed via www.steveearle.com/jt-liner-notes.

33. Justin Townes Earle, interview by Steve Earle, "Hardcore Troubadour Radio," SiriusXM, May 20, 2017.

34. Stephen Deusner, "Justin Townes Earle: The Son Also Rises," *American Songwriter*, June 30, 2011.

CHAPTER 3

This chapter draws on interviews with Melinda Baker, Andrew Colvin, James Crenshaw, Elliot Currie, Willie Domann, Carol Ann Earle, Josh Graham, Chloe Green, Andrew Jacob Holm, Joie Todd Kerns, Jamie Kindleyside, Sean Locke, Erin McAnally, Richard McBride, Ian McCall, Johnny Mark Miller, Andy Moore, Travis Nicholson, David Noel, Michael O'Brien, John Orchard, Jennifer Patten, Derek Pell, James Purcell, Jenn Ramsey, Deidre Randall, Angela Schmidt, Neil Stinson, Jared Tyler, Willie Watson, Dustin Welch, Savannah Welch, Adam Williams, Skylar Wilson, and Cory Younts.

1. The original "Chicken Shack" was built for songwriter Gary Nicholson, the father of a *different* member of the Swindlers: Travis Nicholson. Schleicher also built a Chicken Shack for the musical husband-wife team of country singer Pam Tillis and songwriter Bob DiPiero.

2. Henderson was one of the Swindlers' most revered local musicians. He was also, coincidentally, the man who'd originally built the Chicken Shack on Warfield Drive before selling his house to the Welch family in 1998.

3. Bill Rouda, *Nashville's Lower Broad: The Street That Music Made* (Washington, DC: Smithsonian Books, 2004), 7–9, 13.

4. Gail McKnight and Duren Cheek, "Music City as Tourism Mecca," *Tennessean*, May 30, 1993.

5. Ricky Rogers, "A Look at the Nun Bun of Bongo Java Coffeehouse in Nashville in Photos," Tennessean.com, July 12, 2022, www.tennessean.com/picture-gallery/news/local/2022/07/12/nun-bun-stolen-bongo-java-coffeehouse-nashville-photos/9895154002/.

6. Jacob Sewell has repeatedly told the story of how Harmony Korine cast him in *Gummo*: Jacob Sewell, interview by Casey Doran, "The Bunny Boy from *Gummo*—Jacob Sewell Interview," December 29, 2023, www.thesunisflat.org/jacob-sewell-interview.

7. Justin's brief tenure at Hillsboro High is murky at best. Most friends from that time had vague recollections of Justin's brief presence at the school; several did not

remember him ever actually attending Hillsboro but nevertheless just being around. One friend remembered him appearing midway through the school year; another remembered him showing up at the beginning of a school year before quickly transitioning to homeschooling, before dropping out. It seems likely that he actually showed up to classes for a few weeks or so.

8. Justin claimed in interviews that his last full year of schooling was eighth grade and that he dropped out partway through ninth grade. Academic records from Benton Hall only slightly contradict Justin's own timeline of his dropping out: they indicate he attended Benton Hall the fall semester of his sophomore year of high school at age fifteen before dropping out for the second semester. Steve Earle once claimed Justin repeated the ninth grade. Even Justin's precise sequence of schooling remains mysterious: in Justin's memory, he went from Aiken Elementary School to Benton Hall, then to Fairview Middle School; academic records from Benton Hall appear to contradict this timeline.

9. Joe Hagan, interview with Steve Earle, 2009 (transcript).

10. Both Steve and Justin tended to describe Justin's decision to pursue music in fatalistic terms: "There came a point when it was like, what else were you going to do?" Steve Earle once told his son (Steve and Justin Townes Earle, interview by Steve Inskeep, *Morning Edition*, NPR, December 29, 2008). "At the point I decided that's what I wanted to do, I was really on my way to prison," Justin said that same year. Craig Dodge Lile, "MOKB Interviews Justin Townes Earle," *My Old Kentucky Blog*, March 13, 2008.

11. Jesse Kornbluth, "Justin Townes Earle: Steve's Son? Yes, Just as Talented, but Not Political and Much More Fun," *HuffPost* contributor platform, April 12, 2010.

12. Brian Hiatt, "Justin Townes Earle: The *Rolling Stone* Interview," *Rolling Stone Music Now* (podcast), June 12, 2019.

13. Skip Anderson, "On *Kids in the Street*, Justin Townes Earle Looks Outward—and Backward," *Nashville Scene*, May 4, 2017.

14. Between July and September 1999, a 3:00 p.m. Sunday afternoon set by "Justin Earle" is regularly advertised in *Tennessean* concert listings. He is sometimes described as "blues," sometimes as "acoustic blues."

15. Justin Townes Earle and Samantha Crain, *Live at Pickathon Pendarvis Farm Gallery Barn Stage on 2009-08-01*, released 2009, streaming audio, https://archive.org/details/justintownesearleandsamanthacrain2009-08-01.gallerybarnstage-busmanBASR1.flac16.

16. Steve and Justin Townes Earle, interview by Inskeep.

17. Jewly Hight, interview with Justin Townes Earle, 2012 (transcript).

18. Anderson, "On *Kids in the Street*, Justin Townes Earle Looks Outward—and Backward."

19. There is no concrete evidence (police report, security camera footage) that verifies the tale of Justin's purported gunpoint robbery. It was a consistent story that just about everyone friendly with Justin at the time remembered hearing, either secondhand, as neighborhood lore, or directly, from Justin himself. One friend recalled hearing the story from Justin in such vivid detail that he knew exactly which ATM in which exact

shopping center on Hillsboro Pike Justin claimed he committed such a robbery. Justin never told this story in public, but during his career he frequently made vague allusions to having committed crimes as a teenager.

20. Marah Eakin, "From Rogers Park to Crown Heights, Justin Townes Earle Reminisces on All His Shitty Apartments," *AV Club*, September 17, 2010.

21. Eakin, "From Rogers Park to Crown Heights."

22. Michael McCall, "The Good Life from Now On," *Nashville Scene*, March 27, 2008.

23. Fiona McCann, "Newly Landed Portlander Justin Townes Earle Makes Country Relevant," *Portland Monthly*, May 15, 2017.

24. Michael McCall, Facebook, August 24, 2020, www.facebook.com/michael.mccall.925/posts/pfbid02Cd27WsNyaTTdmAezckiiYoqvPoSPKJ5T1haisckXHFTrZ5jU8a1VFUfBa3SVonEhl.

CHAPTER 4

This chapter draws on interviews with Jim Conway, Darcy Cooke, October Crifasi, Bryan Dowling, Joie Todd Kerns, Charlie King, Andy Levenberg, Colby Maddox, Scotty Melton, Johnny Mark Miller, Susan Moffett, Charlie Pierce, Ed Snodderly, Kevin So, Katie Tuten, and Tim Tuten.

1. Hal Bienstock, "Coming Clean: Justin Townes Earle," *Blurt*, November 16, 2010; Marah Eakin, "From Rogers Park to Crown Heights, Justin Townes Earle Reminisces on All His Shitty Apartments," *AV Club*, September 17, 2010; Chris Talbott, interview with Justin Townes Earle, 2011 (transcript).

2. Justin's time in Johnson City predated the height of the opioid epidemic, but by the late nineties and early 2000s pain pills had already flooded Carter County, Tennessee. Lesia Paine-Brooks, "Pill Began Woman's Road to Addiction," *Johnson City Press*, July 7, 2002; "Pain pill heaven": Talbott, interview with Justin Townes Earle.

3. Jonathan Miles, interview with Justin Townes Earle, 2010 (transcript).

4. Justin's show on March 14, 1999, is the first time his name ever appears in any archival concert listing in either the *Tennessean* or the *Nashville Scene*. Les Honky More Tonkies also played a show with Meghann Ahern a few months prior, in December 1998, and there were differing memories amid band members on whether Justin may have appeared at that show, but he was not billed.

5. Justin told the story of encountering Melton, including his "getting really fucked up" after his "first real show" several times, most vividly: Miles, interview with Justin Townes Earle.

6. Kenny Berkowitz, "Justin Townes Earle on Songwriting, His Idiosyncratic Fingerpicking Style, and Battling Personal Demons," *Acoustic Guitar*, September 2012.

7. Miles, interview with Justin Townes Earle.

8. Peter Cooper, "Malcolm Holcombe: An Appalachian Ghost Story," *No Depression*, January 1, 2008.

9. "Noon Concert Features Nashville Songwriter, Malcolm Holcombe," *Bristol (VA) Herald Courier*, July 25, 1999.

10. Cooper, "Malcolm Holcombe."

11. David Fricke, review of *A Hundred Lies*, by Malcolm Holcombe, *Rolling Stone*, August 3, 2000.

12. Cooper, "Malcolm Holcombe."

13. Justin was so taken with Guy Clark's comment that, years later, he got a pair of sledgehammers tattooed next to his right thumb.

14. Berkowitz, "Justin Townes Earle on Songwriting," 2012.

15. Walter Tunis, "Justin Earle at Lynagh's," *Lexington Herald-Leader*, December 24, 1999.

16. Stephen Deusner, "Justin Townes Earle: The Son Also Rises," *American Songwriter*, June 30, 2011.

17. Holly Gleason, "Interview: Justin Townes Earle," *American Songwriter*, March 15, 2008.

18. Steve Earle, interview with WTTW, Chicago, archival footage, 2000.

19. Lynne Margolis, "Justin Townes Earle Sheds His Namesakes to Be His Own Man," *Boulder Weekly*, February 18, 2010.

20. The full title of Steve Earle's Old Town class is taken from Lauren St. John's *Hardcore Troubadour: The Life & Near Death of Steve Earle* (New York: HarperCollins, 2003).

21. Details of the class as well as the reported number of applicants: Scott Raab, "Steve Earle, Folk Hero," *Esquire*, June 1, 2000.

22. Steve Earle, interview with WTTW.

23. Raab, "Steve Earle, Folk Hero."

24. The listed venues come from a handful of concert listings in the *Chicago Tribune*, *Daily Herald*, and the *South Bend Tribune* for "Justin Earle" in the first half of 2000, which likely represent only a fraction of the shows Justin played while in Chicago. Joshua M. Miller, "Justin Townes Earle Takes Autobiographical Journey on New Album," *Chicago Sun-Times*, May 16, 2017.

25. Like much of Justin's early life and career, exactly when he left Chicago remains a mystery. The last documented show he played in Chicago was in mid-May. Lubbock had another gig in late June, but Crifasi's memory was that Justin had left Chicago, and the band, by then. Around 2018, Justin began telling a story that was likely wildly exaggerated, or perhaps even outright fabricated, about fleeing Chicago in a hurry after stealing tens of thousands of dollars in cash from his drug dealer.

CHAPTER 5

This chapter draws on interviews with Eric Ambel, Brady Blade, Gerry Diaz, Willie Domann, Chloe Green, Christine Hall, Travis Nicholson, David Noel, John Orchard, Derek Pell, Jenn Ramsey, Ketch Secor, David Sickmen, Matt Svobodny, Willie Watson, Dustin Welch, Brian Willis, Skylar Wilson, and Cory Younts.

1. "Steve Earle with the V-Roys—Here I Am (Live at Farm Aid 1997)," YouTube, April 2, 2013, www.youtube.com/watch?v=PiiaKVCN6hM.

2. Rob Simbeck, "How Was Your Day, Dad?," *Nashville Scene*, June 13, 2002.

3. Amoe Poe, *Just an American Boy: A Film About Steve Earle* (New York: Artemis Records, 2003).

4. Jeff Miers, "Club Chatter: Adam Raised a Cain," *Buffalo News*, May 23, 2008.

5. Justin Townes Earle, *Live at Fabrik on 2002-01-25*, released 2012, streaming audio, https://archive.org/details/jte2002-01-25.csb.flac16.

6. Debbie Speer, "Interview: Justin Townes Earle," *Pollstar*, December 9, 2009.

7. Speer, "Interview: Justin Townes Earle."

8. Interview with Justin Townes Earle, WTTW, Chicago, October 2, 2008 (transcript).

9. Stratton Lawrence, "Justin Townes Earle Talks Dope, Bowties, and Subways," *Charleston City Paper*, December 8, 2010.

10. "Other Club Happenings," *Tennessean*, January 3, 2002.

11. Geoff Mayfield, "Over the Counter," *Billboard*, March 30, 2002.

12. Jonathan Bernstein, "*O Brother, Where Art Thou?* at 20: How the Soundtrack Reinforced a Roots Music Myth," *Rolling Stone*, December 4, 2020.

13. Jim Patterson, "*O Brother* Soundtrack Still Driving Bluegrass," Associated Press, October 12, 2002.

14. Justin performed "Decimation of a Southern Gentleman" up until 2007, the last year there's a record of him ever having performed the song in public.

15. Justin's *Nashville Scene* interview about Steve Earle that ran on June 13, 2002, was pegged to Father's Day. If the interview had been set up or conducted a few weeks before the run date, it might have explained his confusion about the date of 2002's Father's Day when touring with the Swindlers in late May.

16. This list of unconventional Swindlers gigs is culled from *Tennessean* newspaper clippings from 2002 to 2003.

17. Steve Earle has told this story many times, namely, in the 2003 film *Just an American Boy* and onstage at the 2023 Justin Townes Earle memorial concert at the Ryman Auditorium. Sometimes when he told the story, it was an unnamed friend making the "parking lot" comment; other times, it was Kevin Welch.

CHAPTER 6

This chapter draws on interviews with Julien Aklei, Eric Ambel, Duane Denison, Gerry Diaz, Willie Domann, Patty Lemay, Scotty Melton, Bob Nastanovich, Mark Nevers, Travis Nicholson, Paul Niehaus, Jenn Ramsey, Matt Svobodny, Dustin Welch, Brian Willis, and Cory Younts.

1. Amoe Poe, *Just an American Boy: A Film About Steve Earle* (New York: Artemis Records, 2003).

2. Descriptions of Steve's drum kit and Justin's outfit on the 2003 tour are taken from photos posted on the German fan site Down by the River: https://down-by-the-river.de/fotos/konzerte2003/STEARLE_2003-03-13/.

3. Brian Hiatt, "Justin Townes Earle: The *Rolling Stone* Interview," *Rolling Stone Music Now* (podcast), June 12, 2019.

4. The account of Justin's 2003 arrest is based on police records from the Portland Police Department.

5. Jonathan Bernstein, "*O Brother, Where Art Thou?* at 20: How the Soundtrack Reinforced a Roots Music Myth," *Rolling Stone*, December 4, 2020.

6. Jim Ridley, "Pick of the Week," *Nashville Scene*, May 31, 2003.

7. David Berman's set was filmed by Travis Keller of Buddyhead Records and can be viewed on YouTube, www.youtube.com/watch?v=J6LkbLRwjFk&t=971s.

8. Nick Weidenfeld, "The FADER's 2005 Interview with David Berman," *FADER*, July–August, 2005. Shirley Street Station is not mentioned by name in the story, but the "crack house [that] also doubled as a music venue" described in the piece is clearly Shirley Street Station.

9. Jim Ridley, "The Year in Review," *Nashville Scene*, December 18, 2003.

10. "Justin Townes Earle—Golden Gate Park—San Francisco, CA, October 6, 2013," YouTube, January 26, 2014, www.youtube.com/watch?v=I5HJBiDA__s.

11. Jenny Upchurch, "Downtown Noise Irks Resident, but All Is Legal," *Tennessean*, February 21, 2010.

CHAPTER 7

This chapter draws on interviews with Willie Domann, Michael Hosty, Molly Jones, Patty Lemay, Sean Locke, Travis Nicholson, Jennifer Patten, Steve Poulton, Lisa Marie Turner, Dustin Welch, and Cory Younts.

1. Amoe Poe, *Just an American Boy: A Film About Steve Earle* (New York: Artemis Records, 2003).

2. Joe Hagan, interview with Steve Earle, 2009 (transcript).

3. Chris Riemenschneider, "Earle Says He'll Miss His True-to-Life Role on *The Wire*," *Minneapolis Star-Tribune*, March 7, 2008.

4. *The Wire*, season 1, episode 9, "Game Day," directed by Milcho Manchevski, aired August 4, 2002, HBO.

5. Michael McCall, "The Good Life from Now On," *Nashville Scene*, March 27, 2008.

6. Chris Talbott, interview with Justin Townes Earle, 2011 (transcript). Justin talks about being twenty years old at this time. It's possible he was either misremembering his age (he was twenty-two in 2004) or actually referring to another earlier period, sometime between 2002 and 2004, where he was living short-term in a motel before being hospitalized. Patty Lemay distinctly remembered there being at least two instances of Justin being hospitalized due to drug use during these years, but there was no definitive evidence of any hospitalizations apart from his admission to the ICU in the summer of 2004.

7. Michael McCall, "Pick of the Week," *Nashville Scene*, March 25, 2004.

8. Peter Cooper, "Get Out Tonight," *Tennessean*, April 8, 2004.

9. Willie Domann has alleged that his former bandmates in the Swindlers, Justin Townes Earle, and Justin's professional associates have all been involved in a yearslong web of copyright fraud, deception, and cover-up. He has alleged he was denied proper credit for cowriting the music to many of Justin and the Swindlers' early songs, an allegation his former bandmates have all disputed.

10. "Get Out Tonight," *Tennessean*, June 24, 2004. This *Tennessean* write-up is the sole documented reference of Khadafi. Willie Domann said he'd never even heard of the band name despite having been in the band.

11. Though the precise medical details of Justin's hospitalization remain foggy, the most thorough account he gave of his July 2004 stint in the Vanderbilt ICU can be found in McCall, "Good Life from Now On."

CHAPTER 8

This chapter draws on interviews with Elliot Currie, Willie Domann, Murielle Dragness, Josh Graham, Christine Hall, Molly Jones, Andy Moore, Travis Nicholson, Caitlin Rose, Travis Stephens, Dustin Welch, Jason Moon Wilkins, Joshua Black Wilkins, Skylar Wilson, and Cory Younts.

1. *Tennessean*, January 29, 2005.

2. Holly Gleason, "Interview: Justin Townes Earle," *American Songwriter*, March 15, 2008.

3. The changes in East Nashville in the '80s, '90s, and early '00s is based primarily on newspaper accounts, from earliest to most recent: Woody Register, "District Races Grow Hotter as Vote Nears," *Tennessean*, August 1, 1983; Renee Elder, "E. Nashville Finds a New Popularity," *Tennessean*, November 3, 1990; Anita Wadhwani and Noble Sprayberry, "Face of East Nashville Changing," *Tennessean*, March 29, 2001; Anita Wadhwani and Noble Sprayberry, "'98 Tornado Sparked Area's Resurgence," *Tennessean*, April 16, 2001.

4. Justin occasionally dedicated one of his "train" songs—"Halfway to Jackson," "The Ghost of Virginia"—to Litz onstage and called him "our pill-poppin' father." Accounts of Litz and Radio Cafe: Jewly Hight, "How Todd Snider, a Freewheeling Barefoot Hippie, Became One of Nashville's Most Respected Musical Exports," *Nashville Scene*, May 31, 2012; Thayer Wine, "Chow Down on Chinese or Mexican," *Tennessean*, May 5, 1995; Thayer Wine, "Cafe Elliston, Radio Cafe Desserts, Light Fare Grounds for Success," *Tennessean*, June 23, 1995.

5. Gerry Wood, "Woodland's World," *Billboard*, May 12, 1979; John Mulvey, "Gillian Welch and David Rawlings: 'Until a Song Is Right, We Basically Exist in a State of Misery,'" *Uncut*, August 31, 2011.

6. Christine Hall is the woman who booked the Swindlers to play the Belcourt benefit show for her community arts space. Much of her life in those years, like those of the Swindlers', revolved around Springwater. Before getting married, she and comedian Craig Smith (the emcee of the Belcourt show) handed out wedding invitations at the bar. When they had a son, the first place they brought him after leaving the hospital was Springwater.

7. Stephen L. Betts, "Hear Miranda Lambert, Steve Earle's New Duet 'This Is How It Ends,'" *Rolling Stone*, June 19, 2017.

8. In the 2010s, the Nashville duo Birdcloud would memorialize Springwater in their song titled "Springwater": "Sang CCR after huffing gasoline / Threw up potato salad on the *care-ee-oak* machine."

9. Jack Silverman, "Cashville Underground," *Nashville Scene*, September 22, 2005; "The Spin," *Nashville Scene*, September 8, 2005.

10. Tracy Moore, "Here We Are Now, Entertain Us," *Nashville Scene*, June 2, 2005.

11. Alison Miller, "Edgefield Restaurant Still Popular amid Influx of Eateries," *Tennessean*, July 29, 2003.

12. Chris Riemenschneider, "Justin Townes Earle: Son of a . . . ," *Minneapolis Star-Tribune*, February 10, 2011.

13. Riemenschneider, "Justin Townes Earle."

14. Jason Wilkins, "London Bridge," *Nashville Scene*, February 22, 2007.

15. Justin had a similarly dismissive attitude toward the Swindlers after that band broke up. Onstage in 2007, he remarked that "you had to be drunk to enjoy" them. Justin on the Distributors: Jim Caligiuri, "The Good Life," *Austin Chronicle*, March 5, 2008.

CHAPTER 9

This chapter draws on interviews with Ian Anderson, Molly Jones, Sara Jean Kelley, June Lehman, Joe Swank, Jason Moon Wilkins, Joshua Black Wilkins, and Jubal Lee Young.

1. Justin started performing "Louisiana 1927" a capella almost every night in 2010, but there is a recording of him performing the song, with guitar, as early as 2007: Justin Townes Earle, *Live at Dorpshuis de Furs on 2007-09-25*, streaming, https://archive.org/details/jte2007-09-25.flac16.

2. "A Desolate Angels Blues" appears on an early Swindlers set list from the Springwater from the late 1990s or early 2000s.

3. Justin Townes Earle and Samantha Crain, *Live at Pickathon Pendarvis Farm Gallery Barn Stage on 2009-08-01*, released 2009, streaming audio, https://archive.org/details/justintownesearleandsamanthacrain2009-08-01.gallerybarnstage-busmanBASR1.flac16.

4. Justin frequently introduced "I Don't Care" onstage circa 2009 by name-dropping Klein's book. In 2012, Justin was asked to curate a series of shows celebrating the centennial of Woody Guthrie and enlisted Klein as a special guest.

5. The mention of the obscure New Mexican village Tucumcari is almost certainly an allusion to Little Feat's "Willin'," a trucking standard both Steve and Justin had previously covered.

6. Nando Cruz, "Justin Townes Earle: Su Vida es Suya y Solo Suya," *Rock Delux*, September 2008.

7. Zack Adcock, "Get the Job Done: An Interview with Justin Townes Earle," *Smile Politely*, March 13, 2009.

8. Jason Wilkins, "London Bridge," *Nashville Scene*, February 22, 2007.

9. Nicole Keiper, "Justin Townes Earle Carries on Family's Musical Success, *Tennessean*, February 27, 2007.

10. Nora Spitznogle, "Web Exclusive: Earle and Wilkins Join Forces," *Nuvo*, April 25, 2007.

11. Steve Wildsmith, "Rewind: Previously, in the *Daily Times* Weekend Edition," *Daily Times* (Blount County, TN), November 29, 2007.

12. Justin Townes Earle, *Live at the Luminaire on 2007-10-10*, streaming, https://archive.org/details/jte2007-10-10.aud.soledriver.flac16.

13. Amy Jones, "They're Real 'Sons of the Guns,'" *Asheville Citizen-Times*, June 14, 2007.

14. Chad Berndtson, "Jason Isbell—*Sirens of the Ditch* (Interview)," *Glide Magazine*, July 1, 2007.

15. Debbie Speer, "Interview: Justin Townes Earle," *Pollstar*, December 9, 2009.

16. Karen A. Mann, "My Justin Townes Earle Article," *Mann's World* (blog), August 9, 2007.

17. Justin Townes Earle, *Live at the Luminaire*.

18. Mann, "My Justin Townes Earle Article."

CHAPTER 10

This chapter draws on interviews with Adam Bednarik, Carol Ann Earle, Julia Haltigan, Molly Jones, Sara Jean Kelley, Dan McCarthy, Richard McLaurin, Rob Miller, Travis Nicholson, Bryan Owings, Caitlin Rose, Amanda Shires, Brenton Stanley, Travis Stephens, Heather West, Bonnie Whitmore, Joshua Black Wilkins, Skylar Wilson, and Cory Younts.

1. Chuck Dauphin, "As Nashville Grows and Gentrifies, David Briggs Sets About Preserving Music Row History," *Billboard*, November 25, 2016.

2. Much of the lore surrounding the history of the House of David can be found on the recording studio's website: www.houseofdavidnashville.com/house-of-david-history.

3. Holly Gleason, "Interview: Justin Townes Earle," *American Songwriter*, March 15, 2008.

4. Marissa R. Moss, interview with Justin Townes Earle, 2019 (transcript).

5. The final two tracks on *The Good Life* incorporate older recordings: a take of "Far Away in Another Town" recorded at Brad Jones's studio in 2006, and a years-old Swindlers recording of "Ain't Glad I'm Leaving," complete with former bandmates like Dustin Welch on backup vocals.

6. Justin's East Nashville home is briefly described in Michael McCall, "The Good Life from Now On," *Nashville Scene*, March 27, 2008, but the majority of its description comes from an interview and corresponding photo shoot specifically about the apartment: Elaine Matsushita, "Finding the Good Life in Too-Short Apartment," *Chicago Tribune*, July 6, 2008.

7. McCall, "Good Life from Now On" (print edition).

8. Holly Gleason, "Interview: Justin Townes Earle," *American Songwriter*, March 15, 2008.

9. Nate Chinen, "At Home with That Nice Couple Next Door," *New York Times*, September 17, 2008.

10. Chris Familton, "Live Review: Justin Townes Earle @ the Annandale Hotel," *Doubtful Sounds*, December 14, 2008.

11. Justin Townes Earle, *Live at the Berkeley Cafe on* 2008-09-28, 2008, streaming, https://archive.org/details/justintownesearle2008-09-28.

12. Justin Townes Earle, *Live at the Turf Club on 2009-04-15*, released 2009, streaming audio, https://archive.org/details/jte2009-04-15.adkTLmtrx.flac16.

13. McCall, "Good Life from Now On."

14. Justin spoke about his time as an adolescent at both Three Springs Wilderness Camp and the Dede Wallace campus of Centerstone in carceral terms, so it is possible he was referring to either of these juvenile institutions when saying he'd spent six months in jail. The unverified lore in the fallout of Justin's 2003 red-hair-dye incident is that not only Justin but his roadie roommate at the time were permanently banned from a hotel chain. Justin performed at Madison Square Garden with his father when Steve Earle opened for Dave Matthews Band in 2000, when Justin was eighteen.

15. Dave Paulson, "Justin Townes Earle: Like Father, Like Son," *Tennessean*, March 27, 2008.

16. Paulson, "Justin Townes Earle."

17. Joshua Hedley (@JoshuaHedley), "Cory Younts just found a recording of our REAL @opry debut, backing up @JustinTEarle. It was the first time for all three of us. I rented a Manuel jacket and spent all day trying to find a pair of pants that were the same weird shade of black," Twitter (now X), November 15, 2020, 12:56 a.m., https://twitter.com/JoshuaHedley/status/1327853017815785472.

18. Kenneth Rollins, "Can Justin Townes Earle Save Country Music?," *Telegraph*, June 20, 2008.

19. "Dow Suffers Its Worst Weekly Drop Ever," ABC, October 13, 2008.

20. Stephen Deusner, interview with Justin Townes Earle, 2008 (transcript).

21. Tom Lanham, "You Don't Need Bad Times to Make Good Songs," *San Francisco Examiner*, April 2, 2009.

22. Duncan Cooper, "Another Country: Justin Townes Earle," *FADER*, August 21, 2014.

CHAPTER 11

This chapter draws on interviews with Ian Anderson, Adam Bednarik, Adams Bellouis (Rachel Keesecker), Sonya Kay Boyd, Carol Ann Earle, Dawn Landes, Sean Locke, Justin Martin, Richard McLaurin, Rob Miller, Shane Nicholson, Travis Nicholson, Angela Schmidt, Amanda Shires, Trevor Silva, Brian Taranto, John Thompson, Bonnie Whitmore, Jason Moon Wilkins, Skylar Wilson, and Cory Younts.

1. Chris Talbott, interview with Justin Townes Earle, 2011 (transcript).

2. Tad Dickens, "Style & Substance," *Roanoke Times*, September 1, 2011.

3. Duncan Haskell, "Interview: Justin Townes Earle," *Songwriting*, December 11, 2014.

4. Michael McCall, "The Good Life from Now On," *Nashville Scene*, March 27, 2008.

5. Brian T. Atkinson, "Earle Doesn't Find the Cactus Prickly," *Austin American-Statesman*, December 14, 2008.

6. Justin Townes Earle, *Live at the Berkeley Cafe on 2008-09-28*, 2008, streaming, https://archive.org/details/justintownesearle2008-09-28.

7. McCall, "Good Life from Now On."

8. Steve and Justin Townes Earle, interview by Steve Inskeep, *Morning Edition*, NPR, December 29, 2008.

9. Joe Hagan, interview with Steve Earle, 2009 (transcript). Steve Earle was unusually reflective and open about fatherhood in his series of conversations with author Joe Hagan in 2009. Hagan was profiling Steve for a story pegged to Steve's tribute album to Townes Van Zandt, so his firstborn son came up quite a bit during the conversation.

10. It's not clear which came first—the song or the interview catchphrase—but Justin says some version of "I am my father's son" at least three times in spring 2008 interviews promoting *The Good Life*. Justin said he worked on "Mama's Eyes" for a long time and may have begun testing out the phrase in interviews while he had the seeds of the idea for the song: James Reed, "Like Father, but More Like Son," *Boston Globe*, April 11, 2008; Lucky Clark, "Earle Surprises with New CD," *Morning Sentinel*, May 30, 2008; Jim Caligiuri, "The Good Life," *Austin Chronicle*, March 5, 2008.

11. Zack Adcock, "Get the Job Done: An Interview with Justin Townes Earle," *Smile Politely*, March 13, 2009.

12. Adcock, "Get the Job Done."

13. Justin Townes Earle, *Live at Newtown Social Club on 2015-04-06*, 2020, streaming, https://archive.org/details/jte2015-04-16.aud.flac16.

14. Thomas Rozwadowski, "After Battling Demons, Father, Earle Finds a Voice of His Own," *Green Bay Press-Gazette*, August 20, 2009.

15. *Pittsburgh Tribune-Review*, 2009.

16. Seth Graves, Facebook, March 29, 2023, www.facebook.com/sethgravy/videos/978409896863315/.

17. Noel Mengel, "He's His Father's Son," *Courier Mail* (Brisbane), September 17, 2009.

18. Stephen Deusner, interview with Justin Townes Earle, 2008 (transcript).

19. Andy Newman, "Police Are Out in Force as a Neighborhood Simmers with Tension Again," *New York Times*, May 22, 2008.

20. Vanita Salisbury, "Justin Townes Earle Makes the Best PB&J in the World," *New York*, November 23, 2011.

21. Wayne Bledsoe, "Second-Generation Singer-Songwriter Makes It on His Own," *Knoxville News Sentinel*, March 6, 2009.

22. Brian Hiatt, interview with Justin Townes Earle, 2012 (transcript).

23. "The March 27–28, 2009, Winter Storm," National Weather Service, www.weather.gov/oun/events-20090327#:~:text=Snowfall%20totals%20of%20up%20to,through%20southwest%20and%20central%20Oklahoma.

24. "Long Shots: Justin Townes Earle & Jason Isbell," *Aquarium Drunkard*, April 10, 2009.

25. Justin Townes Earle, interview by Alison Stewart, *All of It*, WNYC, May 21, 2019.

26. Justin Townes Earle, *Live at Barley's Taproom and Pizzeria on 2009-03-7*, 2009,

streaming, https://archive.org/details/jte2009-03-07.sbd.flac16/JTE-2009-03-07-Barleys-KnoxvilleTN03.flac.

27. Justin Townes Earle, *Live at Horseshoe Tavern on 2009-04-22*, 2009, streaming, https://archive.org/details/jte2009-04-22.mc930.sd702.flac16/jte2009-04-22d1t16.flac.

28. "Pazz & Jop," *Village Voice*, January 20, 2010.

29. Holly Gleason, "Interview: Justin Townes Earle," *American Songwriter*, March 15, 2008.

30. Deusner, interview with Justin Townes Earle.

31. Justin Townes Earle, *Live at the Turf Club on 2009-04-15*, released 2009, streaming audio, https://archive.org/details/jte2009-04-15.adkTLmtrx.flac16.

32. Will Hermes, review of *Midnight at the Movies*, by Justin Townes Earle. *Rolling Stone*. March 3, 2009.

33. Cory Younts, interview with the author, *Rolling Stone* (2020).

CHAPTER 12

This chapter draws on interviews with Justin Borucki, Andrew Colvin, David Noel, Ketch Secor, Willie Watson, Joshua Black Wilkins, and Cory Younts.

1. Alan McGee, "Was Townes Van Zandt Better than Dylan?," *Guardian*, February 26, 2008.

2. Joe Hagan, interview with Steve Earle, 2009 (transcript).

3. The only two instances of Justin and Steve duetting on an officially released recording were both covers: "Candy Man" on 2001's *Avalon Blues: A Tribute to the Music of Mississippi John Hurt*; and "Mr. Mudd & Mr. Gold" on 2009's Steve Earle album *Townes*.

4. Justin Townes Earle and Samantha Crain, *Live at Pickathon Pendarvis Farm Gallery Barn Stage on 2009-08-01*, released 2009, streaming audio, https://archive.org/details/justintownesearleandsamanthacrain2009-08-01.gallerybarnstage-busmanBASR1.flac16.

5. Les Thomas, interview with Justin Townes Earle, *Unpaved*, 2012, https://soundcloud.com/unpaved/justin-townes-earle.

6. Steve's jealousy over "They Killed John Henry": Ben Sisario, "The Album Steve Earle Never Wanted to Make: A Tribute to His Son," *New York Times*, December 29, 2020; Justin claiming Steve hadn't listened to *Midnight at the Movies*: Jewly Hight, interview with Justin Townes Earle, 2009 (transcript).

7. Hight, interview with Justin Townes Earle.

8. Thomas Rozwadowski, "After Battling Demons, Father, Earle Finds a Voice of His Own," *Green Bay Press-Gazette*, August 20, 2009.

9. Allan Wigney, "My Name Is Earle," *Ottawa Citizen*, April 18, 2009.

10. "Ray Lamontagne—Loretta Live 2009 Denver Townes van Zandt cover," YouTube, November 19, 2009, https://www.youtube.com/watch?v=oigMmYF5I2M&list=RDoigMmYF5I2M&start_radio=1

11. Stephen Deusner, "Justin Townes Earle: The Son Also Rises," *American Songwriter*, June 30, 2011.

12. Blake Ells, "Justin Townes Earle Brings Harlem River Blues to Hangout," AL.com, May 18, 2011.

13. "Long Shots: Justin Townes Earle & Jason Isbell," *Aquarium Drunkard*, 2009; the information about Buddy Miller's triple-bypass surgery comes from *Country Standard Time*, February 22, 2009.

14. Wigney, "My Name Is Earle."

15. Ben Sisario, "Polka Music Is Eliminated as Grammy Award Category," *New York Times*, June 4, 2009; Nick Purdy, "Industry Chat: Jed Hilly of the Americana Music Association," *Paste*, July 24, 2009.

16. Rob Bleetstein, "Americana Moves to Another Country," *Gavin*, January 20, 1995.

17. "Americana," *Merriam-Webster*, www.merriam-webster.com/dictionary/Americana; Amanda Andrews, "Now That's Americana: Merriam-Webster Adds Americana to Dictionary," *Nashville Music Guide*, August 25, 2011.

18. "2009 Americana Music Association Awards Nominees Announced," *Country Universe*, May 21, 2009; Justin Townes Earle, *Live at Crystal Bay Casino on 2009-05-21*, 2009, streaming, https://archive.org/details/jte2009-05-21.flac16.

19. "The Top 25 Songs from the '80s, '90s, and '00s," *American Songwriter* (2009).

20. Barry Mazor, "Renegades on the Road," *Wall Street Journal*, August 4, 2009.

21. In an interview, Ketch Secor described the Big Surprise Tour as the final moment, of sorts, before Americana shifted from genuine community to commercial enterprise: "If you were to hold up the Big Surprise Tour [in one hand]," Secor said, "and the Americana Music Association in the other hand, you might feel like I feel: disappointed in the results of all of our hard work."

22. Hight, interview with Justin Townes Earle.

23. Justin Townes Earle (@JustinTEarle), "Cory will no longer be playing with me. He's moved on to bigger and better things and we wish him luck," Twitter (now X), October 14, 2009, 3:46 p.m., https://twitter.com/JustinTEarle/status/4869949208.

CHAPTER 13

This chapter draws on interviews with Eric Ambel, Adams Bellouis (Rachel Keesecker), Bryn Davies, Orsolya Dunai, Josiah Early, Matt Eddmenson, Irakli Gabriel, Tristen Gaspadarek, Julia Haltigan, Rob Heath, Cassidy Holden, Dawn Landes, Gareth Lindsay, Jessica Lea Mayfield, Gerald Menke, Ezekiel Miller, Billy Reid, Allan Sicignano, Brian Taranto, Stephen Thorne, Henry Wagons, and Cory Younts.

1. Justin convinced Keesecker she did not need to pay rent in Crown Heights until her landlord fixed the various problems in the Brooklyn apartment. So when they fled the apartment and moved to Manhattan, Keesecker's mother ended up paying the back rent and various fees.

2. Justin Townes Earle, interview by Alison Stewart, *All of It*, WNYC, May 21, 2019.

3. When one of the Madison Square Gardeners, Aaron Lee Tasjan, started releasing solo records, he memorialized the pub and its ringleader, Kenny O'Connor, in his song "12 Bar Blues."

4. Stephen Deusner, "Justin Townes Earle, Urban Cowboy," *Village Voice*, December 15, 2010.

5. Jesse Kornbluth, "Justin Townes Earle: Steve's Son? Yes, Just as Talented, but Not Political and Much More Fun," *HuffPost* contributor platform, April 12, 2010.

6. Vicki Anderson, *Stuff*, 2009.

7. Thomas Rozwadowski, "After Battling Demons, Father, Earle Finds a Voice of His Own," *Green Bay Press-Gazette*, August 20, 2009.

8. Casey Phillips, "Q&A with Justin Townes Earle," *Chattanooga Times Free Press*, April 29, 2011.

9. Chris Talbott, interview with Justin Townes Earle, 2011 (transcript).

10. Eli Petersen, "Justin Townes Earle Talks to Twangville," *Twangville*, November 30, 2009.

11. Jessica Lea Mayfield, interview with the author, *Rolling Stone*, 2020.

12. Justin Townes Earle (@JustinTEarle), "Almost done writing the new record," Twitter (now X), December 14, 2009, 10:49 p.m., https://twitter.com/JustinTEarle/status/6684801492.

13. Justin Townes Earle (@JustinTEarle), "Still at the ramble. This is the coolest thing I have ever had the pleasure of being a part of!," Twitter (now X), January 2, 2010, 10:19 p.m., https://twitter.com/JustinTEarle/status/7319608585.

14. Kornbluth, "Justin Townes Earle."

15. Joe Pug, interview by Otis Gibbs, "Justin Townes Earle: Remembered—Joe Pug," YouTube, May 12, 2023, www.youtube.com/watch?v=Q8uUX-ImpCk.

16. Justin's fashion comments in this paragraph can be found in Debbie Speer, "Interview: Justin Townes Earle," *Pollstar*, December 9, 2009; and Russell Baillie, "A Quick Word: Justin Townes Earle," *New Zealand Herald*, March 16, 2011.

17. "The 25 Most Stylish Men in the World," *GQ*, February 2010.

18. Chris Riemenschneider, "Suddenly, Justin Townes Earle Is Everywhere," *Minneapolis Star-Tribune*, April 29, 2010.

19. Deusner, "Justin Townes Earle, Urban Cowboy."

20. Justin Townes Earle, *Live at the ArtsCenter 2010-03-09*, released 2010, streaming audio, https://archive.org/details/jte2010-03-09/jte20100309d02t11.flac.

21. Lauren Streib, interview with Justin Townes Earle, 2012 (transcript).

22. Phillips, "Q&A with Justin Townes Earle."

23. Ryan Matteson, *Muzzle of Bees* (2011).

24. Justin Townes Earle (@JustinTEarle), "me and jason are two hillbillies far from home. but i dig this shit!," Twitter (now X), April 8, 2010, 6:27 a.m., https://twitter.com/JustinTEarle/status/11816575050.

25. Matteson, *Muzzle of Bees*; Justin Townes Earle (@JustinTEarle), "its gotta be pho for lunch!," Twitter (now X), April 6, 2010, 8:11 p.m., https://twitter.com/JustinTEarle/status/11726914093; Justin Townes Earle (@JustinTEarle), "oh and seen a dolphin today too! my first," Twitter (now X), April 6, 2010, 2:57 a.m., https://twitter.com/JustinTEarle/status/11686027063; Justin Townes Earle (@JustinTEarle), "have you ever paid 18 dollars for yogurt and fruit? fuck me!" Twitter (now X), April 7, 2010, 7:57 p.m.,

https://twitter.com/JustinTEarle/status/11793853385. *No Depression*: Justin Townes Earle (@JustinTEarle), Twitter (now X), April 6, 2010.

26. Justin Townes Earle (@JustinTEarle), "I think i was born this fucked up, its got nothing to do with the drugs," Twitter (now X), April 20, 2010, 12:57 a.m., https://twitter.com/JustinTEarle/status/12498450149.

27. Jason Isbell, interview by Terry Gross, *Fresh Air*, NPR, September 2, 2013.

28. Garrison Keillor, *A Prairie Home Companion*, NPR, May 1, 2010.

29. Justin Townes Earle (@JustinTEarle), "The girl is still asleep, and It's raining. Westerns and frozen waffles it is. I am goin with the magnificent 7. Jet lag day 3," Twitter (now X), May 3, 2010, 7:20 a.m., https://twitter.com/JustinTEarle/status/13299935233.

CHAPTER 14

This chapter draws on interviews with Rayland Baxter, Adams Bellouis (Rachel Keesecker), Alex Caress, Jordan Caress, Andrew Combs, Derek Hoke, Caitlin Rose, Joshua Black Wilkins, and Skylar Wilson.

1. Robert K. Oermann, "LifeNotes: R&B Musician DeFord Bailey Jr. Passes," *Music Row*, September 20, 2013.

2. Deford Bailey Jr.'s account of the 2010 flood is composed from the oral history he gave as part of the Nashville Public Library's 2010 Nashville Flood Digital History Project: excerpt from Deford Bailey Jr. Oral History Interview, interview by Andrea Blackman, October 14, 2011, Special Collections Division of the Nashville Public Library, audio, https://cdm15769.contentdm.oclc.org/digital/collection/nr/id/3674/rec/16.

3. Background information on the 2010 flood is taken largely from the *Tennessean*'s extensive coverage at the time. But several of the facts from this paragraph are taken from this comprehensive retrospective: Karen Grigsby, "20 Things to Know About the 2010 Nashville Flood," *Tennessean*, April 30, 2015, www.tennessean.com/story/news/local/2015/04/30/nashville-flood-20-things-to-know/26653901/.

4. Peter Cooper, "Soggy Note Hits Music History," *Tennessean*, May 5, 2010.

5. Cindy Watts, "Relocated 'Opry' Show Goes On," *Tennessean*, May 5, 2010.

6. Justin Townes Earle (@JustinTEarle), "Nashville is hurtin!," Twitter (now X), May 8, 2010, 12:29 a.m., https://twitter.com/JustinTEarle/status/13590008371.

7. David Menconi, "Both Earle's Music and His Roots Run Deep," *Raleigh News & Observer*, December 10, 2010.

8. Justin sprinkled in light references to Townes Van Zandt lyrics in many of his songs. In "I Don't Care," from *Yuma*, he sings, "If I had a dollar, boy, I'd find me a game," a clear callback to Townes Van Zandt's "Rex's Blues," a song Justin covered. Townes wrote the song about his friend Rex Bell, and it's a narrative about contemplating suicide that feels like inspiration for both "Yuma" and "Harlem River Blues." In the latter, when Justin sings "tell my mama I loved her / Tell my father I tried," he is seemingly simultaneously referencing Merle Haggard's "Mama Tried" while calling back to the fourth verse in "Rex's Blues" ("tell my mother I did no wrong").

9. Joel Francis, *Kansas City Star*, April 13, 2011.

10. Paul Clark, "Justin Townes Earle Is His Own Brand of Earle," *Cincinnati Enquirer*, September 21, 2010.

11. Jim Carroll, *The Basketball Diaries* (New York: Penguin, 1963), 47–50.

12. Jonathan Miles, interview with Justin Townes Earle, 2010 (transcript).

13. Geoffrey Himes, "Justin Townes Earle: Crossing the Boundary of 30," *Paste*, March 30, 2012.

14. The timeline of the *Harlem River Blues* sessions is reconstructed from Justin's contemporaneous tweets: Justin Townes Earle (@JustinTEarle), "Day one is in the bag hand claps and all. Time to relax baby!," Twitter (now X), May 17, 2010, 10:07 p.m., https://twitter.com/JustinTEarle/status/14199348847; Justin Townes Earle (@JustinTEarle), "Basic tracks done! We got a little Rock n roll on this one folks," Twitter (now X), May 19, 2010, 7:03 p.m., https://twitter.com/JustinTEarle/status/14322160988.

15. Will Hermes, review of *Charlatans at the Garden Gate*, by Tristen Gaspadarek, *Rolling Stone*, March 3, 2011.

16. Kim Severson, "Nashville's Latest Big Hit Could Be the City Itself," *New York Times*, January 8, 2013.

17. Justin Townes Earle (@JustinTEarle), "There's nothin wrong with warm beer," Twitter (now X), May 11, 2010, 9:32 p.m., https://twitter.com/JustinTEarle/status/13822552845.

18. Chris Talbott, "Justin Townes Earle Looks Back at Year of Recovery," Associated Press, October 15, 2011.

19. John Jurgensen, "The Rehab Album," *Wall Street Journal*, January 27, 2011.

CHAPTER 15

This chapter draws on interviews with Sonya Kay Boyd, David Clough, Andrew Colvin, Bryn Davies, Josiah Early, Justin Eshak, Boscoe France, Julia Haltigan, Rob Heath, Derek Hoke, Jamie Kindleyside, Dawn Landes, June Lehman, Jessica Lea Mayfield, Ezekiel Miller, Rob Miller, Jenn Ramsey, Caitlin Rose, Scott Schaefer, Allan Sicignano, Lauren Spratlin, Stephen Thorne, Henry Wagons, and Joshua Black Wilkins.

1. Justin Townes Earle (@JustinTEarle), "I am going insaine! People need to mind there own fucking buisness!!!!," Twitter (now X), June 1, 2010, 6:24 p.m., https://twitter.com/JustinTEarle/status/15207375448; Justin Townes Earle (@JustinTEarle), "I'm not sure of anthing anymore," Twitter (now X), June 2, 2010, 6:02 p.m., https://twitter.com/JustinTEarle/status/15279717346.

2. Justin Townes Earle (@JustinTEarle), "I am in a strange place," Twitter (now X), June 4, 2010, 7:55 p.m., https://twitter.com/JustinTEarle/status/15450818679.

3. Justin Townes Earle, *Live at Memorial Union Terrace–UW Madison on 2010-07-03*, released 2010, streaming audio, https://archive.org/details/JTE2010-07-03.sbd/JTE2010-07-03-SBD-t01.flac.

4. Justin Townes Earle (@JustinTEarle), "Just drove past my old halfway house. Good times!," Twitter (now X), July 3, 2010, 1:00 p.m., https://twitter.com/JustinTEarle/status/17663559276.

5. "Justin Townes Earle Cancels Due to Injury," *Country Standard Time*, August 1, 2010, www.countrystandardtime.com/news/newsitem.asp?xid=4361.

6. Robert Baird, "The Devil's Right Hand," *Stereophile*, October 2010.

7. Mark Wedel, "The Highs, Lows of Justin Townes Earle: Songwriter Looks Back on Addiction, Forward to New Music," *Kalamazoo (MI) Gazette*, August 19, 2010.

8. Justin Townes Earle, interview by Jane Hutcheon, *One Plus One*, ABC, April 3, 2015.

9. Jonathan Keefe, review of *Harlem River Blues*, by Justin Townes Earle, *Slant*, September 12, 2010.

10. Neil Spencer, review of *Harlem River Blues*, by Justin Townes Earle, *Observer*, September 18, 2010.

11. Erik Thompson, review of *Harlem River Blues*, by Justin Townes Earle, *Line of Best Fit*, September 30, 2010.

12. The account of Justin's record-release show at Grimey's is compiled from an audio recording of the full show as well as several YouTube videos: Justin Townes Earle, *Live at Grimey's New and Preloved Music on 2010-09-14*, released 2020, streaming audio, https://archive.org/details/jte2010-09-14.aud.flac16; "072—Justin Townes Earle—'Slippin' and Slidin',"" YouTube, September 14, 2010, www.youtube.com/watch?v=UFptEt4e6O0; "076—Justin Townes Earle—'Christchurch Woman,'" YouTube, September 15, 2010, www.youtube.com/watch?v=fj9FQAxHlL4.

13. Micah Ling, "Justin Townes Earle: Indianapolis, IN," *Beat Jab Reviews*, September 22, 2010.

14. The account of what happened in Indianapolis is composed primarily from the account of four people who were present that night: Jessica Lea Mayfield, Lauren Spratlin, Bryn Davies, and David "Tufty" Clough, as well as police records from the Indianapolis Police Department and Justin's various retellings of the incident immediately afterward.

15. Evan Schlansky, "Justin Townes Earle Arrested for Battery," *American Songwriter*, September 20, 2010; Kyle Coroneos, "Belligerent Justin Townes Earle Arrested in Indianapolis," *Saving Country Music*, September 17, 2010.

16. Selena Frye, "Justin Townes Earle Review: A Night in Jail Can't Keep Him Down," *Louisville Magazine*, September 18, 2010.

17. These tweets of Justin's were seemingly deleted but reported on at the time: Coroneos, "Belligerent Justin Townes Earle Arrested in Indianapolis."

18. "Justin Townes Earle Suspends Tour," *Pollstar*, September 23, 2010.

19. Justin Townes Earle, *Live at Cat's Cradle on 2010-12-13*, released 2010, streaming audio, https://archive.org/details/jte2010-12-13/jte20101213d01t01.flac.

20. Chris Talbott, interview with Justin Townes Earle, 2011 (transcript).

21. Tim Cooper, "Out of the Shadows," *Times*, July 10, 2011.

22. Suzanne Normand Blackwood, "Cumberland Heights Marks 40 Years of Turning Lives," *Tennessean*, August 23, 2006.

23. Hal Bienstock, "Coming Clean: Justin Townes Earle," *Blurt*, November 16, 2010.

24. Justin's rescheduled dates were reported widely, and his new management company announced his signing on October 26: Mick Management, Facebook,

October 26, 2010, www.facebook.com/mickmgmt/posts/pfbid02p3tETYsKJjbDapmh3cjQ2QwN1i4bztouWtnMTD96VLqWCfqEoUvceSJiooRkx5qDl.

25. Talbott, interview with Justin Townes Earle.

26. "Justin Townes Earle Performs 'Harlem River Blues' on Letterman," YouTube, January 6, 2011, www.youtube.com/watch?v=5LLqFF89UtU.

CHAPTER 16

This chapter draws on interviews with Evan Bradford, Bryn Davies, Justin Eshak, Judy Hilton, Jordan Lehning, Colin Meloy, Andy Moore, Michael O'Brien, Ray Rizzo, Amanda Shires, Allan Sicignano, Lauren Spratlin, Dustin Welch, Joshua Black Wilkins, and Skylar Wilson.

1. The account of Jimmie Cox's life is compiled primarily from Gene Anderson's academic article as well as a 1921 letter Cox published in *Billboard*: Gene Anderson, "The Cox Trio: A Study in Black Show Business," in *Legacies of Power in American Music* (London: Routledge, 2022), 43–79; Jimmie Cox, "Jimmie Cox Says Some One Is Impersonating Him," *Billboard*, November 26, 1921.

2. The cover versions of Cox's tune described here are by Pinetop Smith, the Aunt Jemima Novelty Four, and Bobby Leecan, respectively.

3. Justin once explained that his arrangement of "Nobody Knows You" was cribbed from the relatively obscure bluesman named Pink Anderson, a singer perhaps best known as the namesake inspiration for Pink Floyd.

4. Justin Townes Earle (@JustinTEarle), "I grew up not trusting anyone. Should have kept it that way!," Twitter (now X), July 30, 2013, 3:30 a.m., https://twitter.com/JustinTEarle/status/362250812250001409.

5. Gary Graff, "Justin Townes Earle Heading to London to Record Next Album," *Billboard*, February 11, 2011.

6. Stephen Deusner, "Justin Townes Earle: The Son Also Rises," *American Songwriter*, June 30, 2011.

7. Gary Graff, interview with Justin Townes Earle, 2011 (transcript).

8. Justin Townes Earle (@JustinTEarle), "I am going to be homeless for the next six months. to much touring, no sense in paying rent. gotta get ready to ramble!," Twitter (now X), January 30, 2011, 7:47 a.m., https://twitter.com/JustinTEarle/status/31695028627709952.

9. Talbott, 2011 (transcript).

10. Talbott, 2011 (transcript).

11. By his late adolescence, Justin had developed what he believed was an expert pharmaceutical knowledge of drugs both legal and illegal, offering medical advice to friends and colleagues. Amanda Shires remembered Justin trying to convince her to take Seroquel for her ADHD.

12. Salisbury, *New York*, 2011.

13. Garland Harwood, "Justin Townes Earle: Worst Nightmare to Sweet Redemption at Carnegie Hall," *Grass Clippings*, December 7, 2011.

14. Streib, 2011 (transcript).

15. Harwood, "Justin Townes Earle."

16. Aaron Kayce, "Justin Townes Earle Explores Soulful Sounds," *SFGate*, June 27, 2012.

17. Talbott, interview with Justin Townes Earle.

18. The *Nothing's Gonna Change* sessions weren't all doom and gloom: when the band riffed on the Meters' cheery 1970 ballad "Darling, Darling, Darling" in the studio, an enormous smile erupted on Justin's face.

19. Talbott, interview with Justin Townes Earle.

20. Caroline Randall Williams, "Too Old to Die Young," *Native*, February 2013.

21. Brian Hiatt, interview with Justin Townes Earle, 2012 (transcript).

22. Nancy Dunham, "Steve Earle Finds Himself More 'Alive' than Ever," *The Boot*, March 22, 2011.

CHAPTER 17

This chapter draws on interviews with Adam Bednarik, Cory Branan, Alex Caress, Jordan Caress, Andrew Combs, Robert Ellis, Dawn Landes, Kevin Morrow, Michael O'Brien, Amanda Shires, Lauren Spratlin, Joshua Black Wilkins, and Skylar Wilson.

1. Justin Townes Earle, *Live at the Blue Note on 2013-05-02*, released 2013, streaming audio, https://archive.org/details/jte2013-05-02.mk4mk8.flac16.

2. Dwight Garner, "Jason Isbell, Unloaded," *New York Times*, May 31, 2013.

3. Jason Isbell, "Justin Townes Earle, Saturday, July 27, 2013," Newport Folk Festival website.

4. Justin Townes Earle (@JustinTEarle), "I hate to say it but I think I thrive on chaos. Fuck that cant be good," Twitter (now X), January 17, 2011, 4:37 p.m., https://twitter.com/JustinTEarle/status/27117406765719553.

5. Marc Maron, "Episode 482: Jason Isbell," *WTF with Marc Maron* (podcast), March 26, 2014.

6. Justin's original tweet was deleted but preserved through the series of manual retweets it received, several of which Justin personally responded to.

7. Caroline Randall Williams, "Too Old to Die Young," *Native*, February 2013.

8. Justin Townes Earle (@JustinTEarle), "If anyone who follows me works in the middle TN mental health system pleas contact. I have a situation at home. Need help with details," Twitter (now X), May 2, 2013, 5:03 p.m., https://twitter.com/JustinTEarle/status/330065107273015296.

9. Justin Townes Earle, *Live at the Blue Note*.

10. Justin Townes Earle (@JustinTEarle), "New stab!," Twitter (now X), July 30, 2013, 1:03 a.m., https://twitter.com/JustinTEarle/status/362075932342747137.

11. Roland Kay-Smith, "Justin Townes Earle: Finger-Pickin' Good," *The Brag* (blog), January 28, 2013.

CHAPTER 18

This chapter draws on interviews with Cory Chisel, Jenn Marie Earle, Simon Gardner, Mark Hedman, Andy Moore, and Kevin Morrow.

1. Justin Townes Earle (@JustinTEarle), "Woke up to this sitting on my porch? Antique angels must be around," Twitter (now X), September 8, 2013, 3:08 p.m., https://twitter.com/JustinTEarle/status/376784189594431489.

2. Rachel Raczka, "At the Sinclair: Musician as Muse," *Boston Globe*, October 31, 2013.

3. In the year or two following their marriage, Justin began talking up Jenn Marie in nearly every interview, namely, Justin Townes Earle, interview by Jane Hutcheon, *One Plus One*, ABC, April 3, 2015; Benjamin Tilton, "An Afternoon Chat with Justin Townes Earle," *Slug Mag*, September 26, 2014.

4. Andy Moore, interview with the author, *Rolling Stone*, 2020.

5. Jeff Spevak, "Artist Transcends Troubled Landscape," *Democrat and Chronicle*, September 18, 2014.

6. Eric Sundermann, "Justin Townes Earle: Living for the Tiny Revelations," *Vice*, September 5, 2014.

7. The original source of Mumford & Sons' statement on Justin could not be located, but it was reprinted and quoted on several promotional Facebook posts from Los Angeles–area venues before Justin's appearance at a 2013 music festival in Santa Monica: the Echo, Facebook, July 23, 2013, www.facebook.com/EchoLA/posts/10151553605241334.

8. Justin Townes Earle (@JustinTEarle), "I have now learned that you can never trust a bunch of babies that ain't worked a day in their lives. May Shane McGowan kick their asses," Twitter (now X), December 15, 2013, 9:21 p.m., https://twitter.com/JustinTEarle/status/412407207272407040.

CHAPTER 19

This chapter draws on interviews with BJ Barham, Adam Bednarik, Nick Bobetsky, Cory Branan, Alex Caress, Andrew Colvin, Bryn Davies, Jenn Marie Earle, Simon Gardner, Nick Hardy, Mark Hedman, Rich Hinman, Gill Landry, Michael Martin, Erin McAnally, Jim Merlis, Rob Miller, Andy Moore, Aaron Mortenson, Paul Niehaus, Sam Outlaw, Matt Pence, Billy Reid, Adam Roberts, Bryce Roberts, Andy Washington, Joshua Black Wilkins, and Keith Wood.

1. Farah Jasmine Griffin, *If You Can't Be Free, Be a Mystery: In Search of Billie Holiday* (New York: Penguin, 2002), 5.

2. Duncan Cooper, "Another Country: Justin Townes Earle," *FADER*, August 21, 2014.

3. Paul Bowers, "Even in Good Times, Justin Townes Earle Makes His Sorrows Sing," *Charleston City Paper*, November 12, 2014.

4. Author interview with Adam Bednarik, *Single Mothers/Absent Fathers* liner notes (2021).

5. Jonathan Bernstein, "Hometown Blues: A Q&A with Justin Townes Earle," *American Songwriter*, September 2, 2014.

6. Bob Gendron, "Justin Townes Earle Laid It All Out on the Table," *Chicago Tribune*, December 11, 2014.

7. Brian Wise, interview with Justin Townes Earle, 2015 (transcript).

8. Ben Sisario, "Spotify's Revenue Is Growing, but So Are Its Losses," *New York Times*, May 8, 2015. The 2012 subscriber number is taken from the market-research firm Statista: www.statista.com/statistics/222099/spotifys-paid-and-overall-subscriber-numbers-in-the-us/.

9. Justin Townes Earle (@JustinTEarle), "Jack White is such a pussy," Twitter (now X), June 1, 2014, 4:51 p.m., https://twitter.com/JustinTEarle/status/473205155476037632.

10. Nate Rau, "'Nashville' Receives $8 Million from State for Season 4," *Tennessean*, April 29, 2015.

11. Duncan Haskell, "Interview: Justin Townes Earle," *Songwriting*, December 11, 2014.

12. Haskell, "Interview: Justin Townes Earle."

13. Justin is almost certainly referring to George Strait.

14. "Nashville's Million-Dollar Skyscraper, Modern, Massive, Dignified and Elegant," *Nashville Banner*, December 2, 1905.

15. Justin Townes Earle (@justintownesearle), "View from office window. That little slice still kinda looks like Nashville," Instagram, August 1, 2014, www.instagram.com/p/rK6OnlOHfA/.

16. Will Welch, "Meet Three Country Badasses Who Are Shaking Up the Nashville Establishment," *GQ*, January 7, 2016.

17. Jeff Tamarkin, interview with Justin Townes Earle, 2011 (transcript).

18. Justin's increasingly dismissive views of Americana: Marissa R. Moss, "With His Latest, Nashvillian Justin Townes Earle Gives Praise to Single Mothers and Refuses to Be Pushed Around," *Nashville Scene*, September 4, 2014; Hannah Joyner, "How Going Sober Has Reinvigorated Justin Townes Earle," *Tone Deaf*, September 12, 2014.

19. Jeremy D. Goodwin, "Steve Earle Taps Rootsy Sources for His Latest Album," *Boston Globe*, February 5, 2015.

20. James Reed, "Earle Learning to Cope with the Ups, Downs," *Boston Globe*, May 13, 2012.

21. Justin Townes Earle (@JustinTEarle), "Sweet mental stability," Twitter (now X), August 30, 2014, 11:49 a.m., https://twitter.com/JustinTEarle/status/505744090646855680.

22. Raczka, *Boston Globe*, 2013.

23. Phillips, *Chattanooga Times Free Press*, 2011.

24. Debbie Speer, "Interview: Justin Townes Earle," *Pollstar*, December 9, 2009.

CHAPTER 20

This chapter draws on interviews with Cory Branan, Ben Brodin, Cory Chisel, Jenn Marie Earle, Simon Gardner, Adam Roberts, Scott Seiver, and Andy Washington.

1. Linda Stansberry, "The Humboldt 35," *North Coast Journal*, February 1, 2018. For more context on Humboldt County's weed-growing history, see *Murder Mountain*, directed by Joshua Zeman, Netflix (2018).

2. Justin Townes Earle, "Hardcore Troubadour Radio," SiriusXM, 2017.

3. Information from Westport comes from Census data and the archive of the town's newsletter, the *Westport Wave*, during the period Justin was there.

4. Justin Townes Earle (@JustinTEarle), "Between the music business and nashville I became very bitter. So I left nashville and I found it was mostly nashville. So long suckers!," Twitter (now X), July 31, 2015, 1:10 p.m., https://twitter.com/JustinTEarle/status/627164374004838401.

5. Justin Townes Earle (@JustinTEarle), "Heading home for two weeks and I love that the wife and I got a place where there is no phone service and nobody knows where it is," Twitter (now X), September 7, 2015, 12:39 p.m., https://twitter.com/JustinTEarle/status/640927496649744384.

6. Will Hodge, "Interview with Justin Townes Earle," *NoiseTrade*, April 2017; Justin Townes Earle (@JustinTEarle), "Give any life long cubs fan any shit about being a cubs and you will go to hell. Something like the purgatory we live!," Twitter (now X), December 23, 2012, 2:49 a.m., https://twitter.com/JustinTEarle/status/282754679685935105; Sammy Brue, interview with the author, *Rolling Stone*, 2020; Justin Townes Earle (@JustinTEarle), "Come on cubbies. Better be glad that cubs baseball has been one of few constants in my life! Here's to Tinker, Evers, and chance. Go cubs!!," Twitter (now X), August 21, 2013, 9:15 p.m., https://twitter.com/JustinTEarle/status/370353452054216704.

7. Justin Townes Earle (@JustinTEarle), "Saint Jude! The patron saint of lost causes must intervene! She must be a cubs fan!," Twitter (now X), September 8, 2013, 4:29 p.m., https://twitter.com/JustinTEarle/status/376804510309810178.

8. Justin Townes Earle (@JustinTEarle), "I can't focus on anything but the Cubs right now," Twitter (now X), October 24, 2016, 1:06 p.m., https://twitter.com/JustinTEarle/status/790600420477378560; Justin Townes Earle (@JustinTEarle), "I couldn't sing right now if I tried. CUBS!! #FlyTheW," Twitter (now X), November 2, 2016, 4:01 a.m., https://twitter.com/JustinTEarle/status/793724619190435840.

9. Will Hodge, "Interview with Justin Townes Earle"; Sean Jewell, "AST Interview: Justin Townes Earle," *American Standard Time*, December 3, 2016.

10. Chris Talbott, interview with Justin Townes Earle, 2011 (transcript); Duncan Cooper, "Another Country: Justin Townes Earle," *FADER*, August 21, 2014.

11. Steve and Justin Townes Earle, "Hardcore Troubadour Radio."

12. Joanne Will, interview with Justin Townes Earle, 2017 (transcript).

13. Hodge, "Interview with Justin Townes Earle."

14. Will, interview with Justin Townes Earle.

CHAPTER 21

This chapter draws on interviews with Wilson Compton, Jenn Marie Earle, Matt Eddmenson, Simon Gardner, Mark Hedman, Mike Merenda, Andy Moore, and Andy Washington.

1. Justin Townes Earle (@JustinTEarle), "Another new town another new home. Northwest growing on me. I like this rainy motherfucker!," Twitter (now X), November 6, 2016, 12:46 a.m., https://twitter.com/JustinTEarle/status/795125134310797312.

2. Tom Lanham, "Justin Townes Earle Looks Forward with Optimism," *San Francisco Examiner*, May 31, 2017.

3. Steve and Justin Townes Earle, interview by Steve Inskeep, *Morning Edition*, NPR, December 29, 2008.

4. Jewly Hight, review of *Kids in the Street*, by Justin Townes Earle, NPR, May 18, 2017; Glenn Gamboa, review of *Kids in the Street*, by Justin Townes Earle, *Newsday*, May 24, 2017.

5. Press releases from the *Kids in the Street* publicity campaign highlighted Justin "embracing sobriety"; much of the subsequent press coverage of the record emphasized Justin's ongoing sobriety despite the fact that he was beginning to accelerate his substance use outside of marijuana at the time. Justin went along with this narrative, discussing his sobriety in interviews while stressing that he relied on what he called the "marijuana maintenance program." He told one journalist he'd resumed drinking occasionally. Fiona McCann, "Newly Landed Portlander Justin Townes Earle Makes Country Relevant," *Portland Monthly*, May 15, 2017.

6. Dacey Orr Sivewright, "Catching Up with Justin Townes Earle," *Garden & Gun*, April 20, 2017.

CHAPTER 22

This chapter draws on interviews with Nick Bobetsky, Ruby Boots, Blake Brown, Andrew Colvin, Jenn Marie Earle, Chris Frayer, Simon Gardner, Lilly Hiatt, Paul Horvath, Gareth Lindsay, Lydia Loveless, Andy Moore, Alden Peace, Viktoria Safarian, Josh Taylor, James Van Cooper, Katie Vanderpool, and Andy Washington.

1. Danielle Street, "Interview: Justin Townes Earle Talks Murder and Parenthood," *Under the Radar*, October 4, 2017.

2. Justin Townes Earle (@JustinTEarle), "Fellas! We will never know what a woman goes through during pregnancy. No way no how," Twitter (now X), August 14, 2017, 3:09 p.m., https://twitter.com/JustinTEarle/status/897173275511373824; Justin Townes Earle (@JustinTEarle), "Great name! Congrats! Girls are the best!," Twitter (now X), August 18, 2017, 2:16 p.m., https://twitter.com/JustinTEarle/status/898609457072132096; Justin Townes Earle (@JustinTEarle), "Whenever I get wound up and worried about the state of America today, I stop and look at my daughter and it only makes it worse," Twitter (now X), August 22, 2017, 9:17 p.m., https://twitter.com/JustinTEarle/status/900165099247222785.

3. Street, "Interview: Justin Townes Earle Talks Murder and Parenthood."

4. Tom Fish, "These Cities Have the Most Bars Per Capita in America," *Newsweek*, September 26, 2021.

5. Justin Townes Earle, *Live at World Cafe Live on 2018-05-23*, released 2017, streaming, https://archive.org/details/jte2018-05-23.mk6.edtyre/justintownesearle2018-05-23.mk6.edtyre.t18.flac.

6. Jonny Fritz, interview with the author, *Rolling Stone*, 2020.

7. Justin Townes Earle, *Live at the Factory Theatre in Marrickville on 2017-10-17*, released 2017, streaming, https://archive.org/details/jte2017-10-17.aud.flac16.

8. Justin Townes Earle, *World Cafe Live*.

9. Justin Townes Earle, interview by Garret K. Woodward, YouTube, May 9, 2018, www.youtube.com/watch?v=gpEZ0fpW2ng&t=226s.

10. The account of Justin's arrest and charge of fourth-degree assault is based primarily on court records, police documents, and audio of court proceedings from Multnomah County and the Multnomah County District Attorney's Office. Several interviews—with Josh Taylor, Andy Moore, Jenn Marie Earle, and Justin's court-appointed attorney, Viktoria Safarian—helped corroborate and contextualize the case.

CHAPTER 23

This chapter draws on interviews with Adam Bednarik, Brady Blade, Nick Bobetsky, Jonathan Buske, Andrew Colvin, Darcy Cooke, Terry Currier, Jenn Marie Earle, Simon Gardner, Chloe Green, Rosemary Haskins, Laurens Kusters, Gareth Lindsay, Ian McCall, Johnny Mark Miller, Paul Niehaus, James Overbee, Stephen Phillips, Jon Radford, Viktoria Safarian, Clare Shamier, Amanda Shires, Brian Taranto, Josh Taylor, Lisa Marie Turner, and Henry Wagons.

1. The dismissal of Justin's case, and Jenn Marie's reasoning for requesting the case be dropped, is based on records from the Multnomah County District Attorney's Office. Additional context was provided, via interview, by Viktoria Safarian, Justin's court-appointed attorney, who said it was unusual, at this time, for the Multnomah County district attorney to drop a case of this nature, and with this level of evidence, even if the alleged victim no longer wanted to proceed.

2. Justin Townes Earle, *Justin Townes Earle and the Sadies at Central Park Sessions, 8-9-18*, WORT, 2018, streaming, https://soundcloud.com/wort-fm/justin-townes-earle-and-the-sadies-at-central-park-sessions-8-9-18.

3. Matt Innes, "Justin Townes Earle: The Saint of Lost Causes," *Scenestr*, July 9, 2019.

4. Marissa R. Moss, interview with Justin Townes Earle, 2019 (transcript).

5. Jenn Marie Earle, interview with the author, *Rolling Stone*, 2020.

6. Earle, interview with the author.

7. Moss, interview with Justin Townes Earle.

8. Justin Townes Earle, interview by Alison Stewart, *All of It*, WNYC, May 21, 2019.

9. Bruce Headlam, "Justin Townes Earle: In Memoriam," *Broken Record* (podcast), August 25, 2020.

10. Justin Townes Earle, interview by Stewart.

11. Brian Hiatt, "Justin Townes Earle: The *Rolling Stone* Interview," *Rolling Stone Music Now* (podcast), June 12, 2019.

12. Moss, interview with Justin Townes Earle.

13. Justin Townes Earle, *Live at World Cafe Live on 2018-05-23*, released 2017, streaming, https://archive.org/details/jte2018-05-23.mk6.edtyre/justintownesearle2018-05-23.mk6.edtyre.t18.flac.

14. Justin Townes Earle, *Central Park Sessions*.

15. Duncan Haskell, "Interview: Justin Townes Earle," *Songwriting*, December 11, 2014.

16. Geoffrey Himes, "Justin Townes Earle: Crossing the Boundary of 30," *Paste*, March 30, 2012.

17. Chuck Armstrong, "Interview: Justin Townes Earle Talks New Album, Comparisons to His Father + the Future of America," *The Boot*, May 24, 2019.

18. Brian Wise, "Justin Townes Earle—Our Final Interview," *Rhythms*, August 30, 2020.

19. "Justin Townes Earle—Live at Mojo's, Fremantle 08/09/2019," YouTube, January 22, 2021, www.youtube.com/watch?v=K0PZP2IKyG4.

20. Description of Justin's stage banter in Australia comes from various live recordings, including Justin Townes Earle, *Live at the Lansdowne Hotel on 2019-09-04*, 2019, streaming, https://archive.org/details/jte2019-09-04.aud.flac16/2019-09-04+++08.flac; and Justin Townes Earle, *Live at Caravan Music Club on 2019-08-28*, 2019, streaming, https://archive.org/details/jte2019-08-28.aud.flac16/17+-+Justin+talks.flac.

21. Footage of Justin on his fall 2019 US tour is often disturbing and upsetting to watch. "Justin Townes Earle," YouTube, October 8, 2019, www.youtube.com/watch?v=4Gh4_F9aRR4.

CHAPTER 24

This chapter draws on interviews with Adam Bednarik, Brady Blade, Jonathan Buske, Lee Calvin, Nick Dryden, Jenn Marie Earle, Irakli Gabriel, Chloe Green, Rosemary Haskins, Laurens Kusters, Paul Niehaus, Michael O'Brien, Alden Peace, Jenn Ramsey, Anna Rose, Zach Shoffner, Alex Smith, Travis Stephens, Josh Taylor, Joe del Tufo, Dustin Welch, Mike West, and Skylar Wilson.

1. Katie Scott, "Live Nation Pauses All 2020 Tours Due to Coronavirus," *Global News*, March 12, 2020.

2. The account of Justin's final show in Wilmington is compiled from several interviews and accounts of the show from those who attended, as well as several YouTube videos, some of which have since been deleted: "Justin Townes Earle—If You Ain't Glad I'm Leavin—3/12/20—The Queen," YouTube, March 15, 2020, www.youtube.com/watch?v=aXa3zyxbAeA; "Justin Townes Earle 'Let Him Roll' (Guy Clark) 3/12/20 @ The Queen," YouTube, March 21, 2020, www.youtube.com/watch?v=3_Ira_NhOgM.

3. This paragraph is based on headlines in the March 13, 2020, edition of the *Tennessean*. Springwater Supper Club & Lounge, Facebook, March 17, 2020, www.facebook.com/photo?fbid=2834607926575152&set=a.224363917599579.

4. The long list of half-formed ideas Justin floated in the last year of his life is compiled primarily from conversations with Justin's closest musical collaborators and associates like Adam Bednarik and Paul Niehaus, conversations with people Justin spent time with in Nashville over his last year like Rosemary Haskins and Mike West, and conversations with Jenn Marie Earle. Some of these projects were ideas that Justin himself

mentioned publicly during interviews and privately via text messages to collaborators in his last year.

5. Brittney Baird, "Curfew for Nashville Restaurants That Serve Alcohol Now in Effect," WKRN, July 24, 2020.

6. Steve Poulton, interview with the author, *Rolling Stone*, 2020.

7. Ben Sisario, "The Album Steve Earle Never Wanted to Make: A Tribute to His Son," *New York Times*, December 29, 2020.

8. Jenn Marie remembered making a flurry of emergency out-of-state phone calls to Nashville requesting a welfare check. Nashville's Department of Emergency Communications has documentation of a call from Jenn Marie on the morning of August 23 but has no documentation of any prior calls. It is possible Jenn Marie called other people or other governmental entities prior to the twenty-third or that she made earlier calls that, for whatever reason, were not logged.

9. "U.S. Overdose Deaths Decrease in 2023, First Time Since 2018," CDC, May 15, 2024, www.cdc.gov/nchs/pressroom/nchs_press_releases/2024/20240515.htm.

10. Justin Townes Earle, *Central Park Sessions*, 2018.

11. Mariah Timms, "Opioid Deaths Soar amid Coronavirus Outbreak," *Tennessean*, July 19, 2020; "Drug Overdose Mortality by State," CDC, www.cdc.gov/nchs/pressroom/sosmap/drug_poisoning_mortality/drug_poisoning.htm.

12. Marissa R. Moss, interview with Justin Townes Earle, 2019 (transcript).

INDEX